The Broken Spell

Series in Fairy-Tale Studies

General Editor

Donald Haase, Wayne State University

Advisory Editors

Cristina Bacchilega, University of Hawai'i, Mānoa
Stephen Benson, University of East Anglia
Nancy L. Canepa, Dartmouth College
Anne E. Duggan, Wayne State University
Pauline Greenhill, University of Winnipeg
Christine A. Jones, University of Utah
Janet Langlois, Wayne State University
Ulrich Marzolph, University of Göttingen
Carolina Fernández Rodríguez, University of Oviedo
Maria Tatar, Harvard University
Jack Zipes, University of Minnesota

A complete listing of the books in this series can be found online at wsupress.wayne.edu

THE BROKEN SPELL

Indian Storytelling and the Romance Genre in Persian and Urdu

Pasha M. Khan

WAYNE STATE UNIVERSITY PRESS
DETROIT

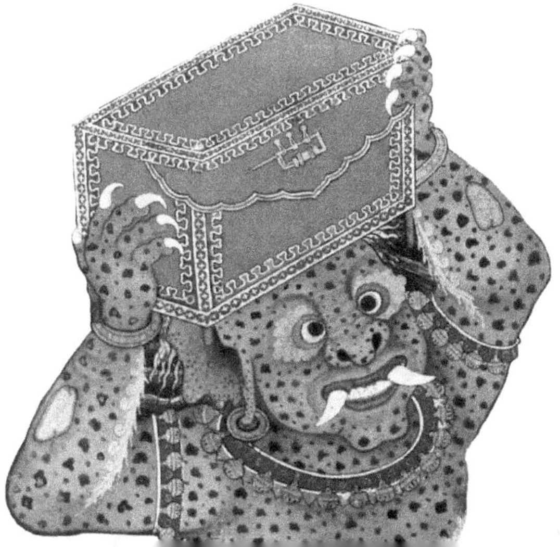

ISBN 978-0-8143-4599-3 (paperback); ISBN978-0-8143-4598-6 (case);
ISBN 978-0-8143-4600-6 (ebook)

Library of Congress Control Number: 2018964988

Published with the assistance of a fund established by Thelma Gray James of Wayne State University for the publication of folklore and English studies.

Wayne State University Press
Leonard N. Simons Building
4809 Woodward Avenue
Detroit, Michigan 48201–1309

Visit us online at wsupress.wayne.edu

Contents

Note on Transliteration *v*

Acknowledgments *ix*

Introduction 1

The Need to Revisit the Romance 2
Outline of the Book 6
On Genre 10

1. The Persian Storytellers of India 23

The Worth of Romances and Their Producers 24
Poetry and Storytelling in the Hierarchy of Genres 27
The Multiple Sources of Storytellers' Worth 32
How Storytellers Increased the Worth of Romances 43

2. Telling the Tale of Amīr Ḥamzah in Urdu 53

Storytelling and Language Education at Fort William College 56
Storytelling and Shi'i Performance in Lucknow and Rampur 61
The Naval Kishore Storytellers between Orality and Print 67
Mīr Bāqir 'Alī: The Decline of Patronage and the Struggle for Worth 72

3. The Storytelling Craft 91

Faḵhr al-Zamānī: A Storyteller's Life 97
The Storytelling Manual and Performance 109
Textual Fragments and Memory in the Romance 117
The Uses of the Multigenre Romance 122

4. Marvelous Histories 133

Ġhālib and the Simurgh 136
The *Shāhnāmah* as History in India 140
ʿAqlī and Naqlī Historiography 147
The Sincerity Effect 152

5. Reason and Romance in the Age of the Novel 163

In Search of Bakāwalī 165
Epistemologies of the Intellect and Heart 181
Equating *Qiṣṣah* and Romance 186
The Rise of the Novel 194

Conclusion 209

The Forgotten Storytellers 211
Survival and Revival 214

Appendix: The Preface and Introduction to the Ṭirāz al-akhbār 219

Notes 265

Works Cited 283

Index 299

Note on Transliteration

MY TRANSLITERATION SCHEME, DETAILED below, is largely a modification of the one adopted by Frances Pritchett in *Nets of Awareness* (1994). Readers who are used to Iranian Persian may find the vowels less familiar, because I find it important to be faithful to the likely pronunciation of Persian in India (and the eastern Persophone world in general, probably including at least parts of Iran) up to the nineteenth century. I have almost uniformly respected the *majhūl* vowels (o, e). However, in the case of twentieth-century Iranian texts, I have treated all vowels as *ma'rūf* (ū, ī).

ا	a, i, u, ā
ب	b
پ	p
ت	t
ٹ	t̥
ث	ṡ, th
ج	j
چ	ch
ح	ḥ
خ	ḳh
د	d
ڈ	d̥
ذ	ẕ, dh
ر	r

ڑ	r̥
ز	z
ژ	zh
س	s
ش	sh
ص	ṣ
ض	ẓ, ḍ
ط	t̤
ظ	z̤
ع	‘
غ	ġh
ف	f
ق	q
ک	k
گ	g
ل	l
	m
ن	n
ں	ṅ
و	w, ū, o, au
ہ	h
ھ	h
ء	’
ے ی	y, e, ai

Acknowledgments

My thanks are due first and foremost to Frances Pritchett for the groundwork that she laid for this book with her scholarship, the humane guidance and advice that she has given me, and her friendship over the years. *The Broken Spell* is a continuation of the work that she began in the 1970s and 1980s, when she roamed the streets of Indian cities on the hunt for old *qiṣṣah*s. I am grateful to her for sharing with me her knowledge, the stories of those days, and the tales that she discovered along with her collaborator Shamsur Rahman Faruqi, whose own work was influenced by her love of *dāstān*s.

My central insight regarding the participation of multiple genres in the *qiṣṣah* took its final form while I was in the arrivals terminal of JFK Airport, waiting to meet Shamsur Rahman Faruqi for the first time. During his subsequent long visits to New York, whether at Fran's apartment in Morningside Heights or on the way to a bookshop on the Lower East Side, he was kind enough to chat with me about Faḳhr al-Zamānī's storytelling craft and Ġhālib's fondness for *qiṣṣah*s. Like so many other books, this one is heavily indebted to Faruqi Sahib, his conversations, and his critical writings on the *Dāstān-i Amīr Ḥamẓah.*

Research for this book was supported by a Social Sciences and Humanities Research Council of Canada Doctoral Fellowship, a travel grant from the American Institute of Pakistan Studies, a Mellon/ACLS Dissertation Completion Fellowship, and a Startup Grant from McGill University. Some of the ideas for this book were rehearsed in articles in the *Indian Social and Economic History Review* and *Comparative Studies of Asia, Africa, and the Middle East* and in chapters of the edited volumes *Tellings and Texts* and *Urdu and Indo-Persian Thought, Poetics, and Belles Lettres*. I am grateful to the editors of these publications, as well as to my colleagues who invited me to give talks on my work at SOAS University of London (Francesca Orsini), Carleton University (Mohammed Rustom), Harvard University (Sunil Sharma), Yale University (Abbas Amanat the first time, Salimeh Maghsoudlou the second), the University of Toronto (Ajay Rao and Mohamad Tavakkoli), and the Max Planck Institute for Human Development (Margrit Pernau). The British Library kindly granted me copyright permission for several figures used here. All translations are my own unless otherwise marked.

I am very grateful to Allison Busch, Farina Mir, and Maria Subtelny for reading and commenting upon an earlier version of this book. Francesca Orsini, Margrit Pernau, and Katherine Butler Schofield have been inspirational models of scholarship and collaboration. Sunil Sharma's generous hand has been behind many of the successes that brought me to this stage. I thank him profusely. I must thank Owen Cornwall, Arthur Dudney, Usman Hamid, and Abhishek Kaicker for their collegiality and friendship. Manan Ahmed Asif, Prasad Bidaye, Afshan Bokhari, Juan Cole, Purnima Dhavan, Thibaut D'Hubert, Jennifer Dubrow, Zara Faridany-Akhavan, Musharraf Ali Farooqui, Walter Hakala, Sonam Kachru, Prashant Keshavmurthy, Razak Khan, my late *ustād* Sohail Ahmad Khan, Paul Losensky, Christine Marrewa-Karwoski, Adil Mawani, Matthew Melvin-Koushki, the late Steven Millier, Jane Mikkelson, Charles Melville, Azfar Moin, Rabea Murtaza, Christina Oesterheld, Neeraja Poddar, Muhammad Salim-ur-Rahman, Pegah Shahbaz, Rifaqat Ali Shahid, Sean Swanick, Anand Taneja, and Travis Zadeh have all contributed, as colleagues, patrons, and/or friends, to the creation of this book, whether they know it or not. Danish Husain, with his new Qissebaazi project, has given me hope for the survival of the *dāstāngo'ī* craft, as have other new Indian and Pakistani *dāstāngo*s who have contacted me over the years.

Librarians in various archives opened their bookshelves to me. I especially thank Leena Mitford, formerly at the British Library; Jim Nye at Regenstein Library at the University of Chicago; Hamid Ali at the Punjab University Library; Mohammad Shah Bokhari at the National Museum of Pakistan; and Mehdi Hassan and the other helpful staff members at the Ganj Bakhsh

Library in Islamabad. The team at Wayne State University Press has been truly marvelous and meticulous. Thank you so much to Marie Sweetman, Rachel Ross, Emily Nowak, Kristin Harpster, and Kristina Stonehill, and especially Anne Taylor for her careful copyediting. Any errors in this book are my own.

The Sufism students of 2014 whom I have kept up with to the present deserve my special thanks. They include such ascetics and dervishes as Arezu Radjaei Riahi, Ida Mahmoudi, Margaret Gilligan, Melis Cagan, Nadir Khan, Nazish Mirza, Ralph Haddad, Reda Berrada, Samantha Larocque, and Sayema Badar. The students in my 2016 Tales of Wonder course engaged with some of the materials and arguments I present in this book. I thank them for putting up with the obsessions of their professor, especially Niyousha Bastani, Nadia Javaheri-Cabrera, and Zain Mian, all three of whom are destined to become great sorcerers. *The Broken Spell* owes a great deal to my graduate students and their works' intersection with my own. David Wong kept me alive to the importance of the materiality of lithographs and manuscripts. Zahra Sabri provided me with crucial sources. From conversations with Odile Schürch concerning her work on the tale of *Kalīlah wa Dimnah*, I was able to better understand the political exemplarity of *qiṣṣah*s. Geneviève Mercier-Dalphond diverted me with her *ʿayyār*-like trickery and provided a model of openness and sociability. The book owes a tremendous amount to my wonderful editorial assistant Jessica Stilwell, who was the first audience for most of the book and who critiqued nearly every paragraph. It is a hundred times better thanks to the care that she bestowed upon it.

This book is dedicated to the memory of my maternal grandmother, Nasreen Khan (née Dar), who passed away in 2016. Thank you to my parents and to my sister, Sana, and her husband, Farrukh, in whose home I found enough focus to write much of chapter 2. And thanks to Kanita for her love and the strength she gave me in the end.

Introduction

THE *DĀSTĀN* OR *QIṢṢAH* is a genre of verbal art that once flourished in India, edifying and entertaining audiences in villages and bazaars and patronized at imperial and subimperial courts and the salons of wealthy urban elites. Although it was not confined to a particular tongue, in this book I analyze its manifestations in the Persian and Urdu languages. In English, it is often referred to as the "romance" genre—but this is a translation that must be scrutinized, for it is symptomatic of a view of the *qiṣṣah* that has more to do with epistemological developments in eighteenth-century Western Europe than with the *qiṣṣah*'s own merits or demerits. *Qiṣṣah*s were woven into existence in oral performance. They were spoken and bodied forth by the *qiṣṣah-k̲h̲wān*s or *dāstāngo*s, the storytellers of India, like the Mughal emperor Akbar's courtier Darbār K̲h̲ān in the sixteenth century or the late Urdu storyteller Mīr Bāqir ʻAlī (d. 1928). These traditions, along with the older perception of the romance, were all but lost until the "Dastangoi" Urdu storytelling revival that began just before the second decade of the twenty-first century. Even the written romance tradition is indelibly marked by the formative traces of oral performance. For this reason, in this book when referring to romances I will frequently refer not to "writing" or "literature" but to "verbal art," a term used by the folklorist William Bascom (1955) to refer to certain forms of folklore. Its later use by Richard Bauman (1975) to emphasize its performativity is important to understanding why it is suited to the present discussion. Nevertheless, here it is primarily a translation of the Perso-Arabic terms *suk̲h̲an* and *kalām*. The term "verbal art" has the added advantage of being capable of adjectival use: it is with the "verbal artistic" genre of the *qiṣṣah* that this book is primarily concerned.

To understand further what the *qiṣṣah* is, or was, it is necessary to examine the process of the institution of genres more generally. There is, however, a dominant imagination of the *qiṣṣah* genre that tends to be assumed by South Asians. While Francesca Orsini (2009, chap. 3) has rightly stressed that some romances in the nineteenth century represented relatively mundane events, some of the best-known *qiṣṣahs* were tales of wonder. Before their audiences, storytellers arrayed marvelous beings and events rich with imaginative force. Romance heroes like Amīr Ḥamzah, the doughty uncle of the Prophet Muḥammad, did battle with sorcerers sporting snakes twisting around their necks and with magicians speeding across the battlefield astride their trusty pigs and ferocious bears. One sorcerer's age is recorded as 1,085,989 years and four months. But for all their experience and power, the villainous magicians are rendered powerless by counter-magical weapons gifted to the Muslim heroes by the Prophet Ḳhiẓr. Protagonists destroyed enchanted worlds (*ṭilisms*) forged by great infidel sages who claimed equality with God Himself. The stories' terrain was planted with strange trees bearing in place of fruit the cackling heads of fairies (*parīs*); it was populated by anthropoglot beasts and beautiful half-human birds mating with men, and it was strewn with magical objects, hidden in the stomachs of dragons or in demons' dwellings, waiting for a hero to discover them. Through the mouths of storytellers or the pens of the Urdu-Hindi or Persian literati, romances yielded up their marvels to astonished audiences.

The Need to Revisit the Romance

The importance of the *qiṣṣah* genre faded, like many other things, with the coming of Western modernity and the influx of colonial ideas into the minds of Indian elites. At the end of the nineteenth century, the Urdu literati were already calling for their fellow Indians to move beyond the romance, as if it were an absurd and childish relic of the past. Indians' understanding of the genre changed; it became an embarrassment, like a doddering old relative to be confined discreetly to a sickroom. The task of this book is to examine, but also to move past, the colonial-era decline of the romance genre and to excavate the extent of its worth as well as its reception and understanding prior to the twentieth century. I do not claim to show that it was the most highly regarded genre among all of the verbal artistic genres of India, for there were always limits to how well it was received. But I will show that the romance genre was accorded worth, by the storytellers of India themselves and by their patrons and audiences, and that its very structure, as revealed by the manner of its performance, demonstrates *how* a *qiṣṣah* could have had worth, and could even have been seen as useful, by means of the combined properties of other genres coursing through it.

I make no claim to impartiality. If the devaluation of the genre occurred due to a particular ideology that came along with colonialism, the project of recovery is also propelled by an anti-colonial ideology that seeks, as per Allison Busch's (2010, 14–15) formulation, to go beyond diagnoses of the postcolonial malaise and show what alternatives might have been possible before our minds, bodies, and art were altered by colonization.[1] To do so, it is crucial to question the ideas that have lowered the *qiṣṣah*'s worth, such as the absolute primacy of a rationalist epistemology; the exclusive emphasis on the entertainment, rather than the uses, provided by the *qiṣṣah*; and the clear separation of the romance from other genres, such as that of history.

The Rebellion of 1857 is often taken as a point of rupture with the chain of previous worldviews that ran through India's intellectual history. It is particularly after this series of events that the value of the *qiṣṣah* faded among Indian reformists, as British worldviews infiltrated elite minds. There had never been a pristine and paradisiacal precolonial time when the *qiṣṣah* had not drawn criticism. Its marvels had long exposed it to attacks from those who saw its representations as antithetical to the dictates of the intellect, even before the arrival of the British flavor of rationalism. But there was a particularly strong revulsion of feeling at the end of the nineteenth century and the beginning of the twentieth. At this time the genre was in its heyday in the Urdu language. Lithography had made *qiṣṣah*s more widely available and more popular than ever. This was the era of the great masterpiece of Urdu prose, the forty-six-volume *Story of Amīr Ḥamzah* (*Dāstān-i Amīr Ḥamzah* or *Ḥamzah-nāmah*). Totaling more than forty-two thousand pages, the *Ḥamzah-nāmah* was published from the beginning of the 1880s until 1917 by Naval Kishore Press with the cooperation of storytellers of Lucknow: Muḥammad Ḥusain Jāh, Aḥmad Ḥusain Qamar, and Taṣadduq Ḥusain. Despite the final disappearance of Mughal patronage of storytellers with the ousting of the last Mughal emperor, Bahādur Shāh Z̤afar, after 1857, storytelling in Urdu continued to flourish at local courts such as those of Rampur, Bahawalpur, and Hyderabad. It was during these halcyon days of the romance that its enchantment began to fail among the elite. Its critics were to be found particularly among the same men who wished to reform Urdu poetry, and especially the *ghazal*—men like Muḥammad Ḥusain Āzād and Alt̤āf Husain Ḥālī.[2] They took the logic of their devaluation from the British view of the romance as a genre that belonged to a bygone age of credulity.

The British had already in the eighteenth century established the difference in value between the genre of English literature thaṭ they called the romance and a closely related genre, newly emerging, that came to be called the novel. The triumph of the novel in this genre war is so much a fait accompli as to be nearly invisible to us now. By the end of the nineteenth century, novels also began to appear in Urdu. In reality they were not always easily distinguishable from *qiṣṣah*s, but like English novels they came to be held up as exemplary works of literature that most commendably mirrored the world of reason and sense. Against the novel, its more virtuous sister, the *qiṣṣah* was discovered to be a disgrace. Its worldview was an old and obsolete one, credulous and primitive, incompatible with the new and correct way of thinking.

In the twentieth century, in spite of the surge of anti-colonial activity and thought, the romance continued to be badly understood. Indeed, the desire among anti-colonial thinkers to be taken seriously on the colonizer's terms meant that among them the image of the *qiṣṣah* could not but be disfigured. There was no dearth of studies of the Urdu romance genre in the mid-twentieth century, written by great scholars of Urdu literature such as Waqār ʻAẓīm, Farmān Fatḥpūrī, and most importantly Gyān Chand Jain, whose *Urdū kī nas̱rī dāstāneṅ* (Urdu prose romances) is a trove of information regarding the Urdu romance tradition, beginning in the days when the strain of Urdu-Hindi we usually call "Dakkanī" was producing a flourishing literature in the south of the subcontinent. Yet even through the best of these studies there ran the traces of the assumptions that had solidified at the end of the nineteenth century, such as Kalīm al Dīn Aḥmad's conclusion that the romance, while important to literary historians, was essentially an artifact of a less enlightened, intellectually backward time.

The lowering of the *qiṣṣah* genre's worth has led not only to the decline of elite storytelling but also to the disappearance of materials. According to Urdu literary scholar Muhammad Salim-ur-Rahman, things have come to such a pass that fifty thousand pages of unpublished Naval Kishore *qiṣṣah*s in the Amīr Ḥamzah cycle have been rubbished.[3] Volumes upon volumes of manuscripts by the storytellers of Lucknow, as well as by ne'er-do-well *qiṣṣah-ḳhwān*s born into the family of the Mughals, lie unstudied in the Rampur Reza Library. Before the present century, the masterpiece of the genre in Urdu, the complete set of the Naval Kishore *Ḥamzah-nāmah* volumes, had not been collected by any library. It was only through the efforts of Frances Pritchett and Shamsur Rahman Faruqi that Columbia University acquired the full set in 2011. The correction of the devaluation of the *dāstān* has been undertaken by Shamsur Rahman Faruqi in his multivolume study of the *Ḥamzah-nāmah*: *Sāḥirī, shāhī, ṣāḥib-qirānī* (Sorcery, kingship, lordship of the auspicious conjunction). He has stressed that the romance reflected a worldview proper to the India that existed prior to and during the early part of the British Raj period but that was replaced through the seeping in of British ideas. And, most centrally, Faruqi has developed a poetics of the romance genre on the basis of the orality (*zabānī-pan*) that he believed was shared by orally performed and written romances alike. The present study agrees with Faruqi's diagnosis, his identification of a shift of worldview that brought about the devaluation of the romance, and his emphasis on orality. Otherwise, however, my approach to the study of the genre is quite different, though it is, I hope, complementary. Whereas Faruqi gives readers the benefit of his deep reading of the Naval Kishore *Ḥamzah-nāmah* and an interior analysis based on structuralist critical tools, I will look at the genre largely from the outside in. I will do so on the basis, to be elaborated later in this introduction, that to analyze any genre *as a genre* one must understand how it was seen by historically situated commentators.[4]

Outline of the Book

The most concise answer to the question "What was the *qiṣṣah*?" is simply that it was a genre of verbal art. However, this answer raises a multitude of other questions. Immediately, the question arises: What is a genre? In the latter half of this introduction, I will argue in detail that a genre is a historically instituted grouping of texts whose identity is encoded according to a set of common marks. The code defining the genre is ideologically produced by the texts' consumers, who may also include the producers. At any given historical moment, the ideology or worldview of a group of audience members positions the genre within a system of genres against which it is relationally defined and hierarchically valued. What we are examining, when we examine the identity of the romance genre, is the process of the institution of the genre code.

Before considering the ideological forces behind the institution of the romance genre, I will narrate, in chapters 1 and 2, the lives of the most important storytellers who worked in Persian and Urdu in India from the fifteenth to the twentieth centuries. It was not only audiences, critics, and connoisseurs who raised the worth and shaped the code of the *qiṣṣah* but also the storytellers who embodied the *qiṣṣah* in performance and whose own fortunes were bound to the fortunes of the genre. Given the *qiṣṣah-ḳhwān*s' identification with their work, their worth in the eyes of patrons and audiences provides a clue to the worth of the *qiṣṣah* itself. The strategies whereby they raised the genre's worth were enriched and enabled by the fact that the storytellers were not storytellers alone but also political players, poets, panegyrists, munshis, reciters of laments for the Prophet's family members martyred in Karbala, chapbook vendors, and so on. By utilizing these roles—presenting the *qiṣṣah* as useful in its political and linguistical exemplarity, catching hold of younger patrons, cross-fertilizing *qiṣṣah* performances with elements from other popular oral-performative genres, supplementing oral *qiṣṣah*s, as per Orsini's (2009) formulation, with manuscripts and lithographs, and putting it forward as a source of knowledge—these performers were able to work within a mostly favorable epistemological climate to elevate the worth of the genre. This was true even during the tumultuous nineteenth century, when storytellers had to deal with new textual technologies, new socioeconomic and political configurations, and, ultimately, the new colonially derived worldview of the younger elites.

Chapter 3 focuses on the extensively recorded life of the most important of the Persian-language storytellers of India, 'Abd al-Nabī Fakhr al-Zamānī. Along with other evidence, including the descriptions of the late Urdu storyteller Mīr Bāqir 'Alī's performances, Fakhr al-Zamānī's storytelling manual the *Ṭirāz al-akhbār* shows us how romances were produced in oral performance in what Shamsur Rahman Faruqi has called a "patchwork" fashion (Faruqi 1999, 411). Text fragments, both newly created and previously existent hypotexts, were woven together into the fabric of the *qiṣṣah*. An understanding of this process makes the thorough intertextuality of *qiṣṣah*s visible and makes possible a series of further insights regarding genre and its reception, valuation, and codes. Like the genre of the *roman* in Mikhail Bakhtin's theory of so-called novelization (Bakhtin 2004, ch. 1), any given *qiṣṣah* text was the bearer of multiple fragment genres aside from its dominant genre, insofar as it was shot through with various hypotexts whose sources would have been recognized by the audience. The reception of the *qiṣṣah* is therefore affected by the audience's recognition of the genre of each textual fragment and by their perception of its particular effects and uses in relation to the genres that surround and envelop it as the romance unfolds.

Historiography (*tārīkh*) was the most important genre in relation to which the *qiṣṣah* was defined before the late nineteenth century. Chapter 4 investigates this relation within the genre system of India, or rather in two contradictory genre systems based on competing worldviews. Using the examples of the *Shāhnāmah* and the *Qiṣṣah-i Ḥātim Ṭā'ī* (Tale of Ḥātim Ṭā'ī), it examines history as a genre external to the *qiṣṣah* in the genre systems and internally, both as a genre that marked textual fragments running through *qiṣṣah*s and as a genre whose texts were scored with hypotexts bearing the *qiṣṣah* genre. Scrutiny of the *qiṣṣah*/history relation reveals that the two were implicitly regarded by many as twin genres, while historians and other writers of a rationalist bent argued strongly against the similarity of the history and romance, averring instead that romance was precisely what history ought not to be. These writers excoriated what they saw as pseudohistories that were too close to being romances, were bedecked with marvels that defied the everydayness of the real world, and defied reason. For them, the *qiṣṣah* was most easily definable by its mendacity, as against the sincerity of history. But for others, the interweaving of romance and history was unremarkable. The existence of competing epistemologies meant the formation of two different genre systems in the same milieu: a powerful but probably minor system according to which the romance was lower in the hierarchy, and a subtler but dominant system in which the boundaries between romance and history were not always clear.

The primacy of the definitive dichotomy or similitude between the *qiṣṣah* and history waned only with the appearance of the novel at the end of the nineteenth century in Urdu. It is instructive, however, to look first at a late dichotomization of these two genres during a period of incipient intellectual colonialization. The example of Sir Richard Temple's purported quest, at the head of a troop of British elephant riders, to discover the truth behind the *qiṣṣah* of the fairy Bakawali shows that the authors of the Urdu "histories of Bakawali" were indebted to a still powerful nonrationalist epistemology, even as they bowed before the growing dominance of a rationalism of colonial origin. By the end of the century, Urdu-writing elites had imbibed British ideas of the superior value of the novel, which supposedly conformed in its representations to what is possible according to reason and sense, as against the irrational and frivolous romance. The very name "romance" ties the *qiṣṣah* to the history of the romance genre in Britain, which involved a gradual bifurcation of the romance from the upstart genre of the "novel," whose glorification over the course of the eighteenth century in Britain was the precedent for the appreciation of the novel in India. Ideas about the inferiority and backwardness of the romance—and its Oriental-ness to boot—gradually saturated the discourse surrounding the *qiṣṣah*. This process culminated in the mid-twentieth-century production of our present "genre code" or definition of the Indian romance, achieved through the canonical studies of *qiṣṣah*s carried out by such scholars as Gyān Chand Jain, Kalīm al-Dīn Aḥmad, and Waqār ʻAẓīm. Sympathetic though many such studies may have been, they retained the depreciative principles that had been articulated by nineteenth-century writers like Āzād and Ḥālī. It is the survival of this depreciation of the *qiṣṣah* genre that necessitates reevaluations such as this one. In the conclusion, however, I will consider another kind of survival: the survival of the traces of the worldview undergirding the former station of the *qiṣṣah* into the postcolonial period.

The range of the original genre terms should be noted before moving forward. By way of Persian, the Urdu language possesses a number of words that are understood to be names either of a single genre that we are calling the "romance" or of a number of subgenres differentiated according to length. The terms *dāstān*, *qiṣṣah*, and *ḥikāyat* are undoubtedly the most frequently used of these genre names, as a glance through a library catalog will confirm. But bound up with each of these words is a vague idea of a narrative of a particular length, which puts some pressure on the idea of the romance as a unified genre. The term "*dāstān*," especially in the present, often refers to lengthy narratives such as the *Dāstān-i Amīr Ḥamzah*, the *Shāhnāmah*, or the *Bostān-i Ḳhayāl*. Yet the long story of Ḥamzah was much more likely to be referred to as the *Qiṣṣah-i Amīr Ḥamzah* before the nineteenth century, and *qiṣṣah*s were sometimes subdivided into *dāstān*s, indicating that the *dāstān* could be a shorter unit. It was not until the nineteenth century that Urdu storytellers sought to increase their prestige by referring to themselves as *dāstāngo*s rather than *qiṣṣah-ḳhwān*s, indicating that by this time the term *dāstān* carried greater value and may have connoted greater length. On the other hand, "*ḥikāyat*" is frequently used to designate very short narratives, sometimes consisting of no more than a few phrases, and yet it sometimes names moderate-length narratives as well. Thus, the possible objection that *dāstān* and *ḥikāyat* refer to specific forms of narrative is difficult to corroborate; we can only say that the preponderance of evidence suggests that the definitions of both words slide toward each other along a continuum, at the center of which there is a considerable area of overlap in the term *qiṣṣah.*

On Genre

To understand what the *qiṣṣah* genre was, one must first understand what genre is. Why bother with genre in the first place? Twentieth-century theorists of genre had to contend with Maurice Blanchot's dismissal of its usefulness, particularly for the analysis of modern literature, and with Benedetto Croce's outright rejection of it.[5] The case against genre countered its totalization with a dispersivity. Works of literature were supposed by Blanchot to belong simply to the genre-less genre of literature itself, with no intermediate terms between Literature and the individual work. Thus, works would be apprehended by scholars as autonomous objects to be read closely and carefully, gleaming brightly in their difference from other works rather than having their meaning bounded by the prison walls of literary genres that corralled them in with texts deemed to be similar. Genres imposed sameness upon the works that supposedly belonged to them, assimilating every individual work to the model of something called the "lyric poem," the "science fiction novel," or the "sonnet." For Blanchot and Croce, literary modernism provided a chance to break this tyranny of the same. Such an objection to genre had its virtues. But Tzvetan Todorov (1990, 196) very convincingly dismissed the idea that this attitude could allow us to dispense with genre altogether by conjuring an insight of Gérard Genette: for even the boldest modernist work to make its transgression, there must be a norm for it to transgress. Blanchot himself would concede that in straining against the boundaries of genre, the literary work makes visible the borderlines of the genre of which it seeks to break free.

But let us leave the realm of theory for a moment and consider our everyday experience of genre. A genre is a barely noticeable thing. Oftentimes it is only slightly more prominent than the texture of the paper from which a book is made or the width of the margins surrounding the text. One does not think very much about a novel's being a novel; it simply is so. More than that, genre is often experienced as something not only "given" but singular. Take the question of whether a certain novel belongs to the genre of historical fiction or of mystery, for example. Perhaps this problem can be solved by putting the two possibilities together and calling the novel a historical mystery. But some works, which seem to play with the borders of conventional genres, may give rise to an argument between two readers, with one saying that it belongs to this genre and the other saying it belongs to another. In such a case, how can the true answer be decided and the argument put to an end? Is there a true answer? Is it possible to determine the genre of a text, a film, a painting, a work of music, once and for all, as we determine the species to which an animal belongs? We have noted that genres constitute norms against which artworks arise. But these questions regarding how genre is determined cannot be answered without thinking in detail about how genre works.

Consider the genre mark. We call a novel a novel, a history a history, because of certain telltale characteristics possessed by the text in question. "Marks of genre" is the term that Jacques Derrida uses in his essay "The Law of Genre," although he also calls them "remarks" of genre (1980, 64–65). With his emphasis on this latter term, *re*mark, Derrida draws attention to a couple of important points about genre marks that must be borne in mind: most importantly, the fact that any given genre mark is repeated or at least repeatable over a number of texts, all of which are said to belong to the same genre by virtue of having that repeated mark, either alone or in combination with other marks. The genre mark itself is intertextual.

We know that Mīr Ḥasan's *Siḥr al-bayān* (Sorcery of expression) is a *maśnawī*. How do we know this? It is because of one genre mark in particular, shared by all such texts: it is composed entirely of rhyming couplets, with the exception of prose section headings and so on, which we would put aside as marginal components, or "paratexts." Other genres may require the presence of multiple traits for such an identification to occur, and traits need not be as formal as they are in the case of the *maśnawī* and *ġhazal*. Consider the following passage from the nineteenth-century poet Dayā Shankar Nasīm's Urdu *Gulzār-i Nasīm* (Nasīm's flower garden):

> There stood a demon—one hell of a guard.
> His teeth were like gravediggers, by Death bestowed,
> his nostrils were pathways to Nothingness' road. . . .
> For days the damn slob had found nothing to gnaw;
> and, starving, he'd chucked the dirt into his maw.
> "I'll have me a taste of this human!" he said,
> "Thank Almighty God for this, my daily bread!"
> The prince was in peril's own mouth standing there,
> feeling quite stressed out and shuddering with fear. (Surūr 2008, 160)

Like the rest of the text, this selection is in *maśnawī* form, and I have highlighted its form by translating the poem into English rhyming couplets, at the expense of literalness. But it is also a *qiṣṣah*. It is understood as a *qiṣṣah* due to several traits. It presents a narrative: a famished demon has encountered a tasty-looking prince, who does not relish the idea of being turned into a kebab and who will, we imagine, put up some sort of resistance. The narrativity of the passage is one mark of genre. The presence of the demon provides the passage with another genre mark or two: marvelousness and fictionality (if we believe that demons are not beings in the real world). Insofar as we interpret these two or three traits as signs that the passage is part of a romance, it does not matter whether it is in verse or prose, since a romance can be either or a mix of the two. Some would go so far as to say that form is entirely separate from genre, though this is not one of the assumptions of the present work (Derrida 1980, 61–62). Unlike the case when identifying a *maśnawī*, a single mark alone would probably have been insufficient to identify this passage as part of a romance. For most audiences, the simple fact of the marvelousness of the subject matter could not mark the text as a romance without the trait of narrativity also being present, while the mere fact of its being a narrative could cause it to be identified with any one of a large number of genres.

What is it that allows the presence of a mark or combination of marks to lead to the conclusion that a text is a member of this or that genre? Evidently, for the marks of narrativity and marvelousness to lead us to assign the genre of *qiṣṣah* to the *Gulzār-i Nasīm*, there must already exist an idea of the marks that a text must have in order to be a *qiṣṣah*. This idea is what we may call the "code" of genre—the law that gathers together one or more marks as identifiers of a given genre. Todorov (1990, 198) describes the process and defines genre as follows: "In a society, the recurrence of certain discursive properties [i.e., what I am calling "marks" or "traits"] is institutionalized, and individual texts are produced and perceived in relation to the norm constituted by this codification. A genre, literary or otherwise, is nothing but this codification of discursive properties."[6] We will return to the idea of the code as an "institutionalization" shortly, but the crucial axiom to which Todorov's idea should alert us is that *genres are not pre-given or natural*. The code that produces a genre by allowing certain marks of a text to identify the text as a novel or a prosopography is itself produced by members of a society and especially by the producers of texts. Indeed, insofar as the code is inseparable from the marks that it must gather, we can say along with Todorov (1990, 198) that the genre *is* the code.

Throughout this book we will see examples of the production of the genre code (or, simply, the genre) of the romance. The clearest occurrence from our vantage point came in the middle of the twentieth century, with the appearance of books like Gyān Chand Jain's *Urdū kī nas̤rī dāstāneṅ* and Farmān Fatḥpūrī's *Urdū kī manẓūm dāstāneṅ* (Urdu verse romances), which set out to explain what traits a *dāstān* should have in order to be identifiable as a *dāstān* and to clarify which Urdu texts are romances. Expressions of the genre code need not come in the form of book-length scholarly pronouncements, however. We may find them in any metatextual texts (texts that reflect on themselves or other texts), such as reviews, prefaces, interviews, or everyday conversations. Aside from being metatextual, these are also texts of the sort that Genette (1997b) called "paratexts," meaning that they provide limits to the text without (necessarily) being part of it.[7] Paratexts surround and define the text like a fine skin over its body.[8]

Genre appears as a description of the text but acts prescriptively to regulate the received meaning of a text. The meaning of Abdullah Hussein's *Udās nasleṅ* (The weary generations) is controlled by our assuredness that it is a novel, not a work of history, in spite of, say, its descriptions of World War I. We would read Muṣṭanṣar Ḥusain Tāraṛ's *Pyār kā pahlā shahr* (The first city of love) very differently if it were presented to us as a *safar-nāmah* (travelogue) rather than a romantic novel about a Pakistani in Paris. A horizon of expectations comes with each genre, controlling our reception and limiting the proliferation of meaning that can issue from the text assigned to the genre. And genre reduplicates itself by providing a convention within which more texts—new autobiographies, new "Muslim social" films, new hymns to the Prophet—can be produced.[9]

It bears repeating: genres are not natural. There is no pre-eternal, innate, or given genre. But widely accepted genre codes come to appear natural. Therefore, it seems that when we call *Ivanhoe* or the Pakistani writer Bano Qudsia's *Rājah giddh* (The king vulture) a novel, all we are doing is *identifying* its genre. This identification usually seems scientific and obvious, as if one were saying, "We all know what a novel is, and clearly this is a novel!" But to reject the idea that genre or genre code is natural is to be aware of the contingency of identification. To accentuate this contingency and "instituted-ness" of the genre of a text, it may be better to say that we *assign* the genre of a text rather than identify it. For the most part I will therefore refer henceforth to the "assignment" of genre in the hopes that doing so will maintain our awareness of the fact that the genre code is instituted, made. The code and genre itself, as we have seen above, are more or less the same thing, but I reserve the right to talk of the "code" when it is necessary to stress genre's non-givenness, whereas I will say "genre" otherwise.

The genre code is instituted by the metatextual remarks made, let us say, by members of a society. When a scholar writes an essay about the genre of the *tazkirah* (biographical dictionary), when someone in a park shares her remarks about Hindi modernist *chhāyavād* poetry, or even when a subtitle states "*Qiṣṣah of the Four Dervishes*" and leads the reader to surmise its reasons for using the word *qiṣṣah*, a genre code has been instituted that will regulate the meanings of texts, set up expectations for texts, and shape future texts.[10] What is the process behind such expressions regarding the code? How and by what force is a genre instituted?

There may be many reasons. Commercial forces are strong drivers of genre production, as when, for instance, a music store capitalizes on the success of an album by displaying it side by side with other albums that are supposed to be similar (and therefore similarly buyable) and by fabricating a genre name to designate the assemblage and make its commercialization more convenient. It is not difficult to imagine something similar occurring in the case of romances even before the late capitalist period. In the eighteenth century, Mīr Taqī Ḳhayāl (n.d., fol. 10ff.) composed and, it seems, performed his gargantuan *Bostān-i Ḳhayāl* (Garden of imagination) to silence an insufferably vain storyteller in a Delhi coffeehouse and demonstrate that the *Dāstān-i Amīr Ḥamzah* could be equaled and even bettered. While on the face of it this demonstration was a denial of the *Ḥamzah-nāmah*'s value, it can just as easily be seen as an effective tribute to this exemplar of the romance genre. By allying itself to the genre, the *Bostān-i Ḳhayāl* strengthened the case for its own worth to elite audiences, of whom Ḳhayāl's subsequent patron Mu'taman al-Daulah was a member. It is very rare for a genre code to be instituted only once; this fact will be made clearer below. Indeed, every addition to the genre, every new text that is assigned to the genre, is a new instance of the institution of the genre code (cf. Cohen 1986, 209). Press advertisements appended or prepended to Urdu lithographs similarly articulated genre codes for commercial reasons. In the advertisements inserted into its *Dāstān-i Amīr Ḥamzah* volumes, the great Lucknow publisher Naval Kishore categorized certain books as *qiṣṣah*s, generally either "prose *qiṣṣah*s" or "verse *qiṣṣahs*."[11] Fredric Jameson (1981, 107) suggested that it was only after the disappearance of "institutionalized social status" for artists (such as the status of patronized storyteller or poet laureate, one imagines) that genre could be instrumentalized by commercial forces.

Even in the cases in which genre codes serve profitable ends, it is possible to discern the force of a *worldview* that is the precondition of the possibility of the genre. It is Jameson's contention that ideologies stand behind genres. He claims, for example, that the post-twelfth-century chivalric romance in Europe was shaped by the emerging class solidarity and shared ideology of the feudal elite (Jameson 1981, 118–19). Ideology as Jameson understands it, "a representational structure which allows the individual subject to conceive or imagine his or her lived relationship to transpersonal realities," is a wide-ranging force (Jameson 1981, 30). And yet it seems too narrow for our purposes. When I say that genres are shaped by the "worldviews" of the societies that produce them, I mean for the term to include or have as its appendages not only ideologies in Jameson's or Louis Althusser's (2008) formulations but also epistemologies, philosophies, systems of knowledge and belief, and so on.

Even the very name "romance," the English word that I have in the end hazarded to keep for *dāstān* and *qiṣṣah*, is the result of a particular worldview. In the particular case of the name "romance," this worldview included Orientalism in Said's (1979) sense of the term. As we will see in chapter 5, at least as early as the eighteenth century there was an Orientalist impulse to group together what were in Britain called "romances"—the Arthurian tales or the *Chanson de Roland*, for example—and marvelous narratives from the Orient, such as the *Thousand and One Nights*. At this time the novel, with its mirroring of the "real world" of reason and sense, was succeeding in establishing itself as a finer genre of prose fiction than the far-fetched (European) romance. But it was precisely in being pitted against one another that the two genres were being created, practically for the first time. The annexation of the "Eastern romance" to the romance genre, with its implications of feverish imaginativeness, marvels for the credulous, and primitiveness, was only possible against the backdrop of a worldview according to which reason was paramount, and Orientals were slow to emerge into the light of reason from their slumberous imprisonment in the cell of superstition.

The annexation to the romance genre of certain narratives produced in Britain and in France's colonies occurred during the propitious historical moment in which the European romance itself was increasingly becoming defined against the new genre of the novel. In this regard, this process is identical to other genre assignments, all of which are made within and enabled by the circumstances obtaining in a particular historical time and context. Insisted upon by Todorov (1990, 198), the historical origin of genre is given supreme importance by Ralph Cohen (1986, 204), who makes a method out of the fact that "genre concepts in theory and practice arise, change, and decline for historical reasons." It could hardly be otherwise given that the ideologies, epistemologies, and so on that cause a genre code to be produced are themselves historical, as Jameson's aforementioned explanation of the chivalric romance bears out. Within the term "historical moment" we should also comprehend the social, cultural, and linguistic particularities of a time and place in which a genre is codified.

Genre, therefore, is historical, not primal or timeless. The genre code is always put into operation in a context. Any study of a work or works with an eye to genre must be a historicist study, paying as much or more attention to how context imprints itself upon the text as it does to scrutinizing the text "alone." For this reason, a study such as this one cannot be a close reading of *qiṣṣah*s from beginning to end. Genre theory of the kind that Todorov, Jameson, Cohen, and others have articulated is a space of relation between history and the texts to which genres are assigned.

Genre is clearly intertextual in that the marks of genre must be repeated through a series of texts for someone to be able to say, with the authority of a certain genre code, that those similar texts all belong to the same genre. *Gulzār-i Nasīm*, *Ẕahr-i 'ishq* (Love's poison), and *Siḥr al-bayān* are all *maṡnawī*s because they share certain distinctive marks. But the genre code not only establishes this relation between texts; it is also affected by various relationships between it and other genre codes. In other words, genres always exist in a system, an ecosystem, or a matrix similar to that proposed by Saussure (1986) and made famous by the Structuralists. A genre cannot be richly understood in isolation from other genres existing in the same context, because its code is partly determined by its relation to other genres in the same genre system.

The most obvious example of a defining relationship within a genre system is that of opposition—for instance, the opposition between the poetic genres of satire (*hajw*) and praise (*madḥ*). These genres can be said to be defined by their difference from one another. Similarly, we have the example of the situation to which we alluded when we began, that of the opposition between the novel and the *qiṣṣah*. The two genres were considered to be opposed to one another in that one represented the possible and the other represented the far-fetched; and they defined one another by means of their opposition to each other. Other relations are, of course, possible. Praise and satire, as subgenres of verse, are considered to be similar to one another in opposition to subgenres of prose. The novel and *qiṣṣah* are known to be like one another in that they are both subgenres of narrative, and indeed it is perhaps their "dangerous proximity" that makes it all the more necessary to underline their differences.

Bear in mind that this opposition itself, between the *qiṣṣah* and the novel, was posited as a result of a certain worldview or worldviews that had gained strength by the turn of the century. Genre codes, as I have already said, are molded by the force of such worldviews, and the same is true of the genre system as a whole. We might think of the genre system as a complex of symptoms whose interpretation will lead us to an image of the worldview that shaped it. Its every detail reveals something about the intellectual climate of the time in which it exists. Folklorist Dan Ben-Amos's (1976, 225) idea of the genre system as a system by which "society defines its experiences, creative imagination, and social commentary" is an important precursor to the one I am putting forward. However, we should be wary of assuming that a given genre system gives us knowledge of some all-powerful and singular worldview behind it, as if it were a puppet animated by an all-encompassing zeitgeist, like a God of monotheism ordering Creation. There are many such gods, each with a certain measure of power. At any given historical moment, there might be any number of worldviews at play in a society, each of which might build up a differently configured genre system. Therefore, we should think about genre systems themselves in the plural number.

As we think about ideological and other forces in intellectual history and their impact upon genre systems, we should remember the role of the *value* that people placed upon genres. The genre system has a vertical dimension; for instance, in the genre system that we have been talking about, the novel occupied a higher tree branch than the *qiṣṣah*. The *ġhazal* was perched still nearer to the canopy. Topping or even transcending most genre systems in the history of the Islamicate world, there would have been a genre containing only a single text: the Quran. The Quran is not only sui generis; it is supposed to possess the unique property of inimitability (*iʿjāz*). Yet this transcendent text, holding aloof from all others, was also conceived of as the origin of various genres. Certain writers of *qiṣṣah*s, for example, seized upon the Quran's designation of its own narration of the story of the prophet Yusuf as the "best of stories" (*aḥsan al-qaṣaṣ*) to provide the *qiṣṣah* genre with a source in the Quran (Ġhulām Rasūl ʿĀlampūrī 2000, 17–18).[12] The Quran is a very unique example of a genre of unlimited worth, but the logic that finds a Quranic origin for genres such as the *qiṣṣah* or the history is also an example of a strategy for the raising of the value of such genres. Valuations are tied to worldviews, have their role in the formation of genre codes, and are especially visible when we think about genres as part of a system. Worth is not static, however, and shifts in value can bring about the metamorphosis of the entire genre system.

One way of transforming a genre system is to alter the value of one or more genres in relation to one another. Alterations in value are often if not always the result of diachronic flux undergone by single genres themselves. Generic flux over time is the dynamic that Ralph Cohen refers to as "processuality." Processuality is, for Cohen, based on the fact that new texts are continually being added to genres. To accommodate the new text assigned to the genre, the genre code undergoes a modification. With each appearance of, say, a new mystery novel or ballad that puts pressure on the definition of the genre to which it is assigned, the genre changes (Cohen 1986, 209). An interesting example of this process in South Asia is the one that altered the *shahr-āshob* (city disturber) genre of poetry.[13] It began as a catalog of the perilously beautiful boys who inhabited a particular city, but, particularly from the eighteenth century onward, poems lamenting the historical despoliation of cities like Delhi were assigned to the genre, culminating in the post-1857 collection *Fug̣hān-i Dihlī* (The lament for Delhi). By the time Na'īm Aḥmad (1968) wrote his classic study and anthology of the genre in the 1960s, critics' preoccupation with mining literature for historical references had ensured that the later poems defined the entire genre, whereas the itemization of "city disturbing" boys became problematical, unless it were made exterior to the genre.

As we will see in my discussion of the *Shāhnāmah* later in this book, texts also shift their generic alliances, being made to defect from one genre and enlist in another, as the *Shāhnāmah* was shuttled between a certain type of historiography and the romance genre. Differences in worldview, whether over time or simultaneously in one historical moment, may alter the allegiance of a text so that it is assigned to or removed from a genre without any necessity for the appearance of a wholly new text. We should, of course, reaffirm with Cohen the importance of the addition of new texts for the formation of genres. Yet in theory it is not even necessary for a text to be added to a preexisting genre for the genre to change over time. The genre code could conceivably change due to ideological forces and new valuations even while the corpus of texts assigned to it remained the same; one can imagine only very few genres that are not "alive" in the sense of having texts assigned to them in the present.

The premises that I have outlined with regard to genre can be summed up as follows. Genre is not innate or natural but rather instituted in a particular historical moment. More specifically, what is instituted is the genre code. Each genre is organized by such a code, which specifies the marks or generic traits that a text must reproduce to belong to the genre. The code justifies the assignment of texts bearing the requisite marks to the "correct" genre. This assignment appears in most cases to be merely a commonsensical identification, yet it is in fact impelled by the force of an ideology or worldview that is present at the moment of the institution of the code. Because it is instituted in a historical moment, by the force of ideas that arise out of a particular context, every genre is always located at the intersection of art and history. Studying the institution of the genre tells us about the worldview of the time in which it was instituted. Genres exist not alone but in "genre systems" wherein they are related to and valued against one another. Like individual genres, genre systems are historical, becoming transformed over time. And since in any given time and place many worldviews may be prevalent, multiple genre systems may exist in a single historical moment. Single genres themselves, aside from being contested by the force of competing worldviews in a single historical moment, also change over time, when new or old works are assigned to or subtracted from the genre or when shifting worldviews work to revalue it.

1

The Persian Storytellers of India

If we did not have access to its pieces, now scattered across the world, we would find it almost inconceivable that a book as luxurious and as valuable as Emperor Akbar's illustrated *Ḥamzah-nāmah* should ever have existed. On pages of outsize dimensions, the stories of Amīr Ḥamzah are beautifully, and sometimes whimsically, depicted by master artists in the imperial atelier. The sleeping king of India Landhūr bin Sa'dān is lifted by a demon determined to fling him into oblivion. Two adversaries do battle wearing armor that sparkles like precious turquoise and carnelian. A party gets out of control, and one drunkard can be seen dropping his trousers to relieve himself (Seyller and Thackston 2002, 95, 235, 248). Art historians believe that this masterpiece was not meant to be bound; its leaves would have been kept loose in boxes in the imperial library (Faridany-Akhavan 1989, 28; Seyller and Thackston 2002, 35, 42).

On one side of the folio were illustrations, and on the other side was often text describing a separate illustration. As in the Iranian storytelling practice of *pardah-khwānī*, it is likely that Akbar's storytellers displayed the images to the audience as they told their tales, perhaps also using the written text as a guide, though they could do without it just as easily (Seyller and Thackston 2002, 41–42; Faridany-Akhavan 1989, 5).[1] Notwithstanding the importance of the stories of Amīr Ḥamzah that have come down to us in writing and in painting, it must not be forgotten that for Akbar, his descendants, and their nobles, *qiṣṣah*s were experienced through oral performance. The vivid images of Akbar's *Ḥamzah-nāmah* were only materializations of the pictures that storytellers sought to paint in the imaginations of their audiences. By now, art historians have written much about the illustrated *Ḥamzah-nāmah*, and its great worth has become obvious to us. But to understand how much or how little romances were valued in the Mughal period, we must ask: *what were storytellers worth?*

The lives of the storytellers of India are tales that have barely been told. Few have bothered to write about them or even to remember their names. What would be the value in doing so, even for a study such as this one, which appears to deal with the worth not of the storytellers but of the texts that they created, the texts that make up the so-called romance genre? The tangibility and material power of a text like Akbar's *Ḥamzah-nāmah*, or the forty-six volumes of the Naval Kishore version, veil from our sight the fact that this genre is inseparable from the voices and bodies of the storytellers who produced, voiced, and embodied *qiṣṣah*s in their performances. If we want to know whether and how much the *qiṣṣah* or *dāstān* was valued prior to the coming of the novel to India, it is therefore necessary to ask how storytellers themselves were recognized and valued, both by their patrons and other contemporaries and by those who did remember them in later generations. In this chapter and the next, I will uncover the lives of the Persian- and Urdu-language storytellers of India, evaluating their worth in the eyes of those who recognized them. A survey of Indo-Persian storytellers demonstrates that, while the romance did not rank as highly as certain other genres, especially poetry, it was prized and valued thanks to the efforts of the storytellers who embodied it.

The Worth of Romances and Their Producers

I use the terms "worth" or "value" as shorthand for the quantity of cultural capital possessed by a romance or a storyteller. Cultural capital refers to cultural competencies that are accumulated through labor. It may be objectified in the form of a text like Akbar's *Ḥamzah-nāmah* or embodied in the storyteller (Bourdieu 2007).[2] Upon being recognized, cultural capital can be converted into other forms of capital—especially, but not exclusively, economic capital. On certain occasions, storytellers were rewarded in cash and in kind, as in one 1617 instance in which the emperor Jahangir showered a storyteller with gifts:

> Mullā Asad the storyteller, one of the servants of Mirzā Ġhāzī, came in those same days from Thattha and waited on me. Since he was skilled in transmitted accounts and sweet tales, and was good in his expression, I was struck with his company, and made him happy with the title of Maḥẕūẕ Ḳhān. I gave him 1,000 rupees, a robe of honor, a horse, an elephant in chains, and a palanquin. After a few days I gave the order for him to be weighed against rupees, and his weight came up to 4,400 rupees. He was honored with a rank [*manṣab*] of 200 personal, and 20 horse. I ordered that he should always be present at the gatherings for a chat [*gap*]. (Nūr al-Dīn Muḥammad Salīm Jahāngīr, Mu'tamad Ḳhān, and Hādī 1914, 187; Ḳhwājah Kāmgār Ḥusainī 1978, 240)[3]

This valuation of Mullā Asad is made in strikingly precise terms: Jahāngīr recognizes his cultural capital and converts it into 5,400 rupees, a *manṣab*, a horse, a robe, and so on. Similarly, it is recorded that on the seventeenth of Rabī' al ākhar 1015 H (August 21, 1606), 5,000 rupees were bestowed by Jahāngīr upon the storyteller Niẓām Shīrāzī (Nūr al-Dīn Muḥammad Salīm Jahāngīr, Mu'tamad Ḳhān, and Hādī 1914, 37). But usually the sources provide us only with noneconomic recognitions and valuations, like Jahāngīr's acknowledgment, in the passage above, of Mullā Asad's skill. That Mullā Asad is mentioned at all in Jahāngīr's imperial history is a form of recognition.[4] Because the conversion of cultural capital into cold, hard rupees is so often hidden from us, or present only as an indefinitely deferred possibility, describing the quantity of cultural capital can seem like an inexact science. But it is quite possible to grasp the worth of storytellers and the genre of verbal art that they produced *relative* to other genres and their producers. And it is possible to recognize the power of Jahāngīr's statements to elevate Mullā Asad the storyteller and to prop up the romance genre in the hierarchy of the genre system.

We have already seen that a genre system takes the shape of a hierarchy, structured by ideological forces. A genre's position in the system is dictated by its worth—that is, the quantity of cultural capital assigned to it, most obviously by its audience, on the basis of the ideology in play. Professional storytellers, insofar as they can be reduced to their storytelling role, can be said to have derived their own cultural capital from the preciousness of the romance genre and its resulting height in the genre system.

However, storytellers must not be seen as passive winners or losers in a one-sided game in which audiences single-handedly determined the worth of the romance and thereby that of the romance's producers. Storytelling was inescapably transactional. The storyteller was always immediately before his or her audience, reacting to their feedback, interpreting for them, and playing for the reward—monetary, symbolic, or otherwise—to be received from the audience and in particular from the patron who was possessed of means. This was the case with the storyteller Takaltū Ḳhān, who refrained from killing off a character to earn the Iranian ruler Shāh Ismā'īl's reward. Storytellers participated in the process of increasing their own cultural capital, raising their worth by magnifying that of the romance genre. The performed tale puts on display the cultural capital that the storyteller already possesses, but that this capital exists, in the form of the romance, is recognized and valued thanks to the storytelling performance.

At this point the relation between the worth of the romance genre and that of storytellers may seem straightforward. However, it will become abundantly clear from our examination of storytellers' lives that we cannot simply assume a closed circuit in which cultural capital flows between the romance and its producer without complication. Those who told stories also derived their worth from other roles that they played and for which they were remembered: from other arts that they practiced, other genres of verbal art that they produced, political functions that they carried out, their social connections, and even from eccentricities of character. Rather than seeing storytellers' playing of multiple roles as a diluting factor in the evaluation of the romance's worth, I will seek to understand how it contributed to the romance's value. Enabled by the spiderweb of roles upon which they moved, storytellers acted in strategic ways to magnify the worth of their stories and of the romance genre.

Two groups of professional storytellers have emerged most prominently out of the archive: those who performed in Persian from the sixteenth to seventeenth centuries and those who produced *qiṣṣah*s in Urdu from the nineteenth century to the early twentieth. Notices of Persian storytellers in biographical dictionaries (*taẕkirah*s) tend to lead to information regarding other Persian storytellers, and similarly within the mentions of Urdu storytellers. It is rare for the Persian-language storytellers accounted for here to be mentioned in Urdu sources, and storytellers working in Urdu are practically never mentioned in Persian sources. Yet, there is an isomorphy between the sets of information that we have on storytellers working in each language. In each case the sources tend to be either court histories or poetical biographical dictionaries, and the storytellers whose lives they reveal are overwhelmingly elite, performing in subimperial or even imperial settings.

Poetry and Storytelling in the Hierarchy of Genres

While the worth of the romance genre suffered a precipitous decline at the end of the nineteenth century and the beginning of the twentieth, it was never the case that it was perched comfortably upon the treetops of the hierarchy of genres. It might seem to have occupied a lofty position from the beginning of the Mughal period, given that the first Mughal emperor, Bābur (r. 1526–30), provided a storyteller for his son Humāyūn—we know this only because the hapless teller of tales was killed in a crossfire during an Indian campaign in 1526, possibly by a stray arrow from Bābur's own side (Babur and Ḳhān-i Ḳhānān 1993, 318). However, when the poet Mīr Sarbarahnah composed verses along the lines of the tale of Amīr Ḥamzah, Bābur regarded his romancing as a waste of time (Babur and Ḳhān-i Ḳhānān 1993, 366). Bābur's disapprobation was directed not at Mīr Sarbarahnah's versification itself but at its subject matter. He was not objecting to the verses as representatives of the genre of poetry but scoffed at them insofar as they belonged to the genre of romance. Poetry itself was a genre of verbal art that occupied a persistently elevated position in the hierarchy of the genre system, for it was a well-accepted currency in the Persianate social world, a versatile and portable medium through which individuals could gain recognition and all sorts of capital: social, cultural, and economic.

At least one storyteller, however, attempted to contest the idea that the romance occupied a lower position than the genre of poetry. In the seventeenth century there lived in Patna a storyteller who had emigrated from Iran to India, ʻAbd al-Nabī Fakhr al-Zamānī of Qazwin, whose well-documented life we will examine in chapter 3. He wrote a manual for storytellers that he entitled the *Ṭirāz al-akhbār* (Embroiderer of accounts). The *Ṭirāz al-akhbār* was not the first text of its kind. In 1545 the storyteller Muẓaffar Ḥusain had written a similar handbook. Muẓaffar Ḥusain was well acquainted with the storytelling craft. He was both the son of the storyteller Darwesh Muḥammad Samarqandī, renowned for his intimate relation with the governor of Khurasan Amīr Khān Turkmān (r. 1516–22), and the teacher of one of Jahāngīr's storytellers, Mīr Qiṣṣah (Qāṭiʻī Harawī 1979, 135). A copy of the *Abū Muslim-nāmah* calligraphed by Muẓaffar is extant, but his storytelling manual, the *Majmaʻ al-laṭāʼif* (Collection of subtleties), is now lost—possibly in a private collection somewhere or consigned to a Pakistani rubbish heap.[5] Given the loss of Muẓaffar's book, we are fortunate to possess Fakhr al-Zamānī's *Ṭirāz al-akhbār*, which refers to the *Majmaʻ al-laṭāʼif*, among many other texts.

The introduction to the *Ṭirāz al-akhbār* contains a section entitled "On the Superiority of the Storyteller to the Poet, Shown by Two Proofs." Fakhr al-Zamānī's arguments for the greater value of storytellers such as himself are as follows. (1) Storytelling is not merely the composition and recitation of words but an artful performance encompassing an outpouring of prose as well as verse that must be not only fluent and eloquent but also suitable (*munāsib*) given its place in the narrative stream. Besides the oral aspect of this performance there is also the physical: gestures and actions suited to the repertoire undergirding the phase of the story and illustrating the events being narrated. (2) The poet has the luxury of manipulating and revising verses as many times as is necessary to polish them to perfection before exposing them to an audience. The "poor storyteller," by contrast, must surrender himself to extemporaneity, a situation in which, Fakhr al-Zamānī suggests, revision is impossible (Fakhr al-Zamānī Qazwīnī 1633, fol. 20a).[6] Effectively, Fakhr al-Zamānī's plea is that the greater worth of storytelling is founded in its more complex performativity and its extemporaneous and transactional production.

Fakhr al-Zamānī's arguments can be read as an attempt to reshape the existing hierarchy in a way that would be beneficial for storytellers. It is because poetry is acknowledged to be a superior form of verbal art that the storyteller must challenge its superiority to gain value as a storyteller. The difficulty of producing an excellent romance contributes to its value, in Fakhr al-Zamānī's view. But this very same difficulty means that few storytellers will be compared favorably to poets. "I do not know," he writes, "whether in the whole wide world there are even two such storytellers who can undo the ignominy [of storytellers as against poets] with such color and fragrance that it would cause the wise ones of the times to be enraptured with their stories and their enchantments" (Fakhr al-Zamānī Qazwīnī 1633, fol. 20a). Excellent romances are hard to find, for the storytelling craft is a difficult one to master. Excellent poetry, being more easily produced (among its other advantages), will therefore be the cynosure of audiences' attention, and, because of the two forms' relative rates of production, poetry will barely be juxtaposed with those few excellent examples of the neglected *qiṣṣah* genre.

Versification was an established and relatively more secure way to gain capital. Persian storytellers in Mughal India therefore participated in the production of poetry alongside their storytelling, thereby gaining the favor of patrons like 'Abd al-Raḥīm Khān-i Khānān, the great potentate under the emperor Akbar. At least two storytellers in the employ of the Khān-i Khānān were also panegyrists. The first, Mīr Muḥammad Hāshim "Muḥtaram" Qiṣṣah-khwān Samarqandī, came into the Khān-i Khānān's service around 1583. The *Ma'āsir-i Raḥīmī* (Traces of Raḥīm) notices him primarily as a writer of praise poetry (*madḥ*), reproducing a panegyric (*qaṣīdah*) that he wrote for the Ḳhān-i Ḳhānān ('Abd al-Bāqī Nihāwandī 1910, 1004–5).

But most of the biographical dictionaries also mention that Hāshim was a storyteller who worked with the *Mahābhārata*. It is not clear whether Hāshim wrote a new Persian *Mahābhārata* or memorized Akbar's Persian *Mahābhārata* (the *Razmnāmah*). Brindāban Dās Ḳhwushgo affirmed the latter possibility:

> Mīr Muḥammad Hāshim Muḥtaram Qiṣṣah-khwān: Mīr Muḥammad Hāshim, pen name Muḥtaram, famous as a storyteller, from Samarqand. For a long while he was with Mirzā Ḳhān-i Ḳhānān. He was unparalleled in his storytelling, so much so that they write that he had on the tip of his tongue the entire *Mahābhārata*, than which there is no more reliable book in India. It is made up of odd names and strange tales, and composed of a hundred thousand verses. Akbar's man Naqīb Ḳhān translated it from Hindi into Persian at the High Order (of the Emperor). He [Mīr Hāshim] took opium constantly, and had a good grasp of wordcrafting.

Hāshim was active in the year 1602, when Akbar's great courtier and litterateur Abū al-Faẓl was killed. By 1024 H (1615–16) he was at the Quṭbshāhī court in Golconda ('Abd al-Bāqī Nihāwandī 1910, 1005).

Iskandar Qiṣṣah-ḳhwān was the other storyteller in the Ḳhān-i Khānān's service. He came to India probably from Western Iraq, and by 1024 H (1615–16) Jahāngīr had granted him a land assignment. Like Hāshim, he was also a panegyrist for the Ḳhān-i Khānān ('Abd al-Bāqī Nihāwandī 1910, 1042–43). Though both Hāshim and Iskandar were mentioned by 'Abd al-Baqī with the title of "storyteller" appended to their names, they received rewards such as ranks and land assignments and had their names recorded, largely because of their poetry, particularly their praise poetry.

Reception by patrons like the Ḳhān-i Ḳhānān and commemoration in written sources are both reflections of the value of artists for their immediate or near contemporaries. With regard to commemorations, it is noteworthy that storytellers were never remembered as a group in any recorded form in the precolonial period. We do not possess anything like a biographical dictionary or even a filiation of biographical notices of storytellers in any textual work. Instead, storytellers are mentioned in histories, for instance, as prodigies who happened to visit the Mughal court on a certain day, or in biographical dictionaries alongside a miscellany of other persons who wrote poetry. This fact is an indication either of the contested value of storytelling or simply of the paucity of storytellers whose craft was of value to potentates.

The starting point that yields the richest results when it comes to the excavation of storytellers' lives in the period before Shāh Jahān's enthronement in 1627 is the *Maikḥānah* (Winehouse), a biographical dictionary completed in 1028 H (1618–19) by 'Abd al-Nabī Faḳhr al-Zamānī. The *Maikḥānah* is by far the best known of Faḳhr al-Zamānī's works and the only one that has been edited. The reason is apparent: the *Maikḥānah* is a record of Faḳhr al-Zamānī's contemporaries, valued for the proximity of its author to the subjects of the biographical dictionary, many of them men he had met himself. It is for this reason that it is valuable to us as well, and no doubt its manuscripts proliferated after the seventeenth century due to similar attitudes. The Mughal emperor Aurangzeb's courtier, the eunuch Muḥammad Baḳhtāwar Ḳhān, mentions only the *Maikḥānah* and the *Nawādir al-ḥikāyāt* (Rare accounts) among Faḳhr al-Zamānī's works (Muḥammad Baḳhtāwar Ḳhān 1667, fol. 487b). The latter is a collection of historical anecdotes about figures from Adam to Buzurjmihr to Shāh Ismā'īl's minister Mīrzā Salmān in the transmission-based mode of historiography.[7] In contrast to the *Maikḥānah*, one could count the number of known manuscripts of the *Nawādir* on one's fingers. The number of manuscripts of Faḳhr al-Zamānī's storytelling manual the *Ṭirāẓ al-aḳhbār* is even fewer.[8]

It should be no surprise that the *Maikḥānah* should be doubly valued for being a storehouse of verses and for commemorating Persophone versifiers in a widely accepted historiographical mode. After all, it existed in a genre system that was dominated by poetry and in a society in which the production and recitation of verses was a key to building social capital via "networking." Its success has meant that Fakhr al-Zamānī has largely been esteemed as a poet and a sort of cultural historian, though at least cursory attention is always paid to the fact that he was a storyteller. Fakhr al-Zamānī himself stressed his storytelling talent very often, and, as we have seen, he claimed that a good storyteller was worth more than a mere poet. Yet the value of the *Maikhānah* itself, in comparison to the *Ṭirāz al-akhbār* or the *Nawādir al-ḥikāyāt*, shows the superiority of poetry against storytelling in the dominant genre system in which Fakhr al-Zamānī's writings found themselves.

One would imagine that a biographical dictionary by a storyteller would yield a couple of mentions of other storytellers, and such is the case with the *Maikhānah*: Fakhr al-Zamānī writes about the storytellers Muḥammad Ṭanbūrah and Mullā Asad, whose lives I will turn to in this chapter. The difficulty for anyone who wishes to tie these storytellers' representations to the value of the *qiṣṣah* is that they are not remembered in the *Maikhānah* on the basis of their being storytellers. Even Fakhr al-Zamānī represents them because of their worth in relation to poetry or to poets. The superior genre in the genre system, poetry, determined how these storytellers were remembered and indeed enabled them to be remembered at all. Outside of the *Maikhānah* as well, we know of many storytellers from this period, perhaps the majority, because of their role as poets and their consequent representation in biographical dictionaries of poets.

The precariousness of the romance's position in the genre system is one reason to think about its place in the array of strategies that storytellers used to increase their worth. For while their diversified strategy makes it more difficult for us to see the link between their worth and that of the *dāstān/qiṣṣah* genre, this complex action was necessary to raise the value of the romance genre to which storytellers were bound.

The Multiple Sources of Storytellers' Worth

For an example of the multiplicity of functions a storyteller could have, we need look no further than Muḥammad Ṭanbūrah, who is the sole storyteller, apart from Faḳhr al-Zamānī himself, whose *tarjamah* (biographical notice) appears in the *Maiḳhānah*. Ṭanbūrah was something of a jack-of-all-trades, whose skills ranged from storytelling to versification to music making to painting. Born in the Iranian province of Fars, Ṭanbūrah grew up in Qazvin and came to India in the year 1014 H (1605–6). The *Maiḳhānah* may be the only available source in which he is represented, and he is included because he is a *sāqī-nāmah* poet. Apart from Ṭanbūrah's composition of *sāqī-nāmah*s, which are poems addressed to the male cupbearer who serves at wine-drinking gatherings, Faḳhr al-Zamānī places stress on Ṭanbūrah's skill as a composer of humorous verses (*hazl*), quoting some lines that he had written on the Iranian prostitute Ḥūrī Ustād. Ṭanbūrah was also a storyteller of both the *Ḥamzah-nāmah* and the *Shahnāmah* at a time when most Persophone storytellers in India specialized in one or the other. And, as his name indicates, he was a proficient player on the tanpura (Faḳhr al-Zamānī Qazwīnī 1983, 914).

Muḥammad Ṭanbūrah is a prime example of an Iranian émigré who hedged his bets when he came to the Mughal court, finding an impressive number of ways to increase his value in the eyes of patrons. What is remarkable about the amplification of Ṭanbūrah's value, as revealed through the manner of his commemoration, is that it is based not only on the worth of his artistic abilities to his patrons but also upon his *defiance* of patronage and power. Ṭanbūrah's willingness to jeopardize the very relationship whence much of his worth was derived ultimately became the reason he is worth remembering. His skill as a visual artist was significant enough to gain him entry first into the atelier of Prince Ḳhurram (the future emperor Shāh Jahān) and then, by 1028 H (1615–16), into that of the emperor Jahāngīr. Ṭanbūrah had obtained his position in the Mughal atelier through the mediation of the superintendent of the Royal Library, after a dramatic falling out with his previous master, Prince Ḳhurram's courtier Ḳhwājah Waisī Hamadānī.

This conflict had come about in the following manner. Despite being a comely man, Ṭanbūrah had sinned against the behavioral laws of *mirzā*-hood by neglecting his appearance and by being not a gourmet but a gourmand.[9] Upon being taunted about his sloppiness by the habitually high-handed Ḳhwājah Waisī, Ṭanbūrah gave a barbed reply that led Ḳhwājah Waisī to dismiss him from service. Subsequently Ṭanbūrah composed a poem making use of his own name, "Muḥammad," to compare his victimhood in this situation to that of the Prophet Muḥammad in the face of his powerful uncle Abū Lahab, also known as Abū Jahl, in the earliest days of Islam:

> I have heard that in Muṣṭaf's days, Abū Jahl
> struck Aḥmad [Muḥammad] with his fist, in his ignorance.
> 'Alī, Master of Martyrs, heard this and he went
> and broke that cursed apostate's head and legs.
> But Ḥaẓrat Nawwāb Ḳhwājah Waisī dealt a blow,
> to Muḥammad, on behalf of Abu Jahl.

Prince Ḳhurram turned against Ḳhwājah Waisī a month afterward, and Ṭanbūrah found himself on the right side of this domestic political conflict. The storyteller's contrarian investment was made at a considerable risk, but it turned out to be profitable. The measure of renown that he gained, thanks to his retaliatory verses and entanglement in court politics, turns out to be as important or more important for his worth as expressed through commemoration (Faḳhr al-Zamānī Qazwīnī 1983, 914–15).

Muḥammad Ṭanbūrah's case illustrates two separate factors that must be taken into account when assessing the worth of storytellers. First, the patronizable abilities that he cultivated were many, so that there were multiple sources of his value to patrons. Second, his value to Faḳhr al-Zamānī was owing not only to these abilities but also to the interesting political role that he happened to play. For Ṭanbūrah, entanglement in politics was not an explicit requirement of any of his jobs. But in the cases of storytellers like 'Ināyat Allāh Darbār Ḳhān (d. ca. 1569), the political role was part and parcel of their professions. Darbār Ḳhān's value to his patron and to those who commemorated him was grounded in his dual ability as a storyteller and a political emissary, so that he straddled the line, if line there was, between the men of the pen and the men of the sword (*arbāb-i qalam* and *arbāb-i saif*).

Darbār Ḳhān, the best-known storyteller to Akbar, was the son of Zain al-'Ābidīn Takaltū Ḳhān (or Takalū Ḳhān). Takaltū Ḳhān served both Shāh Ismā'īl, the first Safavid emperor, and his son Shāh Ṭahmāsp (r. 1514–76). After entering Shāh Ismā'īl's service, Takaltū Ḳhān became very close to the potentate. Sām Mīrzā, one of Shāh Ismā'īl's younger sons, wrote of the storyteller, and of the emperor, "The jests and witticisms that occurred between him and his Majesty are world famous, and since their occurrence was on account of the frank [relationship between the two men], he did thereby not commit any act of impertinence." At the beginning of the sixteenth century, Shāh Ismā'īl seized the city of Tabriz. Here he decided to construct a new pavilion, and when it was complete he held a celebration. At the inaugural party, Takaltū Ḳhān performed the *Ḥamzah-nāmah* books (*daftars*) of Nūr al-Dahr and Īraj, which he had composed. Shāh Ismā'īl was enthralled and lavished two hundred tomans upon his storyteller, naming the building itself the Pavilion (*kūshk*) of Takaltū Ḳhān.[10]

Shāh Ismā'īl treated Takaltū Ḳhān's performances as omens and named his sons Ṭahmāsp and Alqāṣ after the warriors who bore these names in the *Ḥamzah-nāmah*. The fixing of their names was based on the timing of their births: in 1514 the newborn Ṭahmāsp was brought to Shāh Ismā'īl while Takaltū Ḳhān was narrating a battle in which the warrior Ṭahmāsp played a major role, and such was the case of Alqāṣ Mīrzā (1516–50) two years later. Another anecdote tells of how Takaltū Ḳhān could modify the *qiṣṣah* according to Shāh Ismā'īl's desire. The emperor would save favored characters from their customary deaths upon the battlefield by paying Takaltū Ḳhān the bloodwite that the storyteller demanded; ten tomans to rescue Qahrish and twenty for the life of Ṭahmāsp b. 'Anqawīl Dew (Faḳhr al-Zamānī Qazwīnī 1633, fol. 18b).

It may have been Takaltū Ḳhān's exceptional storytelling that caused Shāh Ismā'īl to value him so highly, including his dexterity in directing the flow of tales and his understanding of the romance's transactionality.

But these abilities may not have been the only sources of Takaltū Ḳhān's worth. It appears that he was involved in some form of warfare; Sām Mirzā notes that Takaltū Ḳhān was a native of Shiraz, who at first "traveled a great deal and spent his time in battle" (Sām Mirzā 2005, 138). His name, connected to that of the Takalū tribe, suggests a Qizilbāsh origin. If that is the case, it would not be surprising if he had some experience warring in the interests of the Safavids as they established their dominion over Iran.

Darbār Ḳhān, who was honored by Akbar with a rank (*manṣab*) of 2,000, was heir both to Takaltū Ḳhān's role as a storyteller and to his guise as a man of the sword (Farīd Bhakkarī 1961, 231). The circumstances of one of his storytelling performances in 1564 reveal this quite clearly. It took place in the morning during the rainy season. Akbar's camp had been struck in the jungle of Narwar, not far from Gwalior. 'Abd Allāh Ḳhān Uzbeg, governor of Malwa, had turned renegade, and the emperor was in pursuit. On this morning the imperial party had returned from an elephant hunt, and they took advantage of the respite to watch Darbār Ḳhān perform the *Dāstān-i Amīr Ḥamzah*. But Darbār Ḳhān was there not only to perform the romance. Shortly afterward, as the imperial camp advanced upon 'Abd Allāh Ḳhān, Darbār Ḳhān was sent ahead with I'timād Ḳhān to Mandu to parley with the rebel. Their efforts to bring the rebel to reason were fruitless, and a battle ensued near the village of Bagh. Darbār Ḳhān was likely among the victorious fighters in that effort (Abū al-Fazl b. Mubārak 1877, 225–26).

Similarly, in the next year Darbār Ḳhān was dispatched alongside Ḳhwājah Jahān to negotiate with the rebellious governor of Jaunpur, 'Alī Qulī Ḳhān, who had encamped at the ford of Narhan on the Ganges. The negotiations took place in boats in the middle of the river, and Badā'unī writes in the *Muntaḳhab al-tawārīḳh* (Selected histories) that it was Darbār Ḳhān who brought the report of the discussion to the imperial ear (Badā'ūnī 1864, 79). Darbār Ḳhān also traveled with the Mughal camp during Akbar's expedition against Ḳhān-i Zamān in the twelfth year of the imperial reign and during the 1568 expedition leading to the siege of Ranthambore Fort (Shāh Nawāz Ḳhān Aurangābādī 1888, 2:1). It seems unlikely that Darbār Ḳhān's role was restricted, in these counter-rebellious missions, to that of storyteller, given the precedents of his diplomatic efforts in the quelling of Malwa and Jaunpur. He need not have always moved with the imperial camp. In 976 H (1569) he was granted leave to remain in Agra when Akbar meant to visit the shrine of the Sufi Muʿīn al-Dīn Chishtī in Ajmer. Soon afterward Darbār Ḳhān died in the imperial capital. Akbar returned from Ajmer and took part in the funeral feast, showing his appreciation of his servant's worth (Niẓām al-Dīn Aḥmad b. Muḥammad Muqīm 1913, 225). The loyal Darbār Ḳhān was laid to rest alongside Akbar's dog (Abū al-Faẓl b. Mubārak 1877, 339; Shāh Nawāz Ḳhān Aurangābādī 1888, 2:1).

Apart from the written record of Darbār Ḳhān's political activities, we are fortunate to have a portrait of the storyteller that speaks strikingly of his double role. In connection with King George V's coronation durbar in 1911, a painting of Darbār Ḳhān was exhibited, on loan, at the Delhi Museum.[11] Darbār Ḳhān is not shown in a seated or gesticulating storytelling pose at all. Instead, he is depicted standing in profile, the right side of his body offered to the viewer's gaze. With his right hand he pulls from his left side a sword, which he is apparently unsheathing from its scabbard. A few inches of its metal are visible. His left hand rests on what appears to be another martial implement, probably a shield. This portrait unmistakably represents Darbār Ḳhān as a man involved in politics and warfare. Everything we know about him indicates that he was a man whose storytelling was by no means his only source of value to his patron or to those who preserved his memory.

Muḥammad Ṯanbūrah's sharp verses and Darbār Ḳhān's diplomacy were not the only ways for storytellers to involve themselves in politics. The storyteller Mullā Asad, whom we saw at the beginning of this chapter being weighed against rupees at Jahāngīr's command, supplemented his cultural capital with social capital, which in turn became a kind of political power by proxy. Prior to his arrival at Jahāngīr's court, Mullā Asad had been found worthy of subimperial patronage in the province of Thatta. Asad, himself an émigré from Iran, served his patron with a social capital derived from his network of acquaintances. He was instrumental in identifying other useful servants from the Safavid domains and bringing them to the subimperial court.

The son of an independent sovereign defeated by Ḳhān-i Ḳhānān, Mullā Asad's patron Mirzā Ġhāzī Beg Tarḳhān (ca. 1586–1612) had taken his hereditary place on the throne of Thatta in 1009 H (1600–1601) under the suzerainty of Akbar. In 1013 H (1604–5) that emperor summoned him to the imperial court. Akbar passed away while Mirzā Ġhāzī was still attending him, but Jahāngīr soon recruited Mirzā Ġhāzī's help in a campaign in Qandahar. Mirzā Ġhāzī was fond enough of storytellers to patronize several of them. There was, for instance, Mīr 'Abd al-Bāqī Qiṣṣah-khwān, an Iranian storyteller who came to Mirzā Ġhāzī's court in Qandahar. Then there was Mullā 'Abd al-Rashīd, or Mullā Rashīd, who seems to have come from Bandar Lāharī, a port city to the southeast of Thatta (Nisyānī Tattawī 1964, 224; Qāni' Tattawī 1959, 242).[12] Like so many other storytellers, Mullā Rashīd had many other skills, in his case an ability to compose good poetry and a strong understanding of jurisprudence (Qāni' Tattawī 1959, 242).

However, the most successful storyteller patronized by Mirzā Ġhāzī while he was still in Thatta was Mullā Asad. Like Darbār Ḳhān, Asad came from a Shirazi family of storytellers.[13] His father, Ḥaidar Qiṣṣah-ḳhwān, and his paternal uncle Fatḥī Beg Shahnāmah-ḳhwān were dependents of the Safavid emperor Shāh 'Abbās. Iskandar Munshī was full of praise for Ḥaidar and Fatḥī Beg in his work on Shāh 'Abbās. He applauded Fatḥī Beg's powers of vocal projection. "Without exaggeration," Iskandar Munshī wrote, "the flame of his voice would stretch its tongue as far as a *farsang*." While this praise might be taken as conventional, it should be contrasted with the chronicler's opinion regarding another storyteller in Iran at the time: "Maulānā Muḥammad Ḳhwurshed Isfahānī was also a good storyteller, but the possessors of discernment would prefer Maulānā Ḥaidar" (Iskandar Beg Turkmān 1956, 191).

With a family practicing storytelling in the service of Shah 'Abbas, Mullā Asad was the beneficiary of both cultural capital, in the form of the storytelling abilities that were passed down to him, and social capital via his identification with the Safavid ruler's court. With a bit of effort,

1. Photograph of portrait of Darbār Ḳhān. Photograph, 1912/1911. Photo 1010/10(148), Delhi Museum (Darbar Loan Exhibition), British Library.

social capital with such a strong basis is apt to multiply. Asad is likely to have made many useful acquaintances in Safavid Iran before coming to Thattha to serve Mirzā Ġhāzī, whose coastal domain and Shi'a inclination would have made his patronage visible and attractive to potential dependents from Iran (Rāshidī 1970). Once in Thattha, Asad deployed his potent brew of cultural and social capital to consolidate the power that he gained through Mirzā Ġhāzī's patronage. To focus on his shrewd investment of social capital, we ought to consider how he made use of his network on his patron's behalf.

An illustration of the way Asad increased his value by putting his network at his patron's disposal can be found in Faḵhr al-Zamānī's rather unflattering mention of the storyteller in the *Maiḵhānah*. From 1607 till his death in 1621, Mirzā Ġhāzī was present in Qandahar, which he governed until the end of his short life. Faḵhr al-Zamānī tells us that one of the Iranian visitors to Mirzā Ġhāzī's court was the poet Hakim Faġhfūr Lāhījī, who was on his way to Hindustan via Qandahar. Despite Mirzā Ġhāzī's own kindness, Faġhfūr was incensed by the importunity of two envious boon companions of the ruler (Faḵhr al-Zamānī Qazwīnī 1983, 456). These troublemakers were the émigré poet Murshid Burojirdī and the storyteller Mullā Asad. They were such a source of annoyance to Faġhfūr in Qandahar, interrupting him at every opportunity, that he left the area in a pique, without giving notice. Upon discovering that this rare bird of poetical talent had flown from his dominion, Mirzā Ġhāzī was much abashed. He wrote a letter to Faġhfūr, in which he apologized for Murshid's and Asad's behavior. The two offenders were admonished and made to write letters of their own (Faḵhr al-Zamānī Qazwīnī 1983, 456). Nevertheless, Faġhfūr continued in high dudgeon and only sent Mirzā Ġhāzī a quatrain by way of reply:

> Alas for anyone whose garment's hem
> should be polluted by a corpse gripped by two vultures' claws!
> An ass who seeks to have a horn is asking for too much—
> two ass's ears upon one ass's head are quite enough. (Faḵhr al-Zamānī Qazwīnī 1983, 457)[14]

The extent to which Asad was favored becomes quite clear when we consider the liberty he was given to annoy a poet of high standing. In spite of the Qandahari governor's tardy admonitions, Faġhfūr's description of Mirzā Ġhāzī as a corpse manipulated by Asad's talons no doubt reflected a real power relation. If we turn our attention to the second "ass's ear," Murshid Burojirdī, we will see how Asad was able to bring his friends under Mirzā Ġhāzī's patronage.

Murshid came from Burojerd in the west of Iran, eventually arriving in Shiraz, where he served the Turkoman Muḥammad Qulī Ḳhān Parnak. He stayed in Shiraz for at least seven years, aiding Muḥammad Qulī Ḳhān in governing the region and thereby burnishing his administrative credentials. It was probably in Shiraz where he met Mullā Asad. Asad recommended Murshid to Mirzā Ġhāzī after Muḥammad Qulī Ḳhān's death, and the storyteller was valued enough by Mirzā Ġhāzī that Murshid soon received a letter of invitation to come to Thatta (Faḳhr al-Zamānī Qazwīnī 1983, 598–99; see 'Abd al-Bāqī Nihāwandī 1910, 781–88). Murshid's divan of poetry includes the panegyric that he presented to Mirzā Ġhāzī upon his arrival in Thatta via Hurmuz. In this poem he lauds Asad as his benefactor:

> Your servant of heavenly stature, Asad—who is
> a brother to me, and a clear example to the world
> by way of the inclination of his generous mind (may it endure!)
> toward people of skill, and especially this lowly beggar—
> wrote an epistle with a message whereby the honey
> of homeland love grew bitter to my taste.
> When I had read the letter, out of desire for the Ka'ba of your lane—
> the path to which was shown by none other than Fate—
> I started on the road. (quoted in Faḳhr al-Zamānī Qazwīnī 1983,
> 599–600)

Mirzā Ġhāzī showed as much favor, or more, to Asad's crony as to Asad himself, investing him with high political powers, including deputyship (*wakālat*). Through Murshid's mediation, Mirzā Ġhāzī patronized artists from Iran, including such poets as the renowned Ṭālib Āmulī, Maḥwī Ardibīlī, and Surūrī Yazdī, as well as other craftsmen such as the calligrapher Shamsah-i Zarrīn Qalam (Rāshidī 1970). Murshid was also fast friends with the storyteller Mullā Rashīd, and he would recite Rashīd's verses before the ruler from time to time. Partly through the mediation of Murshid, Rashīd had grown in Mirzā Ġhāzī's estimation to such an extent that the ruler paid for Mullā Rashīd to be conveyed from his home (Bandar Lāharī, probably) and into his service in Qandahar just after 1012 H (1603) (Khan 2017a, 38).

Both Asad and Murshid remained with Mirzā Ġhāzī in Qandahar until the young ruler's suspicious death. Thereafter, Murshid wended his way to Ajmer to serve Mahābat Ḳhān.[15] Asad, on the other hand, found his way to Jahāngīr's court, where the emperor lavished upon him gifts, rank, and the title "Maḥẕūẕ Ḳhān." The sources differ with regard to the year of Asad's death. Taqī al-Dīn Auḥadī holds that Asad was traveling with Jahāngīr's camp from Gujarat to Agra in 1027 H (1619) and died on the way. Wālih Dāġhistānī says that he died in Jahāngīr's camp a year later. The most reliable source, however, may be Murshid Burojirdī, who wrote a chronogrammatical verse set (*qiṭ'ah-i tārīḳh*) in memory of his old friend:

> Alas, alas! For Maḥẕūẕ Ḳhān has left!
> The lion of the world of art has left the world!
> Who has any tongue? What can be said? He's left,
> so speech has left the tongue; the tongue has left the mouth.
> I am left, though I have seen his death—
> the gain to me is loss, nothing but loss.
> Asad left, and Murshid searched for a chronogram
> of his death. His heart said: "Needlessly Asad has left!" (Faḳhr al-Zamānī Qazwīnī 1983, 600)

The chronogram in the final hemistich, "*Asad rāygān raft*," yields the year 1026 H (1617–18) when the correspondence of its letters to numbers is deciphered.

Mullā Asad was thus valuable to his patron not only by way of his storytelling abilities but also because he provided Mirzā Ġhāzī with the political services of his friend Murshid Burojirdī. In return, without having any formal political position, Mullā Asad possessed a power that was at least derived from his friend's political power, and it was due to the good word he put in for his friend that many other émigrés from Safavid domains came to be patronized.

Muḥammad Ṭanbūrah, Darbār Ḳhān, and Mullā Asad all derived worth not only from their storytelling but also from other crafts and functions. Darbār Ḳhān played a diplomatic role for Akbar, while Mullā Asad was valuable to Mirzā Ġhāzī as an anchor for other useful émigrés. Muḥammad Ṭanbūrah was learned in an array of arts and had his own eccentric role to play in Mughal politics. The examples could be multiplied. The storytellers Mīr Muḥammad Hāshim and Iskandar Qiṣṣah-ḳhwān were also panegyrists to the Ḳhān-i Ḳhānān. Faḳhr al-Zamānī himself was librarian to Mahābat Ḳhān's son in Ajmer. He composed poetry, and we remember him mainly because of his biographical dictionary and the poetry that he recorded therein. We cannot deduce the worth of the romance by trying to measure the appreciation and patronage given to storytellers considered solely as storytellers. Rather, we need to take into account the web of roles, aside from and including storytelling, that constituted the sources of worth of storytellers to their patrons, audiences, and commemorators.

How Storytellers Increased the Worth of Romances

Thus far it may seem as if storytelling, and thus the genre of the *qiṣṣah* or *dāstān*, were of low or peripheral value. The facts established above seem to point in this direction: the higher value of poetry in the genre hierarchy, the reflection of poetry's high value in the reasons for the survival of the traces of storytellers, and storytelling's position as only one in an array of strategies that storytellers used to increase their cultural and economic capital. The evidence regarding the supremacy of poetry is unequivocal. But the multiple sources of storytellers' worth in fact allowed storytellers to better amplify the value of the genre.

Take the storyteller Faḳhr al-Zamānī, for example. Despite having several roles and abilities for which he was patronized and remembered, he placed his storytelling at the center of his arsenal of skills. He avowed that it was due to his storytelling, first and foremost, that he gained patronage and that storytelling, in general, was highly valued by patrons. He pointed to Takaltū Ḳhān and Darbār Ḳhān, for example, to argue that "storytellers are quick to gain proximity to the emperors of the world" (Faḳhr al-Zamānī Qazwīnī 1633, fol. 19b). As we shall see in chapter 3, Faḳhr al-Zamānī had a series of patron-client relationships, probably beginning in a small way with his kinsman Mirzā Niẕāmī, a chronicler at Jahāngīr's court in Agra; then attaching himself to Mirzā Amān Allāh, the son of Mahābat Ḳhān, whose librarian he was for several years; and finally, during his long residence in Patna, enjoying the patronage of the governors of Bihar. In each of these cases, Faḳhr al-Zamānī's initial means of bringing himself to his benefactors' attention was his telling of the *Qiṣṣah-i Amīr Ḥamzah*. As Faḳhr al-Zamānī said of himself in the *Ṭirāz al-aḳhbār*: "In every country that he reached, it was his storytelling that was loudly celebrated. He saw that the rank of the other arts was low, and the rulers of every land troubled this weakling to tell the story of [Ḥamzah b. Abū Muṭṭalib]" (Faḳhr al-Zamānī Qazwīnī 1633, fol. 22b). Recalling his time in Kashmir, he speaks of a certain young nobleman whose praise he won by means of his performance of the story of Ḥamzah. By contrast, his friend Ni'mat Allāh Ṣafāhānī failed to dazzle the noble with his display of skill in the occult sciences, demonstrating the superiority of the *qiṣṣah* even to magic in the eyes of patrons (Faḳhr al-Zamānī Qazwīnī 1633, fol. 19a). In securing patronage, Faḳhr al-Zamānī did use his other skills as well. After grabbing Amān Allāh's attention and arousing his desire with a performance of Ḥamzah's tale, he further interested the young noble by his extemporaneous composition of verses. In Patna, apart from telling stories, he wrote a poem upon Shāh Jahān's coronation, for which he received a reward, and for the governor Saif Ḳhān's mosque, he composed a poem that was inscribed along the inner walls. Yet in no uncertain terms, he privileged his storytelling as the skill that patrons appreciated above all others. His poetry would most often have been a way to ornament his prose *dāstāns*. His librarianship facilitated his production of a manual of storytelling. Each of his roles, not only his role as a storyteller, can be seen to be directed toward raising the value of the genre of verbal art, in which he was most invested.

The abundant, if qualified, cultural capital of the *qiṣṣah* genre from the fifteenth to seventeenth centuries is evidenced by the recognition given to storytellers like Darbār Ḳhān and Mullā Asad by patrons. But a genre's value is produced not only by those who receive it but also by those who produce it. Ideological forces stand behind the position of a genre in the genre system. In the act of raising the worth of the *qiṣṣah* genre, storytellers relied upon and reinforced the ideologies of their milieu. This is demonstrated by their assertion of the usefulness or exemplarity of the *qiṣṣah*, which we will now examine. That this assertion was ideological will be made clear in chapter 4 when we consider its rejection by competing ideologies, especially with the onset of colonialism.

Considering the conjunction of storytellers' non-storytelling roles, we will for the moment inspect three strategies employed by storytellers to raise the worth of the romance through the assertion of its use value. Faḳhr al-Zamānī wrote in the *Ṭirāz al-aḳhbār* of the advantages of *qiṣṣah-ḳhwānī* to storytellers and their listeners:

> First, it makes the speaker, along with the listener, eloquent and fluent and knowledgeable regarding the current speech [*rozmarrah*]. Second, it makes them appear knowledgeable regarding the administration of worldly affairs and activities related to the kingdom, and it makes storytellers dear in the sight of the nation's rulers. In spite of its own vanity, it shakes the people of fortune off of the skein of vain thoughts. There is no better medium for the gaining of intimacy with sultans, ministers, nobles and nobles' sons than the romance.

Faḳhr al-Zamānī's words echo three strategies manifestly used by the producers of romances for raising the genre's worth. (1) Storytellers often targeted younger patrons (nobles' sons) receptive to the lessons of *qiṣṣah*s, and (2) they asserted that *qiṣṣah*s had worth as political examples and (3) as examples of good language use. To discuss these strategies, it will be necessary to discuss not only the cases of the Persian-language *qiṣṣah-ḳhwān*s mentioned above but also others whose lives will be discussed in later chapters.

Storytellers seeking patronage appear to have found it worth their while to attach themselves to younger patrons. The primary advantage of this was obvious: they would thereby gain an intimacy that might have been more difficult to obtain with more senior patrons, and they would then be able to develop that intimacy and power over time. Additionally, storytellers' claims regarding the didactic usefulness of their *qiṣṣah*s were more likely to be effective with a patron who was both persuadable over time and receptive to instruction. There are several examples of storytellers working for younger patrons, beginning with the Mughal emperor Humāyūn's storyteller, killed by a stray arrow in 1526 when Humāyūn was a young man of around eighteen years of age. Akbar was no longer a child when Darbār Ḳhān performed the tale of Amīr Ḥamzah for him on a hunting expedition. Nevertheless, the emperor was only around twenty-two years old, and it is unlikely that this was Darbār Ḳhān's first performance for him. As we have seen, within a year of this performance, Darbār Ḳhān had been entrusted with a political role, probably on the basis of his experience or instruction at the feet of his Qizilbash father. Similarly, Mullā Asad attached himself to Mirzā Ġhāzī early in his patron's life.[16] Through his storytelling role, Asad was able to gain the ruler's confidence to such an extent that Mirzā Ġhāzī summoned Murshid Burojirdī from Iran at his recommendation. When Faḳhr al-Zamānī mentioned the *umarā-zadāgān* (nobles' sons) among the kinds of patrons to whose notice storytellers would come, he may have been referring to patrons like Mahābat Ḳhān's son Mirzā Amān Allāh. Amān Allāh was probably at an age between his late teens and late twenties when Faḳhr al-Zamānī first performed and made the young *mirzā* "desirous" of him, in his words, in the year 1613 (Faḳhr al-Zamānī Qazwīnī 1983, 762). Faḳhr al-Zamānī's great regret at having to leave Amān Allāh's service, due to an apparent venereal disease, was no doubt sharpened by the knowledge that Amān Allāh was likely to rise, as he did under both Jahāngīr and Shāh Jahān, despite his father Mahābat Ḳhān's troublesomeness.[17] After his exile from Amān Allāh's patronage, Faḳhr al-Zamānī used his storytelling to become intimate with an unnamed son of a nobleman in Kashmir sojourn. Urdu storytellers too, Ḳhalīl 'Alī Ḳhān Ashk and Mīr Bāqir 'Alī among them, performed for younger audiences.

In pointing out this strategy, I do not wish to make any assumptions about childhood as it was imagined by this society, much less contribute to the tendency to infantilize the romance genre wholesale. I have yet to come across any pre-nineteenth-century criticism of the romance for being infantile or any hint of its consignment to the realm of "children's literature" alone. The British infantilization of "Eastern romances" in the nineteenth century seems to be without precedent (see chap. 5).

Nonetheless, the pattern that emerges from the historical evidence suggests that, very often, storytellers were attempting to capture the minds and hearts of younger patrons, who may have been more receptive to the various forms of exemplarity that *qiṣṣah*s presented or, in other words, to learning from them and using them. The *Ḥamzah-nāmah*, the romance to which Faḳhr al-Zamānī specifically referred in the *Ṯirāz al-aḳhbār*, was likely to have been especially suitable in this context, given that its first cycle (*daftar*) traditionally deals with Ḥamzah's Herculean exploits as a child or very young man. Later on in the series, similar feats are recounted of Ḥamzah's children as well. What is likely to have been important, however, is not so much the age of the listeners but their receptivity.

In the twentieth century, the Urdu storyteller Mīr Bāqir 'Alī, who performed for college students in Delhi, would place great emphasis in his writings on the importance of listening and receiving knowledge. One kind of knowledge that the *qiṣṣah* contained, according to Faḳhr al-Zamānī, was political knowledge, ranging from military stratagems to methods of administration. We have already seen that a storyteller like Darbār Ḳhān could not only possess such knowledge but also convert the capital of his political knowledge into a political role complementing his role as a storyteller. Later storytellers and storywriters would make the same claim, as when Ashk, and later Ġhālib Lakhnawī, stated that when one listens to *Ḥamzah-nāmah*, "one's memory is filled with stratagems for battles, the taking of forts and the conquest of countries" (see chap. 3). The tales of Ḥamzah are indeed filled with such matters. Ḥamzah, as Lord of the Auspicious Conjunction and defender of Islam, does battle with numerous foes, or 'Amar 'Ayyār does so in his absence, sometimes with magic, sometimes with espionage and trickery, and sometimes with more conventional but equally wily forms of military strategy. On the other hand, kings in the *Ḥamzah-nāmah* like the ill-advised Nausherwān provide a negative example of rulership. The claim to political exemplarity would have been familiar to *Ḥamzah-nāmah* audiences from other *qiṣṣah*s like the *'Iyār-i dānish* (Criterion of knowledge), a version of the stories of *Kalīlah wa Dimnah*, written by Akbar's courtier Abū al-Faẓl in 1584. *Kalīlah wa Dimnah* had taught rulers in India and Iran about "the affairs of the state and of property," according to Abū al-Faẓl, though the actors through which this teaching occurred were mere "tongueless" animals made to speak by the teller of tales (Abū al-Faẓl b. Mubārak, n.d., fol. 9a).

Our modern idea of the romance as a frivolous genre, detached from the world, is an ideological one, contradicted by storytellers who operated in a quite different epistemological climate. It is not difficult to gain a sense from the stories themselves of how they could have been politically exemplary. The multigenre makeup of *qiṣṣah*s meant that storytellers were in fact using political and military passages from histories in their storytelling performances, so that the political exemplarity of textual fragments from these genres was woven into the *qiṣṣah* and strengthened by it (see chap. 3). On occasion *qiṣṣah* passages appear in histories as well, in revealing ways. In his history of Humāyūn, Jauhar Āftābchī recounted a tale of a battle lost by the Muslim protagonists in the *Ḥamzah-nāmah* due to the Prophet's misjudgment in not relying entirely upon God's will to decide the course of the conflict. Āftābchī gave this example to highlight Humāyūn's underestimation of his Afghan rival Sher Shāh Sūrī, who would succeed in taking Hindustan. It is difficult to imagine that Humāyūn's unfortunate *qiṣṣah-ḳhwān* had not told him this tale. What Āftābchī's story and its context suggest is that, had Humāyūn heeded the *Ḥamzah-nāmah*'s political exemplarity, he would have been more circumspect in his maneuvers (Āftābchī 2009, 98–99).

The cultivation of the Persian language in India was another source of the value of storytelling, if we are to believe Faḳhr al-Zamānī's representation. Ṭanbūrah, Darbār Ḳhān, Asad, and many other Persian-language storytellers in Mughal India and the Deccan were émigrés from Iran. In fact, most of the storytellers of whom we are aware from this period were Iranian. Much like the preponderance of Iranians among the Mughal poets laureate (*mulūk al-shu'arā*), the remembered proportion of Iranian storytellers is a fact that points to the well-documented prestige in the subcontinent of forms of Persian that were spoken in Iran (Alam 2003, 161). Faḳhr al-Zamānī wrote that the storyteller's audience is apt to gain a better understanding of the *rozmarrah*, or current speech, in Persian. Orally performed romances that were mainly in prose were more likely than poetry to give audiences a sense of the *rozmarrah* that the storyteller chose to present. There is evidence that Iranian storytellers like Faḳhr al-Zamānī considered their own *rozmarrah*, as opposed to that of other Persophone regions, to be the exemplar of correct Persian. In his discussion of the Indian, Turanian, and Iranian styles of storytelling, Faḳhr al-Zamānī looks askance at the odd phrasing used by Turanian storytellers, stating that they are not bound to use the *rozmarrah* at all, though they excel in other ways (Faḳhr al-Zamānī Qazwīnī 1633, fol. 22a–22b). The emphasis on the refinement of language abilities goes hand in hand with the strategy of capturing the patronage of younger nobles most likely to benefit therefrom.

The importance of linguistic exemplarity to the worth of the romance genre will be easier to see in the cases of Urdu storytellers, particularly Khalil 'Ali Ḳhān Ashk and Mīr Bāqir 'Alī, whom we will discuss in the next chapter. Right down to the twentieth century, Bāqir 'Alī was an authority in the Urdu language. Audience members would appeal to him for the elucidation of words that had grown obscure, sometimes during his storytelling performances. He would correct the Urdu usage of passersby on the street. His chapbook *qiṣṣah*s often contained footnotes in which he took it upon himself to explain words he was using. But Ashk, at the beginning of the nineteenth century, is the clearest example of a storyteller whose job it was to inculcate correct language usage in his audience, for he was hired by John Gilchrist of Fort William College for the purpose of telling stories to the British students and thereby improving their command of the Urdu language. It seems to have been understood at Fort William College that the *qiṣṣah* was an excellent vehicle for language acquisition; the books produced at the college for the benefit of British students learning Urdu-Hindi were mainly romances, including Ashk's *Ḥamzah-nāmah* but also many others, such as the *Qiṣṣah-i Chahār darwesh* (Story of the four dervishes) and the *Qiṣṣah-i Ḥātim Ṭā'ī* (Story of Ḥātim Ṭā'ī).

It is doubtful that this recognition of the linguistic-exemplary potential of *qiṣṣah*s originated with Gilchrist or with anyone else at Fort William. It appears likely that the Indian munshis who were teaching the British had already been using romances for this purpose, and we can speculate that this practice stemmed from the similar use of Persian *qiṣṣah*s by Indians. A 1799 manuscript of an Urdu *Qiṣṣah-i Ḥātim Ṭā'ī* belonging to Gilchrist's student, the Orientalist John Shakespear, contains English translations and glosses in the hand of a probable earlier owner, indicating that it was used for language learning. Either in the 1780s or in 1803, Mihr Chand Khatrī wrote the romance of Malik Maḥmūd and Gītī-afroz (*Nau ā'īn-i Hindī*) for the future Baron Cowley, Henry Wellesley, who wished to learn the tongue (Mihr 1988, 54–56; Gyān Chand Jain 1969, 207).[18] Given the British use of written *qiṣṣah*s for this purpose, even before Fort William College inaugurated Urdu printed books, it does not seem improbable that Gilchrist's "long experience" of the advantages of listening to storytellers was based on methods for language acquisition already known to the British in eighteenth-century India. Nor does it seem far-fetched to guess that these methods were derived from a precolonial tradition of using *qiṣṣah*s as linguistic exemplars, as Fakhr al-Zamānī had hinted in the seventeenth century.

The quantification of the romance genre's worth is an inexact science, especially since its worth must have fluctuated over time. Its worth and its place in the genre system were limited by superior genres such as poetry. Nevertheless, the *qiṣṣah* genre and the performance of *qiṣṣahs* undoubtedly had a worth that was recognized by patrons and commemorators but that was also produced in various ways by storytellers themselves. However, from reflecting upon the lives of Persian storytellers, and of Urdu storytellers in the next chapter, we can appreciate two things about the worth of *qiṣṣahs*. (1) The worth of stories cannot be separated from that of storytellers, who were doing their best to raise the value of their craft for their own benefit using strategies such as the three we have examined. (2) The worth of storytellers is in turn inseparable from the worth that they accumulated through their other roles, whether political, social, or artistic—or even as "characters," as in Muḥammad Ṯanbūrah's case.

In the eighteenth century we have very few mentions of storytellers. None are known by their names, and it is unclear in what languages they performed. Several of these nameless storytellers were at work in Bengal, for example, where Nawab 'Alī Wardī Ḳhān (r. 1740–56) employed *qiṣṣah-ḳhwāns* to tell tales after dinner. Mīr Mīran, the son of 'Alī Wardī Ḳhān's disgraced former governor and eventual usurper of the Bengali nawabate, Mīr Ja'far, is said to have been struck by lightning and reduced to ashes along with his attendant storyteller (Ġhulām Ḥusain b. Hidāyat Allāh Ṯabāṯabā'ī 1897, 688). But, though we hear less and less of Persian-language storytelling, lightning did not fall on the storytelling tradition in India by any means. The nineteenth century would see the rise of a vibrant tradition of Urdu-language storytelling, particularly in the former Mughal province of Awadh, as well as the mass publication of the Urdu *Dāstān-i Amīr Ḥamzah*, which became vastly popular even as the genre began to decline in worth in the minds of the Indian elite.

2

Telling the Tale of Amīr Ḥamzah in Urdu

IN THE DECADES AFTER the Rebellion of 1857, the Delhi-born intellectual Walī Ashraf Ṣabūḥī had left his beloved home city to earn his bread in a troubled time. At last, after many years, he and his family returned to Delhi by train. An imperial durbar was being held in the city in honor of the British monarch, and security was tight. It appears that Ṣabūḥī was nervous about bumping into an undercover police officer in one of the streets of the city (Ṣabūḥī 1963, 35). So, when he found himself accosted by a strange, bent-over man pestering him with a spray of personal questions, he suspected that he was dealing with a covert operation by the Crime Investigation Department. This annoying individual, who according to Ṣabūḥī bore an astonishing resemblance to a dried-up piece of unripe mango, carried two bundles with him. One of them turned out to be full of betel nuts. The other bundle was found to contain a set of small chapbooks, which the man offered to sell him in bulk at the low price of four annas.

Picking up one of the chapbooks, Ṣabūḥī was struck by the name of the author printed on it: Mīr Bāqir ʻAlī Dāstāngo, the storyteller, whom he had once known well. Suddenly, as he turned his eyes to the man before him, Ṣabūḥī realized that the seller and the storyteller were one and the same. Amazed and distressed at Bāqir ʻAlī's diminishment to a mere peddler of betel nuts and discount books, Ṣabūḥī began to question him in his turn: "Do you really sell betel nuts? Have your storytelling days come to an end?" Bāqir ʻAlī answered, "Should I go and tell stories in the graveyard?

There is no interest left among the living! 'It was a light that went away, along with the sun'" (Ṣabūḥī 1963, 36).[1]

He is remembered as the last storyteller of Delhi. Though he was only a boy in 1857, at the sunset of Mughal rule, nostalgic Delhites in the first half of the twentieth century understood his death in 1928 as the severing of one of their last links to a culture from which they were growing estranged. For them, his death marked the death of storytelling in Urdu, and while his biographers—even Walī Ashraf Ṣabūhī—tended to look askance at the romance genre, they hunted for ways to explain the decline that had preceded the end, often pointing accusatory fingers at the newly popular Indian cinema.[2] But "Who killed the *qiṣṣah*?" is not the question I wish to ask in this chapter. If we look at the records of Urdu storytellers in the nineteenth century, right down to Bāqir 'Alī's twentieth-century attempts to hold his own in a period of shifting patronage, the more striking question is, "Why was storytelling so much alive?" That is, in the age of colonization, the transitions from manuscript to print culture and from orality to literacy, the rise of the middle class, and the increasing scarcity of courtly patronage, how did Urdu-language storytellers act to maintain the *qiṣṣah* genre's worth? For it is clear, from the evidence of Urdu storytellers' lives and the popularity of their works, that the *qiṣṣah* had a firm place in the dominant nineteenth-century genre system, perhaps even more so than in the days of Persian-language storytelling.

Part of the answer lies in the continuing stress placed by storytellers and story writers on the usefulness of the *qiṣṣah* in providing political, linguistic, and other forms of exemplarity, a claim to which I will return in the next chapter. Like their Persophone antecedents, Urdu storytellers hedged their bets and made use of multiple roles to gain patronage and remuneration. The Persian *qiṣṣah-ḳhwāns*' practices of ensnaring young audiences and presenting romances as models for linguistic education continued from the time of Ḳhalīl 'Alī Ḳhān Ashk's employment at Fort William College at the beginning of the nineteenth century to Bāqir 'Alī's performances at the university in Aligarh and at the Anglo-Arabic College. In the case of Bāqir 'Alī, we have an excellent example of how storytellers positioned the *qiṣṣah* as a repository of other kinds of knowledge as well; to listen to a *qiṣṣah* was to gain a better understanding of the culture. In their use of these strategies to increase their own cultural capital and that of the romance genre, Urdu storytellers were very much like their Persophone predecessors.

However, the nineteenth century also witnessed new developments as storytellers sought to find success in this age of changing oral literacy. Francesca Orsini has stressed that the nineteenth century was not simply a time when newly arrived print technology broke violently with an oral and manuscript past. Reading took many forms, from reading aloud to other people to reading silently. The most successful print genres were songbooks and romances, showing us that printed books sought to capitalize upon and supplement the experiences offered by India's oral-performative forms of verbal art (Orsini 2009, chap. 1). The careers of Urdu storytellers—from Ashk preparing his tales for Fort William College's pioneering press to the storytellers who produced the wildly successful *Dāstān-i Amīr Ḥamzah* for Naval Kishore Press right down to the chapbook-peddling Bāqir ʻAlī—all bear out Orsini's argument. As print genres grew apace, oral-performative romances did not stagnate and cease to change. Rather, they were bolstered by the production of related forms of verbal art; sometimes written romances but often other oral-performative genres. A remarkable example can be seen in the Shiʻi-ruled nawabate of Awadh, where many storytellers raised their cultural capital by performing *marṡiyah-k͟hwānī* and *naṡr-k͟hwānī*, verse and prose laments for the martyred family of ʻAlī b. Abī Ṭālib. Storytellers cross-fertilized the genres of romance and lament as they took on these two roles. They did not restrict themselves to oral performance. Several of these very storytellers produced manuscripts as well, and they were responsible for the printed Naval Kishore *Ḥamzah-nāmah*.

Aside from new developments in age-old techniques, patronage played an important role in Urdu storytellers' success. Its role was particularly pronounced in more stable milieus such as Awadh, with its successive capitals, Faizabad and Lucknow, or the state of Rampur, to which storytellers flocked after the Rebellion of 1857. About storytelling in Delhi we know little, except that by the middle of the century tales were being told to crowds of hundreds at the Jama Mosque's northern stairs, while Mīr Bāqir 'Alī's grandfather spun his stories in the palace of the last Mughal ruler, Bahādur Shāh II "Ẓafar" (r. 1837–62) (Pritchett 1991, 13–14). The Mughals' interest in storytelling ensured its worth even as the dynasty's political power ebbed. Ẓafar's own grandfather, the blinded emperor Shāh 'Alam II, had dictated a romance called *'Ajā'ib al-qiṣaṣ* (Wonder tales). Shāh 'Ālam's son Mirzā Jawān Bakht (1749–88) was gracious to at least one storyteller; while the prince was in Faizabad, the storytelling of Khalīl 'Alī Khān Ashk came to his attention.

Storytelling and Language Education at Fort William College

Ashk was born in Delhi but left in his childhood and came to live in Faizabad, where he met Mirzā Jawān Bakht. He appears also to have spent time in Lucknow, where he made the acquaintance of the poet Kaẓim 'Alī Jawān, whom Ashk describes as one of his mentors and who would become a munshi at Fort William College in Calcutta. Ashk left Faizabad in 1794 for Bengal, where he continued consorting with the high and mighty, and by 1801 he had reached the British stronghold of Calcutta. But here he had difficulty finding employment. Luckily for him, his friend Kāẓim 'Alī Jawān had recently come to work at Fort William College (Barelvī 1965, 9–13).

Fort William College had opened in Calcutta on May 4, 1801. It was established by Lord Wellesley as an outgrowth of the seminary established in the same city in 1800 by John Borthwick Gilchrist, the intrepid and persistent scholar of the Hindustani (Urdu-Hindi) language.[3] Wellesley's vision had been to establish an institution of higher education in which East India Company servants, usually recruited around the ages of sixteen or eighteen, could learn "all the Indian languages, all systems of laws and jurisprudence, regulations enacted by British government in India, political economy, history, mathematics, geography, botany, chemistry, astronomy, Greek and Latin" (Kidwai 1972, 16). However, the East India Company itself, with whose court of directors Wellesley was perpetually at odds, soon succeeded in reducing the college to a language school. Nevertheless, Gilchrist, as professor of Hindustani at the college, made the most of the circumstances, fighting tooth and nail with the College Council to hire employees and to have books written in and translated into Hindustani. Around sixty books in the language were published by the college's press during his tenure there from 1801 to 1804 (Kidwai 1972, 25). Among these were the very first books printed in the Urdu script, using movable type.

Another of Ashk's friends, Maulwī Sa'īd al-Dīn, told him that Jawān was in Calcutta. The delighted Ashk went to meet Jawān, who had probably already been promised a position by Gilchrist (Barelvī 1965, 13).[4] Jawān was aware that Gilchrist was looking for storytellers and had already written, fruitlessly, to the British resident in Lucknow, Lieutenant-Colonel William Scott, asking him to direct any storytellers to the college (Barelvī 1965, 13). Upon discovering that his friend was in Calcutta, Jawān introduced Ashk to Gilchrist, who encouraged Ashk to begin writing down the *qiṣṣah* of Amīr Ḥamzah in Urdu. Reinvigorated after his period of unemployment, Ashk began the task and wrote several *dāstāns* or chapters of the romance. But as time passed and no position or remuneration was forthcoming, Ashk grew disconsolate. Maulwī Sa'īd al-Dīn again came to his rescue by introducing him to the judge John Herbert Harington, who appears to have intervened on Ashk's behalf with the council of Fort William College. Harington was himself a Persian-language scholar, who may have been a member or even president of the College Council at that time (Barelvī 1965, 14).[5]

Gilchrist had also been leaning on the College Council. On January 4, 1802, he wrote to the council secretary,

> Long experience has . . . proved to me the very great advantages of a Qissu-khaun to attend the students at their own houses, I beg therefore to suggest the expediency of having such a person, attached to my class on a salary of 40 Rupees and that until I can procure a man worthy of such pay I may be allowed to keep two inferior people at 20 Rupees each. (Siddiqi 1963, 120)[6]

Gilchrist was so eager and confident that the employment of a storyteller would improve the pupils' language abilities that he suggested cutbacks to the number of upper-level munshis in case the council saw his plan as financially unfeasible. Harington's intervention may have been efficacious, however, for the following month the council approved the creation of a single storyteller position for Ashk at the college. He was given a salary of forty rupees a month, the same wage that the upper-level munshis received and half of that received by Jawān as a translator (Siddiqi 1963, 123). After he had joined the college staff, Ashk would meet with Gilchrist and the Hindustani language students after dinner on the day of their lesson to tell his tales. Since they were learners, Gilchrist would take it upon himself to translate on the spot while Ashk performed. This method appears to have been successful, judging by the praise that Gilchrist expressed to Ashk. Gilchrist "would often say, by way of encouragement, 'The grace of your company has caused the sahibs [i.e., the students] to make much progress in the language. All of the sahibs praise you.'" Declaring himself very much attached to Ashk, he eventually made him a regular munshi, with the promise of further advancement if it were ever in his power (Barelvī 1965, 14–15).[7] By day Ashk taught the college students, and by night he continued performing the *Ḥamzah-nāmah* and embarked on a work of science (*ḥikmat*), the *Risālah-i Kā'ināt-i jau* (Treatise on the beings between heaven and earth) (Barelvī 1965, 15).[8]

Ashk's compressed version of the *Ḥamzah-nāmah*, which appeared in 1801 or shortly thereafter, is the first known North Indian Urdu *dāstān* of Amir Ḥamzah and probably the first tale of Ḥamzah to be printed in either Urdu or Persian.[9] It was the direct predecessor to the 1866 Ġhālib Lakhnawī version and the later and more popular 'Abd Allāh Bilgrāmī text, in its content as well as its mode of production (Pritchett 1991, 29–32). Neither Ġhālib Lakhnawī nor 'Abd Allāh Bilgrāmī were storytellers, as far as we know, but their dependence on Ashk underlines how even the short *Ḥamzah-nāmahs* in print depended upon and reproduced the voices of storytellers. As Orsini (2009, 109–11) suggests, the neo-literate Indian audiences of the later nineteenth century substituted print romances for performed ones, just as Ashk's British students were doing thanks to Gilchrist's initiative.

Like the other Fort William College romances, the story of Amir Ḥamzah was described by its author as a book for the use of language learners, leading one to expect a brief and basic work (Ashk 1863, 2). Its size, however—four volumes totaling five hundred pages—links it strongly to the prolonged narratives of the oral tradition that Ashk practiced. As Frances Pritchett notes, Ashk seems to have originally intended to render on the page an even longer work. Gilchrist remarked on this intention with some delight in 1802:

> If, as KHULEEL KHAN, one of the learned natives of the College, and who now considers himself the Hereditary Story Teller of the Emperor, Princes, and Nobles of India, asserts, the Historical Romance of Umeer Humzu itself, which he is now translating, will consist of 15 or 20 large Volumes, the patrons and admirers of the Hindoostanee may, in this branch alone, hail an inexhaustible fund of legendary narrative and diversion. (*Hindee Story-Teller*, quoted in Pritchett 1991, 13)

Ashk himself wrote in the postscript to the manuscript of volume 1 that he had hoped to write nine sections (*daftars*) containing a total of twenty-two volumes. The sheer length of Ashk's *Ḥamzah-nāmah*—both the one that he aspired to write and the one that he did write—signals an attempt by the storyteller to make the text stand beside him for the British language learners and other audiences, whether they were reading the book or listening to it being read.

Gilchrist appreciated this attempt and clearly recognized Ashk's cultural capital emanating from both his self-image as a courtly storyteller and his written work. It is a measure of the success of Ashk's strategy—which made use of his oral-performative abilities, their transubstantiation into written form, and print technology—that on August 9, 1803, he was made a munshi with a wage of thirty rupees per month. This salary was a pay cut from the forty rupees he had earned as a storyteller, but Gilchrist also suggested in a letter written on the same day that the College Council give Ashk a special award of five hundred rupees—the largest award suggested for a single author by Gilchrist, who proposed similar awards for other staff members in this letter. Predictably, the council dismissed Gilchrist's request (Siddiqi 1960, 170–72, 194). As the college declined after Lord Wellesley's resignation, Ashk would write other works: the 1805 romance *Nigārḳhānah-i Chīn* (The Chinese picture gallery) and the historical texts *Wāqiʿāt-i Akbar* (Events of Akbar's time) and *Intiḳhāb-i sulṭāniyyah* (The royal selection).[10] His twenty-two-volume *Ḥamzah-nāmah* was never written, but his list of the cycle's *daftar*s demonstrates both its connection to the Persian *Ḥamzah-nāmah* and the extent to which it anticipated the forty-six-volume Naval Kishore version.[11]

Ashk's activities at Fort William College demonstrate that he was able to capitalize on his history of courtly patronage, his oral-performative abilities, his capability to produce written romances, and the established strategy of presenting the oral and written romance as a linguistic model. As I suggested in chapter 1, this last strategy, of activating the linguistic exemplarity of *qiṣṣah*s, did not appear out of thin air. It likely had a pre-colonial pedigree, even if Fort William College is the most visible example of an institution for language education that used *qiṣṣah*s in great number. It is visible in this manner in part because of its innovative and prolific use of print technology to produce Urdu-Hindi *qiṣṣah*s. So, for Ashk, practicing as he did at the dawn of printing in Urdu, the difference between manuscripts and printed books is unlikely to have been a great factor in his projection of his worth as a storyteller, except insofar as it facilitated his strategy of presenting the romance as an educational text by making his *Ḥamzah-nāmah* available to read by the same number of students, or more, who could listen to him recite it in his after-dinner storytelling sessions. It would be many decades before storytellers would help put the *Ḥamzah-nāmah* into print again. When they did, they better understood the benefits of the medium of print and how to exploit this medium. But, between the beginning of the nineteenth century and the rise of the Naval

Kishore *dāstān* in the 1880s, storytellers did not cease to use performance as a part of their successful attempts to reinforce their value to patrons and audiences, with manuscripts performing a secondary role.

Storytelling and Shi'i Performance in Lucknow and Rampur

Fertile ground for storytelling was to be found in Awadh, where Ashk had entertained the Mughal prince before moving to Bengal. 'Abd al-Ḥalīm Sharar's claim that storytelling "had become so popular in Lucknow that there wasn't a rich man to be found who didn't have a storyteller in his entourage" might be far-fetched (quoted in Pritchett 1991, 15), but the names of many storytellers of Lucknow have come down to us. Among these were the men who produced the enormous Naval Kishore *Dāstān-i Amir Ḥamzah*, whose first *daftar*, the *Ṭilism-i Hoshrubā* (Sense-stealing ṭilism), was hugely successful. *Ṭilism-i Hoshrubā* was unknown to Ashk. It did not originate with the Naval Kishore storytellers, however, but with the earlier Lucknow storyteller Mīr Aḥmad 'Alī, who, along with his pupils, was quite successful before the advent of the long *Ḥamzah-nāmah* in print.

In Lucknow, a city where Shi'ism was important from the ruling class down, storytellers' success in stabilizing the worth of their craft was brought about in part by the affinity of the storytelling art to other performative arts among Shi'is, particularly *marṡiyah-ḳhwānī* and *naṡr-ḳhwānī*. The *marṡiyah* is a well-known genre of Urdu verse describing the tragedy of Karbala, at which the Prophet's grandson Ḥusain was killed along with other descendants of 'Alī b. Abī Ṭālib, the Prophet's son-in-law and cousin.[12] Less well known is *naṡr-ḳhwānī*, whose performers are called *naṡr-ḳhwān*s or *naṡṡār*s. *Naṡr-ḳhwānī* refers in this context to the recitation of elaborate prose about the same martyrs with whom *marṡiyah*s deal. The subject matter of *marṡiyah-ḳhwānī* and *naṡr-ḳhwānī* would have been loftier in the minds of Shi'i devotees than that of the *Ḥamzah-nāmah*. But the *Ḥamzah-nāmah*'s worth would have been raised by its association with these genres, in terms of both its subject matter—Amīr Ḥamzah is, after all, another member of the Prophet's family who was martyred in battle—and the similarities in performative style.

What we know about the influential storyteller Mīr Aḥmad ʿAlī and his disciples, Anbā Parshād and Ḥakīm Aṣġhar ʿAlī, demonstrates that their performance of these Shiʿi genres must have played a role in their success, or at least in their strategy for achieving success. This success is shown by the recognition of rulers, who deemed storytelling worthy of their continuous patronage. After the fall of the nawab of Awadh, the patronage of storytellers originating in Lucknow simply shifted to the nawabs of Rampur, in whose records we find evidence of how well storytellers were compensated monetarily.[13] Although their manuscript output increased in the years leading up to the publication of *Ṭilism-i Hoshrubā*, storytellers' worth was still primarily expressed in terms of their mastery of the storytelling craft.

Mīr Aḥmad ʿAlī, the crafter of the *Ṭilism-i Hoshrubā* and the master of some of the most important storytellers of the nineteenth century, was himself the disciple of a storyteller of Lucknow named Mīr Qāsim ʿAlī, with whom he wrote four *daftar*s of the *Ḥamzah-nāmah* in Persian in 1853–54. These *daftar*s, preserved in the Rampur Raza Library, were the *Nausherwān-nāmah*, *Kochak Bāḳhtar*, *Bālā Baḳhtar*, and *Īraj-nāmah* (Gyān Chand Jain 1969, 706). After leaving Lucknow, Mīr Aḥmad ʿAlī was employed by the Rampuri nawab Yūsuf ʿAlī Ḳhān (r. 1855–65) and possibly by his predecessor, Muḥammad Saʿīd Ḳhān (Yazdānī 1952, 6; Aṡar Rāmpūrī 1950, 108).[14] If Rāz Yazdānī (1952, 6) is correct that he received sixty rupees per month from the ruler of Rampur, then the price fixed on the master's craft was greater than that accorded to his disciples.[15] Mīr Aḥmad ʿAlī's great worth was derived from his oral performance; his creation of *Hoshrubā*, which was in all probability mainly oral; and his inauguration of a lineage of disciples.[16] Although he produced *Ḥamzah-nāmah* manuscripts with both his master and his students, his books were a secondary source of recognition for the storyteller. The period described by Orsini (2009) and Margrit Pernau (2013), in which a newly literate middle-class audience would arise to consume printed *qiṣṣah*s, was yet to come. Instead, Mīr Aḥmad ʿAlī was recognized for being able to shape his tales into a successful form within the rich array of oral-performative genres available at the time. As Naiyer Masud has revealed, storytellers and *marṡiyah-ḳhwāns* in Lucknow were paying attention to one another and borrowing each other's techniques. Mīr Aḥmad 'Alī's contemporary, the *marṡiyah* reciter Mīr Muẓaffar Ḥusain, understood the power of the master storyteller's style. He imitated the storyteller's style when he recited his *marṡiyah* plainly or "*taḥt al-lafẓ*," as opposed to singing it (Masud 1990, 14; Ṣafawī 1989, 105). By sharing a common, crowd-pleasing set of oral-performative techniques, Mīr Aḥmad 'Alī and Muẓaffar Ḥusain could ensure the popularity of their respective arts.

Social capital also played a role in the high level of worth continually accorded to Mīr Aḥmad 'Alī. Through his education of some of the most important storytellers of the nineteenth century, including Anbā Parshād Rasā, Ḥakīm Aṣġhar 'Alī, and Mīr Bāqir 'Alī's grandfather Mīr Amīr 'Alī, Mīr Aḥmad 'Alī had a series of conduits for his name and fame, which would have survived through these lineages even had he not produced any books at all. Furthering Mīr Aḥmad 'Alī's lineage, all three of the disciples mentioned had their own disciples, mainly offspring, who could claim to come from Mīr Aḥmad 'Alī's line.[17]

The eldest of the disciples of Mīr Aḥmad 'Alī was Munshī Anbā Parshād Rasā of Lucknow (b. ca. 1788, d. between 1885–87), the son of Lālah Chāndī Parshād (Amīr Mīnā'ī 1982, 147). Originally a Hindu of the Kayasth caste, Anbā Parshād was known by his original name even after he accepted Islam and took the name 'Abd al-Raḥmān. In addition to telling the story of Amīr Ḥamzah, he recited *naṡr* in praise of the Shi'i martyrs and composed poetry.[18] Rampuri records show that Anbā Parshād was first employed by the nawab of Rampur Yūsuf 'Alī Ḳhān (r. 1855–65) on March 4, 1857; his arrival in Rampur seems to be linked to the 1856 departure from Lucknow of the last Awadhi nawab Wājid 'Alī Shāh. During the reign of Nawab Kalb-i 'Alī Ḳhān (1865–87), he drew a salary of fifty rupees per month, less than that reported for Mīr Aḥmad 'Alī, though Kalb-i 'Alī is said to have supplemented his artists' salaries with gifts and rewards (Muḥammad Najm al-Ġhanī 1918, 207).[19]

Anbā Parshād merited such a salary due to his command of both oral performance and the techniques of its instruction. He passed his abilities on to disciples even as the writing of manuscripts became a somewhat more important activity for him and for other storytellers of his time. To maintain his salary he was constrained to be in Rampur, although his principal residence was in Lucknow. He had great difficulty obtaining leave from Kalb-i 'Alī to return to his home—the nawab could not sleep properly without hearing his tales. It is said that if Anbā Parshād fell silent when he thought the nawab was asleep, a drowsy whine of protest would escape the royal lips. But eventually he obtained leave for a certain period, six months according to one account. Before going away, he had been in the middle of narrating a story; in the tale, the owner of the house had lifted the entrance curtain and the hero was crossing the threshold. Anbā Parshād deputized a disciple of his to tell the nawab his nightly romance, instructing him to suspend the action until his return, and so he did. Not until Anbā Parshād returned did the hero step into the house (Ṣafawī 1989, 106; Ḳhwājah 'Ishrat Lakhnawī 1935, 60).[20]

Not unusual for a member of the Kayasth community, Anbā Parshād was also a calligrapher. Thus it is unsurprising that he was the author of about a dozen written *dāstān*s, some of them multivolume (Gyān Chand Jain 1969, 709; As̱ar Rāmpūrī 1950, 111). When his teacher Mīr Aḥmad 'Alī produced an Urdu romance entitled the *Ṭilism-i Ṭahmūras̱ De'oband* (The ṭilism of Ṭahmūras̱ the demon-binder), Anbā Parshād corrected it, and his son Ġhulām Raẓā copied it (Gyān Chand Jain 1969, 706). Ġhulām Raẓā (1833–87), who had come to Rampur and converted to Islam with his father at the age of ten, was also trained as a calligrapher (Yazdānī 1952, 11; Jān Ṣāḥib 1950, 28). After copying the *Ṭilism-i Ṭahmūras̱ De'oband*, he focused on extending Mīr Aḥmad 'Alī's *Hoshrubā*, producing four volumes in 1858–59 and a further ten volumes from 1876 to 1880. From then until his death he wrote six more *dāstān*s (Gyān Chand Jain 1969, 711). The extent of the manuscript output of Anbā Parshād and his son indicates that they were able to capitalize on the increasing popularity of written romances in addition to being recognized for their oral performances.

Apart from writing a great many *dāstān*s, Ġhulām Raẓā was celebrated for his performances at Nawab Kalb-i 'Alī Ḳhān's Jashn-i benaẓīr, a grand *melā*, or fair, that took place in Rampur's Bāġh-i benaẕīr (Peerless Garden) (Jān Ṣāḥib 1950, 28).[21] His brother Ġhulām Mahdī would also be present at the *melā*. He too was famous as a storyteller and a *naṡr-ḳhwān*, though less so than his brother. Every Friday throughout the year, the stooped, clean-shaven, and brown-skinned Ġhulām Raẓa held storytelling soirees in his own home in the Muhalla Katra neighborhood of Rampur (Yazdānī 1952, 11). He went on to have his own disciples as well, including Mirzā Muḥammad Murtaẓà Ḥusain "Wiṣāl," who wrote several *dāstān*s before being killed one morning in 1909 when his elephant charged into a store (Yazdānī 1952, 12; Amīr Mīnā'ī 1982, 395; Gyān Chand Jain 1969, 720).

The other important disciple of Mīr Aḥmad 'Alī was Ḥakīm Sayyid Aṣġhar 'Alī (d. 1878), who was born in Lucknow, where his physician forefathers had lived. Aṣġhar 'Alī had learned medicine, but he found no small measure of success as a storyteller, though like most of the Lucknow storytellers he was forced to shift patrons in the 1850s (Ḥasan 1956, 41–44). Before 1856, Aṣġhar 'Alī probably had the patronage of Wājid 'Alī Shāh, who was himself the author of verse romances in *masnawi* form. While he was living in Lucknow, Aṣġhar 'Alī wrote prose *dāstān*s on the basis of three of these poems, as well as authoring Persian *daftar*s in the Ḥamzah cycle. In 1856, the year that the nawab's rule would come to an end, Aṣġhar 'Alī dedicated his romance the *Qiṣṣah-i Raushan Jamāl* to Wājid 'Alī Shāh (Gyān Chand Jain 1969, 706–7; Aṡar Rāmpūrī 1950, 108). Following the nawab's departure from Awadh and the turmoil of 1857, Aṣġhar 'Alī followed his *ustād* to Rampur, where Nawab Yūsuf 'Alī Ḳhān gave him a wage of fifty rupees per month, greater than that of the storyteller Mīr Nawwāb (b. ca. 1805, d. between 1875–80) but equivalent to that of his colleague Anbā Parshād (Yazdānī 1952, 11; Ḥasan 1956, 44).

Unlike Anbā Parshād and Ġhulām Raẓā, Ḥakīm Aṣġhar 'Alī is not said to have been a *naṡr-ḳhwān* or *marṡiyah-ḳhwān*. But it is told that Aṣġhar 'Alī and Mīr Anīs, the most commemorated composer and reciter of *marṡiyah*s, came to see each other's performances in Lucknow. When his story came to the description of a battle (*razm*) between Amīr Ḥamzah and the sorcerers arrayed against him, Aṣġhar 'Alī would charge his voice with force and bravado. Observing this technique—which, as we will see in the next chapter, is crucial to the romance as performed in the Persian-language tradition in India—Mīr Anīs then appropriated it in his own portrayals of the tragic battle between Ḥusain and his loathsome enemies. On the other hand, after hearing the threatening way in which the *marṡiyah-ḳhwān* Mīr Mūnis recited his martial poetry, Aṣġhar ʿAlī emulated this style to increase the effect of his descriptions of battle over the course of his *dāstān* performance (Masud 1990, 14–15).

Aṣġhar ʿAlī, along with his son the famed poet Ẓāmin ʿAlī Jalāl, was involved in the production of a *Ḥamzah-nāmah* for Nawab Kalb-i ʿAlī Ḳhān. Its *daftar*s were written by several storytellers, including Anbā Parshād (Gyān Chand Jain 1969, 707). But it was his performances, such as his storytelling at the Jashn-i Benaẕīr festival, that were commemorated, while his written work was neglected. Such was the case with other storytellers as well, some of whom were especially known for the skill with which they described the tricks of ʿAmar ʿAyyār and other tricksters. Among these was Muḥammad Amīr Ḳhān, who would tell stories at his home in Wazir Bagh, Lucknow, or in the Haidari Imambargah on Wednesdays. Muḥammad Amīr Ḳhān would boast that he was unsurpassed in the portrayal of the shenanigans of tricksters, but he was rivaled in this art by his fellow citizen Sayyid Ḥusain ʿAlī.[22] Sayyid Husain ʿAlī worked in Rampur for Kalb-i ʿAlī Ḳhān, at whose house he gave performances every Friday. But Ḳhwājah ʿIshrat remembers that Sayyid Ḥusain ʿAlī would return to Lucknow on such occasions as the fair in ʿAish Bāġh. At this event, several storytellers performed from the late afternoon to the evening in a tent near the mosque. Their food would be provided by the noble patrons of the fair, and the audience passed around hookahs. Sayyid Ḥusain ʿAlī, the last to perform, would make the audience split their sides with laughter as he recounted how the tricksters deceived their hapless foes (Ḳhwājah ʿIshrat Lakhnawī 1935, 62). For nineteenth-century audiences who were well acquainted not only with storytelling but also with other genres of oral performance, storytellers' skill in their craft was what gave them their worth. But the production of manuscripts, even if their circulation did not go much beyond the court, became increasingly important as the era of the ascendancy of the Naval Kishore *Dāstān-i Amīr Ḥamzah* dawned.

The Naval Kishore Storytellers between Orality and Print

The first printed volume of the most famous *Ḥamzah-nāmah* narrative, *Ṭilism-i Hoshrubā*, appeared in 1883, published by the press of the great publishing magnate Munshi Naval Kishore.[23] *Hoshrubā*, first narrated by Mīr Aḥmad 'Alī, has gone through numerous printings since its original publication. Its authors were, for the most part, storytellers of Lucknow: Muḥammad Ḥusain Jāh, Aḥmad Ḥusain Qamar, and Taṣadduq Ḥusain. About Jāh and Qamar, we have a great deal of information, yet their lives were largely neglected for a century until Shamsur Rahman Faruqi researched and retold them. His findings show us that, on the one hand, they were practicing oral performers who used strategies similar to those of other Lucknow and Rampur storytellers, such as participating in *nas̈r-ḳhwānī*. On the other hand, it is also clear that they understood the power of print, especially in Naval Kishore's hands. Print supplemented and extended the pleasures of oral performance to the neo-literate audiences of the time and to the nonliterate through their recitation by literate individuals. So had manuscripts and the movable-type books printed at Fort William College, but they had done it for a far more limited audience. In a clearer manner than their predecessor Ashk, the Naval Kishore–affiliated storytellers attempted to exploit print technology to counteract the mounting challenges of acquiring economic capital through their performances.

In the library of the Urdu scholar Naiyer Masud there is an obscure treatise entitled the *Ṭarīq-i nas̈r-ḳhwānī* (The way of Nas̈r recitation) by Mīr Fidā 'Alī "Fidā" Nas̈r-ḳhwān (Faruqi 2006b, 150; Masud 1990, 10). This account of the art of prose panegyrics to the Shi'i imams leads us once more to the seemingly ubiquitous practice of *nas̈r-ḳhwānī* by storytellers, for Mīr Fidā 'Alī was a storyteller of Lucknow. He was the disciple of the storyteller Mirzā Ṭ̈ūr of Lucknow. As the treatise suggests, his own student in storytelling as well as *nas̈r-ḳhwānī* was none other than Muḥammad Ḥusain Jāh. Jāh was the principal creator of *Hoshrubā*, or at least its first four and a half volumes (Ḳhwājah 'Ishrat Lakhnawī 1935, 59; Yazdānī 1952, 10; Faruqi 2006b, 141). Ṭūr, Fidā, and Jāh may all have performed both genres. What is more, Jāh's fellow creators of the Naval Kishore *Dāstān-i Amīr Ḥamzah,* Aḥmad Ḥusain Qamar and Taṣadduq Ḥusain, were trained in *naṡr-ḳhwānī* as well (Faruqi 2006b, 150–51).[24] Taṣadduq Ḥusain (d. between 1911–17) may also have been active as a *marṡiyah-ḳhwān* in Lucknow (Faruqi 2006b, 168). Therefore, in his practice of *naṡr-ḳhwānī* Jāh was not only following the lead of his own master; he was doing what many other Lucknow storytellers did to multiply their chances of earning recognition and money. Unlike them, Jāh threw in his lot with print technology; he understood its reach and perhaps hoped that it would enable him to overcome the difficulties that beset him. However, the success of *Hoshrubā* would not benefit Jāh as he had hoped.

Jāh was the son of a geomancer (*rammāl*) named Sayyid Ġhulām Ḥusain, resident in Lucknow (Faruqi 2006b, 149; Jāh 1874, 7). His *naṡr-ḳhwānī* and storytelling lineage was very strong, and Jāh was very collegial in the acknowledgments he made in his writings, paying homage to other storytellers including Mīr Aḥmad 'Alī, Anbā Parshād, Taṣadduq Ḥusain, and Amīr Ḳhān. He had written a different sort of book early on, apparently related to his *naṡr-ḳhwānī*, entitled *Mātam-i Ḥusainī* (The mourning of Ḥusain).[25] But the first publication of Jāh's that has come down to us is his 1874 romance, *Ṭilism-i Faṣāḥat* (The ṭilism of eloquence), published by Naval Kishore Press. In this book, Jāh praised Munshi Naval Kishore profusely.

It is also in *Ṭilism-i Faṣāḥat* that he claimed he received correction at the feet of his "master" in storytelling, Aḥmad Ḥusain Qamar, who was the other author of *Hoshrubā* after Jāh left off the work. Given Qamar's scornful and self-centered attitude and his complete disregard for Jāh in his writings, Shamsur Rahman Faruqi has expressed amazement that Jāh should have given Qamar such high-flown praise (Faruqi 2006b, 159). Faruqi is disposed to see it, in fact, as a very cunning satire, meant to gently and ambiguously deflate the pompous storyteller. Jāh recounted that despite his own unworthiness he had brought his work before Qamar and had coaxed him into bestowing a glance upon it:

> When I set these ignorant words . . . before him, the following jewels dropped from his miracle-expressing tongue onto the skirt of the state of this broken one [i.e., Jāh]: "Without merit and in vain have you caused me to incline my head in your direction! You have made yourself a target for the scornful fingers of the deer-hunters! Since when is this book worthy of correction? This blabbering of yours is absolutely pointless." But once again I struck the most holy skirt with the hand of my helplessness. Obstinately I petitioned him: "The rose should not be ashamed of the thorn, nor the seacoast of mud and grime. I shall not desist from bothering you—I will show you the whole book!" (Jāh 1874, 278–79)[26]

Assuming that Jāh's praise for Qamar is meant as irony or satire, its ambiguity testifies to his desire for self-preservation, for Qamar was probably his senior and came from a family of relatively high rank. Jāh seems aware that the far reach of the printed text would be a double-edged sword.

There is no record of Jāh's receiving patronage beyond the monetary reward he must have gotten for composing his volumes of *Hoshrubā*. It is likely that the money he received was not as much as he had anticipated. Volumes 1 and 2 of *Hoshrubā* were published in succession in 1883 and 1884. Volume 3, however, did not appear until 1888–89, and in it, without pointing his finger at Naval Kishore Press, Jāh claimed that he was not being appreciated at his worth and threatened to leave off *dāstān* writing. During the interval, tragedy also struck his family life when both his son and his daughter departed from the world. Jāh wrote in volume 3 of *Hoshruba*, "It is with great confusion and anxiety that I have written this volume. Sorrow for my children has remained in my heart, and I was myself ill for a some time" (Jāh 1988, 696; Faruqi 2006b, 145, 147). Nevertheless, he composed a fourth volume, published by Naval Kishore in 1890.

Stricken and disgruntled, Jāh took the fifth volume into his own hands. Both Faruqi and Rifaqat Ali Shahid are of the opinion that Naval Kishore or the publishing staff was tired of waiting for his output and that the publisher's impatience may have been the immediate cause of the breach

(Faruqi 2006b, 143). The Lahore-based press Gulāb Singh and Sons published a portion of volume 5 of *Hoshrubā* in December 1890. Jāh then set up his own printing business, Ḥusainī Press, in Lucknow, and published the volume himself, announcing that he would also publish other cycles such as the *Nausherwān-nāmah* and *Īraj-nāmah*. However, Jāh could not compete against Naval Kishore, and he came back to compose one last book with India's most important publisher: *Ṭilism-i Hoshrubā*, volume 5, part 1, published in 1891. After this, *Hoshrubā* was continued by Qamar, and by 1893 Jāh was dead (Faruqi 2006b, 141–43). His persistent association with the medium of print in spite of his tribulations, including his short-lived entrepreneurship in this field, demonstrates that Jāh understood the power of print, even if he was unable in the end to harness it for his own benefit.

The continuer of *Hoshrubā*, Aḥmad Ḥusain Qamar, had no doubt whatsoever with regard to his own worth. He came from an elite *sharīf* background, but like many Indian elites his family was left destitute after the Rebellion of 1857.[27] Qamar's brothers Bandah Ḥasan and Bandah Ḥusain had been administrators for the prime minister of Wājid 'Alī Shāh. During the rebellion, the two fought on the "wrong" side and were killed. It seems that Qamar, only a youth at the time, was also involved in the rebellion, and though the British pardoned him, they confiscated three lakhs' worth of his family's wealth and property. He later lived in Lucknow near the shrine of Ḥaẓrat Shāh 'Abbās (Qamar 1988, 3; Yazdānī 1952, 10; Faruqi 2006b, 162). When Qamar took to studying law, his qualifying examination was rejected because of his seditious past. Therefore, he was constrained to perform as a *naṡr-ḳhwān* and storyteller, occupations in which he found much approbation in noble gatherings, or so he states (Qamar 1988, 3).

Qamar made it very clear that he was not a hereditary storyteller. His implicit valuation of the storytelling profession is therefore interesting, though it must be taken with a grain of salt. Qamar made himself out to be an unmatched storyteller, and it is likely that Munshi Naval Kishore himself gave him fodder for his self-conceit. Describing a meeting with the publishing magnate, Qamar reports Naval Kishore's supposed words:

> It is incredible that a perfect poet, unmatched *naṡr-ḳhwān*, and expert in all of the arts, such as yourself, should be present right here in Lucknow! How sad that I did not know of it before. . . . if I had, I would have had the first four volumes rendered and written by you. The *daftar* of *Hoshrubā* has become famous due to your magical expression—otherwise, no one even knew its name. (quoted in Faruqi 2006b, 164)

According to Qamar, he himself was the true genius behind the *Ṭilism-i Hoshrubā*. Mīr Aḥmad ʿAlī only gave the world some scraps of a ragged narrative, and Jāh committed an injustice in not revealing that the first few volumes he wrote should in reality be ascribed to Qamar as well. Qamar claimed that all of the volumes of the Persian *Ḥamzah-nāmah* written for Akbar himself were available in Naval Kishore's offices, so that he could bypass any intermediate versions (Yazdānī 1952, 10). In spite of the lengths to which Qamar went to associate himself with *Hoshrubā*, he preferred to be known as a *naṡr-khwan*; indeed, all of Qamar's statements point to the idea that he was much more than a mere storyteller (Faruqi 2006b, 163–64). He multiplied his roles ostentatiously; he was an unfortunate noble, a would-have-been lawyer, a reciter of *naṡr* in praise of the family of the Prophet, an excellent poet, and even a historian.

For the self-consciously elite Qamar, storytelling was a relatively lowly profession, and for the purposes of increasing his cultural capital he clearly felt the need to emphasize his multiple abilities and sources of worth. But storytelling appears to have been at least respectable enough that nobles of royal blood, from both the Mughal family and that of the Awadhi nawabs, took it up as their profession. The best-known storyteller among the "Nishapuri" family of the nawabs of Awadh is Risāldār Nawāb Muḥammad Ḥusain Ḳhān, who would tell his tales in the Shish Mahal. Despite being invited to both Hyderabad and Rampur, he was contented to remain in Lucknow, where the audience for *dāstān*s was, according to him, more appreciative than elsewhere; in any case he held a pension of around fifty to sixty rupees a month. His relative Nawāb Āġhā Ḥaidar

Afsūn would tell stories at the Karbala-i Agha Mir, and a third member of this family, Nawāb Hādī ʻAlī Ḳhān, was similarly employed (Ḳhwājah ʻIshrat Lakhnawī 1935, 59–60).

Within the Mughal royal family, we have traces of three storytellers: the three sons of Mirzā Raḥīm al-Dīn Ḥayā, who was the paternal grandson of Shāh ʻĀlam II. The eldest was Mirzā ʻAlīm al-Dīn Wafā (ca. 1854–1926), who was born in Delhi but moved to Rampur with his father as a child. Interested in storytelling from an early age, he trained under Mir Nawwāb and would give performances on Fridays after the congregational prayer. He wrote a large number of romances over a period of around forty years (Yazdānī 1952, 9–10; Gyān Chand Jain 1969, 722–29; Amīr Mīnā'ī 1982, 395–96; Aṡar Rāmpūrī 1950, 42–43). His illiterate brother Mirzā Amīr al-Dīn "Mirzā Kallan" (d. 1939) also practiced storytelling as a client of the Rampuri nawabs until 1937 and dictated romances to his brother Mirzā Walī al-Dīn "Mirzā Mallan," himself a storyteller (Yazdānī 1952, 12). Qamar's own son, Nādir Mirzā, would have become a storyteller had he not been afflicted with elephantiasis (Faruqi 2006b, 163).[28] Whatever one may think of his posturing, Qamar was the author of nineteen of the forty-six volumes of the Naval Kishore *Dāstān-i Amir Ḥamzah*, more than any other individual. He worked on them beginning in 1890 and continued until March 1901, when he passed away.[29]

Mīr Bāqir ʻAlī:
The Decline of Patronage and the Struggle for Worth

Mir Bāqir ʻAlī, hallowed as the "last storyteller of Delhi," stands apart from his colleagues as an object of special commemoration.[30] Representations of Delhi after 1857 are filled with "lasts," reflecting the Delhi elites' conflicted awareness of how colonial modernization had changed their culture, language, and worldview. Despite their own transformation, they attempted to gather together the scraps of their lost tradition, an activity that veered into an incipient nationalist pride. When we read nostalgic intellectuals of the period reminiscing about Bāqir ʻAlī, we need to bear in mind how nationalist motives impelled their appreciation for the storyteller, as well as a certain depreciation. Young admirers of Bāqir 'Alī had imbibed many of the traditional and colonialist objections to the "useless" romance genre. Thus Ṣabūḥī blows hot and cold over the genre and the storyteller, while Yūsuf Bukhārī argues for the worthiness of the *qiṣṣah* genre by emphasizing Bāqir 'Alī's dedication to the nationalist cause. These writers did not often express directly what was valuable about the art of the man they were commemorating, giving only a vague sense that storytelling was part of a fading culture that must be preserved. This inability on their part raises the question of whether the fact or at least the magnitude of decline was not produced in some sense as fodder for nationalist sentiment.

Yet, all of the accounts of Bāqir 'Alī do not only tell a tale of the declining worth of elite storytelling in the first three decades of the twentieth century. They also implicitly give us our most detailed picture of how a storyteller fought against, and seized the advantages of, the tide of socioeconomic, cultural, and epistemological change to raise his worth and the worth of the *dāstān*. Mīr Bāqir 'Alī emphasized the cultural capital bequeathed to him by the *sharīf* storytelling lineage to which he belonged. Like his forebears, he gained courtly patronage, but he also caught hold of patronage provided by nouveau riche urban patrons in Delhi. He continued the strategy of catching the attention of younger audiences and presented his storytelling as a means to gain knowledge of obsolescent traditions and correct linguistic usage. His mastery of the craft of storytelling, which will be detailed in the next chapter, was a source of appreciation for his admirers. But, like the other Urdu storytellers, he supplemented his oral performances with print publications, which he sold himself, relying increasingly on the success of these chapbooks. In all of these ways, Bāqir 'Alī struggled to maintain his own status and the position of the *qiṣṣah* genre in the new age of the novel's supremacy in the genre system.

The last earthly abode of Mir Bāqir 'Alī Dāstāngo (1850–1928) was his small house in the Bhojla Pahari neighborhood of Delhi, known to strangers by the Gondni tree that grew and flowered in its courtyard (Muḥammad Feroz Dihlawī 2014, 65). One winter's evening, on a Saturday, Walī Ashraf Ṣabūḥī came to listen to Bāqir 'Alī perform a *dāstān* from the Amīr

Ḥamzah cycle. Upon crossing the threshold, he entered a smallish room. He was able to behold the scene through his spectacles only after growing accustomed to the darkness, for it was well nigh nine o'clock. About a dozen men sat drinking tea, perhaps served by Bāqir 'Alī's friend Miyāṅ Fajjū (Muḥammad Feroz Dihlawī 2014, 69). Each audience member would have paid one anna for admission, a price that had fallen steadily through Bāqir 'Alī's lifetime.[31] That night there was a special guest from Lucknow: the son of one of the Naval Kishore *Ḥamzah-nāmah* storytellers was ready to evaluate the "Delhi style" of storytelling. On a low chowki kneeled Mir Bāqir 'Alī, whose thin, bow-backed figure was illuminated in the darkness by a small lantern hanging near his head, while on a shelf or recess to the left shone a small lamp (Ṣabūḥī 1963, 44; Muḥammad Feroz Dihlawī 2014, 69). He was well insulated against the cold in an enormous cotton blanket, with a rough cotton cap warming his head. Beneath his blanket he wore a chintz jacket, black with red flowers, and his pajamas were of khaki denim, with thick red-striped socks pulled over the leg openings. Bāqir 'Alī was avowedly a man who put his own comfort first in the matter of clothing, resenting even the princely command of the Maharajah of Patiala when this patron had bade him wear an intricate *ṣāfa* turban (Ṣabūḥī 1963, 45; Sayyid Yūsuf Bukhārī Dihlawī 1987, 25).[32]

Near the chowki were a jug of water, a few cups, and a box, which contained opium. Bāqir 'Alī's storytelling gatherings seem to have always been charged with some mild substance to ease the mind's flight into the skies of imagination. Chief among these was tea, whose popularization was one thing for which Bāqir 'Alī did not curse the British (Shāhid Aḥmad Dihlawī 1979, 191).[33] In other settings, he might have interrupted his tale with pulls on the hookah snake, and a genteel audience might have passed around a beautiful brass box of paan, the leaf whose consumption was an art that Bāqir 'Alī had taken it upon himself to revive (Sayyid Yūsuf Bukhārī Dihlawī 1987, 25). But this was a gathering of *dāstān*-loving opium devotees, and of them Bāqir 'Alī was not the least devoted. Out of his box, he would have taken a bolus of the substance, which he would have wrapped in a bit of cotton and placed in a bowl or cup of water. Chitchatting with the guests, he would have used his fingers to dissolve the opium, disposed of the cotton in a spittoon if he had one, and then taken a sip of the solution, followed by drafts of hot tea. On other occasions Bāqir 'Alī would warm up with some words in praise of chai: "Tea is excellent when it sews the lips shut, rips them open, and sets them aflame." But Yūsuf Bukhārī opined that this speech was simply a polite substitute to mask his passionate love for opium (Sayyid Yūsuf Bukhārī Dihlawī 1987, 26; cf. Shāhid Aḥmad Dihlawī 1979, 41).

As the intoxication loosened his tongue, Bāqir 'Alī began the story of Amīr Ḥamzah's son, Badī' al-Zamān. The prince had been on a hunting expedition when he came upon a river. All of a sudden, there appeared a flotilla of boats upon the river's waves, with a multitude of beautiful women aboard. In one of the boats, the fairy (*parī*) Queen Gohar and her attendants were traveling. Queen Gohar cast her gaze upon the riverbank and, seeing the handsome human prince, was slain by the saber of his eyebrow. Espying the fairy, Badī' al-Zamān too lost his senses and fell to the ground in a swoon. In some consternation, the nobles in his retinue ordered a palanquin and had the prince carried back to Amīr Ḥamzah, who summoned the sons of the Sasanian vizier Buzurjmihr, as well as the King of Tricksters, 'Amar 'Ayyār. The story that Ṣabūḥī put into Bāqir 'Alī's mouth was a collage of abbreviated scenes from Bāqir 'Alī's *dāstān*, the *Ṭilism-i Hosh-afzā* (The sense-increasing ṭilism), calculated to demonstrate the storyteller's command of all of the elements of the romance, from love to war, magic to trickery. When it ended, the audience showed their appreciation, and even the connoisseur from Lucknow was in raptures (Ṣabūḥī 1963, 63).[34]

Like his guest from Lucknow, Mir Bāqir 'Alī came from a family in which the storytelling craft was well established. His ancestors are said to have been sayyids who had come from Mazandaran in Iran and settled in the vicinity of the Turkman Gate in Delhi. More specifically, they had settled in Ḍomoṅ kī galī—"the Ḍoms' Lane," where hereditary musicians of the *ḍom* community lived. It seems that by the time of Bāqir 'Alī's birth the family, or some part of it, was living there still (Muḥammad Feroz Dihlawī

2014, 63; Ṣabūḥī 1963, 43; Sayyid Yūsuf Buk̤hārī Dihlawī 1987, 19). At any rate, the biographers had reason to hold the Ḍomoṅ kī galī connection to Bāqir 'Alī's credit; he was known for his excellent knowledge of music and would challenge the greatest singers if he thought they were in error (Sayyid Yūsuf Buk̤hārī Dihlawī 1987, 24; Ṣabūḥī 1963, 43). His father, Mīr Ḥusain 'Alī, is said to have worked at the Mughal court as a storyteller (Mullā Wāḥidī Dihlawī 2013, 95; Muḥammad Feroz Dihlawī 2014, 63; Sayyid Yūsuf Buk̤hārī Dihlawī 1987, 19). His *nana,* or maternal grandfather, Mīr Amīr 'Alī, lovingly nicknamed Mīr Peṛā (Sir Lump of Dough), had the distinction of being a storyteller to Ẓafar himself (Muḥammad Feroz Dihlawī 2014, 63; Mullā Wāḥidī Dihlawī 2013, 95; Sayyid Yūsuf Buk̤hārī Dihlawī 1987, 19). He had been trained by Mīr Aḥmad 'Alī of Lucknow, making him the *gurū-bhā'ī* (fellow student) of storytellers like Ḥakīm Aṣġhar 'Alī and Anbā Parshād Rasā (Mīr Bāqir 'Alī Dāstān-go 1892, preface). Bāqir 'Alī's son-in-law Sayyid Ẓamīr Ḥasan went so far as to claim that Mīr Amīr 'Alī performed for Bahādur Shāh Ẓafar every day (Muḥammad Feroz Dihlawī 2014, 63). The prestige of Bāqir 'Alī's lineage cannot be understated.

Several of Bāqir 'Alī's biographers emphasize the hereditary nature of his profession, along with other effects of his bloodline. In Mullā Wāḥidī's emphasis on Bāqir 'Alī's sayyid genealogy and his *sharāfat,* or respectability—both innate and performed—there is an especially strong gesture toward the idea that blood eases or even implies the possession of particular kinds of cultural capital (Mullā Wāḥidī Dihlawī 2013, 96).[35] More than simply highlighting the fact that he was advantaged in his access to cultural capital, emphasis on familial tradition added a sheen to Bāqir 'Alī's worth by producing an aura of innateness around his abilities, suggesting that the quality of the tales he produced was much greater than the labor he had to put in, because competence in his craft flowed in his blood and because the labor had been done beforehand, by his elders. The connection that all of the biographers make between Bāqir 'Alī's lineage and his storytelling also allows them to connect the disappearance of certain cultural competencies and knowledge with the death, especially during the catastrophe of 1857, of Delhite families like Bāqir ʿAlī's, who were their traditional carriers and disseminators.

After the Rebellion of 1857, the British sent the aged Bahādur Shāh Ẓafar into exile in Rangoon, where he would die in 1862. Along with the setting of the sun of the Mughal Empire, many of Delhi's lights were extinguished. One of these lights was Mīr Amīr ʿAlī, who is said to have perished in the rebellion's tumult (Muḥammad Feroz Dihlawī 2014, 63). Mīr Ḥusain ʿAlī had passed away before or at the same time as Amir ʿAlī, and the young Bāqir ʿAlī was left to the care of his mother and his childless *māmū*, or maternal uncle, Mīr Kāẓim ʿAlī, who was a noted storyteller himself (Ṣabūḥī 1963, 41). The family took refuge for a time in the ʿAlī Ganj Shāh-i Mardān area (now Jor Bagh in Delhi), moving to the Farrash-khanah neighborhood when the situation had improved (Muḥammad Feroz Dihlawī 2014, 63; Sayyid Yūsuf Buḳhārī Dihlawī 1987, 19). There Mīr Kāẓim ʿAlī seems to have continued his storytelling. Yūsuf Buḳhārī measures Kāẓim ʿAlī's worth by his elderly informants' claims that *dāstān* lovers would venture from as far as Lucknow and Faizabad simply to hear him (Sayyid Yūsuf Buḳhārī Dihlawī 1987, 20). In his evocatively titled memoir of Delhi's splendors, *Dillī kā sanbhālā* (The death rally of Delhi), Ḳhwājah Muḥammad Shafīʿ described Mīr Kāẓim ʿAlī's superb manipulation of a version of the four traditional storytelling repertoires: war, courtly gatherings, trickery, and magic (Muḥammad Shafīʿ 1938, 110–11). Kāẓim ʿAlī left Delhi for the Deccan, where he was employed by the nizam of Hyderabad (Ṣabūḥī 1963, 41; Muḥammad Feroz Dihlawī 2014, 64).

Before repairing to the Hyderabadi court, however, Kāẓim ʿAlī had continued to train his nephew as a storyteller (Ṣabūḥī 1963, 41). Shāhid Aḥmad suggested that Bāqir ʿAlī was, perhaps at first, the student of his grandfather. But in Kāẓim ʿAlī's own lifetime, Bāqir ʿAlī referred to his uncle, the "Nightingale of India," as his *ustād*, or teacher, in his book from the Ḥamzah cycle, *Ṭilism-i Hosh-afẓā*, which was completed in 1892–93 (1310 H) (Mīr Bāqir ʿAlī Dāstān-go 1892, preface; see also 272). Several sources stress the idea that Amīr ʿAlī had been a "mere" *qiṣṣah-ḳhwān*, or teller of *qiṣṣah*s, whereas Kāẓim ʿAlī was a *dāstān-go*, or teller of *dāstān*s. This supposedly superior ability and the *dāstān-go* title were both passed down to Bāqir 'Alī, who at the end of one of his 1920 recordings for the Linguistic Survey of India can be heard saying his name with a firmness verging on vehemence: "Bāqir 'Alī Dāstāngo, resident of Dehli" (Ṣabūḥī 1963, 41; Muḥammad Feroz Dihlawī 2014, 63; Shāhid Aḥmad Dihlawī 1979, 190; Mīr Bāqir 'Alī Dāstān-go 1920a). Undoubtedly this title acted as a kind of credential, proclaiming the cultural capital possessed by Bāqir 'Alī to anyone who was apprised of the distinction. How material this distinction was, however, is not clear.[36]

While his uncle worked in the south, Bāqir 'Alī was in demand at several northern courts and was retained at the court of the Maharajah of Patiala. Yūsuf Buḳhārī also notes that Bāqir 'Alī performed at the court of Rampur, as well as in Loharu, Dojana, Malerkotla, Jahangirabad, Kashmir, and his uncle Kāẓim 'Alī's territory in Hyderabad (Shāhid Aḥmad Dihlawī 1979, 190; Sayyid Yūsuf Buḳhārī Dihlawī 1987, 22–23). Courtly performances like those that took place in Patiala in the heyday of the Naval Kishore *Dāstān-i Amīr Ḥamzah* were chances for Bāqir 'Alī to network; they were attended by important men who could in turn become patrons, though on one occasion Bāqir 'Alī received a resounding blow to his *sharāfat* when he kowtowed to a showily dressed audience member who turned out to be nothing more than the *paṭwārī* (account keeper) of a nearby village (Mullā Wāḥidī Dihlawī 2013, 94–95). He reportedly took hundreds of rupees for performances at these princely courts, but it is likely that even during this time Bāqir 'Alī was still performing back home in Delhi, where he might only charge a couple of rupees (Shāhid Aḥmad Dihlawī 1979, 192).[37] Approbation and remuneration by royalty, however minor, was a clear validation of Bāqir 'Alī's worth as a storyteller. Therefore, the cessation of his excursions to such courts was a mark of the decline not of the absolute value of the storyteller but of the mechanism by which his worth could be made evident and recognized by Indians in general, and therefore of something like his "market value." The tales of the lowered value of storytelling are all partially stories of political decline, from the fall of Mughal rule to the fading of princely patronage to a final colonially influenced revolution in elite Indian worldviews that sounded the death knell for storytellers. Before this knell could be rung, however, a new urban aristocracy had its turn at validating Bāqir 'Alī's worth. Probably Bāqir 'Alī had never abandoned his Delhi residence; certainly in 1892 or 1893 he was still described as a Delhite (Mīr Bāqir 'Alī Dāstān-go 1892, preface). When his main patron, the Maharajah of Patiala, passed away at the turn of the century, Bāqir 'Alī decided to focus his energies on Delhi entirely.

In and around the city Bāqir 'Alī found new sources of patronage and revenue. Some of these were similar in form to the princely patronage to which he had been used, for brand-new princes were arising from the *ashrāf class*. In at least one case Bāqir 'Alī succeeded in captivating a patron at a young age, a strategy used by many a storyteller before him. The fabric magnate Chhunnāmal had been hearing Bāqir 'Alī's tales from his childhood, and when Bāqir 'Alī returned to Delhi he was able to secure this extravagantly rich man's patronage, attaching himself to Chhunnāmal for forty to fifty rupees per month (Sayyid Yūsuf Buḳhārī Dihlawī 1987, 21; Shāhid Aḥmad Dihlawī 1979, 190). He was still willing to perform outside of the city, as when he did so at the Aligarh residence of Nawab Muḥammad Isḥāq Ḳhān; Buḳhārī also mentions Nawab Faiẓ Aḥmad Ḳhān and Nawab Nannhe Ḳhān as his patrons (Sayyid Yūsuf Buḳhārī Dihlawī 1987, 23). But generally he cleaved to Delhi-based patrons.

Bāqir 'Alī sometimes spun his stories in the Delhi houses of *dāstān* enthusiasts who might not have had the wherewithal or inclination to provide continuous patronage but who had other gifts to bestow. He told tales at the residences of Mullā Wāḥidī and Ḳhwājah Ḥasan Niẓāmī, for instance (Mullā Wāḥidī Dihlawī 2013, 96). These renowned literary personalities were able to give Bāqir 'Alī access to the world of journals and publishing, and through their own writing and the funds of social capital they could make his worth known to others. Ḳhwājah Ḥasan Niẓāmī gave the storyteller the lofty title of *muqarrir-i kā'ināt*, "speaker of the world," not only projecting the fame that Bāqir 'Alī had acquired by virtue of his tongue but also implying that, through speech, the storyteller brought a world into existence (Muḥammad Feroz Dihlawī 2014, 22; Sayyid Yūsuf

Bukhārī Dihlawī 1987, 22).[38] Niẓāmī's charisma as a Sufi master gave his endorsement a kingly ring, and Bāqir 'Alī used the title like a charm. Yet the public approbation of such men was no substitute for the monthly wage granted by Chhunnāmal or the equally important patronage of the physician brothers Ḥakīm 'Abd al-Majīd Ḳhān and Ḥakīm Ajmal Ḳhān.

Ḥakīm Ajmal Ḳhān is well known as an extraordinarily successful practitioner and representative of the Indo-Muslim *Unānī* medical tradition, an important player in the pre-independence *ḳhilāfat* movement to preserve an Islamic caliph after World War I, and the founder of Ṭibbiya College. Yūsuf Bukhārī complained, however, that the physician's artistic patronage went relatively unnoticed (Sayyid Yūsuf Bukhārī Dihlawī 1987, 21). Ḥakīm Ajmal Ḳhān's grand hall for guests, or *dīwān-ḳhānah*, was the setting in which Bukhārī went with his father to hear Bāqir 'Alī tell his stories countless times. Sinuous specimens of calligraphy reposed upon the walls, and the entrances were muffled with patchwork curtains. The floor was covered with a cloth so white it flashed in one's eyes. Sitting on rugs and bolsters, the Hakim's guests passed the hookah around and took paan. Bāqir 'Alī sat on his favorite chowki or against a bolster, carefully preparing his opium in a bowl of water. He would imbibe first the opium and then some tea, and, with his customary speech in praise of tea, he would begin a tale of Amīr Ḥamzah (Sayyid Yūsuf Bukhārī Dihlawī 1987, 25–27; see also Mīr Bāqir 'Alī Dāstān-go 2011, 52).

It is said that, once, Bāqir 'Alī's grandfather Mīr Amīr 'Alī was telling Emperor Bahādur Shāh Ẓafar the tale of a pair of lovers. At the point where they were expected to consummate their relationship, Amīr 'Alī arrested the *dāstān*, describing the room, the lovers' beauty, their clothing, their passion—in short, everything except their lovemaking itself. Where Anbā Parshād's disciple kept up the nawab of Rampur's suspense for six months, Amir 'Alī supposedly kept Ẓafar in suspense for twelve years before His Majesty could bear it no longer and gave his command: "Today the curtain should be lifted!" Like his grandfather, Bāqir 'Alī was an expert in the art of arresting the *dāstān*, or *dāstān roknā*, known three centuries earlier to the storyteller 'Abd al-Nabī Faḳhr al-Zamānī as *pāband-ḳhwānī*.

His admirers who had thronged Chhunnāmal's residence said that they had been hearing him for twenty years and had never heard him finish his story. This was a point of pride for Bāqir 'Alī. It is reported that he was asked, "Have you ever finished the *dāstān*?" He answered, "Once in all my life" (Sayyid Yūsuf Buḳhārī Dihlawī 1987, 22; Shāhid Aḥmad Dihlawī 1979, 190).

His biographers took care that later generations would know that watching Bāqir 'Alī was not like flipping the pages of a storybook. Shāhid Aḥmad recounts a story of his admirers' disdain for mere reading off the page:

> Mīr Maḥmūd 'Alī Ṣāḥib told me: "Once in Calcutta the fame of a certain storyteller of Lucknow was bruited about. One day I too went to see him, but what did I see but a book placed open before the storyteller! He would read from it, and if he became unusually enthusiastic he would go to the extreme of raising one of his hands. I was quite disgusted. I wished that Mīr Bāqir 'Alī would somehow arrive, so that the people of Calcutta would discover what storytelling really is. The next day, out of the blue, I saw Mīr [Bāqir 'Alī] Ṣāḥib himself, walking along in Colootola. It turned out that he was there on some business of his own. To make a long story short, Mīr Ṣāḥib performed a *dāstān*, and the storyteller from Lucknow was left clasping his hands together and saying, 'Dear sir, this is a miracle! Dear sir, this [art] belongs to you!'" (Shāhid Aḥmad Dihlawī 1979, 192)

The memoirists described his modulations of voice, his pronunciation, and especially his physical movements, gestures, and "acting" (Shāhid Aḥmad Dihlawī 1979, 191). This thin, bow-backed man would seem erect and imposing when he told of a powerful emperor. He could become a dacoit, a genteel lady, or a man in his dotage (Mullā Wāḥidī Dihlawī 2013, 96; Ṣabūḥī 1963, 42, 46; Sayyid Yūsuf Buḳhārī Dihlawī 1987, 24). Thanks to Shahid Amin's efforts to retrieve the Linguistic Survey of India recordings from the British Library's depths, we can still hear Bāqir 'Alī's 1920 imitation of a toothless old *ḍom* and the breathless staccato rhythm of his lists—of weapons in the case of the recorded tale, but from the published *Ṭilism-i Hosh-afzā* and the biographers we know that he rattled off many other lists, of foodstuffs, items of jewelry, or wrestling moves.[39]

Near the end of *Ṭilism-i Hosh-afzā*, King Gohar Winedrinker and the hero, Amīr Ḥamzah's grandson Nūr al-Zamān, settle down to enjoy watching a dance. After the dancers are finished, Nūr al-Zamān turns his attention to the dinner cloth (*dastar-ḳhwān*) spread out for them, and now Bāqir 'Alī describes eight types of naan and a kulcha, a six-colored korma, qaliyah kebab, chicken kebab, whole chicken, half chicken, Shami kebab, seekh kebab, four types of pulao and a sweet rice, firni, mango jam, quince jam, pear jam, pineapple jam, and so forth (Mīr Bāqir 'Alī Dāstān-go 1892, 264). Feroz stresses that Bāqir 'Alī not only was a connoisseur of such dishes but also had a consummate understanding of the etiquette of eating with one's hands on the *dastar-ḳhwān* spread out on the floor (he is said to have deigned on occasion to eat at British tables, however) (Shāhid Aḥmad Dihlawī 1944, 40). He once chided a host for not providing a *s̈aqal-dān*—a covered vessel for the polite disposal of small bones and other uneatables (Muḥammad Feroz Dihlawī 2014, 68).[40] In his storytelling, knowledge such as this was on display. As Bāqir 'Alī performed his stories and amazed the audience with his unstammering lists, he would welcome questions from puzzled audience members who might be confused about the difference between a *sar-pech* turban and *jīghā* headwear (Shāhid Aḥmad Dihlawī 1979, 191; 1944, 40; Mīr Bāqir 'Alī Dāstān-go 2011, 54). A deep understanding of weaponry and martial arts was an obvious staple of his art for the purpose of narrating episodes of *razm*, or battle, but, in addition, his descriptions of jewelry were so exquisite that his advice was sought by the *sādah-kār*s, makers of gold and silver ornaments, who practiced their art in Ustad Hamid's Lane (Muḥammad Feroz Dihlawī 2014, 69). Unsurprisingly, Bāqir 'Alī was a particular expert in the Urdu language itself. He was horrified once when a muslin-hatted man in the street omitted to say salaam and assailed him instead with a "*Hā'o ḍū yū ḍū?*" (Mīr Bāqir 'Alī Dāstān-go 2014a, 191).[41] He would correct misuses that he heard when he went for a stroll, filled his chapbook *qiṣṣah*s with explanatory footnotes, and delighted Ḥakīm Ajmal Ḳhān's guests with his adroit explanations of obscure words and idioms (Muḥammad Feroz Dihlawī 2014, 67).[42]

Delhites' recollections of Bāqir 'Alī's feats of memory and his sumptuous lists speak more of his worth than the other techniques of the storyteller's craft. They do not only tell us that his storytelling was valuable for its superiority to the humdrum book reading to which members of the middle class were accustomed. They also validate Bāqir 'Alī as a prodigious repository of knowledge of a fading time and present his storytelling as a means of access to this knowledge. That Bāqir 'Alī was appreciated as a lore master is clear, but to ask why his knowledge was valued at this time is to step into a swirling mire of colonial and precolonial sediments. On the one hand, there is at play the idea that literature is of low worth unless its absurd fantasies are leavened by useful information about the real world, past or present. This notion, connected to colonial epistemologies, assisted the realistic novel's ascent to the treetops of the Indian genre system. Bāqir 'Alī's younger contemporaries accepted the terms of the British valuation of literature but tried to show that Bāqir 'Alī's storytelling was valuable even according to the British standard.

On the other hand, that romances have effects, including the imparting of knowledge, on their audiences is a claim made by storytellers and story writers long before either Bāqir 'Alī or the advent of colonialism. It is an aspect of the elite storytelling tradition that Bāqir 'Alī himself promotes, for example, in his treatise on listening, *Kānā-bātī* (Whispers in the ear). The word "*sun*"—the verbal stem or imperative form of the verb *sunnā*, "to listen"—is also the name of a kind of mirror, he explains. As a mirror interiorizes and reflects what is outside of it, so the ear as it listens gathers and reflects what it hears; the ear (*kān*) becomes a mine (*kān*) of knowledge (Mīr Bāqir 'Alī Dāstān-go 2011, 42, 56).[43] The ear is a supremely valuable organ; Bāqir 'Alī plumes himself on the fact that despite being seventy years of age he has excellent hearing, in part due to his refusal to submit to having his ear wax removed (an operation generally performed by ear wax cleaners known as *kan-meliyā*s, whose use of iron wires is objected to by

Bāqir ʻAlī) (Mīr Bāqir ʻAlī Dāstān-go 2011, 35). In line with the hierarchy of faculties agreed upon by many Muslim thinkers, Bāqir ʻAlī affirms the superiority of hearing to seeing—if someone sees a lion for the first time, how will they know that they are about to be mauled to death? (Mīr Bāqir ʻAlī Dāstān-go 2011, 32; cf. Hujwerī 1978, 564–66). Thus knowledge is but another name for listening and telling (" *ʻilm sunne sunāne kā nām hai*") (Mīr Bāqir ʻAlī Dāstān-go 2011, 55). Like his colleagues in the past, Bāqir ʻAlī raises his worth and that of his craft by presenting storytelling as a conduit for knowledge. There is one aspect of his reflections on listening and telling, however, that appears incalculable in terms of the economy of self-promotion: telling, for Bāqir ʻAlī, is inferior to listening (Mīr Bāqir ʻAlī Dāstān-go 2011, 29, 34, 46). By inference, then, the worth of the storyteller is less than that of the audience. Yet worth therefore rebounds upon the storyteller, on whose speech the high worth of the listener depends. Like the lover in Sufi thought, the one who imparts knowledge through speech is invaluable to the knowledge receiver; their sacrifice raises their worth. It is no wonder, then, that Bāqir ʻAlī would say, "May the life of the one who tells be short, and may the life of the one who listens be long" (Sayyid Yūsuf Buḳhārī Dihlawī 1987, 22).

Bāqir ʻAlī's own education had been informal; he had some training at the Fatehpuri Masjid, and in his old age he sat in on classes at Ṭibbiyah College (Muḥammad Feroz Dihlawī 2014, 67; Ṣabūḥī 1963, 43; Sayyid Yūsuf Buḳhārī Dihlawī 1987, 23). But his connection with Nawab Iṣḥāq Ḳhān of Aligarh led to a speaking engagement at that city's college, at which he told the tale of Bahādur Shāh Ẓafar's elephant Maulā Baḳhsh. It was an occasion of which Bāqir ʻAlī was very proud (Mīr Bāqir ʻAlī Dāstān-go 2014b, 189). The wealthy and well connected were not the only audiences for whom Bāqir ʻAlī performed. He was not averse to doing his storytelling at Humāyūn's tomb, where Rājah Naushād ʻAlī of Jahangirabad reported seeing him perform (Mullā Wāḥidī Dihlawī 2013, 96). But perhaps the most striking strategies of the storyteller are recounted by Yūsuf Būḳhārī: his targeting of youthful audiences and his production of tales in print that reflected the politics of the time.

Bukhārī remembers that he first saw Bāqir 'Alī in 1919, when he was a boy in the sixth standard at Arabic College. At the main gate of the college a throng of students and professors gathered to hear the storyteller tell a tale—not the tale of Amīr Ḥamzah, for once, but the comic story of Gāṛhe Ḳhān and Malmal Jān, with characters entirely of Bāqir 'Alī's own invention. The dim-witted and innocent Gāṛhe Ḳhān, son of Cotton Mouth, whose color is swarthy like that of cotton unseparated from the seed, falls in love with the comely Malmal (Muslin) Jān, daughter of Iron Machine. He proceeds to marry her, despite a few initial qualms about his first wife and the many objections voiced by his faithful servant Charḳhah (Spinning Wheel) Ḳhān. Malmal Jān is fair skinned and slim with thin lips and juicy eyes, known to be forty-two years old but often mistaken for a twenty-six-year-old. Upon marrying Gāṛhe Ḳhān, she appropriates his house and has most of the valuables transported to her parents' home. The stricken Gāṛhe Ḳhān, shut out of the house, wanders into the wilderness, where he receives some solace from a *mahātmā* and realizes that the better mate was the wife from his place of origin (*waṭan*, a word that with the rise of nationalism was coming to mean "homeland"). He returns to the house, where Malmal Jān and her cronies are enjoying themselves in the style of Amīr Ḥamzah's royal gatherings. Upon hearing that Gāṛhe Ḳhān is bent on entering, she threatens to deploy a multitude of weapons, from the sword to the rifle, from the cannon to the airplane. But Gāṛhe Ḳhān manages to enter and pronounces the divorce (Mīr Bāqir 'Alī Dāstān-go 1922).

This is not the place to examine the play of Malmal Jan's perilous European sexuality or her colonization of Gāṛhe Ḳhān's home. Nor is it the place to situate Bāqir 'Alī's thick embroidery of the tale with metaphors relating to fabric and thread at a time when Indians were being exhorted to abandon cloths, like muslin, of British manufacture and in the heady days of the *ḳhilāfat* movement, the rise of Mahatma Gandhi, and the demand for *svarāj*. It will suffice to note that Yūsuf Bukhārī saw the oblique connections quite clearly, and the banning of the *Gāṛhe Ḳhān* chapbooks raised Bāqir 'Alī's worth in his eyes (Sayyid Yūsuf Bukhārī Dihlawī 1987, 22).

Like other Urdu storytellers from Ashk to the Naval Kishore *dāstān-gos*, Bāqir 'Alī tried to use print technology to supplement and boost his worth as a storyteller. As we have seen, he consorted with Delhi's literati, including Mullā Wāḥidī, who claims that he used to give Bāqir 'Alī the titles of stories that the latter would then compose (Mullā Wāḥidī Dihlawī 2013, 96). On the same street as Mullā Wāḥidī's house lived Bāqir 'Alī's good friend, the journalist Mīr Jālib Dihlawī. Bāqir 'Alī wrote for Maulānā Muḥammad 'Alī's journal *Hamdard* while Jālib was an important member of its staff (Shāhid Aḥmad Dihlawī 1979, 192; 1944, 41; Mullā Wāḥidī Dihlawī 2013, 95). He helped another member of this literary circle, Qāẓi Sarfarāz Ḥusain, by writing a passage describing a fight between two *hījṛās* for his novel *Sazā-i 'aish* (Punishment for pleasure) (Sayyid Yūsuf Buḳhārī Dihlawī 1987, 24). Bāqir 'Alī's book-length works never stayed long in print, and thus they have become obscure. In 1892 or 1893 (1301 H), during the heyday of Naval Kishore's *Dāstān-i Amīr Ḥamzah*, the Matba'-i Riẓwī published the first volume of *Ṭilism-i Hosh-afzā*, Bāqir 'Alī's story of Amīr Ḥamzah's son Badī' al-Zamān and grandson Nūr al-Zamān. It was patronized by the Hyderabadi prime minister Wiqār al-Umarā, and the events it recounts take place after those of the *Kochak Bāḳhtar* and *Bālā Bāḳhtar* cycles of the long *Ḥamzah-nāmah* as represented by the Naval Kishore version. It includes much poetry by Bāqir 'Alī, writing under the pen name "Maujid," and its courtly style and subject matter are unlike those of his later works, for it was the only book that he would write in the Ḥamzah cycle. The promised second volume appears never to have been printed (see Mīr Bāqir 'Alī Dāstān-go 1892, preface and colophon).

After *Ṭilism-i Hosh-afzā*, Bāqir 'Alī's books become focused on the same rising middle class upon whom he increasingly depended for his livelihood. To some degree these works bear a resemblance to earlier tales of this sort described by Francesca Orsini, only their style and diction are more complex and challenging, prompting Bāqir 'Alī to indulge in a spate of footnotes that seem to be the print equivalents of his oral asides during storytelling performances. Unlike the Persianate diction of *Hosh-afzā*, however, the wording of these books reflects the everyday language of Delhi

Urdu speakers. The chapbook format and reasonable prices of many of these books also point to Bāqir 'Alī's new audience. The relatively successful *Gāṛhe Ḳhān ne Malmal Jān ko ṭalāq de dī* (Gāṛhe Ḳhān divorced Malmal Jān), whose second printing ran to one thousand copies, provides the prices of his pre-1922 books, all of which are advertised as being procurable at Bāqir 'Alī's Bhojla Pahari house if the prospective buyer failed to encounter him on the streets of Delhi peddling his chapbooks out of a bag. Apart from *Gāṛhe Ḳhān ne Malmal Jān ko ṭalāq de dī* itself, which sold for three annas, the books listed include the more expensive eight-anna *Ḳhalīl Ḳhān Fāḳhtah*, Bāqir 'Alī's scatological tale of an aged buffoon (due to misplaced birth papers he is unaware of precisely how old he is) given to involuntary urination who gets his comeuppance when he seeks the hand of a very young wife—apparently the latest in a long string of them. Its cast of characters includes a cosmetician (*mashshāṭah*) and a bevy of prostitutes.[44] The Gāṛhe Ḳhān chapbooks and *Ḳhalīl Ḳhān Fāḳhtah* are likely to have resonated with middle-class Delhites with a taste for humor and a desire to look into a mirror of sorts.

Shahid Ahmad called Bāqir 'Alī "the last *dāstāngo* of Delhi" (Shāhid Aḥmad Dihlawī 1979, 189). Mullā Wāḥidī and Ṣabūḥī both state that the storytelling tradition ended when Bāqir 'Alī was laid to rest in the Dargah-i Shah-i Mardan in 1928 (Mullā Wāḥidī Dihlawī 2013, 95; Ṣabūḥī 1963, 41).[45] Though Bāqir 'Alī was only a boy when the Mughals' final downfall came, his status as a professional repository of cultural knowledge of a vanished time betokens, for his biographers, the disappearance of the most substantial specters of Delhi's cultural glory. With Bāqir 'Alī', the master-disciple chain was severed; he left no formal disciples. Bāqīrī Begam, the daughter of Bāqir 'Alī and his wife, Wazīrī Begam, went to Ṭibbiyah College and became a physician and midwife. Yet she also had some storytelling talent; Ṣabūḥī and Buḳhārī lament that Bāqir 'Alī never trained his own daughter in his profession (Sayyid Yūsuf Buḳhārī Dihlawī 1987, 20; Ṣabūḥī 1963, 42).[46] Another half disciple was the young Zulfiqar Ali Bukhari, the brother of the famed satirist Ahmad Shah "Patras" Bukhari and a renowned radio broadcaster (Sayyid Yūsuf Buḳhārī Dihlawī 1987, 24).

The strategies and methods for the acquisition of cultural capital employed by Bāqir 'Alī show, on the one hand, the agency that he possessed. He actively widened his social networks, whether of patrons or writers, to secure the continuance of his performances and his writings. Performances for the young aided him in catching hold of a long-lasting audience. Most importantly, Bāqir 'Alī's status as a repository of and conduit for knowledge—of obscure objects, practices, and, in particular, the Urdu language—was a powerful source of worth, particularly as time passed and nostalgia for pre-Raj Delhi grew. Bāqir 'Alī himself linked the transmission of knowledge to his storytelling. His use of storytelling to disseminate knowledge and linguistic models was closely in line with the practice of previous storytellers like Ashk, and we will consider other examples in the next chapter. But in Bāqir 'Alī's time, his role as a knowledge repository reacted powerfully with his younger contemporaries' nostalgia, blended with a new instrumentalism of British origin.

Two points need to be borne in mind, however. First, and most obviously, the memorials of Bāqir 'Alī's worth would not have been made in a climate in which the worth of storytelling and romances was universally acknowledged. The precariousness of Bāqir 'Alī's survival into the age of moving pictures simply shows that, as his art was being devalued all around him, he was minimally able to hold up his head and squeeze the most out of his scarcity value. Second, Bāqir 'Alī's relative destitution demonstrates that the acquisition of cultural capital and the gaining of economic capital do not always go hand in hand and may even exist in an inverse relation, especially in the absence of the social conditions that formerly ensured their mutual reinforcement. Bāqir 'Alī is valued by the nostalgists for his proud poverty and the lessening of the financial reward that his great art deserved. His agency in this kind of disadvantageous cultural capital acquisition seems to lie in the *sharāfat* that he performed: his stubborn pride in his manners, birth, and understanding of the storytelling tradition.

How does Bāqir 'Alī's personal worth reflect the worth of the romance genre? The memoirists say very little about the Amīr Ḥamzah narrative, which he recited. It is likely that they had not seen the *Ṭilism-i Hosh-afzā* and had only heard it from his lips, which only underlines the fact that memoirists understood Bāqir 'Alī's *dāstān*s to be inextricably connected to his bodily presence. Along with the storyteller, the inference is, the romance genre itself had to decline, and, in its courtly form at least, it passed away with its last exponent. While Bāqir 'Alī's role as a storyteller is heavily stressed by his biographers, other roles that he played, from elderly college student to betel nut vendor, are sometimes disparaged by them (Ṣabūḥī 1963, 38, 43; Shāhid Aḥmad Dihlawī 1979, 192). However, even in the case of Bāqir 'Alī, whose identity is represented as being subsumed under his storytelling role, it is possible to see how other roles such as that of political commentator both stood apart from his storytelling and increased its worth. In this sense he was no different from the courtly storytellers of Iran, who came, like Bāqir 'Alī's own forebears, to India to tell the tale of Amīr Ḥamzah.

By Bāqir 'Alī's time, the profusion of oral-performative genres of verbal art that previous Urdu storytellers had tapped into—especially *naṡr-k͟hwānī* and *marṡiyah-k͟hwānī*—was no longer as important, though watching Zulfiqar Ali Bukhari recite a *marṡiyah* for Pakistani television one can imagine that some link remained between storytelling and these other genres. Print had become infinitely more important than it had been in Ashk's time, and Bāqir 'Alī was far bolder than the Naval Kishore storytellers in his experiments with the medium.

The decline of professional, elite storytelling in Urdu was remembered by writers like Ṣabūḥī and K͟hwājah 'Ishrat Lakhnawī in rather tragicomic terms. At least Bāqir 'Alī's reduction to a street vendor of betel nuts is tempered by the storyteller's pride in his own *sharāfat* and his insistence that he was preserving tradition by educating his customers about the correct way to prepare the betel nut. 'Ishrat's 1935 portrait of the contemporary Lucknow storyteller Mirzā Ṭallan shows an uninspiring man, far gone in his opium addiction, who is inconsolable after his favorite quail has its leg mortally bitten by a mouse and who is arrested while trying to bury it in a public park. 'Ishrat depicts storytelling as a profession past its expiry date and beset by mediocrity. The timid Mirzā Ṭallan, hearing the name of a storyteller of a bygone age, pulls his ears in humility and says, "By God, he was a master! I am nothing. I will take his name and tell you a story. I am ignorant; what comparison can be made between him and me?" Mirzā Ṭallan was nevertheless active after the "death of storytelling" with Bāqir 'Alī, narrating his stories with gusto in a tent at the fair on the banks of Moti Lake while spectators munched on sugarcane and ate sweet rice.

While data is sparse regarding storytelling in South Asia between Bāqir 'Alī's death and the *dāstān-go'ī* revival in the twenty-first century, Saeed Bhutta's scholarship on the Punjabi storyteller Kamal Din reveals that forms of storytelling were alive well beyond the decline of the courtly tradition. To study the romance genre beyond its most privileged examples, we must ask what storytelling as a practice in India was, beyond its elite forms (Bhutta 2006). Some of the challenges for the study of storytelling will be laid out in the conclusion of this book. It seems clear, however, that with the decline of courtly patronage the professional, Persianate, and elite strand of storytelling declined to the point of vanishing. The lack of remuneration from nobles could have been counteracted by the other forms of patronage that Bāqir 'Alī successfully exploited at the beginning of the twentieth century, but, under British influence, an epistemological and ideological shift was at work that caused even sympathizers like Ṣabūḥī to deny the use value that storytellers and story writers once ascribed to the romance. The chroniclers of Bāqir 'Alī's life gave us indications of how he performed and crafted his stories, but they did not grasp how the way in which romances were crafted in oral performance affected the structure of texts in this genre in a way that made it quite different from, but not less useful than, the empiricist ideal of the novel genre. Telling of how Mirzā Ṭallan financed his opium addiction, 'Ishrat noted that he spent his days embroidering floral designs upon muslin (Ḳhwājah 'Ishrat Lakhnawī 1935, 62). 'Ishrat seems to have been unaware that professional storytellers had always had other roles and other avenues to cultural and economic capital. Nor have many scholars been able to follow the paths of storytellers' textual embroidery, which gave the romance genre its form and impact.

3

The Storytelling Craft

MĪR BĀQIR 'ALĪ THE storyteller, like any good professional, was keen to upgrade his skills. He went so far as to take classes in subjects that he thought would enrich his descriptive abilities as a storyteller. Medicines, poisons, and cures are often featured in Urdu romances. So, to better describe these elements, Bāqir 'Alī sat in on lectures at Delhi's Ṭibbiyah College, an institution in which his patron the famous physician Ḥakīm Ajmal Ḳhān played a presiding role.[1] We are told that Bāqir 'Alī also took classes in philosophy, mathematics, literature, logic, and astronomy at the college and earned a degree. Bāqir 'Alī's intellectual friend Walī Ashraf Ṣabūḥī was unsympathetic to storytellers who went around getting degrees from medical colleges. Whatever Bāqir 'Alī learned while mingling with the college boys was fine in itself, but Ṣabūḥī could not comprehend why the storyteller had to sprinkle his romances with such a boring ingredient. The romance, he thought, was something like a sweet, with no nutritional value to speak of, cooked in a bygone age of frivolity and idleness. It had no use beyond sheer delectation at the dinner party—but at least the sugar excited the tongue (Ṣabūḥī 1963, 43). This blinkered view of the romance genre caused Ṣabūḥī to disdain romances as empty and useless amusements, crippling his ability to imagine that they could ever be anything else.

Yet time and time again we see the tellers and writers of romances claiming that their productions were *useful.* On the one hand, the *dāstān* of Amīr Ḥamzah was often prefaced with claims that, centuries ago, a Ghaznavid ruler's court intellectuals had produced the story to cure him of a disease. The mysterious storyteller Shāh Naẕar Qiṣṣah-ḳhwān claimed to have been cured of his own ailment by listening to the *dāstān*; Mīr Taqī

Ḳhayāl similarly writes that when he was seriously ill he would repair to the coffeehouse to hear Ḥamzah's tale (Ḳhayāl 1742, fol. 9b). The Urdu storyteller Ḳhalīl 'Alī Ḳhān Ashk (1863, 2) claimed in his romance of Ḥamzah:

> By listening to [the *dāstān*] one comes to know the ways of every kind of creature, and secondly one's memory is filled with stratagems for battles, the taking of forts and the conquest of countries; for this reason it was told to the emperor every day.

This claim was repeated by Ġhālib Lakhnawī in the preface to his 1855 version (3).

Two centuries previously, the storyteller with whom this chapter is concerned, 'Abd al-Nabī Faḳhr al-Zamānī Qazwīnī (fl. 1593–1632), had written in his manual for storytellers, the *Ṭirāz al-aḳhbār*,

> In spite of the fact that [the romance] is a lie, devoid of the form of sincerity, several benefits accrue to the tellers and hearers of the romance. . . . It shows nobles how to manage worldly affairs and the business of the kingdom . . . and in spite of its own falsehood, it turns their minds from vain thoughts. (1633, fol. 19a)

Should we take these statements seriously? Were *dāstān*s, with their twenty-foot violet-colored demons and gossipy jackals, of any use? Or is so-called usefulness merely a pretext for pleasure? Pleasure ought not to be sidelined, but both pleasure and use must be taken into consideration, each in its own way. Twentieth-century critics tried to make use of romances as historical source books, presenting them as direct reflections of the societies in which they were produced, ignoring artistic convention, extrinsic elements, and formalist aspects. Yet the same critics would have rejected the idea that we will examine in the next chapter: that romances *were* histories. The reflective approach, which vampirizes art for the sake of an illusory benefit to history, is to be avoided. But at the same time, it will not do to ignore the use value so often attributed to romances by their producers as part of the definition of the genre. If the romance *were* to be useful, how would it be so?

Like the patched frock of the dervish, a *dāstān* is parti-colored with rags of texts that give it shape even as they are discernibly foreign to the body of the garment. These rags or fragments of other artworks that find themselves in a work of romance are themselves colored with genres of their own, apart from the genre of the whole. The kind of internal variegation that we can see in the romance genre stands as a fact apart from the equally important principles of multiplicity that have already been stated: that is, that changes happen over time to the "genre code" (and therefore to the genre itself) and that the genre or genre code is disputed even within a given historical moment. We will turn our attention in chapters to come to the diachronic and synchronic multiplicity of the *qiṣṣah*. But we must first examine the colorful rags of texts that so visibly bespangle any complete work to which the name *qiṣṣah* or *dāstān* is given. Why must they be scrutinized? If we are to put aside our modern incredulity and take seriously the claim, made by storytellers like Mīr Bāqir 'Alī or by writers of *qiṣṣahs* like Ġhālib Lakhnawī, that the romance is not froth and foam but has practical uses, then the multigenre character of the romance will be key to understanding their confidence in this claim. Though the principle that a work of verbal art is crisscrossed by multiple genres is true not only in the case of the romance genre in India, its operation can be made particularly clear in the romance's case if we consider the oral-performative production of romances by storytellers such as the ones whose lives we considered in the previous chapter.

The very mode of the *qiṣṣah*'s production by the storyteller demonstrates to us how bits and pieces of previously existing works (what Gérard Genette [1997a, 5] called "hypotexts"—i.e., source texts) were woven into the romance during its performance. The need to grasp this weaving process is another reason why an understanding of the lives and practice of storytellers is so valuable to the study of the romance. Research is needed into the history of their lives and practices because without it we are missing the clues to an understanding of the genre that they produced through their performances. The method by which the *Ḥamzah-nāmah* was told in India provides us with a remarkably clear image of a verbal artwork composed of a rich assemblage of genres. And this method is nowhere better glimpsed than in a remarkable and unique manual for storytellers written in the seventeenth century by the storyteller ʿAbd al-Nabī Fak̲h̲r al-Zamānī of Qazvin, entitled the *Ṭirāz al-ak̲h̲bār* (Embroiderer of accounts). It was produced while Fak̲h̲r al-Zamānī was a resident of Patna, presumably living under the patronage of the governor of Bihar, Saif K̲h̲ān. Before examining the *Ṭirāz al-ak̲h̲bār* and its revelations regarding the craft of storytelling, we will consider Fak̲h̲r al-Zamānī's life, better documented than that of any other storyteller of his time, thanks to his habit of writing about himself and his constant allusions to other literary men of his acquaintance, showing his efforts to acquire social capital. We find that, like the storytellers whose lives we examined in chapters 1 and 2, Fak̲h̲r al-Zamānī had several roles that aided him in his accumulation of cultural capital. His worth, in the building of which his storytelling played the most important role, was signaled by his recognition by Saif K̲h̲ān, though one of the most lasting concretizations of this recognition involved Fak̲h̲r al-Zamānī's secondary role as a poet whose verses were inscribed upon a gubernatorially commissioned mosque.

After the coronation of Prince K̲h̲urram as Shāh Jahān in 1627, the city of Patna, in the Mughal province of Bihar, found itself in the hands of a governor whom the sovereign may have regarded with some animosity. Shāh Jahān had been restive when he was only Prince K̲h̲urram, striking poses of power throughout Hindustan and making himself a thorn in the side of his imperial parent Jahāngīr. Fak̲h̲r al-Zamānī was already living in Patna when K̲h̲urram wrested Bihar from the control of his brother Parwez. The storyteller sent the prince a poem predicting his accession to the throne, for which he received a reward. However, K̲h̲urram's ally ʿAbd Allah K̲h̲ān, anathematized as "Laʿnat Allāh" (God's curse) by a wrathful Jahāngīr, was soundly defeated in 1032 H (1623) by Saif K̲h̲ān, then *dīwān* of Gujarat and loyal to the emperor (Nūr al-Dīn Muḥammad

Salīm Jahāngīr, Mu'tamad Ḳhān, and Hādī 1914, 370–74; 'Abd al-Ḥāmid Lāhaurī 1867, 76–78). Yet Saif Ḳhān was installed as governor of Bihar by Shāh Jahān himself. It seems that he had family ties to thank for this. The governor-to-be was the grandson of one of the brothers of Jahāngīr's wife Nūr Jahān, and the governor's own wife Malikah Bāno was the elder sister of Shāh Jahān's wife Mumtāz Maḥal, in whose memory the Taj Mahal would one day be built. After ascending the throne, Shāh Jahān gave orders for Saif Ḳhān to be arrested in Ahmedabad, Gujarat. But it appears that through the machinations of his sister-in-law Mumtāz Maḥal, there was no chastisement of Saif Ḳhān, who was installed as governor in Patna instead. He became governor of Bihar at the beginning of the lunar year after Shāh Jahān's accession (Shāh Nawāz Ḳhān Aurangābādī 1888, 2:416–21; Nūr al-Dīn Muḥammad Salīm Jahāngīr, Mu'tamad Ḳhān, and Hādī 1914, 370). Faḳhr al-Zamānī had already been a citizen of Patna for over a decade.

Information regarding Faḳhr al-Zamānī's relationship with Saif Ḳhān at the time the *Ṭirāz al-aḳhbār* was produced can be gleaned from the preface to the *Ṭirāz* itself. But we also find it in an unexpected place: a public building. At the very outset of his gubernatorial stint, Saif Ḳhān embarked on an ambitious architectural program on the bank of the Ganges River. Catherine Asher (1992, 237–38) has written about the buildings that remain to bear witness to his zeal; fuller information is given by Faḳhr al-Zamānī (Faḳhr al-Zamānī Qazwīnī 1633, fols. 9a–10b; see also Qeyamuddin Ahmad 1973, 228; Patil 1963, 414; Beglar 1878, 29–32). Fresh from a similar building project in Ahmedabad, Saif Ḳhān first built an 'Īdgāh in Patna, in which the faithful could attend Eid prayers. In the following year he really got down to work on an assemblage of public edifices.

Most of them have now disappeared. The five-bayed mosque of brick that still survives was originally the centerpiece of a complex including an attached *madrasah* holding a hundred students, a house of healing (*dār al-shifā'*), and a bathhouse (*ḥamām*). To cover the upkeep of the mosque complex, and apparently to subsidize medications dispensed at the hospital, a serai was constructed adjoining the mosque. The British merchant

Peter Mundy (1907, 159) breathlessly noted the building's splendor when he stayed in Patna, calling it "the fairest Sarae that I have yet seene, or I thinck is in India, not yett finished." Fakhr al-Zamānī was more forceful, claiming that the buildings were not only beautiful but so strong that they would withstand a second Noah's flood if God ever saw fit to visit such a calamity on the denizens of Patna. If we consider the later fortunes of the mosque that Saif Ḳhān built as the central jewel in this group, we find that by the end of the nineteenth century its luster was already dimmed. In 1871 the archaeologist J. D. Beglar visited it. He noted that on the walls surrounding the hall were tiles, glazed and colored, and upon these was a dilapidated inscription. He was denied permission to enter the prayer hall to try to read the words (Beglar 1878, 30). Further attempts were made by Muslims more than forty years later, but by then most of the writing was nearly illegible, so that what they record makes little sense except for the closing portion in which the "decorator" of the mosque, Muḥammad 'Alī Kashmīrī, inscribed his name (Ahmad 1973, 228).[2]

Reading the recorded fragments, however, I have discovered that the inscription must have matched Fakhr al-Zamānī's poem about Saif Ḳhān's mosque and the buildings he constructed around it. This poem is given in the preface to the *Ṯirāz al-akhbār*, and it ends with a chronogram yielding the date of the buildings' construction (1039 H, or 1629–30) (Fakhr al-Zamānī Qazwīnī 1633, fol. 10a). The intended immortalization of Fakhr al-Zamānī's verses in the mosque of Saif Ḳhān indicates that Fakhr al-Zamānī swiftly became a recipient of the governor's favor. If we are to believe Fakhr al-Zamānī, this favor would have merely duplicated the beneficence of previous governors: since the beginning of his residence Bihar had been under the administration of Jahāngīr Qulī Ḳhān, Muqarrab Ḳhān, and the Safavid nobleman Mirzā Rustam (Fakhr al-Zamānī Qazwīnī 1633, fol. 4b).[3]

It may have been his verses that adorned the mosque interior, but Fakhr al-Zamānī frequently insists that his storytelling was his most effective hook for patrons. He declares that wherever his travels took him, he was valued for his telling of *dāstāns* rather than for any of the other arts that he practiced (Faḳhr al-Zamānī Qazwīnī 1633, fol. 4a). He therefore advises his fellow storytellers to recognize the power of their art: "there is no better medium for the gaining of intimacy with sultans, ministers, nobles and nobles' sons than the romance [of Amīr Ḥamzah]," he writes (Faḳhr al-Zamānī Qazwīnī 1633, fol. 19a). He brings up the examples of the storytellers Takaltū Ḳhān and Darbār Ḳhān, the father and son who captivated the potentates Shāh 'Ismā'īl and Akbar, respectively (Faḳhr al-Zamānī Qazwīnī 1633, fol. 19b). Faḳhr al-Zamānī was not, as far as we know, a storyteller to emperors. But according to himself, he had had his successes even before coming to Patna, and they began not long after his migration from his homeland in Iran.

Faḳhr al-Zamānī: A Storyteller's Life

Aside from Mīr Bāqir 'Alī, 'Abd al-Nabī Faḳhr al-Zamānī is the storyteller about whom we have the *means* of knowing the most. Unfortunately, this is different from saying that scholars *do* know very much about his life. Some of his own writings, especially his biographical dictionary the *Maiḳhānah* (The wine shop), have managed to survive; like the traces of other storytellers, they have not necessarily survived because Faḳhr al-Zamānī was valued as a great storyteller but for other reasons, which reflect the variety of roles that men who told *qiṣṣah*s played in society. The *Maiḳhānah*, by far his best-known work, has been preserved and has proliferated because of the prestige of Persian poetry, including the *sāqī-nāmah*s—addresses to the young male bearer of the wine cup (*sāqī*), in whose recording the *Maiḳhānah* specializes. His other writings have fared worse, but they have at least been preserved in manuscript form.

As with every one of the other storytellers, Faḳhr al-Zamānī's life has not yet been fully narrated. The fullest biography was undertaken by the South Asian scholar of Persian Muḥammad Shafī'. In the Urdu preface to his 1926 edition of the *Maiḳhānah,* Muḥammad Shafī' deplored the lack of attention given to Faḳhr al-Zamānī (ii).[4] Muḥammad Shafī''s own groundbreaking contribution, upon which Gulchīn-i Ma'ānī built in his Iranian edition of the *Maiḳhānah*, relied for the most part on the *Maiḳhānah* itself for its account of Faḳhr al-Zamānī's life. In what follows I have also made use of the *Ṭirāz al-aḳhbār* and the first volume of the *Nawādir al-ḥikāyāt.*

Faḳhr al-Zamānī was probably born in Qazvin at the end of the tenth century Hijri or the beginning of the eleventh.[5] He was at least a third-generation Qazvini. His paternal grandfather, Faḳhr al-Zamān, also a man of Qazvin and a purported descendant of Ḳhwājah 'Abd Allāh Anṣārī of Herat, was the kind of ancestor in whom Faḳhr al-Zamānī could take great pride. He was a man of sufficient learning and standing to write in Arabic a certificate from Shāh Ṭahmāsp's brother Prince Bahrām, granting land in the village of Alwand near Qazvin to Bahrām's son Sulṭān Ibrāhīm Mīrzā. Flaunting his skills as a poet, Faḳhr al-Zamān garnished this document with a commemorative Persian verse (Faḳhr al-Zamānī Qazwīnī 1983, 758–60).[6] Faḳhr al-Zamānī's father, Ḳhalaf Beg, was not as accomplished in the verbal arts and seems never to have written a jot of poetry. Nevertheless, Faḳhr al-Zamānī makes him out to be a man of strong mystical and dervish-like inclinations, possessing a certain insight into the future. After making the pilgrimage to Mecca, Ḳhalaf Beg turned his face from worldly concerns for the remainder of his life. At the end of 1001 H (1593) there was an outbreak of the plague in Qazvin. Ḳhalaf Beg calmed the fears of his brothers and relations by predicting that they would all be spared and that only he himself would be taken to his Maker. He further predicted, according to Faḳhr al-Zamānī, that he would die on a Friday during the prayer—and so it happened (Faḳhr al-Zamānī Qazwīnī 1983, 768). Rather than linking himself with his clairvoyant father, Faḳhr al-Zamānī associated himself with his grandfather through the nom de plume that he was apt to use in prose. It seems, however, that the pen name "Faḳhr al-Zamānī" was too unwieldy for poetry. In his youth he signed himself "'Izzatī" in his verse, later opting for "Nabī," plain and simple (Faḳhr al-Zamānī Qazwīnī 1983, 760).

In his homeland he became acquainted with men of ability, perhaps frequenting the barbershop of the poet Ṣafā'ī Tabrezī, which appears to have been a literary salon for the wordsmiths of the city. Perhaps by forming associations at such places he absorbed some of his companions' capabilities himself (Faḳhr al-Zamānī Qazwīnī 1983, 900). Among other skills, he seems to have learned the occult science of *jafr*, but it is poetry and storytelling that he emphasizes (Faḳhr al-Zamānī Qazwīnī 1633, fol. 4a). How did he learn storytelling? In the *Ṭirāz al-aḳhbār*, Faḳhr al-Zamānī takes it for granted that storytelling is a craft transmitted from an *ustād* (teacher) to a disciple, yet in his own case he mentions no particular teacher. He only says (speaking of himself in the third person, as was usual), "in the early days of his youth, he was quite intimate with storytellers" (Faḳhr al-Zamānī Qazwīnī 1633, fol. 17a). From whomever he may have learned, the elements of the craft that he learned must have included the vocal effects, gestures, and postures, which he says are a legacy from the storyteller's *ustād*. But he also picked up the knack of remembering many different *qiṣṣahs*. "Due to the urgings of youth," he wrote, "[I] pursued the knowledge of romances [*qiṣṣah-dānī*]" (Faḳhr al-Zamānī Qazwīnī 1983, 760). Faḳhr al-Zamānī would go on to recognize knowledge of *qiṣṣahs* as a foundational skill: *qiṣṣah-dānī* was crucial to the storyteller who had to be able to perform any story demanded by the patron (Faḳhr al-Zamānī Qazwīnī 1633, fol. 20b). Writing much later in his life, he wistfully recalled his early capacity for remembering stories:

> By the absorptive power of his memory his mind seized the entire romance of Amīr Ḥamzah b. 'Abd al-Muṯṯalib in a single hearing. In those days this beggar's powers of memory were such that if he heard a hundred couplets at a gathering, almost seventy of them would be so ingrained in him that, coming home, he could transfer them all into his notebook. Now, when he is busy in the composition of the *Maiḳhānah*, only a trace of that memory remains. A couplet or two will remain in his mind after a single reading, and that too with a hundred thousand struggles. God be glorified! There is not a creature whose state remains the same. (Faḳhr al-Zamānī Qazwīnī 1983, 760–61)

Given the high value Faḳhr al-Zamānī places upon the "absorptiveness" (*quwwat-i jāẕibah*) of the memory of a good storyteller, the degradation of his own powers must have been a cause of grief to him. It is noteworthy, however, that even a decayed memory can be improved, according to Faḳhr al-Zamānī's guidelines, by various means. The storyteller should control his diet and recite the following *du'ā* (personal prayer) 340 times a day: "O Knower of the Hidden, Who needs no aid for His Memory!" (Faḳhr al-Zamānī Qazwīnī 1633, fol. 19b).

Faḳhr al-Zamānī was nineteen years old when he made a pilgrimage eastward to Mashhad to visit the magnificent shrine of Imām Riẓā, the eighth imam of the Twelver Shi'as. This sojourn, which is likely to have occurred around 1016 or 1017 H (ca. 1608), lasted about a month. During this month, he encountered traders and wanderers who described India in glowing terms, filling him with a desire to push further east to see Hindustan. Traveling through Mughal Qandahar along the way, he arrived in Lahore, weary and not in the best of health, at the end of 1017 H (1609). After recuperating from his journey, he surveyed the city of Lahore. He was struck, so he wrote, at the absence of busybodies in Lahore. This pleasant laissez-faire attitude, which Faḳhr al-Zamānī believed to be characteristic of India in general, convinced him to indefinitely postpone his return to Iran: "I said to myself, 'This, and not Qazvin, is the land in which you ought to make your home!'" (Faḳhr al-Zamānī Qazwīnī 1983, 671).[7]

The events of the next ten years are related by Faḳhr al-Zamānī in some detail. After leaving Lahore he arrived in the capital Agra in 1018 H (1609), where he met with a relative of his, Mīrzā Niẕām al-Dīn Aḥmad Niẕāmī Qazwīnī. Mīrzā Niẕāmī acted as a mentor to his younger kinsman, patiently listening to him reciting the story of Amīr Ḥamzah and encouraging him to smooth the rough edges of his storytelling performance. In particular, Faḳhr al-Zamānī claims that in those days he lacked *mauzūniyyat*, the ability to use words in an appropriate and balanced manner, and evidently he strove to correct this failing.[8] Mīrzā Niẕāmī was at the time a chronicler, or *wāqi'ah-nawes*, connected with Jahāngīr's court, well positioned to help Faḳhr al-Zamānī establish a professional foothold in India by polishing his storytelling abilities to a point where they would be valued by patrons.[9]

No doubt thanks to Mīrzā Niẓāmī, Fakhr al-Zamānī had not been long in Agra before he got a chance to attend the imperial court. From among Jahāngīr's inner circle of luminaries, he made the acquaintance of the renowned historian Najīb al-Dīn Ghiyās al-Dīn 'Alī b. Mīr 'Abd al-Laṭīf b. Mīr Yaḥyà, whose title was Naqīb Khān. It would have been a privilege for the young storyteller to meet the great Naqīb Khān, a scion of an important family of Qazvini Sunni intellectuals who had fled Iran in Shah Tahmasp's time and who had been welcomed to India by Akbar at the beginning of his reign (Fakhr al-Zamānī Qazwīnī 1633, fol. 17b).[10] Fakhr al-Zamānī witnessed examples of his dazzling intellect and incredible memory when Naqīb Khān was quizzed by the emperor. Fakhr al-Zamānī called him the "greatest of the historians of this morsel of time." His profound appreciation for Naqīb Khān's knowledge of history led him to pump the great man for information regarding the origins of the story of Ḥamzah, a problem in which he had long been interested. Undaunted by this seemingly obscure line of inquiry, Naqīb Khān was able to furnish Fakhr al-Zamānī with a history of the *Ḥamzah-nāmah*'s genesis and its progress into the Safavid era, including the information on Takaltū Khān's storytelling for Shāh Ṭahmāsp that has been recounted in the previous chapter.

Naqīb Khān's knowledge of the *Ḥamzah-nāmah* indicates that, for him, it was an artwork worthy enough for him to devote to it some vaults of his memory. Naqīb Khān was elderly at the time of his meeting with the budding storyteller. He had already made his mark during the rule of the emperor Akbar, to whom the story of Amīr Ḥamzah was precious, as we see by the luxurious paintings illustrating the romance and by the storytelling of Darbār Khān, which Naqīb Khān probably heard firsthand (Abū al-Faẓl b. Mubārak 1877, 223). When he tells Fakhr al-Zamānī about Darbār Khān's father, Takaltū Khān, it is possible that his information comes from Darbār Khān himself. It appears that Naqīb Khān had already written about Takaltū Khān before giving Fakhr al-Zamānī his information. From a marginal note on a folio of the *Ṭirāz al-akhbār* manuscript we are given to understand that Takaltū Khān's performative practices are mentioned in the *Zubdat al-akhbār* (Cream of reports), a history written by Naqīb Ḳhān (Faḳhr al-Zamānī Qazwīnī 1633, fol. 19b).[11]

Why were *dāstān*s valuable in the eyes of Naqīb Ḳhān, given that he is remembered as a respectable historian? Naqīb Ḳhān was a principal contributor to the Persian translation of the *Mahābhārata* commissioned by Akbar and entitled the *Razmnāmah*, which was compared by Abū al-Fazl to the *Ḥamzah-nāmah* (see Truschke 2011, 501, 510; 2016). The Jesuit Jerónimo Xavier even indicated that Naqīb Ḳhān read histories aloud to Akbar, an activity perhaps akin to *qiṣṣah-ḳhwānī*, though the comparison should not be taken too far (quoted in Alam and Subrahmanyam 2009, 482). Finally, Naqīb Ḳhān's uncle Mīr 'Alā' al-Daulah is one of our main sources of information on Akbar's illustrated *Ḥamzah-nāmah*, which he mentions in some detail as a work in progress in his history the *Nafā'is al-ma'āsir* (Choice traditions) (Mīr "Alā" al-Daulah b. Mīr Yaḥyà Qazwīnī 1674, fols. 54b–55a).[12] Faḳhr al-Zamānī had seen the *Nafā'is al-ma'āsir* and so probably knew of Mīr 'Alā' al-Daulah's comments on the royal *Ḥamzah-nāmah*, though surprisingly he does not refer to Akbar's copy in the *Ṭirāz al-aḳhbār*.[13] It becomes plain, then, that in Naqīb Ḳhān's world *dāstān*s were not trifles to be ignored. Owing to a range of circumstances—but perhaps especially the value granted to the *Ḥamzah-nāmah* by Akbar—romances occupied a relatively important place in the lives of Naqīb Ḳhān and other people of his time. So we can comfortably believe that he would have been ready to satisfy the curiosity of a young would-be storyteller from his homeland.

Faḳhr al-Zamānī would remain in the capital for four years while the emperor resided there. On the second of Sha'bān 1022 H (1613) Jahāngīr left Agra for Ajmer. He purposed on the one hand to visit the shrine of the saint Mu'īn al-Dīn Chishtī and on the other hand to put down the rebellion of Rānā Amar Singh at Chittor to the south of the town (Nūr al-Dīn Muḥammad Salīm Jahāngīr, Mu'tamad Ḳhān, and Hādī 1914, 123). Along with him went the important nobleman Zamānah Beg Mahābat Ḳhān and his son Mīrzā Amān Allāh Ḳhān "Amānī." Naqīb Ḳhān came too; he was fated to end his days in Ajmer not long afterward. Also among

Jahāngīr's retinue was Mīrzā Niẕāmī, accompanied by Faḳhr al-Zamānī. On the road Faḳhr al-Zamānī encountered another fellow Qazvini named Masīḥ Beg, a dependent of Mahābat Ḳhān (Faḳhr al-Zamānī Qazwīnī 1983, 762). This Masīḥ Beg exerted himself to introduce Faḳhr al-Zamānī into the service of Mīrzā Amān Allāh, who was at the time very much in the emperor's good graces.[14] In Mīrzā Amān Allāh, Faḳhr al-Zamānī found a fan of *dāstāns*. Faḳhr al-Zamānī recounts: "After I had been at his service for a little while, as per his command I presented a section of the tale [of Amīr Ḥamzah] before that Issue of Lords. After he had given ear to this speech, that Master of Speech became, to some degree, desirous of this beggar" (Faḳhr al-Zamānī Qazwīnī 1983, 762). By providing a hint of the storytelling abilities that he had been burnishing with Mīrzā Niẕāmī's aid, Faḳhr al-Zamānī was able to instill a preliminary sense of his worth in the young noble. He followed up this success with another, somewhat different exhibition of his value as a crafter of words.

Amān Allāh traveled onward, taking Faḳhr al-Zamānī along with him among a retinue of Arabs. They journeyed for fifteen days, by which time they had reached Ajmer (Faḳhr al-Zamānī Qazwīnī 1983, 763). On the sixteenth day, Amān Allāh repaired to the picturesque scenery surrounding the Chashmah-i Nūr (Fountain of Light) near Taragarh Mountain. With him was Masīḥ Beg, who whispered a word to the young nobleman to remind him of Faḳhr al-Zamānī. The latter was summoned forthwith and found himself admitted into an intimate gathering by the side of the fountain with Amān Allāh and a few men of artistic talent, all conversing together. Amān Allāh proposed that four of them should recite a verse each on the beauty of the Chashmah-i Nūr to produce a quatrain. He provided the first line himself:

There is no place in existence like the Chashmah-i Nūr.

chūṅ Chashmah-i Nūr nīst jā'e ba-ḥuẕūr

Faḳhr al-Zamānī extemporized a mellifluous verse to match it:

Its waves are an army, as if from a houri's glance.

mauj-ash fauje-st go'ī az ġhamzah-i ḥūr

Upon hearing this Amān Allāh cried, "Mullā 'Abd al-Nabī, I had no idea that you were so *mauzūn*!" Once more Faḳhr al-Zamānī's labors to develop his verbal artistic skill, in this case correcting his imperfect *mauzūniyyat*, gave him worth in the eyes of an important appraiser. Faḳhr al-Zamānī went on to finish the quatrain himself, pleasing Amān Allāh further. The young noble went on to recite a hemistich from a ġhazal by Amīr Ḳhusrau to the assembled poets and suggested that on the morrow they should present to him a *ham-ṭarḥ* verse with the same meter and rhyme scheme as the exemplary half line. Faḳhr al-Zamānī recorded his own verse composed in answer to Amān Allāh's challenge (as well as that of Nūr Muḥammad Anwar of Lahore).[15] Amān Allāh showed his approbation by asking Faḳhr al-Zamānī to repeat his verse. Finally, Faḳhr al-Zamānī expressed gratitude to this poetry-loving patron and credited him with the further increase in his *mauzūniyyat* that occurred during his time in Amān Allāh's service.[16]

So began Faḳhr al-Zamānī's first period of service to a member of the subimperial elite, a time that he recalled with gratitude for Amān Allāh's role in his verbal artistic development and ultimately with regret at how his employment terminated, with the disgraceful taint of venereal disease. The emperor remained in Ajmer for three years, and evidently Mīrzā Amān Allāh was among the nobles who settled there with him (Prasad 1962, 212). Faḳhr al-Zamānī's circle of acquaintance grew wider in the city. He met poets such as Muḥammad Ḥaidar Ḥaidarī, who was in Mahābat Ḳhān's service; the young Maḥwī Ardabīlī, who was in the service of the self-exiled Safavid noble Rustam Mīrzā and who would die young due to diarrhea; 'Abd al-Karīm 'Aṭā'ī Jaunpūrī; Sharārī Hamadānī; and Bāqiyā-i Muṣannif, an accomplished musician whom Faḳhr al-Zamānī would encounter again in Patna in 1028 H (1619–20) (Faḳhr al-Zamānī Qazwīnī 1983, 846, 868–70, 849, 802, 872). During this period Amān Allāh made Faḳhr al-Zamānī his librarian. Having the run of a library allowed him the freedom to peruse the collection and to nourish his mind with examples of prose and verse that he had not previously encountered. It was a valuable opportunity to hoard bits of texts in his memory, and Fakhr al-Zamānī would similarly avail himself of the governor Saif Khān's library in Bihar during his composition of the *Ṭirāz al-akhbār* (Fakhr al-Zamānī Qazwīnī 1633, fol. 11a). In the presence of these tomes, memorials of past litterateurs, Fakhr al-Zamānī developed an anxiety about the impermanence of his own name and fame.

This uneasiness is the reason that he gives for sketching out, during this period, three written works: the *Maikhānah*, the *Nawādir al-ḥikāyāt*, and the *Dastūr al-fuṣaḥā* (Fakhr al-Zamānī Qazwīnī 1983, 768–69). The *Maikhānah* is the best known of these works. Much of what we know of Fakhr al-Zamānī's life is gleaned from its pages, and it reveals the large social network that Fakhr al-Zamānī had built up by the year 1024 H (ca. 1616), for Fakhr al-Zamānī had met quite a few of the poets whom he mentioned. The *Nawādir al-ḥikāyāt* (Rare tales), on the other hand, has been almost completely ignored since the nineteenth century. It is a collection of transmitted anecdotes straddling the line between history and romance, arranged into five chapters, each containing twelve parts in honor of the number of imams recognized by Twelver Shi'ahs. A first volume out of a projected five was completed late in Fakhr al-Zamānī's life, while he was in Patna. In fact it appears that Fakhr al-Zamānī was writing it at the same time as he was writing his *Ṭirāz al-akhbār* (which was also completed in 1041 H). By 1053 H (1643), the second volume seems to have been in existence as well. From the *Ṭirāz al-akhbār* we are able to deduce the existence of a *masnawī* entitled *Bāgh o bahār* (Garden and spring) and possibly a divan by Fakhr al-Zamānī. I have not seen any trace of these. Nor is there any clue to the fate of the third work that Fakhr al-Zamānī planned to write during his halcyon days as a librarian in Ajmer: the *Dastūr al-fuṣaḥā'*.[17]

The *Dastūr al-fuṣaḥā'* (Model for the eloquent) is the vanished precursor to the text that most closely concerns us, the *Ṭirāz al-akhbār*. In the *Maikhānah* Fakhr al-Zamānī described it as a book "about the recitation of the romance of Amīr Ḥamzah and its rules, to stand as a model for storytellers." The chronograms for this book, given in various manuscripts of the *Maikhānah*, are incorrect, but Muḥammad Shafī' has convincingly deduced that it was completed while Fakhr al-Zamānī was in Kashmir from 1025 to 1026 H (ca. 1616–17).[18] The evidence that we have points to the disappearance of this work within Fakhr al-Zamānī's own lifetime. In 1029 H (1620–21), when Fakhr al-Zamānī was living in Patna, there was a fire in his house that destroyed many of his documents. Could it be that the *Dastūr al-fuṣahā* was among them? In the absence of any mention of this book in the manuscript catalogs, we can only guess that it was lost or consumed by fire. The fact of the existence of this manual for storytellers throws out tantalizing possibilities; perhaps it was more detailed than the *Ṭirāz*. Perhaps its descriptions would have greatly enriched our knowledge of the performance of the *Dāstān-i Amīr Ḥamzah* in the Safavid and Mughal realms. As a balm for the ache of regret, we have the *Ṭirāz al-akhbār* in its place, written in Patna around fifteen years later. Before the time came for Fakhr al-Zamānī to write the *Ṭirāz*, he was made to undergo a painful separation from his patron Amān Allāh, retrace his footsteps to Lahore, try his luck in Kashmir, and drop in on Jahangir at least twice, first in Mandu and then in Agra, before settling down at last in Patna.

Fakhr al-Zamānī had planned the *Maikhānah*, *Nawādir al-ḥikāyāt*, and the *Dastūr al-fuṣaḥā* in Ajmer and had gathered fifteen biographical notices for the *Maikhānah* before he was forced to leave Amān Allāh's court due to an untoward illness. He described the termination of his service as follows:

> Suddenly the fearful, froward Sky began its discordance with this valueless one. Thanks to its disorderly revolution—without the medium of sensual enjoyment, without the pleasure of carnal intercourse—it gave rise, in its injustice, to the European pox [*bād-i Firang*], which was like fire in the body and soul of this powerless one. Before the shameful secret of this wound could become known, and the rose [*gul*] of this disease could cause this mean one to be deemed a thorn in the view of his peers and contemporaries, it made him sick and weak. And so for fear lest his master should be informed of the state of this wreck, he

> petitioned the pillars of state to obtain permission for this mean one to depart for another land. (Faḳhr al-Zamānī Qazwīnī 1983, 769)[19]

However much he protested that the malady was not caused by sexual intercourse, Faḳhr al-Zamānī decided to leave Ajmer to escape the ignominy that would have resulted from his contracting this unlucky venereal disease.

In 1024 or 1025 H (ca. 1616) he started off for Lahore and had reached as far as Sambhar, just outside Ajmer, when he chanced to meet his friend Maḥmūd Beg Turkmān. Even in this period of itinerancy, Faḳhr al-Zamānī was able to widen his circle of acquaintance, cultivating colleagues who might have helped him to hone his craft and who certainly would have been useful in finding him a position. Maḥmūd Beg was a particularly good man to know, having recently been given a rank (*manṣab*) by Jahāngīr in Ajmer; following this honor he began to wend his way back to his primary patron, Ilāhdād Ḳhān of Bangash in the Kurram Valley. Faḳhr al-Zamānī wrote in the *Maiḳhānah* that he benefited greatly from Maḥmūd Beg's kindness. The two shared their poetry with one another, and when Faḳhr al-Zamānī went off to Bihar some time later, he had copies of Maḥmūd Beg's poems with him. Regrettably, when Faḳhr al-Zamānī's house in Patna caught fire, most of these copies perished in the conflagration. From Sambhar the pair moved toward Narnawal—joined at some point by a third traveler, Mīr Ni'mat Allāh Waṣlī of Shiraz.[20] They all passed through Sirhind before reaching Lahore, Maḥmūd Beg composing a ghazal describing the sights at each stop along the way and sometimes spurring on Faḳhr al-Zamānī and Waṣlī to the performance of similar poetic feats. Upon reaching Lahore in 1025 H (1616) Maḥmūd Beg moved on to the Kurram Valley, taking Waṣlī along with him (Faḳhr al-Zamānī Qazwīnī 1983, 885).[21]

Faḳhr al-Zamānī himself did not remain long in Lahore, for upon his arrival he found the plague ravaging the city's population, and, fresh from his brush with venereal disease, he quickly resolved to travel on to a less dangerous locale. He stayed just long enough to make the acquaintance of the poet Kaifī Nau-Musalmān, a Jewish convert from Sabzevar, but then moved swiftly on to the healthier climate of Kashmir (Faḳhr al-Zamānī Qazwīnī 1983, 876). Here he reconnected with his kinsman Mīrzā Niẕāmī, who had left Ajmer before Faḳhr al-Zamānī and had been practicing *wāqi'ah-nawesī* in Kashmir at least since 1023 H (1614–15) (Ḳhwājah Kāmgār Ḥusainī 1978, 497). By the time Faḳhr al-Zamānī arrived, Mīrzā Niẕāmī was *dīwān* and *baḳhshī* of Kashmir—influential enough, it seems, with the governor Ṣafdar Ḳhān to arrange a gubernatorial librarianship for the poet Ghafūr 'Aṣrī (Faḳhr al-Zamānī Qazwīnī 1983, 913).[22] Faḳhr al-Zamānī kept plying his craft and gaining favor in Kashmir. He took advantage of his two years in Kashmir (1025–26 H/ca. 1616–17) to complete the *Dastūr al-fuṣaḥā'*.[23] During his time there he sought out more poets, meeting, for instance, the two locals Mīr 'Abd Allāh Mużhah Farebī and Ẕihnī Kashmīrī (Faḳhr al-Zamānī Qazwīnī 1983, 904–5).[24] Perhaps the most notable among the poets he met in Kashmir was the elderly debauchee Nadīm Gīlānī, who spent the great majority of his time playing backgammon and devoting his hours of leisure from this occupation to pouring wine down his throat and cultivating a reckless attitude toward life (Faḳhr al-Zamānī Qazwīnī 1983, 837).[25]

Late in 1026 H (1617–18) Mīrzā Niẕāmī was summoned to Mandu by Jahāngīr for one month, at the end of which he was made *dīwān* of Bihar. Faḳhr al-Zamānī accompanied him on his journey both to Mandu and afterward to Bihar, where Mīrzā Niẕāmī would write his surviving works.[26] By 1028 H (1619–20) Faḳhr al-Zamānī was making noises about moving back to Iran, and in a *sāqī-nāmah* poem he expressed the hope that the noble Sardar Ḳhān Ḳhwājah Yādgār would finance the journey (Faḳhr al-Zamānī Qazwīnī 1983, 778–81). It is unlikely that this plan ever came to fruition; in the next year we find Faḳhr al-Zamānī still resident in Patna. However, when his house in Patna caught fire, among the precious documents consumed in the conflagration were copies of poems by his friend Maḥmūd Beg Turkmān, as we have seen, as well as the poetry of Ṣafī Ṣafāhānī and possibly his own *Dastūr al-fuṣaḥā'*, the predecessor to the *Ṯirāz* (Faḳhr al-Zamānī Qazwīnī 1983, 430n3, 886). In that same year, 1029 H (1620–21), Faḳhr al-Zamānī decided to journey to Agra once more, where he attended Jahāngīr's *darshan* and witnessed the trampling of a servant by a royal elephant run amok (Fakhr al-Zamānī Qazwīnī 1632, fols. 35a–35b).[27] Evidently it was after his Agra sojourn that Fakhr al-Zamānī returned to Patna for good.

The Storytelling Manual and Performance

Fakhr al-Zamānī completed his manual for storytellers in Bihar in the year 1041 H (1631–32). In its preface, he wrote that he had been living comfortably in Patna for the past twelve years, that is, since the disaster of the fire in his home and since his visit to Agra, which may have represented an attempt to settle elsewhere (Fakhr al-Zamānī Qazwīnī 1633, fol. 4b). By the time Fakhr al-Zamānī was completing the *Ṭirāz al-akhbār*, Saif Khān's buildings were part of the cityscape, and at the center of them was the mosque, engraved inside with Fakhr al-Zamānī's verses in praise of the governor's architectural projects.

But the serai that Peter Mundy praised so much was in a sense the really important structure, since the revenues from it funded the school and hospital. Here traveling merchants, perhaps wending their way from Safavid Iran, could rent quarters by the month and store their goods. Their lodgings were located in the upper portions, while below was a bazaar in which the merchants could presumably rent shops as part of the monthly rate (Fakhr al-Zamānī Qazwīnī 1633, fol. 9b). Travelers from Iran would have brought with them their fascination with coffee, the dark drink that at that time was beautified by a rainbow slick of oil floating upon its surface (Hakala 2014, 379). For their enjoyment, the serai complex in Patna seems to have contained a coffeehouse. Fakhr al-Zamānī described it as a den for the habitués of the liquid that "repels sleep from the eyes of the wise" (Fakhr al-Zamānī Qazwīnī 1633, fol. 10b). Travelers may even have come from beyond the Safavid realm, like the Arab inhabitants of a famous serai in Delhi. This was described by Dargāh Qulī Khān (1993, 75) in the eighteenth century as a place where visitors could drink large servings of over-sugared and indigestible coffee while feasting their eyes on unkempt boys. At Saif Khān's coffeehouse, musical performances were probably held in which storytellers would have entertained the coffee drinkers with tales in Persian, just as they were doing in the famous coffeehouses of Shāh 'Abbās's Iran (see Falsafī 1954). Perhaps Faḳhr al-Zamānī himself would have performed his specialty, the *Dāstān-i Amīr Ḥamzah,* at the café.

Posturing before a rapt audience of coffee-sipping merchants, voicing and embodying tricksters at the court of the governor—what would a performance by Faḳhr al-Zamānī have been like? Thanks to the *Ṭirāz*, we have clues to the mechanics of storytelling performances in the seventeenth century and, consequently, to the structure of romances. Faḳhr al-Zamānī mentions that there were other practitioners of *qiṣṣah-ḳhwānī* in the city, some in attendance upon Saif Ḳhān. With the writing of the *Ṭirāz al-aḳhbār* Faḳhr al-Zamānī makes himself out to be the most experienced and knowledgeable of them all, claiming that when he listened to his fellow storytellers in Saif Ḳhān's company he rarely heard anything that he had not heard or read before (Faḳhr al-Zamānī Qazwīnī 1633, fol. 11a). Great storytellers are, according to Faḳhr al-Zamānī, very rare in any case. In principle, a storyteller exceeds a mere poet, because the storyteller needs not only to compose prose as well as verse but also to compose it extempore. But storytellers who could do this well and thereby prove the superiority of storytelling to poetry were few and far between (Faḳhr al-Zamānī Qazwīnī 1633, fol. 20a). Perhaps Faḳhr al-Zamānī counted himself as a superior craftsman, but he represented the *Ṭirāz* as a humble offering to his fellow storytellers in the service of Saif Ḳhān, the better to delight Saif Ḳhān with their performance. Perhaps, he wrote, they might even praise him, Faḳhr al-Zamānī, in the august presence of their patron (Faḳhr al-Zamānī Qazwīnī 1633, fol. 11b). The *Ṭirāz* would ameliorate their performances not only by teaching them some of the principles of storytelling but also by giving them the raw materials with which to build their *qiṣṣah*s.

The *Ṭirāz al-aḳhbār*, the successor to Faḳhr al-Zamānī's lost *Dastūr al-fuṣaḥā*, has been a sadly neglected text. It was never printed, and, strange to say, all of the known manuscripts are in Iran rather than India. However, the great Iranian *qiṣṣah* scholar Muḥammad Ja'far Maḥjūb (1991) reproduced some of the important portions of its introduction, and Shamsur

Rahman Faruqi (1999, 419ff.), in his magnum opus on the *Dāstān-i Amīr Ḥamzah*, later used Maḥjūb's article. Muḥammad Shafī'ī-Kadkanī (2002) also described the body of the work. Though Faḵhr al-Zamānī did distinguish between the Indian style of storytelling and his own Iranian style, as well as isolating a "Turanian" style, it should be no surprise to find his own storytelling style reproducing itself in the twenty-first-century *dāstān-go'ī* performances of Shamsur Rahman Faruqi's nephew and his colleagues, with their seated postures and stylized gestures. Twenty-first-century *dāstān-go'ī* is the most powerful and most recent effect of this manual for storytellers. But there are also indications that prior to our own time, in the nineteenth century, the guidelines that the *Ṭirāz* articulated were still circulating. In particular, we find traces in this century of the *Ṭirāz*'s four repertoires according to which intertextual elements, shreds of written works, gestures, postures, and so on were deployed.

The main body of the *Ṭirāz* was made up of bits and pieces of prose and poetry taken from a variety of sources and organized thematically into sixty-seven sections called *ṭirāz*es. The *ṭirāz*es were themselves grouped into four chapters called "*ḵhabar*s," plus a conclusion (*ḵhātimah*). Faḵhr al-Zamānī intended these textual fragments to be studied by storytellers and recited at appropriate junctures in the storytelling performance. But to weave a fragment from some hypotext into the romance most appropriately, the storyteller needed to recognize the particular narrative situations that called for a particular kind of text to be read. The four *ḵhabar*s were meant to enable this kind of recognition. The very names of these repertoires signaled the situations in which the pieces of text were to be recited: *razm*, *bazm*, *ḥusn o 'ishq*, and *'ayyārī*—battle, courtly gatherings, beauty and love, and trickery. The four repertoires were the engines by which a storyteller like Faḵhr al-Zamānī would construct the edifice of the *qiṣṣah*.

Before looking more closely at the repertoires and how they were meant to be used, we might look briefly at the longevity of the idea that the *qiṣṣah* was made up of these four elements, lest it be dismissed as an obscure notion lying forgotten in a rare manuscript. We see traces of the repertoires in many places, including the opening poem in the Urdu *'Ajā'ib al-qiṣaṣ* (Wonder tales) composed by the Mughal king Shāh 'Ālam II, which announces that in the romance to come there will be love, battles, and courtly gatherings, as well as magic and *ṭilisms* (enchanted worlds). *Ṭilisms*, rather than *ḥusn o 'ishq*, were also mentioned in Ġhālib Lakhnawī's important 1855 version of the *Dāstān-i Amīr Ḥamzah*. While Ġhālib Lakhnawī was not himself a storyteller, the mid-nineteenth century was, as we have seen, a time when storytelling flourished in Lucknow, and the idea of the four repertoires could have reached him from any number of informants. Ġhālib remarked, "There are four things in this *dāstān*: battle, courtly assemblies, enchanted worlds and trickery" (Ġhālib Lakhnawī 1855, 3). The rise of the *ṭilismī* romance was a relatively late development, gaining increasing traction in the eighteenth and nineteenth centuries and culminating in the *ṭilism* mania fostered by the late nineteenth-century storytellers of Lucknow and Rampur.[28] Compared to these storytellers' astounding works, Ġhālib Lakhnawī's book was quite mundane. After Ġhālib, the Lucknow-based litterateur 'Abd al-Ḥalīm Sharar reverted to Faḳhr al-Zamānī's formula in his description of storytelling in Lucknow: "*razm*, *bazm*, *ḥusn o 'ishq* and *'ayyārī*" were for him the elements of the romance, while Mīr Bāqir 'Alī in his verse preface to *Ṭilism-i Hosh-afzā* explicitly mentioned *razm*, *bazm*, and *siḥr* but alluded as well to the *'ayyārī* of the master trickster 'Amar's son, Āshob (Mīr Bāqir 'Alī Dāstān-go 1892, 1).

To be sure, the survival of these categories seems odd if we attempt to follow the trail of writings alone, without factoring in oral transmission. We do not know, after all, of any copies of the *Ṭirāz al-akhbār* in South Asian libraries.[29] But a manuscript Persian *Ḥamzah* romance entitled (as many *Ḥamzah-namahs* were) *Ẓubdat al-rumūz*, authored by the mysterious storyteller Shāh Naẓar Qiṣṣah-ḳhwān, betrayed a link to the *Ṭirāz al-aḳhbār* by plagiarizing its introduction. Whenever and wherever this text may have been composed, it was copied in 1857 by a scribe with a remarkably Awadhi name: Shaiḳh Muḥammad Ḥusain "Miṭṭhan." I suspect that it was meant for the Lucknow market, though it is now in Tehran (Shāh Naẓar Qiṣṣah-ḳhwān, n.d., fol. 224b). So it is plausible that non-storytellers like Ġhālib Lakhnawī could have had access to Faḳhr al-Zamānī's ideas even in their written form.

How would the repertoires have been used? A book like the *Ṭirāz al-akhbār* was meant to be memorized piecemeal; storytellers might begin by browsing through it and committing to memory passages that caught their fancy. With a passage, the storyteller's memory would associate the category of repertoire to which it belonged—or, what is the same thing, the narrative situation in which it ought to be recited. Then, during the performance, these texts in the memory of the storyteller would be woven into the *dāstān* in conformance with whether the narrative dealt with battle, courtly gatherings, love, or trickery. This intertextual practice was called *munāsib-khwānī*, or appropriate recitation. Intertexts for use in storytelling could come from any number of oral or written sources, and the *Ṭirāz* would not have been the only anthology of textual fragments. The storyteller's *bayāẓ*, or notebook for verses, might serve the same purpose, or a compendium of stories like the *Jāmiʿ al-ḥikāyāt* (Gatherer of tales) might be a rich source of narratives. The Englishman John Malcolm (1827, 61), in his travels in the Safavid Empire, was friendly with a storyteller named Adīnah Beg, who told him that he had a book from which he drew his tales. It is possible that the categories in Muẓaffar Qiṣṣah-khwān's lost verse anthology *Majmaʿ al-laṭā'if* (Gathering of subtle accounts) were the result of this fifteenth-century storyteller's orderly mind, for he, like Fakhr al-Zamānī, grouped verses together under headings such as "union," "separation," "the beard," "description of the beloved," and so on (see chap. 1). The value of the *Ṭirāz* was to further classify such texts and to point, in its introduction, to how they could be used via *munāsib-khwānī* and related subcategories of intertexual practice.

We can imagine specific uses of these repertoires in a performance by Fakhr al-Zamānī with the help of the *Ṭirāz*, and some of the gaps and deficiencies in our knowledge can be filled in by referring to Mīr Bāqir 'Alī's similar practices. Fakhr al-Zamānī mentions four styles of storytelling: Iranian, Turanian, Indian, and Rūmī (i.e., Western Turkish) (Fakhr al-Zamānī Qazwīnī 1633, fol. 21a). An Iranian storyteller like Fakhr al-Zamānī would begin the *dar-āmad*, or introductory speech, with verses incorporating a comprehensive mixture of *razm*, *bazm*, *husn o ʿishq*, and *ʿayyārī*. After this he would sing the praises of the hero Amīr Ḥamzah and introduce the narrative with a device called *barā'at-i istihlāl*.[30] A brief prefatory passage from one of the repertoires would be recited, and through it the thrust or tenor of the coming account would become evident to the hearer (or reader). Examples of this device can be found in much later *Ḥamzah-nāmahs* such as ʿAbd Allah Bilgrāmī's; for example, Ḥamzah's first dalliance with his beloved Mihr-nigār is introduced with a love poem:

> Love is ever fertile in ploy and stratagem,
> Ready with a new trick for every occasion:
> Sometimes it becomes a contagion of tears,
> Sometimes it reads like a fable of blood and gore,
> Sometimes it becomes the salt with which a wound is sealed
> Sometimes it is the seeker, sometimes the sought,
> An engaging subject it is in any guise. (Bilgrāmī and Ġhālib Lakhnawī 2007, 170)

Passages to be used in *barā'at-i istihlāl*, most often descriptions of sunset and sunrise, were marked as such in the *Ṭirāz*.

In the introduction to the *Ṭirāz*, Fakḥr al-Zamānī makes it clear that apart from fragments of previous texts, there are also non-textual (gestural, tonal, etc.) elements specific to each repertoire (Fakḥr al-Zamānī Qazwīnī 1633, fols. 21b–22a). The term "orality" does not sufficiently characterize *qiṣṣah-ḳhwānī*, which was fully *performative*, loaded not only with vocal effects but with gestures and postures as well. The English word "acting" is how Sabūḥī chose to describe Mīr Bāqir ʿAlī's performance, for he would become, Sabūḥī said, a "picture" of a combatant in war. The lean, bent Bāqir ʿAlī would grow into an imperious ruler as the wonderstruck Mullā Wāḥidī sat watching his performance (Ṣabūḥī 1963, 42; Mullā Wāḥidī Dihlawī 2013, 96). Perhaps the storyteller using the *Ṭirāz* would embody the Lord of the Auspicious Conjunction, Ḥamzah, with his troops ranged against the enemy sorcerers, and the narrative would build toward the drawing of the swords. He would reach into his memory of the passages on *razm* in the *Ṭirāẓ* and describe the sword using words chosen from the *Tāj al-ma'āsir*:

> On the surface of its sky-colored body the forms of the stars arose, like bubbles. You would say that they were bits of diamonds resting on a blue branch of the heavens, or scraps of silver fallen on an emerald ring, or that luscious rose leaves were decorated with dewdrops, or a necklace of jewels was stretched out over wet vegetation. (Fakhr al-Zamānī Qazwīnī 1633, fols. 94a–94b)

The storyteller would initially be seated on one knee, but as he spoke of the battle, voice raised in martial ardor, he would lift himself up until he was elevated upon two knees. The *Ṭirāẓ* specifically identified this posture with the battle repertoire, and Fakhr al-Zamānī indicated that military actions such as the pulling of a bowstring or wrestling should be conveyed by acts (Fakhr al-Zamānī Qazwīnī 1633, fols. 21b–22a).

The romance would go on, and the enemy would approach. To describe the stalwart chieftain of the sorcerers, the storyteller could dive into his memory of the *'ayyārī* repertoire, containing all sorts of outré matters, and retrieve a passage from the *Tārīkh-i mu'jam*:

> He was a sorcerer who with his knowledge of magic could bring the pole star down from the sky and make it spin. Or with the sleights of his enchantments he could keep the prayer bead of the planets from journeying, as if they were fixed stars. (Fakhr al-Zamānī Qazwīnī 1633, fols. 492b–493a)

One of the recordings that we have of Mīr Bāqir 'Alī rattling off a list of weapons in a short *qiṣṣah* conveys to us the staccato rhythm that he might have used for battle descriptions (Mīr Bāqir 'Alī Dāstān-go 1920a). As in Bāqir 'Alī's case, Fakhr al-Zamānī stressed that the storyteller should enact the form of the character, whether it was an imperious sorcerer or a coquettish beloved. Love scenes were quite different from scenes of battle;

the *Ṭirāz* suggested a softened voice and a mimicry of the couple's *nāz o niyāz*, the confident blandishments of the beloved, and the abject desire of the lover (Faḳhr al-Zamānī Qazwīnī 1633, fol. 22a). Perhaps the overeager lover would be too hasty in seeking what he wanted. A proper admonishment might come from Mīrzā Ja'far Āṣaf Ḳhān's poem *Ḳhusrau-Shīrīn*, excerpted in the *Ṭirāz*'s section on love and beauty. Voicing the coy beloved, the storyteller would say,

> Drink less wine. You're such a drunken man
> that you don't know the wine cup from your hand!
> Have patience and at last you'll have your way.
> You'll have what you desire one day—but not today! (Faḳhr al-Zamānī Qazwīnī 1633, fol. 451a)

And if indeed the lover and the beloved married at last, the birth of the child could be described by a passage from the *Akbar-nāmah* excerpted in the same section of the *Ṭirāz* (Faḳhr al-Zamānī Qazwīnī 1633, fols. 355a–356a). The intertextual and performative protocols for battle, scenes of love, and so forth should not be mixed. Faḳhr al-Zamānī frowns upon undue movement between two different repertoires, seeing it as evidence that the storyteller is scattered and unfocused (Mahjub 1991, 192).

At the end of a sitting, the storyteller would be careful to follow the rules of the *bar-āmad*, or termination of the episode. Like Shahrzād of the *Thousand and One Nights*, the storyteller would leave the audience craving more by stopping at an especially suspenseful point. This would help to ensure the presence of future audiences, to extend the duration of patronage, and to secure ongoing remuneration. This prolongation of the suspense, by the storyteller's refusal to resolve the matter or end the episode, was called by Faḳhr al-Zamānī *pāband-ḳhwānī* in Persian, while in Urdu it was called *dāstān rokna* (arresting the *dāstān*) (Faḳhr al-Zamānī Qazwīnī 1633, fol. 22b; Shāhid Aḥmad Dihlawī 1979, 190; see also Pritchett 1991, 20; Faruqi 1999, 430). Faḳhr al-Zamānī admits that once the audience cannot control its eagerness, the tale should continue (Faḳhr al-Zamānī Qazwīnī 1633, fol. 22b).

Textual Fragments and Memory in the Romance

The case of the *Ṭirāz al-aḳhbār* and the manner in which it and other such intertextual sources were used by the crafters of romances provides a particularly striking explanation for the heavy intertextuality of romances. It allows us to see clearly that romances were constructed from preexisting bits and pieces juxtaposed with one another in thematic harmony. Shamsur Rahman Faruqi (1999, 439), in his exposition of the poetics of the *dāstān*, refers to this as the *silsilah-jātī*, or the "paratactic" structure of romances. Stories, in other words, are made up of smaller stories, which storytellers have in their memory or produce extemporaneously. They string these narratives together during the performance, often without the kind of causal relationship that we would expect from a novel but according to other logics, such as that of the four repertoires.

If Shamsur Rahman Faruqi is correct, storytellers may have had a technical name for narrative modules as they existed before being woven into the narrative in the storytelling performance or in story writing. He believes that they were referred to as *patah*s (indications). In a review (*taqrīẓ*) of the second volume of *Ṭilism-i Hoshrubā*, Ja'far Ḥusain Hunar Faiẓābādī had explained the origins of *Hoshruba*, the most famous portion of the Urdu *Ḥamzah-nāmah*:

> This romance was written in Persian by Faiẓī (upon whom be mercy), every section of whose version was merely a *patah* of the larger romances. Mīr Aḥmad 'Alī the storyteller took this Ṭilism from [Faiẓī's work], and wrote it according to the *patah*s for the sake of [other] storytellers. But even to get a hold of that was extremely difficult. With fathomless effort and much searching [Muḥammad Ḥusain] Jāh has provided it. But to understand its marks and its *patah*s and to comment upon them was very difficult. The truth is that to write

them with elegance, beauty and excellence was Mīr [Aḥmad 'Alī]'s work. (quoted in Faruqi 1999, 438–39)

The attribution of authorship to Abū al-Faiẓ Faiẓī, the younger brother of Akbar's right-hand intellectual Abū al-Faẓl, is no doubt spurious. It is possible that Hunar was referring to Akbar's illustrated *Ḥamzah-nāmah*, whose large paintings (around 27 inches × 21 inches, not including borders) were matched on facing pages by written texts with the narratives to which the paintings referred (Faridany-Akhavan 1989, 18). Perhaps it is these texts that were referred to as *patah*s. For example, one of the paintings at the Metropolitan Museum of Art attributed to Keshav Dās and Māh Muhammad depicts a lithe 'Amar 'Ayyār, the trickster companion of the hero Amīr Ḥamzah, draped in blue, subduing an enemy *'ayyār*. The facing text begins,

> When Khwājah 'Amar overthrew this foot-soldier and sat on his chest, he looked. It was one of Faulād's *'ayyār*s named Haibat. 'Amar was about to kill him, but he said, "Khwājah 'Amar, don't kill me, for I will do you a good service! I will show you the way to the castle."[31]

It is generally agreed that the Akbar *Ḥamzah-nāmah* illustrations were used during storytelling performances as visual accompaniments, as in the case of Iranian *pardah-khwānī*, or Indian picture storytellers, such as the Bengali *pāṭū'ā*s and the *chitrakathī*s of Maharashtra.[32] As Zahra Faridany-Akhavan (1989, 252ff.) has written, the accompanying text in Akbar's volumes seems too sparse to have been read verbatim by the storytellers, but it is possible that they provided basic "draft" modules that would be embellished and expanded by the *qiṣṣah-khwān* in performance. Faruqi is at any rate convinced that, strung together, *patah*s were the seeds of the paratactic romance. Like the textual fragments collected in the *Ṭirāz al-akhbār*, *patah*s would have been building blocks in the intertextual construction of the *dāstān*. Such modules could have been taken out of any collection of short tales, such as Sa'dī's *Gulistān* or 'Aufī's *Jawāmi' al-ḥikāyāt*, or passed down orally from master to disciple.

2. Amar 'Ayyār kicks enemy *'ayyār* to the ground outside Faulād Castle. Attributed to Keshavdās and Māh Muḥammad, ca. 1570. Ink, opaque watercolor, and gold on cloth, mounted on paper. 28¾" × 22¼". Rogers Fund, 1923. 23.264.2. Metropolitan Museum of Art.

Agglomerations of narrative modules or *patah*s as well as heaps of textual fragments from various sources are examples of hypotexts. Hypotextuality, the state of being a source text, is relative. If a storyteller quotes some lines of 'Attār's poem *Manṯiq al-ṯair* (Conference of the birds) in a romance, these lines are hypotextual in relation to the romance, while the complete *Conference of the Birds* out of which the lines have been taken is a hypotext or source text in relation to both the excerpted lines and the romance in which they have been used. The *Ṯirāz al-akhbār* and any collections that might have been used in the same way are what we might call repositories of hypotexts. However, the memories of various written or non-written texts that the crafters of tales had encountered throughout their lives were the real "hypotext repositories" that formed the ground for their romances.

The concept of a mass of texts available in the memories of individuals is important not only when we consider the production of romances but perhaps even more so when it comes to their reception. Let us say that we are all members of Fakhr al-Zamānī's audience in a Patna coffeehouse or that we have gathered at Bāqir 'Alī's home in the Bhojla Pahari neighborhood of Delhi. As he weaves together his romance from whatever textual fragments his memory possesses, the romance affects us in part on the basis of associations that our own memories make with texts that *we* have experienced in the past. Mīr Bāqir 'Alī is relating the romance of Ḥātim Ṭā'ī. The hero, out for a ride on his trusty steed, is inconveniently accosted by a lion bent on devouring his flesh. Ḥātim, the exemplar of generosity, declines to turn his sword on the beast. Instead (to the audience's amazement), he freely offers his body for the now rather embarrassed lion to dine upon. In case his own meat is no longer palatable, he suggests his horse as an alternative dish (Ḥaidarī 1972, 22–23; "Haft sair-i Ḥātim" 2007, 62). Hearing this wonderful tale of exceptional largess, we in the audience might allow precedents to flash through our minds. Potential hypotexts that might surface in our memories include the story of King Shibī's gift of his own flesh in the *Mahābhārata* and similar tales of the Buddha in the *jātakas*, of Moses in the *Ṭūṭī-nāmah* (Parrot's tale), and, most obviously, of Ḥātim in the well-known *Bostān* of Sa'dī, in which he gives the meat of his famous and valuable horse to an unexpected guest (Sa'dī Shīrāzī 1977, 134–36).

If we take a few steps back from this role play, we will soon realize the difficulty of knowing the textual memory of any given individual of Bāqir 'Alī's or Fakhr al-Zamānī's time. Yet what we can say is that the potential hypotexts I have mentioned were *available* to Persian and Urdu romance audiences in North India and also that some were particularly well known and *visible* in their minds. We can ascribe especial visibility, for example, to some version of the *Mahābhārata* and certainly to Sa'dī's *Bostān* or his *Gulistān*, which was a foundational text for relatively elite students in the Indo-Islamicate educational system. These students or former students were the same kind of Indians who were likely to listen to these romances.

Cultural historians can only acquire a blurry idea of Indians' textual memories by gaining a sense of the texts that would have been available and visible among a certain segment of society. In the case of written text, the researcher might consider the frequency of their appearance in manuscript archives, their presence in *madrasah* curricula, and the number of times they were mentioned, alluded to, or cited by authors of the time. On this basis we might expect elite Muslims living in nineteenth-century Lahore to have read the Quran and perhaps a Quranic commentary, the poems of Ḥāfiẓ, the *Gulistān* of Sa'dī, and the ethical manual *Akhlāq-i Muḥsinī* (Muhsinian ethics) and to have heard Wāris̤ Shāh's *Hīr* or another version of the same romance and possibly the latest faddish poem by Dayā Shankar Nasīm. More speculatively, they were likely to be up to speed on the current jokes and insults, the proper formulas by which to address their parents and superiors, and popular *ġhazal* verses. They may have studied one of the prevalent manuals of letter writing (*inshā*) to attain epistolary proficiency, and perhaps they had read a widely available history like the *Rauẓat al-ṣafā* (Garden of purity). Of course, memory fluctuates; throughout their lives individuals will go on adding texts to the archive in their brains and losing a great many of them through forgetfulness. But we can guess at the makeup of an individual's textual memory—if we have some sense of who she or he is.

After all, the texts swirling around in a particular reader's or hearer's memory will not be the same as those present in the memory of every other reader or listener. We can, however, assume the existence of groups of individuals sharing a common trait or role who are likely to be familiar with a similar set of hypotexts and who are therefore likely to experience *qiṣṣah*s in a similar way. For instance, social class and educational experience are likely to determine whether a reader is familiar with the intricate poetry of 'Abd al-Qādir Bedil in Persian or with the popular poems of Wāris̤ Shāh in Punjabi. Also important are the linguistic communities to which one belongs; without a knowledge of Persian, Bedil can only be known secondhand, and the same goes for Punjabi with regard to Wāris̤ Shāh. Geographical location, religion, occupation, gender, and a host of other sociological factors come into play in the formation of these communities of textual memory. And, of course, any given individual may belong to any number of these communities.

To understand how the textual memory of a group of audience members would have affected their reception of romances, we must think more about the consequences of the romance's being made up of many different textual fragments. Understanding these consequences will lead us to understand how it might have been possible for romances to have practical effects, apart from giving pleasure.

The concept of the *patah* and the evidence of the *Ṭirāz* serve to underscore the heavily intertextual construction of the romance, a necessary result of the storytelling craft in which text fragments lodged in the artist's memory would be recited or embellished extemporaneously in a paratactic fashion. The textual fragments of which romances were constructed could have come from hypotexts of any genre. Based on the *Ṭirāz al-akhbār*'s list of quotations, we know that in Fakhr al-Zamānī's romances, excerpts from the *Shāh-nāmah* and *Conference of the Birds* might mingle freely with epistolary specimens (*inshā'*), *sāqi-nāmah*s, and the moral fables of Kalilah and Dimnah. History is well represented: Mirkhwānd's history the *Rauẓat al-ṣafā* (Garden of purity), Hātifī's *Timūr-nāmah*, the *Tāj al-ma'āsir* (Crown of great deeds), the *Ḥabīb al-siyar*, Amīr Khusrau's *Qirān al-sa'dain* (Conjunction of the two felicitous planets), and the *Tārīkh-i mu'jam* are all quoted in the *Ṭirāz al-akhbār* (see Fakhr al-Zamānī Qazwīnī 1633, fols. 15a–16b). The effects of such genres as ethics (*akhlāq*), panegyric (*madḥ*), and often history (*tārīkh*)—to edify, praise, inform, warn, or exemplify—are easier to gauge than those of the supposedly ineffectual *qiṣṣah* genre. But the presence of eminently effectual genres *within* the dominant genre of the romance might enable us to take storytellers' and story writers' claims about romance's effects more seriously. Fakhr al-Zamānī's *qiṣṣahs* themselves do not survive, but we have a sense of how they were produced. With this sense and by looking at romances that were written down, we can feel the "multigeneric" or multigenre texture of romances and guess at how the effects and uses associated with the genres marking each textual fragment would make themselves felt through the *qiṣṣah*.

The Uses of the Multigenre Romance

Genre strikes us not only at the level of the work but also at the level of the episode, the phrase, and even the word. What I have been provisionally calling a "textual fragment" is any text that is part of a larger text, the "work." An individual volume of the *Dāstān-i Amīr Ḥamzah*, for instance, might be perceived as a work, while any of its episodes, phrases, interpolated poems, and so forth is a textual fragment. Genre theory has focused not on the textual fragment but upon the work, as if only an entire book could be marked by a single genre. But, following an analysis of the romance that takes into account the role of a very tangible hypotext repository like the *Ṭirāz al-akhbār*, we cannot escape the conclusion that textual fragments are equally branded with genres.

How do fragments stand out as participants in a particular genre—which might not be the same as the genre that the audience assigns to the work as a whole? A genre establishes a horizon of expectations for its audience—a contract whereby the audience will understand the text within the bounds of the rules established by the genre to which the text supposedly belongs. Hans Robert Jauss (1982, 79) provides a succinct statement of the necessity of genre and the way it works:

> It is . . . unimaginable that a literary work set itself into an informational vacuum, without indicating a specific situation of understanding. To this extent, every work belongs to a genre—whereby I mean neither more nor less than that for each work a preconstituted horizon of expectations must be ready at hand (this can also be understood as a relationship of "rules of the game" to orient the reader's (public's) understanding and to enable a qualifying reception).

The reader of a text in the genre of Sufi poetry, like *Conference of the Birds*, expects to encounter allegory, edificatory discourses, and so on. Within a work understood to participate in such a genre, the sudden appearance of an enumeration of poetic devices is an unexpected and, at least initially, extra-generic event. Unless the way is paved for it in some manner, the fragment genre is jarring and leaves the reader with a sense of transgression; until the reader's expectations about the genre have been readjusted, the genre assignment is deemed to be incorrect or the genre code itself begins to undergo change. Yet a third possibility is for the audience member to continue to consider the jarring element to be in some manner extraneous, sometimes with the judgment that the integrity of the work has been marred but sometimes with a sense of pleasure at the piquancy of the unexpected placement.

For example, it is well known that Islamicate works, including romances, often begin with such "extra-generic" fragments: the *ḥamd* (praise of God), *naʿt* (praise of the Prophet), *madḥ* (general panegyric), and so on. Despite their extra-genericity, these opening fragments, readily recognizable as paratexts, are so conventional that they do not interrupt the audience's equanimity. They are often taken, often unjustly, to be sealed off from the rest of the work. But other extra-generic passages as well are fenced off. Suddenly, near the end of the *Tale of the Bakāwalī Flower* (*Qiṣṣah-i Gul-i Bakāwalī*), a historical anecdote appears, about the Mughal emperor Jahāngīr's death and the internecine rivalry that ensued between the princes Ḵhurram and Parwez:

> Listen: Nur al-Din Muhammad Jahangir, the crowned head of India, had made his younger son Parwez the heir to the throne. He ordered that his elder son Ḵhurram should be incarcerated in one of the prisons of the Deccan. When Nur al-Din Muhammad Jahangir made his journey away from this perishing world, one of his nobles named Mahābat Ḵhān went to the Deccan in the manner of a merchant. He met with the emperor of the Deccan and with wiles and subtilizings he received the emperor's permission, and had a meeting with Prince Ḵhurram, in which he told him of Parwez's rulership. Ḵhurram sought some stratagem from Mahabat Ḵhān. Mahabat Ḵhān taught him a trick: "You must make yourself out to be ill, and after a few days you must make it seem as if you have died, so that I can ask the Shah of the Deccan for your casket, and take it to Hindustan. Other than this I cannot imagine any way for you to release yourself from this prison." In short, Ḵhurram pretended to be dead, and was released from the Shah of the Deccan's prison. He reached Hindustan, gathered a force,

> did battle against Parwez, sat upon the Throne of Command, and gained the title "Shah Jahan." ('Izzat Allāh Bangālī 2007, 721)

To those familiar with the general outline of the history of Jahāngīr's succession, this fragment of the romance would certainly strike them as a text bearing the genre of history, which was a genre that was sometimes even definitionally opposed to the romance. That the passage could easily have been taken as historical is, I think, shown rather than refuted by the comments, seventy years later, of the Urdu translator Nihāl Chand Lāhorī, who tells the reader that he has omitted the story of Prince Ḵhurram in his version of *Bakāwalī* because it "turned out" to be contrary to the account in the *Jahāngīrnāmah* (Nihāl Chand Lāhorī 2008, 156). Precisely because the textual fragment would otherwise be identified as factual, the translator decided to make the comparison to the *Jahāngīrnāmah* and report the incongruity of the two accounts.

Who can say what the genre of a text is? Who "identifies" or assigns it? Understanding the workings of the genre of textual fragments means turning once again from the producer of the romance to the consumer, from the storyteller or writer to the hearer or reader. A storyteller like Faḵhr al-Zamānī could only have guided the reception of their performance. Ultimately the responsibility for assigning genres to the texts he produced would have fallen to the lot of the listener, usually on the basis of the potential hypotexts buried in her memory. Of course, this genre assignment does not necessarily take place because the reader connects a certain textual fragment in the tale being told to a specific hypotext that she remembers. It is equally possible that she has internalized norms relating to how one identifies a text as belonging to a certain genre—that is, a genre code. Or it is possible that on the basis of her experience of a number of texts, she herself has an idea of a genre and relates the new text she is experiencing to the genre code that she has synthesized.

Just as often, if not more often, the genre identification of the newly experienced work refers not to a free-floating genre itself (the genre code) but rather to previously experienced works in that genre, and particularly to its most visible works. For example, we can think about possible genre associations in the story of Ḥātim Ṭā'ī's offering first his own flesh and then that of his horse to the lion. There are several potential hypotexts in the genre of *akhlāq* (ethics), which recount some narrative of Ḥātim giving his famous and valuable horse as food in exemplary hospitality. The most "visible" and obvious *akhlāq* work to which the audience's mind would turn upon hearing this account is Sa'dī's *Bostān*, a very well-known text among Indian Islamicate elites.[33]

If the listener made this genre association and assigned the genre of *akhlāq* to this passage of the *Qiṣṣah-i Ḥātim Ṭā'ī*, the *akhlāq* genre would effectively infiltrate the romance work. Along with the genre of *akhlāq*, the *effects* of *akhlāq* would therefore have an opportunity to make themselves felt. When a textual fragment bearing the *akhlāq* genre appears in a romance, the audience is able to experience the ethical exemplarity of the munificent Ḥātim Ṭā'ī or the just Sasanian king Nausherwān. Through the multiple genres coursing through it, the *qiṣṣah* is able to have effects including but not limited to the pleasure that it brings. It is able to convey the ethical exemplarity of *akhlāq*, use potent historical examples, or showcase the storyteller's social capital through an opening panegyric for a patron.

The obvious objection to the idea that romances are multigeneric is that in the end the genre of the work swallows up and assimilates the genre of any textual fragments inside it. A modern reader, with an acute sense of the division between "true" history and "false" romance, might hear the story of Ḥātim Ṭā'ī and be confronted by a passage alluding to the historicity of Ḥātim, who lived just before the Prophet Muḥammad. He would say to himself, "Ḥātim Ṭā'ī was real—so this really happened?" Then he would come to realize: "No, it's only a tale." The genre of truthful history that he had associated with the name of Ḥātim had been buoyed up in his mind before perishing beneath the waves of the false romance. Undoubtedly there tends to be a genre that audiences assign to the work as a whole, a "master genre" that partially controls the reception of minor, fragment genres within the work. But apart from the fact that the genres of history and romance have long had an especially tense relationship, we should not be hasty in assuming that the suppression of fragment genres is what happens all the time, every time.

The relation of a fragment genre to the master genre of the work in which it is found depends on a judgment that the audience makes regarding the extent to which a fragment and its genre are "outside" or "inside" the larger text and its genre. Take, for example, the case of 'Izzat Allāh Bangālī's *Gul-i Bakāwalī*. 'Izzat Allāh's version of the romance is interspersed with commentarial passages leading away from the narrative itself and into Sufistic speculation of the kind that eighteenth-century Indians would find in the *Revelation of the Veiled* (*Kashf al-maḥjūb*) of 'Alī 'Us̤mān Hujwerī or in the writings of Abū Ḥāmid and Aḥmad Ġhazālī. For instance, to smuggle a secondary character, Bahrām, into the home of his beloved, the fairy Rūḥ-afzā, his mother, Saman-rū, disguises him as a lady's maid: "Saman-rū dressed him up in women's clothes and decorated him with studded jewelry. Because Bahrām was a beardless man, he became like a pretty-faced young maid" ('Izzat Allāh Bangālī 2007, 712). The relatively common motif of cross-dressing, used to humorous effect by the mischievous *'ayyār*s of the *Dāstān-i Amīr Ḥamzah*, is not left without a remarkable commentary in *Gul-i Bakāwalī*:

> Let it not remain hidden from the minds of the wise that had Bahrām not donned the garment of womanhood, he would never have gained his heart's desire—union with his beloved—with such speed. It is for that reason that the Prophet (blessings of God be upon him), enjoining the refinement of morals, said, "*Take on the attributes of God*"—that is, take on God's qualities. From the string of lovers, the Beloved takes that lover who colors himself in the Beloved's color. ('Izzat Allāh Bangālī 2007, 715)

This passage displays many characteristics that would put the audience in mind of a manual for the Sufistically inclined. It refers to a hadith in which the Prophet Muḥammad enjoins humans to take on God's attributes: "*takhallaqū bi-aḳhlāqi Allāh*." Depending on the communities of textual memory to which they belonged, audience members would recall that the hypotext, this prophetic saying, is often a subject of commentary by the Sufis. They would also remember that the concomitant ideas of "coloring" and "union" are regularly expounded by Sufis. If their memories worked in this manner, they would "recognize" the passage as something bearing the genre of a Sufi teaching on approaching the Divine Beloved. Thenceforward in the romance of Bakāwalī, the *'āshiq* and *ma'shūq*, lover and beloved, could hardly be understood in their worldly senses alone.

What is the relation of this Sufistic commentary to the romance? It is within the work and yet aloof. It stands apart from the romance narrative, and yet, if it sets alight the audience's imagination, it can control the way in which they understand the romance. In this sense it is like the texts that Genette (1997b) calls "paratexts." These are textual elements lying at the threshold of a text, simultaneously within it and without it, and helping to control how we read it, like prologues and prefaces, appended chronogrammatical verses (*qiṭ'āt-i tārīkh*), colophons, laudatory reviews (*taqrīẓ*), and marginalia.[34] Paratexts were implicitly conceived by Genette as being set off from the work in some way and not enclosed within it as 'Ināyat Allāh's commentary is. Nevertheless, a textual fragment like this, bearing a genre separate from the master genre and providing a guide to reading the romance, fulfills the most prominent conditions of paratextuality. Depending on the hearer's perspective as shaped by her memory of texts, the passage might seem to fit seamlessly within the romance, or it might appear strangely foreign to the romance. More likely, it will appear to be both simultaneously. The same can be said of the genre with which it is marked. Paratextuality is in a sense the nature of any hypotext—which in the final analysis means every single part of any text, since all language is ultimately intertextual; "After Adam there are no nameless objects nor any unused words" (Todorov 1984, x).

The *para*textuality of hypotexts means that there is no single mode of relationship between the genre of a text fragment and that of the work that it inhabits. It depends on one's reading, which is in turn controlled by one's memory of potential hypotexts and the genre identifications that one is likely to make. The relationship of myriad genres within a work—both to each other and to the master genre—also reflects in microcosm the "genre system" of the milieu in which the work is heard or read. If history and romance are opposing genres according to the prevalent genre system, and this opposition is accepted by the reader of a particular romance, then, at first reading, a historical passage within a romance will appear to jar. Thenceforth the reader might leave the passage suspended in its paratextual ambiguity, or she might make a decision. The minor genre may be seen to be contained and neutralized by the master genre, or it may remain foreign, "contaminating" the genre of the host text.

Not all pairs of genres in a genre system are opposed to one another. Non-oppositional relationships take a wide variety of forms; a panegyric within a romance might merely signal the work's status as an item of exchange in a patron-client relationship, or it might go further and shade the romance with its presence, making the entire work doubly readable as romance and panegyric. A hemistich of a *ġhazal* quoted in a romance might stand aloof from the romance genre, or, cleverly used, it might form part of the narrative like a Bollywood song, assimilating itself to the genre. Assimilation or neutralization of the fragment's genre by the master genre is always possible, but it does not always happen, and it is only one possible outcome of the hearer's or reader's reception of the multigenre romance.

As Shamsur Rahman Faruqi has said, romances are patchwork texts, made up of many different fragments (Faruqi 1999, 411). Faḳhr al-Zamānī's prescribed use of the *Ṭirāz al-aḳhbār* is only the tip of the iceberg. Each fragment constituting this patchwork could bear its own genre apart from the romance genre, and thus the romance could have diverse effects on the basis of the variety of other-genre-bearing texts within it. It should be said that all works, no matter what their master genre, are multigeneric. No work or genre is pure, and genres cannot be studied in isolation from one another. We cannot ask what the romance is without asking at the same time about other genres like the history, panegyric, or ethical manual. And we cannot dismiss the claims of Faḳhr al-Zamānī, Ġhālib Lakhnawī, and others about the uses of romances when we consider the uses of the genres running through it.

When the rags of texts (*patahs*, episodes, etc.) making up the *qiṣṣah* are seen in the specificity of their various genres, we can see that there is no pure and flawless romance. There is no romance that is uninhabited by other genres in the form of its constituent fragments, which allow it to be apprehended and used, at least in part, as something other than a romance. In the next chapter, we will see the most radical example of this principle: the presence of history in the "romance" allows, under certain ideological circumstances and given a certain genre code, the possibility of reading the whole work as history.

THE BIOGRAPHERS MAKE NO mention of our last traces of Faḳhr al-Zamānī, whose *Ṭirāz al-aḳhbār* elucidates the structure of *qiṣṣahs* and the mode of their performance so well. Despite the generosity and solicitude of his patron Saif Ḳhān, the storyteller was distressed by poor health as he finished the *Ṭirāz*. Afraid that he might not live to complete his work, he forced himself to do a rushed job. He complained bitterly of his condition:

> Even though this least of the servants of God is preserved from the weakness of penury and the pain of possessionless-ness by the fortune of the fortunate one [Saif Ḳhān] with whose renowned name and honored title this book is ornamented, yet . . . for some time he has been seized by the misery of a continuous colic disorder [*qaulanj*]. Due to intimacy with this chronic disease he is weary of his life. He tastes nothing when eating his food, and senses no sweetness when drinking. If he drinks even a tiny draft he fills up with air like a bellows. If he takes a cup of wine he becomes thirstier than an ironsmith's furnace. His stomach cannot digest even the thought of bread, and he cannot stand even the idea of broth. His head cannot abide a turban, nor can his body abide his clothes. His existence is a pain; the heat and cold of everything bring no benefit, only damage. His misery is such that even if the Messiah were to descend to the earth from the Fourth Heaven to treat him, he would not succeed. (Faḳhr al-Zamānī 1632, f. 617b)

But he lived at least long enough to complete the first volume of the *Nawādir al-ḥikāyāt*, a collection of anecdotes of a historical nature, and I suspect that the Iranian Majlis Library's copy of the *Ṯirāz*, copied in Patna for an "Aḥmad Ḥusain Bahādur" two years later in 1043 H (1633), may be in Faḳhr al-Zamānī's own hand.[35]

It was probably in that very year, 1043 H, that Saif Ḳhān left Bihar for Allahabad to take up the governorship of that province (see Khan 2017a). The new governor of Bihar would have been particularly repugnant to Saif Ḳhān's loyalists, for he was none other than Saif Ḳhān's old foe 'Abd Allāh Ḳhān.[36] It would not be surprising if individuals like Faḳhr al-Zamānī, who had written in praise of Saif Ḳhān's victory over 'Abd Allāh Ḳhān, should decide to join their patron, who in 1045–46 H (ca. 1635) left Allahabad for his old position as governor of Gujarat, with his capital at Ahmedabad (Shāh Nawāz Ḳhān Aurangābādī 1888, 2:420). It is interesting, therefore, that the next dated manuscript is the 1053 H (1643) *Nawādir al-ḥikāyāt*, copied in Ahmedabad. Was Faḳhr al-Zamānī alive and resident in Gujarat? We cannot tell. But if other volumes of the *Nawādir* are extant, there may be more to the tale of 'Abd al-Nabī Faḳhr al-Zamānī.

4

Marvelous Histories

THE *QISSAH* MUST BE examined not only in its adjacency to other genres but also as a thread running through texts dominated by other genres and as a fabric embroidered with threads of a multitude of genres. A study of the genre of any *qiṣṣah* would need to take into account the genres running through it in a dazzling array of intertextual forms. The hypotextual presence of the *akhlaq* (ethics) genre in a *qiṣṣah* might alert the reader to the possibility of its ethical exemplarity. Panegyrics (*madḥ*) to specific patrons, lodged paratextually in the *qiṣṣah*, might activate its exemplarity. Strands of Sufistic commentary might make possible an interpretation of the *qiṣṣah* that would have remained latent otherwise. To understand any one of these genres running through the *qiṣṣah*, it is also helpful to observe the reverse situation. A genre participating in the *qiṣṣah* and the *qiṣṣah*'s participation in that genre are two sides of the same coin.

The clearest and most definitive relation into which the *qiṣṣah* genre can be placed is that of opposition to other genres. At the end of the nineteenth century, the *qiṣṣah* was subject to a reconfiguration of its genre code when it came to be defined in opposition to the novel. But before India's formal integration into the British Empire, the genre to which the *qiṣṣah* was most radically opposed was that of historiography (*tarīkh*). Yet bits and pieces of history strayed through many *qiṣṣah*s, interacting with other fragment genres like *akhlāq* and the panegyric in productive ways. The *Qiṣṣah-i Ḥātim Ṭā'ī*, *Abū Muslim-nāmah*, *Qiṣṣah-i Tamīm Anṣārī*, *Khāwarān-nāmah*, *Bostān-i Khayāl*, and *Ḥamzah-nāmah* are all examples of *qiṣṣah*s whose protagonists would have been recognized by audiences as historical.

More disturbing for some was the opposite case—passages in histories that would have been recognized by audiences as resembling fragments of *qiṣṣahs*. An alternative *Jahāngīrnāmah* from the seventeenth century recounts the Mughal emperor's investigation into a cave in Ajmer. In the cavern's darkness, Jahāngīr and his retinue observed a faint red glow. Upon examining its source, they found it to be the glint of red gold, illumined by fire. A dragon was sprawled out in the dark in a nest of the precious metal, sound asleep and flicking forth tongues of flame as it snored. Wisely, the royal party made haste to remove themselves from the cave, but Jahāngīr returned to vanquish the beast and liberate the country from the monster's hateful presence. Such passages in the *Jahāngīrnāmah* led its cataloger Charles Rieu to state dismissively that it was "of little historical value" (Nur al-Din Muhammad Salīm Jahāngīr n.d., fol. 138bff; Rieu 1879, 254). Most Indians would have recognized the presence of the *qiṣṣah* in this *tārīkh*, whether they believed that this history was illegitimate or not. But Indians were not united in their condemnation of such *qiṣṣah*-like histories, nor did everyone understand the two genres to exist in an opposition. In other words, two differently configured genre systems existed in Islamicate India. One system, shaped by a rationalist worldview, defined the mendacious *qiṣṣah* in opposition to the veracious *tārīkh*. But another system, perhaps a more prevalent one, if less familiar to us, treated the *qiṣṣah* and history as close cousins with porous limits.

Not content to see decline everywhere in the history of "the East," Orientalists grieved over the decline of Oriental historiography itself. Their stance is recounted in Velcheru Narayana Rao, David Shulman, and Sanjay Subrahmanyam's study *Textures of Time* (2003). Orientalist scholars understood the early Islamic hadith histories to possess an admirable historiographical method. But they supposed that, as the ranks of the intelligentsia increasingly swelled with non-Arab, and particularly Persian, *mawālī* and as Islamicate historiography began to be written in the New Persian language, history writing came under the malign influence of Persianate tastes and ideas, becoming superfluously ornate in its style and careless in its method. Furthermore, it increasingly became entangled with far-fetched legendary accounts. The new histories consisted of historical narratives illegitimately muddled with marvelous accounts that properly belonged to the poorly regarded *qiṣṣah* genre. The adulteration of "pure" history by elements of this lower genre was an indication of historiography's increasing bastardy.

This view was challenged effectively toward the end of the twentieth century by scholars such as Julie Meisami, on the basis of whose work the authors of *Textures of Time* also present their critique. Meisami examines the rhetorical aspects of histories in Persian, showing at length how they served courtly functions (Meisami 1999; Narayana Rao, Shulman, and Subrahmanyam 2003, 209ff.). The relationship between *qiṣṣah* and history has been less carefully studied. To understand their relation, it will be useful to consider what was perhaps the most prominent of the generically ambivalent *qiṣṣah*s in India: the *Shāhnāmah*. The *Shāhnāmah*, now usually seen as a romance or epic, was formerly received as a historical text instead of or in addition to what is now its obvious genre. These ambivalent identifications were enabled by the existence of a methodological split between rationalist (*'aqlī*) and transmissionist (*naqlī*) historiography, the latter allowing for the accommodation of marvelous and *qiṣṣah*-like elements, even as the former method rejected such a possibility.

Though the *Shāhnāmah* is a text associated strongly with Iran, Sunil Sharma's (2013) scholarship has recently detailed several appearances of *Shāhnāmah* versions in India. Though we do not always know what storytellers in India were reciting, we may speculate that Iranian émigrés like Mullā Asad Qiṣṣah-k̲h̲wān did much to whet the appetite of Indian courtly audiences for the *Shāhnāmah*. We do not know what Mullā Asad was reciting to his patron, Mirzā Ġhāzī Tark̲h̲ān, but we have seen that he came from a family that was renowned for its devotion to the performance of the *Shāhnāmah* at the court of the Safavid emperor Shāh 'Abbās I. Courtly storytellers were not the only reciters of the work. At the end of the next century (or the beginning of the eighteenth), there were, for example, individuals like Lālah Āsā Rām Sāth, who is mentioned by Mīr Taqī Mīr (1979, 77) as having memorized Firdausī's narrative.

The *Shāhnāmah* is often regarded as the source from which other long *dāstāns* sprang. The most notable of these are the Persian romances of Amīr Ḥamzah and the *Bostān-i Ḳhayāl*, but other examples include the *Dārāb-nāmah*, *Garshāsp-nāmah*, *Ḳhāwarān-nāmah*, and other romances that were mainly popular elsewhere in the Persianate world and that borrow characters as well as narrative structures from the *Shāhnāmah*. Along with the *Shāhnāmah*'s performance context, its relation to other subsidiary *qiṣṣah*s marked the *Shāhnāmah* as a *qiṣṣah* itself.

But why attempt to prove the obvious? It seems obvious to modern readers that the *Shāhnāmah* is a romance or epic—certainly not a history. There are important exceptions to this viewpoint among modern scholars; Julie Meisami (1993, 253ff.), for instance, insists that Firdausī wrote his *Shāhnāmah* primarily as a historical work. Her article should be referred to for a general explanation of this genre identification; my own purpose in this chapter is to extend her argument and to localize it by focusing on responses to the *Shāhnāmah* within the Mughal Empire. The *Shāhnāmah*'s genre was a field for battles of ideology, which Meisami characterizes as conflicts over whether "Islamic historiography" was the sole mode of history or whether "Persian histories" like the *Shāhnāmah* were also legitimate. By the time of the *Shāhnāmah*'s completion, Meisami notes, the ongoing shift in genre perceptions toward the triumph of "Islamic historiography" meant that the *Shāhnāmah* was already "something of an anomaly: not quite literature and not quite history" (Meisami 1993, 263). Almost a millennium later, the ambiguity of the *Shāhnāmah*'s genre is still discernible in the comments made upon it by the nineteenth-century poet of Urdu and Persian Mirzā Asad Allāh Ḳhān Ġhālib.

Ġhālib and the Simurgh

On April 4, 1865, the elderly Ġhālib was reading the *Awadh Aḳhbār* newspaper when he came across an advertisement for the newly printed romance *Paristān-i ḳhayāl* (Fairyland of imagination). Written by Ġhālib's friend and student Sayyid Farzand Aḥmad Ṣafīr Bilgrāmī, the *Paristān-i ḳhayāl* was an abridged Urdu translation of an eighteenth-century Persian romance that Ġhālib had read before, the *Bostān-i Ḳhayāl* (Garden of imagination) by Mīr Taqī Ḳhayāl. According to the advertisement, the book had been published in two volumes by the Aẕīm al-maṭābiʿ press in Patna, and it was available for one rupee and twelve annas, plus postage. Ġhālib wrote immediately to the director, Mīr Wilāyat ʿAlī, with an urgent order for two volumes of the romance. From his letter, it is clear that Ġhālib was eager to get his hands on the book:

> I just found out about this today, and today I'm sending off this letter and the postage. I ask you—indeed, I *urge* you—to act with similar promptness, and to send out the parcel on the very day that follows the arrival of my letter. In case of expedition, I am most grateful, and in case of delay, I make ready my complaint!

After he had sent this letter, Ġhālib discovered that in his eagerness and haste, he had forgotten to send the postage. The next day he sent, along with the postage, a letter of apology for the decline of his mind, which he blamed on his declining years: "I'm seventy years old, my memory is extinct, forgetfulness reigns!" (Ġhālib to Mīr Wilāyat ʿAlī, Delhi, April 5, 1865, in Ġhālib 1984, 1572; see also Ġhālib 1969a, 931).[1] Ġhālib's persistence in procuring this romance is one of the many proofs of his partiality for the genre that one finds in his letters (see especially Ġhālib to Mīr Mahdī Ḥusain Majrūh, Delhi, ca. September 1860, in Ġhālib 1967b, 176–79).

The *Paristān-i ḳhayāl* was an Urdu translation of Mīr Taqī Ḳhayāl's eighteenth-century Persian romance—it was probably Ḳhayāl's original that Ġhālib had read before. Ġhālib was well acquainted with Ṣafīr, and he showed great respect to the young man, who belonged to an important Sufi family. Indeed, on the very day that he sent his initial order to Mīr Wilāyat ʿAlī, Ġhālib (1993, 1580–81) also sent a letter of congratulation to Ṣafīr. But there were many translations other than Ṣafīr's, and Ġhālib was certainly familiar with at least one other. In 1866, a year after the publication of Ṣafīr Bilgrāmī's volume, the Delhi-based press Akmal al-maṭābiʿ published the first volume of what would subsequently become the most famous Urdu *Bostān-i Ḳhayāl*, written by Ġhālib's adoptive nephew (*bhatījā*) Ḳhwājah Badr al-Dīn Amān. This first volume was entitled *Ḥadā'iq-i anẓār*, and it boasted a preface by Ġhālib himself.

The genre could not have found a more eloquent champion. What concerns us here is Ġhālib's manner of mounting the genre's defense, which involves an example that must have appeared very odd indeed to many twentieth-century readers. Ġhālib takes the romance's alleged inferiority to the genre of history as his starting point:

> You may see in biographies and histories what happened hundreds of years before you. You may listen, in stories and romances, to what no one has ever seen or heard. Though the wakeful brains of intellectual men will incline by temperament toward histories, nevertheless in their hearts they will admit to the tastefulness and delightfulness of romances and tales. (Ġhālib 1967b, 449, trans. in Khan 2017b, 92)

The division between the two genres seems quite clear. Histories portray events that have occurred in the past. *Qiṣṣah*s, on the other hand, present events that have always been non-observable because they have never occurred. The inclination of the intellect (*ḳhirad*) is toward historical fact. The heart, however, inclines toward the delectation afforded by *qiṣṣah*s. Delectable as they are, however, there is no gainsaying the fact that *qiṣṣah*s are lies—*jhūṭī kahāniyāṅ*, as Ġhālib says himself (1967b, 450).

What we see in Ġhālib's preface is a genre system in the form of a hierarchy. By inventing roots for this system in an analogous hierarchy of faculties, *qiṣṣah* and *tārīḳh* corresponding to the heart and the intellect, Ġhālib strengthens the hierarchy a great deal. Strength was needed, for this was an unstable and contested genre system. The relationship between the romance and history genres is apparently a relationship of opposition between a genre to which mendacity (*kiẕb*) is central and one in which sincerity (*ṣidq*) is paramount. Each gives the other its identity in a radical way, and their separate identities are thrown into relief in every expression of their conflict, no matter which genre happens to have the higher value under the particular circumstances. When Ġhālib lifts the romance above the history, he does not alter the mode of their relation or the nature of their identities. He reverses the hierarchy without appearing to disturb the conflictual premise on which the genre division is based.

All that Ġhālib has to do to place the *qiṣṣah* above the *tārīḳh* is to elevate the heart over the mind—a quite standard epistemological move at the time. But as his review of Ḳhwājah Amān goes on, Ġhālib does something else that is quite provocative. He puts the very division between history and romance into question. "Aren't impossible tales narrated in histories?" he asks. "You are unjust, it isn't so!" (*Kyā tawārīḳh meṅ mumtana' al-wuqū' ḥikāyāt nahīṅ? nā-inṣāfī karte ho, yih kuch bāt nahīṅ*) (Ġhālib 1967b, 449, trans. in Khan 2017b, 92). The word that Ġhālib uses is more precise than the English word "impossible." Something that is *mumtana' al-wuqū'* is something whose *occurrence* is strictly barred, an impossible event. Recall that Ġhālib has just described history as a genre that recounts that which has *occurred* (*jo wāqi' hu'ā*), and it will become clear that if, as he claims, there is a history narrating events whose occurrence is impossible, this history is a traitor to its own genre. The effect of this surprising move is to demonstrate that historical works are, at least potentially, as blameworthy as romances in regard to their fantastic quality.

The purportedly historical account that Ġhālib singles out for discussion is the description of the adoption of the albino hero Zāl by a bird possessed of occult powers, the Sīmurġh. Throughout his life Zāl carries the feathers of the Sīmurġh, which he only has to burn to summon his foster parent. When the enemy Isfandyar wounds the great hero Rustam, son of Zāl, Zāl uses a feather to summon the Sīmurġh, who gives Rustam a special weapon with which to slay his foe. Ġhālib recounts this episode with some hilarity:

> When Rustam despairs of his fight with Isfandyār, Zāl calls out that name without a named, and the Sīmurġh comes directly upon hearing the sound of the whistle, just like a trained pigeon. With a daub of its droppings, or some other medicine, it heals Rustam's wound, and,

giving him a double-shafted arrow, it takes its leave. (Ġhālib 1967b, 449, trans. in Khan 2017b, 92)

Most cultured individuals of Ġhālib's time would have been able to identify this episode with great ease as forming part of the *Shāhnāmah*. In contrast to our modern understanding of the *Shāhnāmah* as a *dāstān*, and in agreement with Julie Meisami's assessment, Ġhālib implies that the *Shāhnāmah* was a history, albeit one with marvelous episodes. To modern eyes, Ġhālib appears to have grossly misidentified the genre of the *Shāhnāmah*. But the nature of genre makes it necessary to approach the question of the *Shāhnāmah*'s genre with an eye to the historical specificity and flux of genre identification.

Once they have been accepted as normal, genre identifications tend to be resistant to alteration, although this may have been a shade less true of Ġhālib's time than of the age of physical bookstores and music stores, in which the bookseller cannot shelve a novel like *Robinson Crusoe* under "Travel" without thereby making it more difficult to sell. In these terms, Ġhālib appears to have mis-shelved the *Shāhnāmah* in the "History" section. But if Meisami is right about Firdausī, or at least about the impression that he gave to his readers, then Ġhālib's seeming ineptitude in the science of genre identification could be forgiven, and the confusion might be traced to a historical shift in the *Shāhnāmah*'s generic allegiance. One might speculate that it was widely considered to be a history in Ġhālib's time but came to be regarded primarily as a romance by the twentieth century due to a shift in thinking. In reality, it is unlikely that there was any historical moment in which the *Shāhnāmah* was not identifiable as a romance, but it is possible that for much of its existence it possessed a double identity and that at times its historiographical identity was privileged.

The *Shāhnāmah* as History in India

Genre identifications are rarely new; for the most part they are based on precedent, adhering to the say-so of previous audiences, until transformations in the new audience's worldview cause them to change. But would the idea that the *Shāhnāmah* was a historical work have been available to Ġhālib in the 1860s from any source other than his fecund imagination? It is true that many later dynastic histories in verse were modeled upon the *Shāhnāmah*. Sunil Sharma presents several examples of such histories: Mustaufī's *Ẓafar-nāmah*, the *Shahanshāh-nāmah* of Aḥmad Tabrīzī, and Abū al-Malik 'Iṣāmī's *Futūḥ al-salāṭīn*, among others (Sharma 2002). In addition, it is certainly the case that episodes from the *Shāhnāmah* are recounted in many Persian and Arabic books describing themselves as histories (*tārīḳh*). Ṭabarī's *Tārīḳh al-Rusul wa al-mulūk*, the *Tārīḳh-i Bal'amī*, and Mīrḳhwānd's *Rauẓat al-ṣafā* all contain a significant amount of material gathered from the *Shāhnāmah*, and Ġhālib is likely to have read Mīrḳhwānd at least. Just as the *Shāhnāmah*'s influence on romances like the *Ḥamzah-nāmah* and *Garshāsp-nāmah* points to its inclusion within the romance genre, the presence in these histories of information garnered from the *Shāhnāmah* might retroactively mark the *Shāhnāmah* as a history itself. The trouble is that none of these histories makes any mention of the episodes featuring the Sīmurġh, which are the ones that Ġhālib singles out for comment. Even the *Rauẓat al-ṣafā* omits the Sīmurġh, despite its pointed inclusion of other marvels, particularly in its opening sections.

The marvelous Sīmurġh narrative does find a place in one Arabic history, the *Ġhurar aḳhbār mulūk al-Furs* (Choice reports of the Persian kings) by Abū Manṣūr al-Tha'ālibī. Writing just after Ġhālib's time, the Indian intellectual Shiblī Nu'mānī shows his familiarity with Tha'alibi, but whether Ġhālib himself knew of Tha'alibi's work is a moot question (Shiblī Nu'mānī 1962, 111). To find the Sīmurġh in a Persian historical work, we must turn to a history produced within the Mughal Empire in the year 1063 H (ca. 1653). Shāh Jahān's domains extended to Ghazni in the west, where Shamsher Ḳhān was posted as governor. Shamsher Ḳhān's chronicler (*wāqi'ah-nawes*), Tawakkul Beg b. Tūlak Beg, wrote a history for his patron. Tawakkul Beg describes the genesis of this history as follows: One day Shamsher Ḳhān said to his companions, "If a book of history could be had, which one could use to very briefly pick out and learn the particulars of past monarchs and to be informed of all of their qualities, this would be very nice!" The men present in the gathering replied, "There is no better book than the *Shāhnāmah* for the attainment of this object." The genre identification being made in this courtly scene is clear: Shamsher Ḳhān asks for a *tārīḳh*, and his companions give him the *Shāhnāmah*. But Shamsher Ḳhān complained of the *Shāhnāmah*'s prolixity and of Firdausī's emphasis on poetic virtuosity, and therefore Tawakkul was commissioned to write a summary in prose (Tawakkul Beg 1999, 15).[2] This work was called the *Tārīḳh-i Dil-gushā-i Shamsher-Ḳhānī* (Heart-opening history, for Shamsher Khan), later referred to simply as the *Shamsher-Ḳhānī*.

According to both its title and the story of its origin, the *Shamsher-Ḳhānī* is a book of history. But unlike many other histories, it includes the stories of the Simurgh as well as of the various demons that populate Firdausī's work. So we see that in 1653, as in 1865, these unusual beings were characters in at least one history book. Could Ġhālib's views on the *Shāhnāmah* have been influenced by the *Shamsher-Ḳhānī*? Many seventeenth-century books had been forgotten by the nineteenth century, but the *Shamsher-Ḳhānī* remained popular and prestigious. Charles Melville (2009), who has studied the work closely, has viewed at least four eighteenth-century manuscripts in British archives, including two from Murshidabad, and has drawn attention to an early Edinburgh manuscript from 1697.[3] That these were probably acquired by the British from the late eighteenth to the nineteenth century suggests that they were in circulation during this period. Aḥmad Munzawī's (1988, 148–51) union catalog lists eleven *Shamsher-Ḳhānī* manuscripts from the eighteenth century and a remarkable twenty-six from the nineteenth century in Pakistani archives alone (out of a total of fifty-three, many undated). British Orientalists in the nineteenth century were well acquainted with the abundant work; in 1832, James Atkinson (1892, xxiv–xxv, quoted in Melville 2009) declared it to be the best-known version of the *Shāhnāmah* in India. A measure of the value attached to it is its reproduction as an illustrated manuscript in Punjab during the reign of Ranjīt Siṅgh (r. 1801–39). First, we may note the two illuminated "*Shāhnāmahs*" in the Punjab State Archives and the National Museum in New Delhi. They are both prose works and likely to be *Shamsher-*

Ḳhānī manuscripts. The first was supposedly copied by Tawakkul Beg for Shāh Jahān and entered Ranjit Singh's library in 1244 H (1828–29), while the second appears to have been produced in Lahore around 1830 (Payeur 2010, 236; Lafont 2002, 22–23). Second is the much more clear-cut case of the Lilly manuscript, an illustrated *Shamsher-Ḳhānī* that in the 1830s was in the possession of the Italian Jean Baptiste Ventura, a general in Ranjīt Siṅgh's employ. This manuscript, the object of a study by Brittany Payeur, is housed in the Lilly Library at the University of Indiana, Bloomington.

It is unclear whether there were any printed copies of the Persian text, but Ġhālib could certainly have had access to a manuscript *Shamsher-Ḳhānī* given the abundance of copies. Besides, as we will see, the apparent paucity of Persian *Shamsher-Ḳhānī* lithograph copies was offset by a good number of Urdu translations in print. At any rate, what matters is not whether he had read it or even heard of it but rather its general popularity, as demonstrated by Atkinson's testimony and by its frequent and sometimes prestigious reproduction. Its popularity raises the likelihood that it was able to saturate the cultural discourse (in which Ġhālib participated) regarding the genre of the *Shāhnāmah* with its own representation of the narrative as a historiographical one. To complete the evidence of its popularity in Ġhālib's time, let us consider two Urdu translations from the nineteenth century.

The first was composed in 1810 or 1811 (1225 H) by one Mūl Chand Munshī, who translated the *Shamsher-Ḳhānī* into Urdu verse at the urging of an unnamed friend (Munshī 1844, 7–8). Its chronogrammatic title is *Qiṣṣah-i Ḳhusrawān-i ʿAjam* (Tale of the kings of Persia). The earliest printed copies of which I am aware date from 1844 and 1846. The latter of these is a typeset copy by Ġhulām ʿAlī of Hooghly, who writes that he undertook the reprinting for the benefit of the Urdu-learning students at the schools administered by "Captain George Turnbull Marshal Bahādur" (Munshī 1844, 1–2). By dint of its very title, the *Qiṣṣah-i Ḳhusrawān-i ʿAjam* presents us with a generic ambiguity. The title points to its being a *qiṣṣah*, and many of the chapter headings refer to the accounts as *dāstāns*, yet it is a translation of a "history," and indeed it simultaneously keeps up the genre identification presented by the *Shamsher-Khānī*. The terms *qiṣṣah*, *dāstān*, *ḥikāyat*, and so on are vexatious in that while they are common identifiers of genre, they may also refer simply to narrative units and do not necessarily carry connotations of fictionality.

In his *sabab-i tālīf* (exposition of the reasons for the work's composition), Munshī recounts the story of the *Shamsher-Khānī*'s genesis at the governor's court in Ghazni and repeats Tawakkul Beg's characterization of it as a history:

> That assembly was the envy of the field's springtime.
> Every minute, poetry was being mentioned.
> Once, when histories were mentioned too,
> Everyone expressed themselves as follows:
> "The *Shāhnāmah* is a wonderful book,
> "Marvelous, with enthralling verses, and powerful.
> "But it is not accessible to everyone—
> This happy history is not available everywhere." (Munshī 1844, 7)

The "too" in the third line of my translation expresses a break between two genres. Poetry proper is constantly mouthed at Shamsher Khān's court on the one hand, and on the other hand history is also mentioned by way of a change. A history like the *Shāhnāmah* can be in verse (*naẓm*), but in this account *tārīkh* stands slightly apart from *shi'r* (poetry), perhaps in the sense that the latter was construed as a mendacious genre. When Ġhulām Ḥaidar reprinted the *Qiṣṣah-i Khusrawān-i 'Ajam* for Captain Turnbull in 1846, he did not dismiss Mūl Chand Munshī's "mis-shelving" of the *Shāhnāmah* under "History" either. In his preamble to his reprint, Ġhulām Ḣaidar writes, "Though this history may be old, its tales are yet so interesting and attractive . . . but you will have to read them to find out" (Munshī 1846, 2). The identification with historiography is there in Ġhulām Ḣaidar's comment, even if he simultaneously allies the text with the romance, as does Munshī himself. Here, commercial or at least promotional impulses stand half-veiled behind the double genre identification.

The audience for Munshī's book will receive whatever they wish: romance, if they fancy romance; history, if they desire history.

The year after Ġhulām Ḣaidar had republished Munshī's translation, the most important *Shamsher-Ḳhānī* translation was completed. Aside from being the best-known and probably the most frequently printed translation, it was written by a prominent Urdu litterateur who was an esteemed acquaintance of Ġhālib. This was the prose writer Mirzā Rajab 'Alī Beg Surūr. Surūr's translation, entitled *Surūr-i Sulṭānī* (The sultan's joy), was dedicated to the Awadhi nawab Wājid 'Alī Shāh, and the first edition was printed by the royal press in 1847, less than twenty years prior to Ġhālib's writing. Ġhālib showed great respect to his senior colleague in his letters (Ġhālib to Hargopāl Taftah, Delhi, June 26, 1858, in Ġhālib 1969b, 212–13) and in the preface that he wrote to a later romance composed by Surūr (Ġhālib 1967a). Therefore, it seems very unlikely that Ġhālib was unfamiliar with the *Surūr-i Sulṭāni*. Rajab 'Ali Beg Surūr was and is chiefly known as a writer of romances, such as the *Fasānah-i 'ajā'ib* (Tale of wonders). But the preeminent twentieth-century Urdu critic Gyān Chand Jain (1969, 507) was perspicacious enough to exclude the *Surūr-i Sulṭāni* from his list of romances, objecting that "one cannot call it a *dāstān*, since on the face of it it is referred to as a history of a particular period in Iran." Surūr's (1975, 54–55) own preface mentions the genre of his book:

> That which has been versified by the poet Firdausī is also the subject of the *Tārīḳh-i dil-gushā-i Shamsher-Ḳhānī*. However, the present writing is another matter, since [in the previous work] the genealogies of famous kings have not been attended to. A mere picture album has been made with the force of [Firdausī's] poetry, and with every hemistich, a painting caught in writing has been put on display. Therefore, I have looked in the trustworthy works of history, whose names will be cited at the proper occasion and place, so that the readers will regard it as authoritative, so that there will be no doubt left, and so that the book will be worthy of trust.

We see that it is Surūr's ambition to make the *Surūr-i Sulṭāni* an augmented historical transcreation of the *Tārīkh-i dilgusha* by citing "trustworthy works of history." He fulfills his promise by referring throughout the book to canonical histories such as the *Tārīkh al-rusul wa al-mulūk*, *Murūj al-dhahab*, *Rauẓat al-ṣafā*, *Tārīkh-i mu'jam*, and *Tārīkh-i guzīdah* (Surūr 1975, 29–30). Given these references, it seems obvious that Surūr does not read his material as unhistorical. Implicit in his claim that he will improve Tawakkul Beg's version is a critique: that the *Shamsher-Khani* is lacking as a historiography. But clearly this flaw does not lead Surūr to treat the *Shamsher-Khānī* as a non-history. He accepts its historiographical nature and founds on this basis his own attempt to increase the concentration of historiography within it by intertextual means. Surūr's clear act of genre identification makes Ġhālib's possible as well.

The surprise evinced by Ġhālib's assumption that the *Shāhnāmah* is a history can thus be attributed to our own alienation from the history of genre identifications preceding Ġhālib's. Based on the evidence presented above, Meisami's characterization of the *Shāhnāmah*'s genre appears correct. However, what remains strange is Ġhālib's suggestion that, while it is historical, the *Shāhnāmah* also contains beings and events that are *mumtana' al-wuqū'* (barred from occurring). How was it possible, then, for Ġhālib to believe that a history may contain impossible events? Was he expressing his amusement at the illegitimate infection of the truthful history genre by the mendacious romance genre, or is he guided by a vision of a historiography that is not characterized primarily by its truthfulness? How substantial was the line between these two genres, the history and the romance, in the first place?

What is in question when we read Ġhālib's comments is the mode of interiority of the impossible to the sincere—or, one might say, of the romance elements to their containing history. Recall Ġhālib's question: "Aren't impossible tales narrated *in* histories?" We may ask whether the history can *contain* the elements of romance within it, such that the line between history and romance is maintained despite the relationship of interiority. Or does the romance within the history spill over into the history and dye it in its own color? The third alternative is that, in contrast to the notion of history that we most often espouse today, there was not necessarily a line between history and romance—they were not always opposed as a sincere genre against a mendacious one at all. It would be difficult to corroborate the second option of spillage in Ġhālib's reading of the *Shāhnāmah.* At first blush, it seems likely that when Ġhālib asked his rhetorical question, he had in mind a contained interiority. In other words, the *Shāhnāmah* was a history into which romance had crept as a foreign body or excrescence—ludicrously but without altering the containing text's status as history. This principle would then have to apply, of course, to texts like the *Tārīkh-i dil-gushā* and the *Surūr-i sulṭāni* as well. However, it is equally possible that Ġhālib was simply possessed of a conception of history that somehow did not exclude the romantic *mumtanaʿ al-wuqūʿ*. Was it possible for the genre of history to include the impossible?

ʿAqlī and Naqlī Historiography

The code or definition of the genre of historiography was riven by differences among its producers and its audiences on the basis of conflicting or simply divergent ideologies. This heterogeneity of Islamicate ideas of history is the organizing principle of Tarif Khalidi's work, *Arabic Historical Thought in the Classical Period*, and disputes over the quiddity of *tārīkh* similarly enable Julie Meisami's revisionary study *Persian Historiography*. We will require the insights of both scholars when we consider two particularly important historiographical methods competing with one another in the Islamicate world, which I will call the *ʿaqlī*, or intellect based, and the *naqlī*, or transmission based. The preponderance of evidence suggests that this methodological conflict, hinted at by Khalidi, was probably more crucial than the less frequently attested belittlement of marvelous histories on ethno-religious bases (see the argument in Meisami 1993), as when Abū Raiḥān al-Berūnī disparaged the Persian language as fit for nothing more than tale telling (quoted in Meisami 1993, 264). Berūnī's comment criticizes a language and by extension its speakers, but arguably the real target of his excoriation is not the Persian language itself but the methodological deficiency of historiography produced by the Persophones.[4]

The important historian Abū al-Faẓl Muḥammad Baihaqī both undermined and affirmed these sentiments when he wrote an important history in Persian—one that was, however, distinctly rationalist in its method, unlike the Persian-language histories frowned upon by Berūnī. Meisami and the *Textures of Time* authors both refer to Baihaqī's grand Berūnī-esque condemnation of the tall tales (*ḵhurāfāt*) beloved of the credulous multitudes, who are inattentive to rationally acceptable history and "prefer impossible falsehoods [*bāṯil-i mumtana'*]," such as "reports of demons, fairies, and ghouls of the desert, mountains and sea" (Baihaqī 2009, 713; see Meisami 1993, 265; Narayana Rao, Shulman, and Subrahmanyam 2003, 216). No doubt he would not have countenanced simurghs either. The fourth-century Hijrī, inhabited by Berūnī, Baihaqī, Firdausī, and T͟ha'ālibi, was a fertile time for rationalism. Mu'tazilism, often caricatured now as a hyperrationalist ideology, still held some sway a century after the sympathetic Caliph Al-Ma'mūn had instituted an inquisition (*miḥnah*) on its behalf. But, more to the point, most theologians (*mutakallimūn*) were seen as rationalist to a greater or lesser extent, Mu'tazilī or no, if we believe their characterization by the critical Sufi Muḥyī al-Dīn Ibn 'Arabī, for example. By this time the concept of the intellect was imbued with Greek and specifically Aristotelian meaning, particularly through the various translations of and commentaries on Aristotle's *On the Soul* (*Kitāb fī al-nafs*), where the intellect was given lordship over the faculties. Ġhālib subordinated the intellect to the heart, a commonplace position in his time, thanks to the long-standing Sufi critique of the intellect, to be examined in the next chapter. Baihaqī (2009, 715) took an opposing view in his *History* (*Tārīḵh-i Baihaqī*):

> The eyes and the ears are the heart's spies and watchman, who convey to the heart whatsoever they see and hear, . . . and the heart lays whatever it has found out from them before the intellect, who is a judge, in order for him to separate truth from falsehood.

The method of historiography that Berūnī and others set themselves against was what I am calling the *naqlī*, or transmission-based method. This method was in fact probably dominant in most places at most times, having a well-regarded pedigree in the methods of the *hadith* scholars. *Naqlī* histories reproduced and collected historical reports from the oral testimony of witnesses (often handed down via chains of authorities) or from "trustworthy" written documents; in this they conformed to Baihaqī's own requirements. The difference was that they bracketed questions of whether a given report conformed to reason. This understanding of *naqlī* historiography puts it very close to what Khalidi refers to as "hadith historiography"—depending on what precisely the latter is. Hadith historiography often seems to be exclusively underpinned by the use of the chain of transmission (*isnād*), but Khalidi notes, for instance, that Ibn Isḥāq's eighth-century *Biography of the Prophet* does not always provide chains of transmission but sometimes refers simply to a named or unnamed informant (Khalidi 1994, 39). Later historians like Mīrḵhwānd, who practiced source citation referring to earlier texts rather than to oral testimony, should also be understood as *naqlī* because their textual sources are in effect links in a chain of transmission.

A kind of manifesto of *naqlī* historiography can be found in Muḥammad b. Jarīr al-Ṭabarī's canonical *Ta'rīkh al-rusul wa al-mulūk* (History of prophets and kings):

> We rely in most of what we describe in this book of ours on traditions and reports from our Prophet—upon whom be blessings and peace—and from pious ancestors before us, to the exclusion of rational or mental deduction since most of it is an account of past events and present happenings, and these cannot be comprehended by rational inference and deduction. (Ṭabarī 1960, 58, quoted in Khalidi 1994, 76)

This quotation is well chosen by Khalidi for its explicit rejection of the role of the intellect (*'aql*) in historiography. The notion of a self-subsistent transmission, unsullied by judgments made by reason, is central to Ṭabarī's conception of historiography. As Khalidi points out, Ṭabarī places historiography squarely in the category of the transmitted sciences (*manqūlāt*) as opposed to the intellectual sciences (*ma'qūlāt*) and denies the intellectual faculty the right to submit historical reports to a trial on its own terms. The reality of a report could be established only by means of a transmission (*naql*) that either was well attested by a number of transmitters or was attested to by a trustworthy authority (the Prophet or ʿAlī b. Abī Ṭālib, for example). Therefore, even reports that were repugnant to the intellect were allowable (*jāʾiz*) as long as they were well transmitted (Khalidi 1994, 76–77), a point that needs to be borne in mind when we consider reports of apparently impossible events and beings like the Sīmurġh.

Given that Firdausī's *Shāhnāmah* could be understood as history, it was possible for it to be the basis for derivative histories such as the *Tārīkh-i dil-gushā* and the *Surūr-i sulṭānī*, both of which can now be identified as *naqlī*. Thaʿālibī's *Choice Reports of the Persian Kings* has been mentioned above as one of the few histories aside from these two that included the Sīmurġh. *Choice Reports* is much older than Tawakkul Beg's and Surūr's histories; it was written for the Ġhaznawid governor of Ḳhurāsān, Abū al-Muẓaffar Naṣr b. Sabuktagīn, in the tenth century CE.[5] Nearly contemporaneous with Firdausī's *Shāhnāmah*, it is not derived from Firdausī's book but probably drew upon the same sources.[6] It also drew upon Arabic histories that are well known to us. According to its editor, Thaʿālibī lists his sources in the unpublished portion of the work, and they include canonical histories such as those of Ṭabarī, Ḥamzah al-Iṣfahānī, and Ibn Ḳhurradādhbih (Zotenberg 1900, xixff.). Thaʿālibī is less firm than Ṭabarī when it comes to accepting marvelous accounts, but he submits to the principles of the *naqlī* method. Consider, for example, his comments regarding the piece of history ridiculed by Ġhālib, the Sīmurġh's foster parentage of Zāl:

> I do not take any responsibility for this story. If it had not been for its fame in every place and time, and upon every tongue, and its use as a means to delight and amuse kings into wakefulness, I would never have written it. In those first times, many strange things happened, such as the attainment of the age of one thousand years by a single person from among his family, and the subjection of the jinns and satans by kings. (Thaʿālibī 1900, 69–70)

Tha'ālibī seems to have a difficult time swallowing the Sīmurġh's existence, and yet he yields to the necessity of including the report on the basis of the abundance of its transmitters. He leaves his readers to form their own conclusions, after chiming in with his caveats. Despite his qualms, he is unwilling to submit entirely to rational norms. He argues that, in faraway times, things that his contemporaries would have found far-fetched *did* happen.[7] Tha'ālibī's wavering is remarkably similar to Yāqūt al-Rūmī's reluctance to credit some of the accounts that he records, although he submits to the wide field of possibility that God's power provides. He writes, "I am skeptical of such things and shrink away from them, discharging myself to the reader of responsibility over the truthfulness of these matters"—this is followed by his vindication of his own sincerity even in transmitting what might be identifiable as a lie (quoted in Zadeh 2010, 36). Tha'ālibī, in the same boat as Yāqūt, Ṭabarī, and many others, was merely submitting to *naqlī* methods when he included the Sīmurġh in his history, and in both cases the *sincerity* of the authors was not in question because marvelous beings and events were possible, however far-fetched.

When we come to examine instances of historiographical intertexts in the *qiṣṣah* of Ḥātim Ta'i, it will become clearer how *naqlī* histories and romances could be "mistaken" for one another. Or, rather, it will become apparent how what one audience member would identify as a romance could be identified by another as history. The principle enabling their inter-identifiability, however, should already be clear. Because transmissionist historians simply provided transmitted reports without making definite claims regarding their truth or falsehood according to rational judgment, what mattered was simply the transmittedness of the reports. Ġhālib's levity with regard to the *mumtana' al-wuqū'* portions of the *Shāhnāmah* may at first glance appear to be evidence that he considered these portions as *qiṣṣah*-ish misfits in what was otherwise a history. But, given that he later writes about Rustam as a *historical* model for Amīr Ḥamzah in the *qiṣṣah* of Amīr Ḥamzah, it seems that ultimately Ġhālib accepts the Sīmurġh as "historical" in the bare sense that it appears in a history, and the absurdity of its real existence and its having reared Rustam as its chick is a secondary consideration. As Zadeh (2010, 35) observes, what matters is not the truth or falsehood but the narration itself. Human reason was in any case deficient and exceeded by the divine creative decree, as partisans of the *naqlī* method like Ṭabarī, T͟haʿālibī, and Yāqūt affirmed. Therefore, that which broke with custom (*ḳhāriq al-ʿādah*), and even that which defied reason, was not to be brushed aside altogether.

Factuality, the representation of what has incontrovertibly happened in the past, was not necessarily the goal of *naqlī* historiography at all. What was important was the sincerity of the narrator, and narrations could be sincere without being factual. We can do no better, in that case, to seize upon sincerity rather than factuality as the differentiating criterion between the two genres of *qiṣṣah* and *tārīkh*, at least for nonrationalist audiences. But how was sincerity recognized, and why would any reader be convinced of the sincerity of a historian like Firdausī or Surūr?

The Sincerity Effect

In his thirteenth-century cosmography, Yāqūt al-Rūmī wrote, "I have mentioned many things which rational minds would reject. . . . Yet, nothing should be deemed as too great for the power of the Creator or the wiles of creation [*qudraṭ al-ḳhāliq wa ḥiyal al-maḳhlūq*]" (quoted in Zadeh 2010, 34).[8] The power of the divine creative decree obviated, for many Muslims, any "procedure by which one can separate the true from the false in history since the command must always be admissible" (Khalidi 1994, 76). Thus a historian like Ṭabarī or Yāqūt did not need to be concerned with such a separation. They only needed to be taken as sincere. Yāqūt was quite explicit in this regard: "I am sincere [*ṣādiq*]," he wrote, "in adducing [falsifiable accounts] the way I have adduced them, so that you know what has been said, whether it be true or false" (quoted in Zadeh 2010, 34).[9]

It is impossible to judge the intention of a writer or narrator when they claim sincerity. The purported writer of the *Ḥātim-nāmah*, Mullā ʿAbd Allāh, claimed in his preface that he constructed the narrative out of "trustworthy" histories:

> It so happened that this lowly slave of God, the dust of the foot of God's creation, Mullā 'Abd Allāh, desired to compose a book of histories. Meanwhile one of the friends of this grape plucker of the field of speech arrived and said, "I want you to apprise me of the qualities of Ḥātim b. Ṭai, who risked his head and his life in the path of God." This wretch said, "If God the Exalted wills, I will busy myself with the compositions having to do with that Yemeni king's particulars, and I will write down whatever I am able to verify on this subject from the trusted histories." (Mullā 'Abd Allāh 1799, fol. 1a)

It is possible to view Mullā 'Abd Allāh as a hustler who thought it was good marketing to present a tale of *ṭilism*s and woman-faced birds as a historical account. Certainly the usual reception of the *Ḥātim-nāmah*, evidenced in its alternative title, the *Qiṣṣah-i Ḥātim Ṭā'ī*, was as a *qiṣṣah*, at least in terms of the genre that dominated the work. Whether Mulla 'Abd Allah's claim to sincerity was intended to be sincere or not does not matter so much as the fact that he made the claim as well as his ability or inability to produce the *effect* of sincerity.

Whether or not Mullā 'Abd Allāh or Yaqūt al-Rūmī are in fact sincere, they attempt to produce what I am calling a "sincerity effect." In the vocabulary of John Austin's speech act theory, we might say that we are dealing basically with "illocutionary" sincerity. For Austin, an illocution is a speech act, like the act of promising, that is effectively accomplished whether or not the speaker intends it to be accomplished (Austin 1975).[10] In his preface, Mullā 'Abd Allāh in effect *claims* to be sincere, no matter whether he is in fact sincere or not. Therefore, he may be able to produce a sincerity effect, if the mode of the claim or the context in which he makes the claim does not cause his readers to doubt him. If it is successful, the sincerity effect of a narrative should allow the narrative's audience to identify and receive it as a history rather than as a romance. And as we have seen, it was possible for narratives that might otherwise have been received as romances to be taken for *naqlī* histories. This was because of the presence in the narrative of elements that, in the minds of the audience, made claims to sincerity and produced a successful sincerity effect. What were these elements?

At the very beginning of the *Ḥātim-nāmah*, we find a device that would have been able to produce a sincerity effect due to its resemblance to historiographical devices. Following the opening genealogy of Ḥātim—or, in certain manuscripts, immediately following the divine and prophetic praises—there appears what I will call the transmission claim: "The narrators of reports and transmitters of surviving accounts narrate that . . ." Numerous prose romances would begin with a formula of this kind, ranging from a simple "they have related" to highly ornate versions such as those in the early eighteenth-century *Maḥbūb al-qulūb* (Beloved of hearts): "The fruit of this little matter came into my hands thanks to a certain arborist of the orchards of reports and surviving accounts, in the date-palm grove of speech and expression" (Mumtāz 1957, 148). Implicit in these formulas is the assertion that the account to follow is merely being *retold* by the narrator, who received it from another transmitter. In his study of the marvel-laden twelfth-century history the *Chachnāmah*, Manan Ahmed (2008, 118–19) has called short transmission claims of this kind "pseudo-*isnād*s," that is, "broad, generic *isnād* . . . , which follow literary conventions." These *isnād*-like objects, while they may not be as impressive or authoritative as long chains of transmission, can help to produce the sincerity effect of a history or *qiṣṣah*.

Among the key devices of *naqlī* historiography, the *isnād*, or chain of transmission, has been particularly seductive to scholars reflecting on the genre (see, e.g., Khalidi 1994, 22–23).[11] The fascination with it is understandable, for this device, which legitimates the entire corpus of hadith, represents the historical endeavor at its most optimistic. The name of each transmitter is a link interlocking with its predecessor, forming a chain that recedes further and further into the past, culminating in the original authority who was contemporary with the Prophet himself. This eyewitness, usually one of the Companions, anchors the whole skein in the firm ground of the first century Hijri. Khalidi (1994, 22) remarks that "the *isnad* was in reality a chain of *authorities* appended to each hadith" to compensate for the loss of the original witness—hence, the importance of the "science of men" (*'ilm al-rijāl*) for *ḥadīth* critics who needed to establish transmitters as authorities by proving their trustworthiness.

The hadith genre exerted an influence over histories written during the 'Abbāsid period, many of which used *isnāds*. Abū al-Faraj al-Iṣfahānī's *Book of Songs* (*Kitāb al-Āġhānī*), which in the tenth century gathered together reports of Ḥātim as well as numerous other poets, presented its reader with an impressive forked chain of transmission for an account in which Ḥātim's daughter Saffānah was taken prisoner by the Muslims and interviewed by the Prophet:

> This was reported to me by Aḥmad b. 'Ubaid Allāh b. 'Ammār. He said: "I was told by 'Abd Allāh b. 'Amr b. Abū Sa'd, who said: 'I was told by Sulaimān b. Al-Rabī' b. Hishām the Kūfan. . . .'" Besides, I found [the report] in some Kūfan manuscripts by Sulaimān b. Al-Rabī', more complete than the former [narration], so I copied it and composed the two together. He [Sulaimān] said: "I was told by 'Abd al-Ḥamīd b. Ṣāliḥ al-Mauṣilī al-Burjamī, who said: 'I was told by Zakariyā b. 'Abd Allāh b. Yazīd al-Ṣuhbānī, who had it from his father, who had it from Kamīl b. Ziyād al-Naḳh'ī, from 'Alī—upon whom be peace!'" (Abū al-Faraj al-Iṣfahānī 1970, 6694)

It would be easy to describe the history of Islamicate historiography in terms of a steady diminution of authority chains to merely formulaic transmission claims, signifying the degradation of historiographical rigor. But this would be a caricature, for there was no golden age in which every historical report was upheld by a felicitous chain of authority. Nevertheless, it is only natural that chains of authority should be increasingly replaced by more bibliographical modes of source indication. As we can see in the case of the *Kitab al-Āġhānī*'s chain of authority for the report of Saffānah bt. Ḥātim's captivity, reliable books could be auxiliary components of *isnāds*. Abū al-Faraj al-Iṣfahānī uses Sulaimān b. Rabī''s manuscript to *reproduce* the chain of authority leading back to 'Alī b. Abī Ṭālib. What we see as time passes is the practice of citing books to *point to* chains of authority without going to the length of reproducing those chains—for once a chain has been established and recorded, it is only necessary to direct the audience to the record. This change was already occurring in the tenth century; Peacock's (2007, 76–77) study of Bal'amī's Persian *Translation of Ṭabarī's History* (*Tarjamah-i Tārīḵh-i Ṭabarī*) makes much of the fact that Bal'amī forbore from copying the *isnād*s that Ṭabarī included in the *History of Prophets and Kings*.[12] Just as often, however, a bibliographical citation would point to an *isnād*-less report that derived its authority in some other manner.

If, for "hadith historiography," the authority empowering historical reports was the sincere witness at the end of an *isnād*—Muḥammad, 'Alī, 'Ā'ishah, and so on—this authority soon transferred itself to books like Ibn Isḥāq's *Biography of the Prophet*, whose venerability was often but not always derived from hadith-historiographical methods. Mullā 'Abd Allāh and other writers wrote vaguely of a corpus of "trustworthy histories" (*tawārīḵh-i mu'tabarah*); this phrase is used in many a romance as well as in histories. As in the case of the storyteller's *isnād*, the appeal to trustworthy histories is double-edged. On the one hand, it is airy enough to appear evasive and to signify a *qiṣṣah*-fied nonseriousness; on the other hand, it indicates the existence of a well-established canon that is too well known to require detailed description. Mīrḵhwānd, the fifteenth-century historian attached to the court of the Timurid ruler Sulṭān Ḥusain Bāyqārah, is an example of a writer who does describe a canon of great historiographical works, mentioned throughout his history the *Rauẓat al-ṣafā*. His list of trustworthy histories in Arabic and Persian includes many of the fixtures that we would recognize today: the *tārīḵh*s of Ibn Isḥāq, Ṭabarī, Ibn Kat͟hīr, Baihaqī, Dīnawarī, and so forth (Mīr Ḵhwānd 1959, 17). The canonicity of these histories would likely be corroborated by a survey of the frequency of their manuscripts in the archives.

Such a canon of historiography is an excellent indicator of the makeup of that part of the hypotextual repository of elite readers that was understood according to the expectations tied to the history genre. That is, reports, even if they were embedded within works understood as *qiṣṣah*s, would be recognized as historical if they were repetitions of reports given in a historical work within the audience's hypotextual repository. The genre identification of such reports could be effected even without source indication because of the power of visibility. Passages from canonical books, at the zenith of their success and visibility, become recognizable without any hints to the memory apart from their own words, particularly among the cognoscenti within oral-mnemonic cultures. Books like the Quran or the Bible or corpuses of works such as those of Sa'dī and Shakespeare are prime examples.

In the Islamicate world, the best example of the power of recognizability without source indication (*tanbīh*) is the Quran—so much so that entire intertextual "crafts" or figures (*ṣanaʿāt*) were consecrated to intertextual situations involving the divine Lecture. The figures most frequently enumerated were *ʿiqd*—verse paraphrase of fragments of the Quran, with optional source indication (*ishārah*)—and *iqtibās*—word-for-word citation of fragments from the Quran, without source indication. In the case of *ʿiqd*, source indication was permissible because of the possibility that the process of recognition might be impaired by the looseness of the paraphrase. An instance of *iqtibās* was likely to be recognized, because Muslims placed such a high value upon memorization (*ḥifẓ*) of the Quran. Where Quran memorization had been a part of an individual's education, *iqtibās* was almost sure to be successful, and even otherwise the discursive air was so thick with fragments of the Quran that they would have become lodged in the memories of many if not most Muslims, as well as some non-Muslims.

While *iqtibās* is a particularly efficacious and clear example of the process of intertextual recognition without source indication, it also had its more general, non-Quranic counterpart in the intertextual craft of *taẓmīn*, described by Taftazānī (2001, 725) as follows:

> [*Taẓmīn* occurs when] the poem incorporates something of another poem within itself . . . , with an indication of the source, provided that the other poem is not well known among the poetic savants. If it is well known, there is no need to indicate the source.

In the case of *taẓmīn*, a distinction is made between intertexts that require source indication to make the intertextuality (i.e., the *taẓmīn* itself) work and those that, like the Quran, can be assumed to be well known (*mashhūr*) enough to be recognizable without any such hints, at least to a certain class of aesthetes whose business it is to carry around the cited verses in their memories. The fame or visibility of a work is concomitant with its canonicity, and in the cases of canonical works of poetry like the *Bostān* of Sa'dī, the *Haft paikar* of Niẕami, and the *ġhazal*s of Ḥāfiẕ, *taẓmīn* would be successful without source indication.

A similar principle would apply to a historiographical canon such as the one that Mīrḳhwānd describes. Even without the aid of a chain of authority or source indication, a report from a canonical historical work would have been recognized as "historical" by any reader or listener with a memory of its presence within the canonical source text. For example, the captivity of Ḥātim Ṭ̈ā'ī's daughter as described in the *Qiṣṣah-i Ḥātim Ṭ̈ā'ī* is not materially different from the historical account given in Mīrḳhwānd, as Duncan Forbes noted in his translation (Ḥaidarī 1972, 244; Mīr Ḳhwānd 1959, 497–98; D. Forbes 1830, 181). And, as we have already seen, it had long been available in the *Kitab al-Āġhānī* with a lengthy chain of authorities. In Arabic it would also have been available via Ibn Kat͟hīr's (1964, 108–9) and Ibn Isḥāq's (1963, 1000–1001) histories of the Prophet, as well as in any derivative biographies of the Prophet that may have been based on these works. Similarly, the sequel to the *Ḥātim-nāmah*, the *Seven Deeds of Justice of Ḥātim Ṭ̈ai* (*Haft inṣāf-i Ḥātim*), uses as its framing narrative the story of the courtship of Ḥātim and his wife, the princess Māwiyyah bt. 'Afzar ("Haft inṣāf-i Ḥātim" 2007, 19–31). This story is recounted in the *Āġhānī* as an account narrated at the request of the caliph Mu'āwiyah (Abū al-Faraj al-Iṣfahānī 1970, 6715–20). For an audience with a recollection of the historical genre of previous texts in which the account has appeared, the account would likely be accepted as sincere. This memory acts as a surrogate for a more explicit historiographical device such as an *isnād* or source indication.

The sincerity effect of the romance is enhanced, on the one hand, by such recognitions of *substantial* intertexts, in which the content of the element recognized as historical is traceable to a hypotext that is understood by the audience as a history. On the other hand, it is also possible to recognize *formally* historiographical intertexts. The transmission claim that begins most romances is a special instance of this form of intertext, as are some of the formulas used by the Iranian storyteller Mashdī Galīn Ḵhānum (2011). Another example is the genealogy (*nasab*) found in the *Ḥātim-nāmah*:

> The narrators of reports and conveyors of records relate that the account of the parentage of Ḥātim Ṭai is as follows: Ḥātim son of Ṭai son of Kahlān son of Rasn son of Naḵhshab son of Qaḥtān son of Hūd son of Umāyā.

This genealogy is followed by an account of Ḥātim's forbears from Umāyā down to Ṭai. Umāyā's son Hūd, who has inherited the chieftaincy of a village from his father, leads a coup against the Yemeni ruler of the previous dynasty and becomes king in his stead. Hūd and his descendants rule Yemen in peace until Naḵhshab's iniquitous reign, which is emulated by his son Rasn, who gives his father a taste of his own medicine by rebelling against him. Finally, Kahlān, son of Rasn, restores tranquility to the country and begets Ṭai, the father of Ḥātim ("Haft sair-i Ḥātim" 2007, 59–60). Seven generations of Ḥātim's forebears are presented to the audience in a form that many would have recognized as a standard genealogy. The *nasab* genre is well established as a historiographical subgenre prevalent in the Islamicate world from the 'Abbasid period onward. A footnote in Duncan Forbes's translation apprises us of the translator's low opinion of Ḥātim's genealogy as offered in the *Ḥātim-nāmah*. "This account," writes Forbes, "is rather questionable; at least, the translator has not been able to find any account of [Ḥātim] that agrees with this description" (D. Forbes 1830, 1). Indeed, the *Ḥātim-nāmah* version differs vastly from the version of Ḥātim's genealogy given in the eighth/ninth century by Ibn Kalbī.[13] On the authority of Ibn Kalbī and Ibn A'rābī, Abū al-Faraj al-Iṣfahānī repeats the same genealogy, with some lacunas, in the tenth century (Abū al-Faraj al-Iṣfahānī 1970, 6691). Even as late as 1486, Kāshifī (1941, 6) was able to reproduce the genealogy more or less correctly. The *Ḥātim-nāmah* is not completely off the mark; the names of Ṭai, Kahlān, and Qaḥṭān appear in the genealogy that it presents, as they do in Ibn Kalbī, Abū al-Faraj al-Iṣfahānī, and Kāshifī.[14] But for the most part the genealogy cannot be traced in its substance to any previous version of which I am aware. It is its *form*, then, that is important, along with the historiographical genre that its form announces. The simple recognition of the genealogical form would trigger the suspicion of historicity, and in this manner the genealogy, like the transmission claim or the presence of historiographical narratives in the *Ḥātim-nāmah*, is able to strengthen the romance's sincerity effect.

We have seen that the sincerity effect or appearance of *ṣidq*, which is generally consecrated to historiographical works, can make itself felt in works widely identified as romances, such as the *Ḥātim-nāmah*s, and it can be broadly stated that it does this through either formal or substantial intertexts. It would be rash to suppose that such localized manifestations of the history genre necessarily saturate the entire work and give it a uniformly historical coloring. We might say that the strongest effect that devices such as nameless transmission claims have on the genre of the work may rather be to invest it with their own indeterminacy. On the other hand, the possibility of saturation remains. The question is open: do these splashes of apparent sincerity continue to seep unchecked through the audience's reception of the work, or are they insoluble in its fluid, and do they therefore remain local?

At first glance, these historiographical grafts do appear to be incapable of spreading, because of the unhistoriographical nature of the work in which they are implanted. But where does this impression come from? First, it comes from the apprehension of metatextual genre designations such as the title "*Qiṣṣah-i Ḥātim Ṭā'ī*" or from orally expressed statements with the same effect. Where these are not available or in question, however, a sliver of history such as the account of Ḥātim's daughter and the Prophet Muḥammad appears incongruous in its "host text" because of a perception of the incredible nature of the events between which it is sandwiched. The story of Ḥātim's daughter is recounted in the context of an exchange between Ḥātim and the fairy king Shams Shāh, who claims to have rebelled against the prophet Sulaimān and to have been turned into a serpent for his insubordination, until the time of his salvation at Ḥātim's pious hands (Ḥaidarī 1972, 242–43). The introductory chapter begins with the conventional *isnād* and a genealogy of Ḥātim that appears unproblematically historical but ends with the shamed retreat of a hungry lion at Ḥātim's generous readiness to offer himself and his horse to satisfy the predator's appetite ("Haft sair-i Ḥātim" 2007, 62).

These events are incredible to modern readers who have learned to bow to certain epistemological strictures and for whom factuality, rather than sincerity, is paramount. These readers would consider absurd the very existence of serpent fairies or the ability of a lion to understand human speech and express his humiliation. For them, epistemological dogmas preclude the possibility of either of these episodes' being factual or historical. It is not immediately clear, however, that such apparent absurdities would have been absurd to all Indian readers. For them, much more may have seemed to be possible than it is for "us," if we are the kind of people who do not believe in fairies.

5

Reason and Romance in the Age of the Novel

THE TRANSLATION OF THE terms *qiṣṣah* and *dāstān* by the English word "romance" reproduced in late nineteenth-century India a century-old British genre system that had already devalued the romance genre in relation to the Western novel. It had done so on the premise that the romance was marred by its conformity to an outdated and irrational epistemology. The romance/novel binary determined both genre codes in a very focused manner, despite the principle that a genre's position in the genre system is always determined by its relationship to a multitude of genres, never merely by a dyadic relation. Similarly, we may say that the *qiṣṣah*'s place in the genre systems across much of the Islamicate world had been most clearly locatable relative to the proximate genre of history. But the *qiṣṣah*/romance's devaluation at the end of the nineteenth century took place as another proximate but opposing genre appeared in the Indian genre system: the novel.

Before the incursion of colonial epistemologies onto the Indian scene, the *qiṣṣah* had been able to maintain a respectable position in the genre system that had prevailed among Persian-knowing and Urdu-speaking elites. Its ability to do so was in large part due to its resonance with dominant precolonial epistemologies that circumscribed the role of the intellect (*ʿaql*) and privileged the heart as the organ best placed to encompass reality. It should not be imagined that epistemologies privileging the heart were simply antirationalist or opposed to the intellect altogether; the intellect was nearly always given its place. As the previous chapter has shown, it is also naive to think that nonrationalist epistemologies had the run of the place. In fact, they always coexisted with and clashed against precolonial Islamicate rationalisms. By the middle of the nineteenth century, a new rationalist thought system was taking shape among Indian elites, through the influence of British ideas. For a while, the main effect of British intellectual dominion was primarily to provide a new authority under which precolonial epistemologies congregated in a new formation. We see the power of British authority in the historicizations of the *qiṣṣah* of Princess Bakāwalī (*Qiṣṣah-i Gul-i Bakāwalī*) from the 1870s to the 1890s. Both the critiques of the mendacious *qiṣṣah* genre and the truth-finding moves discernible in the histories of Bakāwalī were less colonial than they were reactive to the challenge of colonialist thought and the splendor of the technology to which it gave rise. Yet these developments, however conservative in a sense, signal the rise to prominence of a new epistemology compounded of pieces of the colonial thought system and the intellectual reactions of the colonized. This epistemology, most often identified with Sir Sayyid Aḥmad Ḳhān, made reason and "nature" touchstones for the evaluation of reality. It was coming into its own at the same time that the genre of the novel made its appearance in the Indian genre system. Urdu verbal art (now beginning to be understood in Western-derived terms as "literature") became subject to a critique based on rationalist and *necharī* (naturalist) principles. While the blight of naturalism upon the Urdu *ġhazal* is by now well known thanks to Pritchett's study (1994), the most prominent new literary critics, including Ḥālī, Āzād, and Sharar, also subjected the poetic and prose *qiṣṣah* genre to attacks on the basis of its nonconformance to nature and its inability to present audiences with an effective exemplarity because of its representation of a world contrary to the world of reason and sense.

As the power of the new epistemology waxed, it elevated the novel genre over and against the now devalued "romance." The formation of a genre code is a process driven by ideology. This principle is exemplified by the shifting hierarchy between the *qiṣṣah* and novel genres, amounting to a reconfiguration of genres within the system. The formation of the *qiṣṣah*/novel hierarchy was symptomatic of an epistemological and ideological shift introduced thanks to colonialism. But this shift was an echo of one that had already occurred in Britain itself in the eighteenth century, the reactivation of which reveals itself in the translation that equates "romance" with *qiṣṣah/dāstān/ḥikāyat*. We need to grasp the history of this mistranslation to understand why we need to jettison or resignify the term "romance" as it applies to texts like the *Dāstān-i Amīr Ḥamzah*, the *Shāhnāmah*, or the *Qiṣṣah-i Gul-i Bakāwalī*.

The deformation of the *qiṣṣah* genre that was effected in the late nineteenth and early twentieth centuries would not have mattered a great deal to us today had it been corrected between then and now. Of course, there is nothing "correct" or "incorrect" about generic flux from the standpoint of genre criticism; insofar as a genre is historically formed, one needs to accept and then to inspect its formation. Genres are made to change all the time. But we can certainly disagree with the ideology, and in this case the epistemology, that made the change. The new epistemologies brought by the British and accepted by Urdu-speaking elites unfortunately continued to affect critics' understanding of the *qiṣṣah* genre through the middle of the twentieth century, when the great studies of the Urdu *qiṣṣah* were made by men like Gyān Chand Jain and Waqār 'Azīm. These studies, especially those of Jain and Farmān Fatḥpūrī (*Urdū kī manẓūm dāstāneṅ*), were brilliant, monumental, and extremely influential upon practically everyone who cared about the Urdu *qiṣṣah* genre. But despite their general sympathy toward the genre, these critics evaluated it not in terms of the epistemologies of the periods prior to the nineteenth century but according to the devaluing ideology of their immediate predecessors. Their studies therefore only perpetuated the devaluation of the *qiṣṣah* genre as a grouping of primitive, absurd, and ineffectual texts.

In Search of Bakāwalī

The wonders proffered by texts of the *qiṣṣah* genre had always had their critics. Criticism was present even before the coming of the colonial thought systems that played such havoc with the genre's value at the end of the nineteenth century. A couple of decades after the Rebellion of 1857 and the establishment of British imperial rule over India, new critiques of the *qiṣṣah* were emerging that were clearly indebted to a rationalism of colonial origin but that did not go as far as later rationalist or "naturalist" critiques. A set of critiques made from the 1870s onward targeted the popular *Tale of the Bakāwalī Flower* (*Qiṣṣah-i Gul-i Bakāwalī*) and its representation of the escapades of *parī*s and the follies of their demonic associates. We find these critiques in the Urdu accounts of Sir Richard Temple's quest to infiltrate the swamp-encircled fortress of the *qiṣṣah*'s eponymous hero, Princess Bakāwalī, in the Central Provinces of India. The attempts to correct and historicize the *Tale of the Bakāwalī Flower* echo precolonial rationalist critiques of the dangerous proximity of the genres of *qiṣṣah* and *tārīkh*, while they lean heavily on the authority of British wisdom and respond to colonial developments.

In 1866, Sir Richard Temple was chief commissioner of the Central Provinces of British India. Scholars of *qiṣṣah*s are more familiar with Temple's son, Richard Carnac Temple, the author of *Legends of the Panjab*, a three-volume collection of tales from throughout the Punjab (Mir 2010, 101–3). Urdu histories, however, suggest that the father had a taste for adventure to rival the son's. They inform us that, in 1866, Temple Senior launched an expedition with 100 to 125 Englishmen riding elephants to traverse an enchanted swamp and gain entry into the fortress of a princess of old.[1] The swamp-encircled fortress, located near Amarkantak in the *ẓila'* of Mandala, was known as the Fortress of Bakāwalī. Of an evening, mysterious vapors would be seen lifting up from the swamp, and in the fortress itself fires could often be seen burning, as if lit by ghostly inhabitants. The princess who had once dwelled therein had been a princess of no ordinary kind. It was alleged that she had been the "fairy" (*parī*) Bakāwalī, the protagonist of the *Tale of the Bakāwalī Flower*.

Along with the elephant-riding Englishmen and their "doctors," the expedition was accompanied by members of the Gond community. The Gonds and other locals living around the Maikal hills believed that the swamp was ensorcelled, protected by a powerful *ṭilism*—an enchantment thousands of years old. The swamp itself had been created as part of this enchantment to safeguard the Fortress of Bakāwalī from intruders (Muḥammad Ya'qūb Lakhnawī 1876, 18–19). The inquisitive Sir Richard Temple (so allege the Urdu histories) believed that, in sufficient numbers, a horde of white men on elephants could penetrate the *ṭilismī* swamp. But hardly had they gone seven miles into the muck before the slimy denizens of the swamp—snakes, scorpions, and leeches—attacked the elephants with such ferocity that the expedition was sent scurrying back to the outer limits of the *ṭilism*. After the failure of this attempt, Temple pondered the merits and demerits of sending observers above the fortress in a hot-air balloon (Muḥammad Ya'qūb Lakhnawī 1876, 20). But this plan, too, was abandoned, and the *ṭilism* of Bakāwalī withheld its mysteries from the colonial administrator, as it had done for so many thousands of years.[2]

The historical studies of Bakāwalī written in Urdu were framed as refutations and responses to one of the best-known *qiṣṣah*s in the Urdu language. The first written version of the *Tale of the Bakāwalī Flower* was composed in Persian in the eighteenth century. Its author, 'Izzat Allāh Bangālī, initially told the tale orally to his beloved, the handsome Naẓar Muḥammad. After hearing it, Naẓar Muḥammad advised his lover to write it down in Persian and wash the *qiṣṣah* clean of the "stench of the language of the people of India," leading Rashīd Ḥasan Ḳhān to venture that 'Izzat Allāh may have initially narrated the *qiṣṣah* in Bengali rather than in Persian ('Izzat Allāh Bangālī 2007, 609–10; Ḳhān 2007, 11–67). True to his beloved's behest, 'Izzat Allāh began writing the tale down, but to his infinite distress, Naẓar Muḥammad passed away in 1134 H (1722). Friends convinced the bereaved 'Izzat Allāh to abandon the idea of tearing his manuscript to shreds in his grief, and he completed the tale. In the nineteenth century, many prosaic and poetical versions were penned. The most famous of these were the 1803 Fort William College prose *Maẕhab-i 'ishq* by Nihāl Chand Lāhorī along with Dayā Shankar Nasīm's maṡnawī written in 1254 H (1837–38). Nasīm's poem, the *Gulzār-i Nasīm* (Nasīm's flower garden), was one of the best-known Urdu maṡnawīs of the nineteenth century. Into the twentieth century, a controversy raged regarding the *Gulzār-i Nasīm*'s rhetorical features, a battle of critics that can only have increased the maśnawī's visibility (Ḳhān 2007, 124–40; Ryan 2013).

The Tale of the Bakāwalī Flower begins with the story of Prince Tāj al-Mulūk's quest to find a cure for the blindness of his father, King Zain al-Mulūk. This cure is the Bakāwalī flower, which lies within a pond in the impenetrable garden of the fairy princess Bakāwalī. After an unplanned encounter with a hungry demon (*de'o* or *dew*), Tāj al-Mulūk avoids the division of his flesh into a multitude of kebabs by cooking halwa for the famished creature. The grateful demon directs Tāj al-Mulūk to the residence of his younger sister, the demoness (*de'oni*) Ḥammālah. After some dalliance and marriage with Ḥammālah's human housemate Maḥmūdah, the prince obtains the aid of Ḥammālah in constructing a tunnel into the Garden of Bakāwalī. Once in the garden, he finds the pool and plucks the flower. On his way out, he comes across the princess's bed. He stops to gaze upon the beauty of the sleeping Bakāwalī and is unable to resist slipping her ring off of her finger and replacing it with his own before going back to cure his father. Upon awakening, Bakāwalī is vexed at the flower's disappearance; she dons the raiment of a man, discovers the prince, saves him from some difficulties into which he has fallen, and befriends Ḥammālah and Maḥmūdah. Unfortunately, Bakāwalī's mother, Jamīlah, discovers that Bakāwalī has fallen in love with a son of Adam. She traps Tāj al-Mulūk inside a *ṭilism* and imprisons her daughter.[3] Tāj al-Mulūk undergoes some odd adventures, becoming a woman for some time and giving birth to a child. However, he escapes with the help of another fairy and enlists the aid of that fairy's mother, Ḥusn-ārā. Ḥusn-ārā cleverly shows Jamīlah a picture of Tāj al-Mulūk and draws her attention to his fine moustache. The moustache convinces Jamīlah and soon Tāj al-Mulūk and Bakāwalī are married.[4]

Like many of the Fort William College *qiṣṣah*s, the *Tale of the Bakāwalī Flower* was very popular and quite widespread both in its printed forms and in its oral retellings. Pritchett shows that *qiṣṣah*s printed in the early years of commercially viable print (between 1849 and 1852) initially sold at a sluggish rate. Yet the Muṣṭafā'ī Press edition of *Gul-i Bakāwalī* (Kanpur,

1852) sold 200 copies in its first year, achieving much greater success than other *qiṣṣah*s from the same period, which sold from 10 to 78 copies in the first year of their printing (Pritchett 1985, 24). The wide circulation of the tale can be gauged from the evidence of a British folklorist, who heard a local telling of the story, very close to Nihāl Chand's version, as far south as Ceylon (Digby and Harrow 2000, 283). And clearly the story, taken as a description of local events, was well known in the Central Provinces of India, in the area surrounding the source of the Narbada River. The writers of several accounts of the "true story" of Bakāwalī were thus able both to critique the *qiṣṣah* as a mendacious representation of local history and to bank on the story's prominence, in *qiṣṣah* form, when they did so.

Several lithograph treatises on Temple's mission and the "truth" of Bakāwalī's life were printed from the 1870s to the early twentieth century.[5] The titles of the books provide their most prominent genre designations. The first such treatise of which we are aware was the 1876 *Guldastah-i Ḥairat, ma'rūf bah Tawārīkh-i Bakāwalī* (Bouquet of bewilderment, known as the Histories of Bakāwalī) by Muḥammad Ya'qūb Lakhnawi. The second part of the title clearly designated the account as a historical one, and on the title page the reader was also informed that "this matchless, worthy, and accurate treatise is well-established [*mustanad*] like other histories of the ancients" (see fig. 3). Muḥammad Ya'qūb put the work forward as a history on the basis of his local information gathering. He obtained the testimony of the local *taḥsīldār*, who possessed Temple's notes on the expedition, as well as the accounts narrated by the local Pinda community (Muḥammad Ya'qūb Lakhnawī 1876, 6).[6] The map of the Garden of Bakāwalī provided by the Amarkantak forest warden Mīr Qudrat 'Alī is another proof by which the book asserts that its genre is history (fig. 4).

The double title activates a double genre code, however. Muḥammad Ya'qūb's book was printed in his bustling hometown of Lucknow but deals with occurrences in the mysterious jungly Indian heartland. It is likely that some Lucknow city slickers were ready to believe that hidden wonders abounded in such forbidding regions of their country, even if their own deposed ruler Wājid 'Alī Shāh had been disappointed in discovering that his

3. *Guldastah-i Ḥairat* title page.

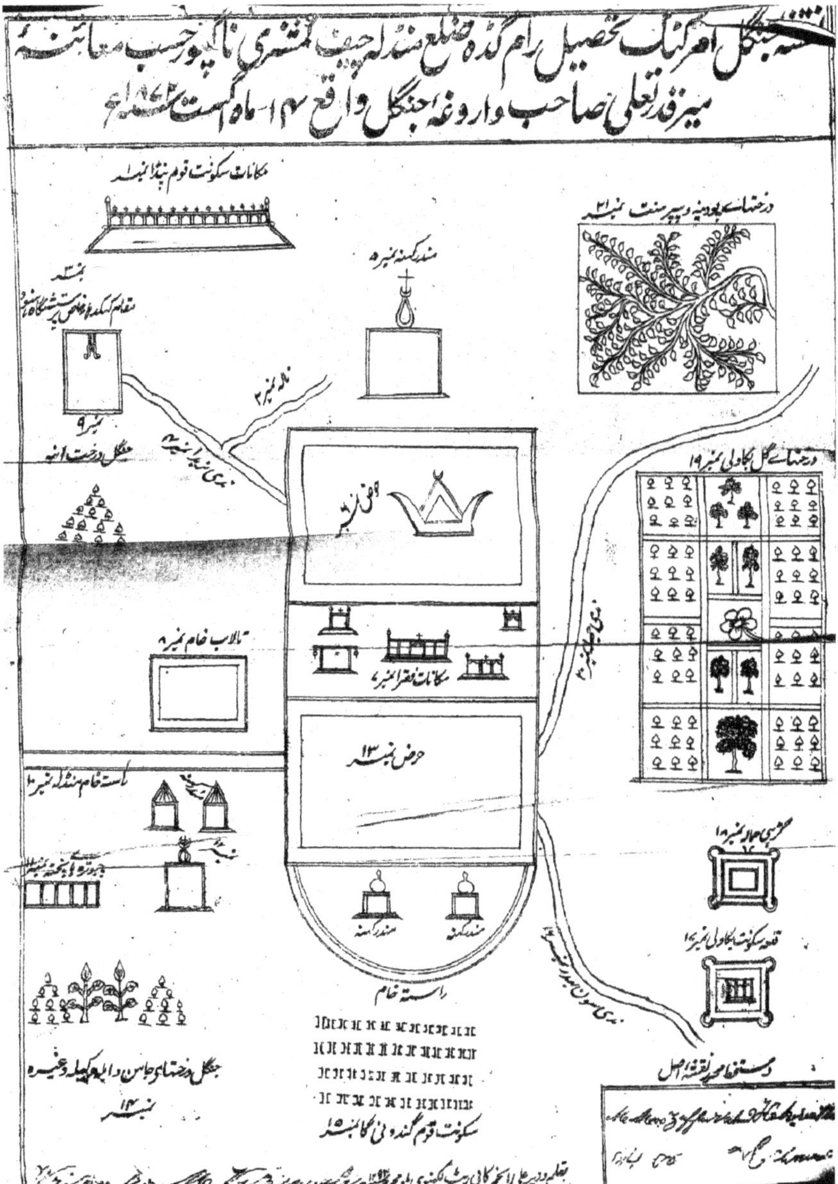

4. Map of Amarkantak jungle, including the Garden of Bakāwalī. *Guldastah-i Ḥairat*, appendix.

meetings with the king of the Jinn were attempts at extortion (Ṣafī 1984). The first (chronogrammatical) title, *Guldastah-i Ḥairat*, points the reader or the hesitant book buyer to the connection between Muḥammad Ya'qūb's history and the marvelous *qiṣṣah* that it seeks to supplement and emend. The book's self-description further disturbs the distinction between *qiṣṣah* and history, beyond the insinuations of its double title. Muḥammad Ya'qūb writes that the captivating *qiṣṣah* of Bakāwalī is well known in verse and in prose. But the "true reality" of Bakāwalī, her birthplace and residence, has never been written; only a story (*afsānah*) has been written (Muḥammad Ya'qūb Lakhnawī 1876, 3–4). This statement seems to contrast truthful histories and mendacious *qiṣṣah*s. But later on, Muḥammad Ya'qūb calls his book a "*qiṣṣah-i ġharīb*," a strange *qiṣṣah*. Even if we take this as a convention or wish to reduce the word *qiṣṣah* in this context to its most colorless meaning, we must note that the writer then proceeds to juxtapose the two genre designations in an unmistakable way. "The name of this *qiṣṣah* is the *Bouquet of Bewilderment*, known as *The Histories of Bakāwalī*" (Muḥammad Ya'qūb Lakhnawī 1876, 4). The intercontamination of the *qiṣṣah* and history genres that had already been common before colonialism was thus maintained even in this late British Raj-era text. Generic ambiguity was maintained even though certain *'aqlī* moves were employed in the treatise, as we shall see. It is quite likely that such an ambiguity was commercially profitable.

The other treatise that I have been able to see is the 1895 edition of *Tārīkh-i ṭilism-i Bakāwalī* (History of the ṭilism of Bakāwalī) written by Sayyid Muḥammad Ismā'īl Ḍāsnawī in 1888 and first printed at the end of 1894 and the beginning of 1895. According to Farmān Fatḥpūrī's (2006, 50–58) report on this treatise and its editions up to the year 1922, it appears to be the most detailed and successful account of the "reality" of Bakāwalī.[7] Muḥammad Ismā'īl's *Tārīkh* is longer and much more polemical than the *Guldastah-i Ḥairat*. Indeed, Muḥammad Ismā'īl presents the *Tārīkh* as an improvement not only upon the *qiṣṣah* but also upon the *Guldastah-i Ḥairat* itself, which is alleged to have misrepresented the history surrounding Bakāwalī in several places (Muḥammad Ismā'īl Ḍāsnawī

1895, 8). The title of the 1895 edition is clear with regard to the text's genre (see fig. 3), and this clarity is upheld by the body of the text, in which the *qiṣṣah* is disavowed with great energy.

Both the *Guldastah* and the *Tārīkh-i Ṭilism-i Bakāwalī* can be said to present the *Qiṣṣah-i Gul-i Bakāwalī* as a distortion of real historical events. Precolonial proponents of rationalism such as Fā'iz Dihlawī can be said to have dismissed unhistorical *qiṣṣah*s and *dāstān*s such as Firdausī's *Shāhnāmah* and Jāmī's *Yūsuf o Zulaikhā* in much the same manner in the eighteenth century. In this sense, what the "histories" of Bakāwalī were doing was a continuation of a previous trend. What was novel about the late nineteenth-century reduction of the *Tale of the Bakāwalī Flower* to an *'aqlī* history was its recourse to the authority of British ways of thinking.

The edition of the *Tārīkh-i Ṭilism-i Bakāwalī* cited here was printed in Meeruth by the Gulzār-i Muḥammadī Press. The director of the press, Muḥammad Khalīl, informs the reader in the book's opening pages of the mendacity of *The Bakāwalī Flower* and other such *qiṣṣah*s:

> The books *Gul-i Bakāwalī* and *Gulzar-i Nasīm* were written by Indian poets who used their ingenuity to make up fables and romances [*fasānah o qiṣṣah*], exaggerations and lies [*lughw o duroġh*]; the fashionings of their own fancies [*man-gharat*]. In the eyes of the public they could never have taken place [*kuchh bhī wuq'at nahīṅ rakhte*]. The public regards them as lies and exaggerations, just like the tales of the four dervishes, Ḥātim Ṭā'ī, etc. (Muḥammad Ismā'īl Ḍāsnawī 1895, 2–3)

Perhaps thanks to the press's understanding of the changing tastes of elite readers in the new era of the novel, the *Tārīkh-i Ṭilism-i Bakāwalī* is much more explicitly dismissive of *qiṣṣah*s than the *Guldastah-i Ḥairat*. But Muḥammad Ismā'īl goes further than simply calling the *qiṣṣah* mendacious. He counters the *qiṣṣah*'s lies with rationalistic alternatives. Some of these alternatives had already been presented by the *Guldastah*. For example, both books describe the Bakāwalī flower itself. This white flower was found growing to the north of the Garden of Bakāwalī's eastern water reservoir (see fig. 4). Its trees, probably *Sesbania grandiflora*, were no more than two and a half feet tall (Muḥammad Ismā'īl Ḍāsnawī 1895, 65).[8] Muḥammad Ismā'īl claims that in fact he was able to procure some of the Bakāwalī trees that grew in the Garden of Bakāwalī and have them transplanted in the Bāġh-i Nishāṭ (Garden of Delight) in Bhopal, though he laments that the keeper of the garden has destroyed these plants through his carelessness (Muḥammad Ismā'īl Ḍāsnawī 1895, 71). His affirmation of the reality of the Bakāwalī trees does not mitigate Muḥammad Ismā'īl's contempt for 'Izzat Allah Bāngālī's "lies" and his "simply incorrect" claim that the Bakāwalī flower could cure blindness. He makes a much-reduced claim regarding its medicinal properties, which include the ability to soothe irritated eyes (Muḥammad Ismā'īl Ḍāsnawī 1895, 65–66).

This diminution of the effects of the flower effectively demolishes the chains that bind the narrative of the first part of the *Tale of the Bakāwalī Flower*, in which Tāj al-Mulūk quests for a cure to his father's blindness. In that sense, the *Tārīḳh-i Ṭilism-i Bakāwalī* sets itself squarely against the *qiṣṣah*, the kind of demolition that was occasionally undertaken by upholders of the *qiṣṣah/tārīḳh* divide before the coming of British forms of rationalism. A more colonial form of antagonism toward the *qiṣṣah* can be seen when the *Tārīḳh* turns from the question of the plant's genus to that of the species of its characters. Muḥammad Ismā'īl writes lividly in defense of Tāj al-Mulūk's friend Ḥammālah: "'Izzat Allāh Bangālī has written in his *Tale of the Bakāwalī Flower* that Ḥammālah was a demoness. God forbid! She was a beautiful, elegant woman!" (Muḥammad Ismā'īl Ḍāsnawī 1895, 60). Bakāwalī was not a fairy, nor was Ḥammālah a demoness; what else were they but humans? (Muḥammad Ismā'īl Ḍāsnawī 1895, 15). He does not so much deny the other demons of *The Bakāwalī Flower* as much as he reorients the word "demon." The term *de'o* is synonymous, according to the author, with the Sanskrit-derived *rākshas.* On the authority of "book research" he informs the reader that "*rākshasa*" was a word used by the Aryans to refer to the people whom they found already inhabiting India when they arrived—"ugly, black, savage peoples." These people were used by the Aryans to perform unclean labor and also to protect the Aryans' lives and property (Muḥammad Ismā'īl Ḍāsnawī 1895, 54–55). Given that the identification of *rākshasa*s with the indigenous non-Aryan peoples of India had been made by British Indologists like Monier-Williams, Muḥammad Ismā'īl almost certainly harvested the fruits, through his "book research," of the colonial fascination with the Aryan race and its incursion into India. His hermeneutical movement itself is similar to that of the British Indologists, though the latter worked, at least initially, with "high" Sanskrit verbal artworks such as the *Māhābhārata* and *Rāmāyana* (Monier-Williams 1863, 9–10). Like Monier-Williams, Muḥammad Ismā'īl looks past the absurdities of the tale and attempts to wipe the dirt from it to reveal a shining historical reality. It seems difficult to escape the conclusion that when he explained away the demons of *The Bakāwalī Flower* as non-Aryan savages, Muḥammad Ismā'īl reproduced the conditions of knowledge production increasingly accepted by Indian elites following the imposition of British knowledge systems in the late nineteenth century.

Before Muḥammad Ismā'īl wrote his work, the authority of British thought had already been visible in Muḥammad Ya'qūb's *Guldastah-i Ḥairat*, with its glorification of the chief commissioner's intrepid though abortive quest. Temple's adventure functioned as a pattern, in fact, for what the historians of Bakāwalī were themselves attempting to do: to clear away the improbable accretions upon veritable history by inspecting the local theater of the occurrence of that history—though they were constrained to do so without an army of elephants. The waning credulity of the post-1857 generation of British-influenced elites meant that the spell of the *qiṣṣah* genre was lifting for this class of Indians. Amazement was giving way to disgust and contempt. A more limited sense of wonderment had now to be evoked by revealing the further stretches of experience and scientific fact. If these uncharted waters for the ship of the intellect could be shown to exist within India itself, the more was the wonder. Nevertheless, it would be incorrect to assume that during this period British epistemologies had taken hold of the minds of Indian elites completely. What is rather more important for the historians of Bakāwalī is the *figure* of the British sahibs, which authorizes their production or dissemination of knowledge regarding the truth buried beneath the *qiṣṣah*'s lies.

In an apparent attempt to situate his study within a trustworthy lineage (never stated in detail) of British works, Muḥammad Ya'qub claims that "many" English authors have written of the *ṭilism*s of the area surrounding the Fortress of Bakāwalī (Muḥammad Ya'qūb Lakhnawī 1876, 6). He highlights the reported conclusions of the English doctors (*ḍākṭar*) who accompanied Temple into the *ṭilismī* swamp. The Gonds of the area bade Temple take heed of the stories their ancestors had passed down to them regarding the vapors that arose from the swampy terrain and the strange lights that could be seen burning within Bakāwalī's fortress. They were products of a magical spell of great antiquity, which would prevent the party from reaching the fort. Only the Garden of Bakāwalī remained accessible. But the doctors, riding their elephants uncomfortably into the muck, were impatient with this talk of magic. There were perfectly satisfactory scientific explanations: the rising smoke was a product of the swamp's natural heat. The lights were merely a lot of fireflies.

However, as they went on, the doctors changed their tune. When they noted the fortress and its situation within the swamp, they admitted to the chief commissioner that even their Feringhee intellects were at a loss:

> In fact, this place was made by a powerful engineer [*injīnīr*], and it appears to be a kind of sorcery [*siḥr*]. It seems to us that the creation of a habitation in such a place must be the work of a great mathematician and engineer. Who knows by the power of what science [*'ilm*] this fortress has been raised, and upon what foundation it rests? The intellect is of no use here. Now that we see these *ṭilism*s, the *qiṣṣah* of Bakāwalī appears to be quite correct.

In reply, Sir Richard Temple said,

> That's all right, but the writer of the *qiṣṣah* didn't write about any of these marvels, nor did he write about the engineer. We are seeing

more of the effects of the *ṭilism* than there are in the *qiṣṣah* itself! (Muḥammad Ya'qūb Lakhnawī 1876, 19–20)

Thus in the reported statements of the English doctors, we find three hermeneutical movements. First, they reduce to natural causes whatever can be so reduced (the smoke and lights). Second, regarding the position of the fortress, they suggest that only a superior technological skill, resting on a knowledge of mathematics and engineering, could have placed such an edifice in such a location. Third, and most surprisingly, they affirm the existence of the *ṭilism* and its connection to sorcery. This affirmation simultaneously confirms sorcery as a legitimate science with a grounding in mathematics and physics and expresses the distance of this science from the grasp of their intellects in the current state of knowledge.

This distance is itself temporal and therefore bound up with the genre of history in which Muḥammad Ya'qūb and Muḥammad Ismā'īl have chosen to write. The *Tārīkh* implies that the power of the intellect is limited by the moment within which it operates and that, given time, the power of the intellect and the breadth of its knowledge will increase. This increase will occur in the future. But the same can be said of the past, in some cases, and this is precisely what Muḥammad Ismā'īl contends. According to the *Tārīkh-i Ṭilism-i Bakāwalī*, Princess Bakāwalī lived in the distant past, several thousand years before the *Māhābhārata* hero Yudhishtra, who was alive 4,800 years ago (Muḥammad Ismā'īl Ḍāsnawī 1895, 36). Her father, Rāja Maikal Jog, after whom the local Maikal Hills are named, was the younger son of the Sūrajvanshī Rāja Karanjot, and upon the division of Rāja Karanjot's kingdom, Maikal Jog received only the wilderness surrounding Amarkantak as his domain. The newly propertied ruler despaired of his kingdom. But his rani was not so quick to abandon hope of a prosperous reign.

Rāja Karanjot had a prime minister named Khanḍā Khaṛak. This prime minister was a great sage, the most powerful sorcerer and *ṭilism* crafter of his time, and the commander of the royal army. Several hundred magicians and *ṭilism* makers danced attendance at the court of Khanḍā Khaṛak at all times, for they were devoted to him. Maikal Jog's queen advised her husband to take Khanḍā Khaṛak into his service. And so Khanḍā Khaṛak came to the court of Maikal Jog, who sought his advice regarding the establishment of a center of government. Khanḍā Khaṛak's magicians flew about the kingdom and discovered a body of undrained water in the vale by Amarkantak Hill. At Khanḍā Khaṛak's order, his sorcerers created the fortress for the raja and his army in the midst of the water, and the *ṭilism* makers transformed the water into the enchanted swamp to protect the fortress. After the birth of Princess Bakāwalī, the fortress was called by her name. At the same time as Bakāwalī was born, Khanḍā Khaṛak's wife gave birth to a daughter who would be named Jabālah (later corrupted into "Ḥammālah"). In time Rāja Maikal Jog's eye alighted on Jabālah, and the two desired one other. So Khanḍā Khaṛak built a prison for his daughter that could also be seen in the swamp's midst, called by the locals Gaṛhī Ḥammālah. All of these matters, older even than the war between the Kauravas and Pandavas, had left their memorials in the shadow of the Maikal range of the Vindhya Mountains (Muḥammad Ismā'īl Ḍāsnawī 1895, 33–74). As fantastic as these events may seem to Muḥammad Ismā'īl's readers, his contention is that they puzzle the intellect only because they are enveloped so thickly by time. As Tha'ālibī suggested regarding the Sīmurġh, temporal distance had led to defamiliarization.

If the intellects of even the British doctors are powerless to comprehend the construction of the *ṭilism* and Fortress of Bakāwalī, it is because the sciences of the ancient Indians have passed out of Indians' memories and into oblivion, not because these sciences are beyond the intellect's potential grasp. Muḥammad Ismā'īl states that it is recorded in books of history that the "Hindu" rulers founded their power upon the arts of astrology, *ṭilism* creation, and magic. These potentates employed large numbers of experts in the occult sciences, or *'ulūm-i ġharībah* (Muḥammad Ismā'īl Ḍāsnawī 1895, 6). Maikal Jog, through Khanḍā Khaṛak, commanded hundreds of them. Bakāwalī's suitor Son Bhadra was another puissant ruler; himself a great mage, he sent a delegation of sorceresses riding dragons to ask Maikal Jog for his daughter's hand, and when he was accepted, he came to collect his bride with ten thousand magicians in train (Muḥammad Ismā'īl

Ḍāsnawī 1895, 77–79). *Ḥakīms* or sages no longer existed in such numbers at the end of the nineteenth century, but Muḥammad Ismā'īl averred that India had once been "a mine of all of the sciences" (Muḥammad Ismā'īl Ḍāsnawī 1895, 6).

Implicit in the English doctors' affirmation of sorcery and *ṭilisms* is the long-standing idea that the occult sciences were based upon mathematical principles. Matthew Melvin-Koushki (2017) has argued that these sciences were heavily mathematicalized from the "High Persianate" period onward.[9] The mathematical basis of sorcery (*siḥr*) is the reason for Muḥammad Ya'qūb's insistence that Khaṇḍā Khaṛak was a great mathematician and that the *ḥakīms* and sorcerers under his command were similarly mathematically adept (Muḥammad Ismā'īl Ḍāsnawī 1895, 8). The occult science that is most prominent in the histories of Bakāwalī is the science of *ṭilisms* (*'ilm al-ṭilismāt)*, which was classified by encyclopedists as a natural science rather than a mathematical one. Yet the creation of *ṭilisms* is inconceivable without mathematical bases. As the *Durrat al-tāj* of Quṭb al-Dīn Shīrāzī explained, the *ṭilism* maker would join celestial virtues to the virtues of certain earthly bodies to produce an extraordinary action in the world (Melvin-Koushki 2017, 147). While it was based on the natural principle of the correspondence between the celestial and earthly realms, the creation of *ṭilisms* could not be effected without the inscription of mathematical figures and designs onto an earthly medium (Melvin-Koushki 2017, 23; Lory 2003, 536). This device was well known to *dāstān* audiences as the *ṭilism*'s "tablet" (*lauḥ-i ṭilism*) (Lory 2003, 536). While *ṭilisms* are used to influence humans or to protect treasures and so forth by means of illusory appearances, in the *dāstān* tradition these *ṭilism*ically produced illusions take on the proportions of entire worlds in which the protagonists find themselves trapped until they are able to discover the tablet and conquer the *ṭilism* (Faruqi 2006c, 286). Indeed, Muḥammad Ismā'īl suggests that if the *ḥakīms* of old had not assiduously hidden the tablet controlling the *ṭilism* of Bakāwalī, it would have been possible to break its spell.[10]

If the grounding of sorcery in mathematics was a well-established idea, clearly its identification with engineering was not.[11] But this terminology, put quite suitably into the mouths of the British, is what one would expect of an Indian elite increasingly overawed by the technology of the colonizer: trains, telegraphs, photographs, and the hot-air balloon in which Temple considered surveying the *ṭilism*. This interest in technology can be seen in Muḥammad Ismā'īl's references to the flying machines (*uṛan khaṭole*) used by Khanḍā Khaṛak's sorcerers as the only means of entering and leaving the fort (Muḥammad Ismā'īl Ḍāsnawī 1895, 33, 50).[12] The implication that the Indians also had their engineers long before the coming of the British suggests a quiet one-upmanship together with a fairly standard declinist reading of Indian history. One of the reviews (*taqrīẓ*) appended to the *Tārīkh-i Ṭilism-i Bakāwalī*, written by the press's scribe, gives the "experimenters of India and China" their place alongside the great "sages of Greece and Rome" and the "intellectuals of Europe" (Muḥammad Ismā'īl Ḍāsnawī 1895, 87). The *Tārīkh* claims to give the reader a "photo of the intellect" of a bygone era (*'aql kā foṭo*) and stresses the existence of the traces of the ancient intellect throughout India, from the Fort of Bakāwalī to the Jantar Mantar (Muḥammad Ismā'īl Ḍāsnawī 1895, 5–6). But though the histories of Bakāwalī play with Indian chess pieces, the game and its rules belong to the colonizer. They foreshadow the most grandiose claims of the postcolonial Hindu Right, as well as a certain Islamic modernist triumphalism regarding Muslim achievements in science. These are stances that, while anti-colonial in their impulse, are profoundly reactive and fail to escape the colonial intellectual frame in that they accept the dominant epistemology of the West.

The historians' rejection of the *qiṣṣah* and its attendant "lies," therefore, does not negate the existence of magic and *ṭilism*s in the world, as one would expect. Muḥammad Ya'qūb and Muḥammad Ismā'īl demolish the *qiṣṣah*'s assertions to a limited extent. But they affirm much of the sorcery connected with the Fortress of Bakāwalī, and they inquire into the basis of its existence. Implicit in their critique is the idea that the *qiṣṣah* fails to carry out such inquiry and to perform verification (*taḥqīq*), not that it presents a strictly absurd image of the world. Whether they demolish or affirm, the historians of Bakāwalī take their cue from the British and their intellectual authority.

That the histories of Bakāwalī are reactions to colonial epistemologies does not however mean that they are simply reducible to those epistemologies or that they have no relation to precolonial modes of thought. They deploy some of the telltale strategies of the *naqlī*, or transmission-based mode of historiography, alongside *'aqlī* strategies. For example, in recounting God's transformation of Bakāwalī into the Narmada River, they rely on the testimony of local pandits and the *purānas*, which are understood as historiographical works themselves (Muḥammad Ismā'īl Ḍāsnawī 1895, 80–82). Along with other metamorphoses, the liquefaction of Bakāwalī is left unexplained. Although the intellect is an important arbiter of the mendaciousness of the *qiṣṣah* of Bakāwalī, the *Tārīkh-i ṭilism-i Bakāwalī*'s scribe, Muḥammad 'Abd Allāh Ḵhān Naṣīr, reminds the reader in his appended review that the intellect is bestowed upon humans by God, Who is not rationally comprehensible Himself (Muḥammad Ismā'īl Ḍāsnawī 1895, 87). In their recognition of the primacy of Divine Power over the intellect, the ideas of the Gulzār-i Muḥammadī Press's scribe are close to precolonial epistemologies.

Epistemologies of the Intellect and Heart

It is important to recount, at least in a preliminary fashion, the shapes of the epistemologies that preceded the irruption of British ideas and education onto the Indian scene, for these epistemologies were the lifeblood of the *qiṣṣah* before its value was challenged by the elevation of the novel in the genre hierarchy. If we accept, along with Frederic Jameson, that genres are formed by the ideologies of the milieus in which they appear, we can say that the *qiṣṣah* genre conceals the working of a precolonial, nonrationalist epistemology or set of epistemologies. What makes the delineation of these epistemologies so difficult is that they do not arise purely out of philosophical thought. Rather, what stand behind the *qiṣṣah* genre are "folk" epistemologies that must be abstracted laboriously from the traces of the milieu. I do not claim to do so rigorously here; I will only provide a brief outline. If we look beyond philosophical and scientific works and consider texts with a wider reach, such as poetry and the texts of the Sufis, the epistemological limits of the intellect become clear. The precolonial epistemologies that remained powerful through to the end of the nineteenth century were ones in which the intellect was not always the ultimate arbiter of truth and in which the Western scientific concept of the "natural" had not yet appeared.

However, there are many dangers involved in talking of precolonial "nonrationalist" epistemologies. First, there is the danger the phrase will be taken to refer to the absolute rejection of the faculty of the intellect, which is hardly the case; reason always had a place in the thought systems undergirding the *qiṣṣah*'s former place in its genre system. Second, as I have shown, no one can deny the existence and doggedness of precolonial rationalist thought, particularly at the elite level, that formed the basis of opposition to the *qiṣṣah* genre before the coming of colonialism. Third, while British rationalism is important because of its appeal to a society with an already booming rationalist tradition, it is important not to reduce British thought to a pure rationalism. Thus in speaking of rationalisms, whether Islamicate or British, I refer to epistemologies that privilege the intellect as the arbiter of what is true or possible, however else they may differ and whatever ancillary strands of ideology they may incorporate.[13] Finally, we should be cognizant of the fact that the British may not have been as bound to the rationalist epistemology as they claimed.[14]

Wonderment (*ta'ajjub, ḥairat*) is key to the *qiṣṣah* genre's epistemological background. As Roy Mottahedeh (1997, 30) has pointed out with reference to the *Thousand and One Nights*, wonder was defined by Al-Rāġhib al-Iṣfahānī and later authors as a state coming upon a person who is faced with a thing whose cause is unknown. The cause may ultimately be discoverable; in this sense, the wonderful was not contrary to reason. When the authors of the various texts that went by the name of *'Ajā'ib al-makhlūqāt* (Wonders of creation) proclaimed that "nothing should be deemed too great for the Power of the Creator," this dictum can be taken to imply that wonder may be a challenge to the intellect, to inquire and probe into the cause of the wondrous thing (Zadeh 2010, 32). However, Divine Power, infinitely exalted in this statement, constituted a limit to the intellect's power.

An acknowledgment of this limitation upon the power of the intellect is visible even in the *Tārīkh-i ṭilism-i Bakāwalī*, whose scribe, Naṣīr, answered Muḥammad Ismāʿīl's history by faithfully reiterating the well-known idea that God is "*be-chūn*" (without "how") (Muḥammad Ismāʿīl Dāsnawī 1895, 87). The "how-ness" of God is not to be contemplated, as Maḥmūd Shabistarī's influential Sufi poem the *Gulshan-i rāz* (Rosegarden of secrets) put it: "His Essence is purified of 'how many,' 'what,' and 'why,' / His Glory is exalted above what they say" (*munazzah ẕāt-ash az chand o chih o chūn / taʿālà shānu-hu ʿam-ma yaqūlūn*) (Shabistarī 1978, v. 111).[15] At the level of the Essence (*ẕāt*), intellectual inquiry must cease, for it is ineffectual. The inability of the intellect to comprehend the Divine is so obvious a feature of Sufi thought that it is perhaps needless to adduce further examples of this idea. However, Shabistarī's long poem formulates it in particularly striking ways, comparing the intellect to the eye of a bat trying uselessly to gaze at the sun of the Essence (Shabistarī 1978, v. 118). Muḥyī al-Dīn Ibn ʿArabī had explained in his *Ringstones of Wisdom* that the intellect is a fetter upon the ability of human beings to accept the reality of phenomena as the self-manifestations (*tajalliyāt*) of God (e.g., Ibn al-ʿArabī 1966, 122, trans. in Dagli 2004, 130).

What is it that causes the intellect to falter? Ibn ʿArabi gave an example in the *Ringstones*: the intellect cannot accept the idea that something caused can cause its own cause. Yet, he explained, the science of the self-manifestations of God (*ʿilm al-tajalliyāt*) tells us this very thing: that what is caused causes what causes it (Ibn al-ʿArabī 1966, 185; 2004, 234). This reality cannot be known by the human intellect but rather only through an experience of Divine self-manifestation, a witnessing (*mushāhadah*) or tasting (*ẕauq*). These experiential methods generally involved the shedding of the intellect as an obstacle on the path to knowledge of the Real. In the process, the intellect is lifted into a state of bewilderment (*ḥairat*) that is heavily valorized in Sufi texts, most notably Farīd al-Dīn ʿAṭṭar's *Conference of the Birds*, but also in the *Ringstones* and in the verses of Punjabi-language Sufi poets such as Sulṭān Bāhū, Bullhe Shāh, and Miyāṅ Muḥammad Bakhsh (2002, vv. 650–59), who devotes a portion of the preface to his nineteenth-century

Tale of Saif al-Mulūk to a discussion of bewilderment. The celebration of the bewildering multiplication of meanings (meaning creation, or *ma'ni-āfirīnī*) in the poetry of the so-called Indian style in Persian and Urdu is arguably in harmony with a nonrationalist epistemology.[16] Bewilderment in this context is not so much an invitation to the intellect to continue its work as before as it is a transformative experience that takes the partial, creatural intellect beyond itself. The intellect that has been so dazzled will realize its own Reality—its ipseity, or *huwiyyah*. Thus it is clear that non-rationalist epistemologies were not anti-rational or anti-empirical. They did not reject the workings of the intellect or the senses. Rather, they put forward the possibility of something along the lines of the hyperrational and hyper-empirical: the filling of the intellect and the senses with the knowledge of the One to Whom they belong.

Given the depreciation of the intellect and the valorization of bewilderment not only in Sufi texts but also in the *ġhazal*, the most powerful genre of the Mughal period, it is very difficult to deny the pervasiveness of this set of epistemological assumptions. However, an objection could be made on the basis that rational and nonrational inquiry had separate fields of application: the physical and the metaphysical, respectively. If it is incapable of comprehending God, reason is certainly capable of comprehending nature, one might say. The modernist idea of nature requires reexamination, however. Pritchett (1989) has shown how a two-pronged British idea of nature deformed the Urdu *ġhazal* after 1857. It is telling that both the Urdu-speaking proponents and critics of this naturalism wrote in Urdu of the fixity of "*nechar*" or the sins of the "*necharīs*." The idea of nature as an unchangeable law, a closed system governing all creation, does not appear to have been very prevalent in India prior to its appearance in the late nineteenth century, especially through the immensely powerful advocacy of Sir Sayyid Aḥmad Ḳhān. For Sir Sayyid, God and nature could be reconciled through a more or less deistic logic: the law of nature is a promise made by God, and God cannot break His own promises (Aziz Ahmad 1967, 46–47). Sayyid Aḥmad Ḳhān's British-derived understanding of nature stands in stark contrast to Ibn 'Arabī's reading of the Quranic verse, "Every day He is upon some work" (Quran 55.29). Ibn 'Arabī took this verse to refer not simply to God's continuous involvement in the world but to the continuous Divine renewal of the process of existentiation (*takwīn*) itself.[17] This sentiment was not an uncommon one. We find it even in the comments of the *Tārīkh-i ṭilism-i Bakāwalī*'s scribe, when he tells us that God is the increaser of astonishment (*ḥairat-afzā-i hosh o hawās*), Who has frustrated the intellect's workings throughout human history (Muḥammad Ismā'īl Ḍāsnawī 1895, 87). While the concept of nature has now been thoroughly normalized in the Urdu language, the words used in the present to denote the English "nature" all had other, better-recognized meanings in the nineteenth century. *Qudrat*, perhaps the most common modern word for "nature," is better translated in most pre-twentieth-century texts as "Divine Power." In the twentieth century, the *qiṣṣah* was criticized or celebrated as supernatural (*fauq al-fiṭrat*). *Fiṭrat*, however, had long referred to the primordial human constitution. The category of *fauq al-fiṭrat* is a late one that would not have held much water in the precolonial era of Indo-Islamicate thought.

Rather than a pervasive idea of "nature" as a closed system, the idea of *'ādat*, or custom, was prevalent. Much more germane to the thought systems of this period is the term *kharq al-'ādat*, or custom breaking, which is still sometimes used unreflectively as a criticism of the *qiṣṣah*, alongside the compromise term *fauq al-'ādat* (super-normal, super-customary) that the novelist 'Abd al-Ḥalīm Sharar used (n.d., *Florā Florinḍā*). As an alternative to the concept of nature and a partner to the rational, the concept of *'ādat* is an extremely important one. In the eleventh century, the Ash'arī Abū Bakr al-Bāqillānī had defined *'ādat* as referring to recurrence and to the patterns that come to be expected by experienced observers (Khalidi 1994, 156–57). That which breaks with custom, the *khāriq al-'ādat*, is an important and much-discussed category, since it comprehends the miracles of prophets and saints as well as marvelous occurrences. Those who thought deeply about *'ādat* recognized, however, that even the binary opposition between customary and custom breaking was valid only from the perspective of a community of creatural observers (humans, jinn, or angels), not from the perspective of the Real. Bāqillāni himself affirmed this fact, noting that insofar as God was concerned, no repetition was possible. Ibn 'Arabī explained non-repetition in terms of the *tajalliyāt* (Divine self-manifestations). There is no repetition (*takrār*) in the self-manifestations of God. Every moment of creation, which is an unceasing act carried out by God, is radically new. Everything, or nothing, is therefore *khāriq al-'ādat*, or custom breaking (Ibn 'Arabī 2004, 31).[18] *'Ādat* is therefore a matter of perspective, and its openness to being "broken" makes it quite different from the more rigid concept of natural law, exceptions to which would have to eventually be resubsumed into it. Thus, the possibility—which is not necessarily to say the probability—existed of there being strange creatures, sorcery, and *ṭilismī* worlds in the universe that God was constantly creating.

The power of this epistemology for precolonial Indians, and even for non-elite Indians during and after the colonial period, enabled the *qiṣṣah* genre with all of its wonders to escape absolute devaluation by precolonial rationalist critiques. However, with the arrival of British education in India, the increasing permeation of British ideas into the worldview of elite Indians, and rise of the novel in the Urdu language, the *qiṣṣah* genre did undergo a devaluation. This devaluation was made especially powerful because it had been rehearsed before in Europe itself, when the novel genre was separated by critics from the romance on ideological or epistemological grounds that were strikingly similar to those that were applied in India at the end of the nineteenth century.

Equating *Qiṣṣah* and Romance

A brief history of the equation between *qiṣṣah* or *dāstān* and "romance" will shed light on the otherwise suspect terminology used in these pages. Why, after all, refer to *qiṣṣah*s as romances? The great peril of this translation is that the reader may assume that the answer to the central question of this study—"What is or was the *qiṣṣah* genre?"—is simply that the *qiṣṣah* is and was the same as the British/French romance. Not only would such an assumption be a mischaracterization of the *qiṣṣah*, but it would also do a disservice to the European romance genre by taking for granted a frozen idea of what it is and neglecting to probe into its history.

With the arrival of the novel in Urdu in the late nineteenth century, the *qiṣṣah* genre underwent a devaluation, along with its producers, the storytellers themselves. We have seen that the value of even courtly storytelling (*qiṣṣah-khwani*) in Persian and Urdu had always been contested. But in the time of Mīr Bāqir 'Alī its value underwent a marked decline, partly for socioeconomic reasons related to the scarcity of older forms of patronage. But at the epistemological level as well, something was happening to reform—or deform—the genre system. The subordination of the *qiṣṣah* to the novel in this period mirrors the devaluation of the romance in the genre hierarchy of eighteenth-century Britain, just as its genre code was being solidified against that of the novel. As in the case of the novel/*qiṣṣah* genre distinction in India, the lower worth of the romance in Britain was based on the probability of events and beings represented in the novel and the improbability of events and beings represented in the romance. The equation between the European romance and the "Eastern" *qiṣṣah*, along with British speculations regarding the reasons for the popularity of the *qiṣṣah* genre in India, fed the Orientalist image of the irrational Indian.

Regardless of the existence of a conceptual distinction, most European languages still do not distinguish between the romance and the novel. The French term *roman* is the designation of choice in many of the languages of Europe apart from English. Even in English, the two genres appear not to have been well distinguished until the efflorescence of the novel genre in the eighteenth century. And even during that pivotal century, the idea of the novel genre was in its birth throes and had not extricated itself from the midst of the heap of genre designations that were available at that time. It is not clear that the works of a writer like Henry Fielding would have been understood as novels, though we now understand them as such. Fielding's *History of the Adventures of Joseph Andrews* (1742) was apt to refer to itself as a history, as the title indicates, or as a "comic romance," or as a biography. It referred to itself in this manner despite that it presented itself as a new kind or genre of writing: a "comic epic poem in prose" (Fielding 1986, 25).

This latter designation is also found in *Tom Jones* (1749), which, however, is more fully entitled *The History of Tom Jones, A Foundling* and more frequently calls itself a history. *Tom Jones* does hint, unlike *Joseph Andrews*, at its being a "novel," but such hints are so sparse and so well counterbalanced by other designations that they can only be made much of by tendentious critics who seek them out retrospectively as proof of the novel genre's pedigree.

What is striking about *Tom Jones*, however, is that while it does not present itself unambiguously as a "novel," it does make it clear that whatever it is, it should be distinguished from "romance"—though even this distinction is made by Fielding (1998, 423) because he feels that he must do so to escape censure. Fielding had been quite content to refer to *Joseph Andrews* as a romance, not once but repeatedly. His making this distinction in *Tom Jones* was symptomatic of the split that was taking place in the middle of the eighteenth century between romances and other forms of prose fiction. It is highly important to understand the basis of this split. In the seventeenth century there already existed a distinction between false romances and true histories. Pierre Daniel Huet's essay "Sur l'origine des Romans" (1670) had been adapted into English in 1715 by Stephen Lewis as "The History of Romances." Lewis had assured the reader that the term "romance" should not be taken to comprehend histories—not even histories that contained falsehoods (Herodotus, for instance). While the essay had acknowledged that histories could have false information within them and that romances could contain truths, the one genre was by and large veracious and the other generally mendacious (Williams 1970, 47).

The term "novel" very gradually came to designate writings intermediate between romances and histories. Though novels, like romances, may have been fictitious, it eventually came to be thought that, of the two sister genres, the romance generally represented improbable things, while novels represented what was probable. In other words, novels were closer to "history," in the sense of a faithful record of events. Writers like William Congreve and Marie de la Rivière Manley had characterized the novel in these terms early on, in 1695 and 1705, respectively (Williams 1970, 27, 33–35). Nevertheless, the distinctions between the three terms—romance, novel, and history—were far from settled until the end of the eighteenth century, as the example of Henry Fielding shows. In 1762, Hugh Blair could still write about the romance/novel as "fictitious history" with impunity (Williams 1970, 247). But as the difference between the romance and the novel grew better accepted, a struggle arose between the proponents of the two genres, from which, as we know, the novel emerged victorious.

Fielding's choice of nomenclature may have been made under duress, but the prefaces of each book of *Tom Jones* are quite explicit regarding the desirability of writing prose fiction that represents the probable over the representation of the improbable and impossible that was increasingly coming to be the sign of the romance genre. "As for elves and fairies, and other such mummery," Fielding wrote, "I purposely omit the mention of them, as I should be very unwilling to confine within any bounds those surprising imaginations, for whose vast capacity the limits of human nature are too narrow." Going further, Fielding (1998, 348) proclaims, "nor is possibility alone sufficient to justify us; we must keep likewise within the rules of probability." Eventually such sentiments were to be challenged, often by conservatives, but in 1750 even such a Tory literatus as Samuel Johnson was eager to pooh-pooh the narratives that would become known as romances. Johnson made the withering remark in the *Rambler* that "almost all the fictions of the last age will vanish, if you deprive them of a hermit and a wood, a battle and a shipwreck." The aim of the new kind of fiction as popularized by Fielding, Tobias Smollet, Samuel Richardson, and so on was deemed by Johnson to be representation of the natural, not the improbable, however agreeably wondrous the latter might be:

> Its province is to bring about natural events by easy means, and to keep up curiosity without the help of wonder; it is therefore precluded from the machines and expedients of the heroic romance, and can neither employ giants to snatch away a lady from the nuptial rites, nor knights to bring her back from captivity; it can neither bewilder its personages in deserts, nor lodge them in imaginary castles. (Williams 1970, 142)

Increasingly, the primacy of reason and sense was being established in Britain, and personages as different as Johnson and Fielding were united in depreciating improbable narratives, however far apart these two men may have been on other points. By the last decades of the eighteenth century, the hierarchical opposition between probable novels and improbable romances had become well established.

A remarkable scholar and proponent of the romance genre during this period was Clara Reeve. Her book *The Progress of Romance*, which appeared in 1785, was both a history of the genre and a reflection upon its properties. Reeve (1930, xi) mentioned a few British critics who gave the romance its due, but she made it clear that the proponents of the romance were in a decided minority. She adhered to the definition of the romance that had come to distinguish it from the novel, suggesting that it was an extreme fiction, at a far remove from probability and fact (6). One of the purposes of her writing was to challenge the romance's opponents. Yet, even so, she added the caveat that the genre would benefit readers only if its use were properly regulated, particularly in the case of juvenile readers (Reeve 1930, xvi). Reeve conceded, too, that the romance was moribund and that its sister, the novel, had sprung from its "ruins" (1930, 8). The genre code that placed the novel above the romance can be shown to be powerful indeed when we consider that even a champion of the romance should accept all the same that the genre was improbable, in need of fencing in, and a decaying relic that was giving way to the more vital novel genre.

The Progress of Romance also touches upon the question of whether the romance was a Western genre alone. The very fact that we are discussing romances at such length in a study of the *qiṣṣah* genre shows that the idea of the romance as a worldwide genre came to be well accepted and that the *qiṣṣah*, along with various other narrative genres, came to be equated with the romance. It is to the development of this "genre equation" that I will now turn. Along with *The Progress of Romance*, Reeve also published a translation, from French, of an Egyptian tale that she entitled *The History of Charoba Queen of Aegypt*. She did so to prove the existence of "Eastern romances" to a skeptical friend. But the idea of the Eastern romance was already well established in the minds of British critics and readers. Galland's *Les Mille et une nuits*, a version of the *Alf lailah wa lailah* (*One Thousand and One Nights*), had been rendered into English a number of times over the course of the eighteenth century, and its popularity led to the confabulation of other "Oriental romances" such as *Almoran and Hamet*, written by John Hawkesworth and published in 1761.[19]

This equation endured through the nineteenth and twentieth centuries, with the effect that most scholarly works in English on the *qiṣṣah*, *dāstān*, or *ḥikāyat* have referred to texts of this genre as "romances"—William Hanaway (1970), Frances Pritchett (1985), and Aditya Behl (Manjhan Rājgīrī 2000), for instance, have all done so. Northrop Frye (1973, 307) sounds like a twentieth-century echo of Clara Reeve when he asserts that the romance, in contrast to the novel, was not merely Western but "world-wide." The value assigned to the *qiṣṣah* genre has therefore been a reflection of that which was assigned to the romance—and, by extension, the novel, since the valuation of the romance has, since the later eighteenth century, been tied to the rising fortunes of the novel.

Not only were Western and Eastern "romances" understood as belonging to a single, worldwide genre, but very often the former was understood as a descendent of the latter. The theory that the Eastern romance was the mother of the Western romance had a long history. It was probably already available in the sixteenth century, when Giammaria Barbieri postulated that Arab verses had led to the rise of troubadour lyrics as a result of Christendom's contact with Moorish Spain (Boase 1977, 11). In 1671, Huet similarly suggested that the prose romance originated with the Asians (Boase 1977, 13). We have already seen that Huet's "De l'origine des romans" was translated into English in the eighteenth century, and it appears to have been quite influential. One of the English critics it influenced was Thomas Warton, who wrote in the latter half of the eighteenth century that the Western romance possessed a double ancestry. Its first origin was in Gothic-Germanic narratives, but this was eventually superseded by a second, Hispano-Arab source (Boase 1977, 15–16; see also Reeve 1930, 10). Warton in his turn had a great influence upon Reeve, who, as we have seen, wholeheartedly accepted and controverted in favor of the "Eastern origin" thesis and who was an advocate for the romance, Eastern or Western, within certain bounds. Romances, according to Reeve (1930, 16), were a "universal growth." More specialized Orientalists agreed that Indian and other Asian narratives were indeed romances, and so the genre equation was settled, for better or for worse.

The notion that the romance belonged to a defective past and the novel to an improved present becomes, in the writings of the Orientalists, entangled with the idea that India suffers from a case of arrested development. The fact that India continued to produce romances could be explained by the altogether common assertion that this region of the Orient was stuck in a past that Europe had thankfully escaped. This assumption is evident in the Orientalist scholar Duncan Forbes's introduction to his translation of the Indo-Persian *Tale of Hatim Ta'i* (*Qiṣṣah-i Ḥātim Ṭā'ī*), which he translated in 1830 under the title *The Adventures of Hatim Tai: A Romance.* "In Europe," Forbes wrote,

> the last three centuries have wrought mighty changes in the state of society, while Asia remains, comparatively speaking, unaltered. Among the natives of Persia and Hindustan, the belief in demons, fairies, magicians with their enchanted palaces, and talismans and charms, is as prevalent as it was in Europe in the chivalrous ages that succeeded the crusades. Hence the most celebrated works of fiction in the East abound with the incredible, the wild, and the marvelous, like the productions of the bards and story-tellers of Provence and their imitators, which enchanted Europe from the twelfth to the sixteenth centuries. (v)

The Adventures of Hatim Ta'i, according to Forbes, contains elements that British readers in the nineteenth century would have thought incredible and uninteresting because it was produced within a culture that lacked the solidity of reason and sense that Europe had gained since the Enlightenment.

In this statement, there was both condemnation and apology. The preposterous romance genre's time was thought to be long gone, and in this sense it was devalued against the novel. But Forbes implied that the genre was at least useful as a museum piece in the case of Western romances or, in the case of the "romances" of India, as a symptom that helped Orientalists to understand Indian culture and what ailed it. As one writer put it, in a review of Forbes in the *Asiatic Journal*, "The literature of a nation affords the best guide to researches into its character, manners, and opinions; and no department of literature contains a more ample store of data in the respect, than the light and popular part, consisting of tales, romances, and dramatic pieces" ("Review" 1830, 67).

National literatures were supposed to disclose the "national character" even in the cases of European nations. Nineteenth-century literary criticism was very much wedded to this principle (Jauss 1982, 6–8). But, unlike the European, the Indian's character was disclosed as that of the "half child." A later review of Forbes's *Adventures of Hatim Ta'i* argued that, to enjoy the book, the reader must become as a child once more:

> There is no use whatever in our sitting down to read the adventures of Hatim Taï, unless we first revive in our souls the rainbow-hues of youth, and recall that inexperienced ardour which prompted us easily to believe in the mystic potency of talismans, and in the obedience rendered to them by genii of earth and air and ocean. ("Review" 1883, 506)

The sympathy of the reviewer should not obscure the logic of the review: modern British readers cannot appreciate this "Eastern romance" as Eastern readers would, because the latter are childish in the liberty they give to their imaginations, whereas the former are bound by a mature rationalism. This infantilization of the *qiṣṣah* and therefore of its audience appears to have no equivalent in pre-1857 India. We have seen in chapter 1 that storytellers were certainly aware of, and availed themselves of, the value of the *qiṣṣah* to potential patrons who might be receptive to its examples, whether those examples were linguistic, political, or otherwise. Such patrons were often younger, though not necessarily; the advantage of nabbing a youthful patron was the possibility of the storyteller's establishing a long-term and deep power relation with them. What seems to be missing entirely, even in the screeds of the genre's precolonial critics, is an identification of the *qiṣṣah*'s audience as juvenile or an identification of the *qiṣṣah* genre itself as what the British would call "children's literature."

As little as the translation of *qiṣṣah* as "romance" has been questioned or examined by scholars of South Asian literature, we have seen that the equivalence between the two genres is not arbitrary but rather historically conditioned. When we examine the equation, we get a glimmer of the worldview locked up within the eighteenth-century hierarchical genre binary novel/romance and let loose upon the Indian genre system first by British Orientalists and later by Indian elites themselves. Following this revelation, it would seem as if the project of decolonizing the genre code of the *qiṣṣah* necessitates a repudiation of the label "romance" and an insistence upon the use of the Urdu/Punjabi/Persian/Arabic term. Doing away with the terminology of the "romance" altogether might appear to be the safest option, yet without recalling this equation, we would have been unable to expose it and critique it. The question is whether it is not better, however, to rethink and resignify the term "romance" itself. It is not only the Indian *qiṣṣah* genre that is dehistoricized and misunderstood thanks to the epistemological shift of the British eighteenth century and its reflection in the literary criticism of the period. A disservice is done, for instance, to the literature of medieval Europe as well, through the depreciation of the medieval epistemologies that were supposedly overcome in the West but not in the East.

The Rise of the Novel

The epistemological critique concomitant with the British equation of the exploded romance genre and the *qiṣṣah* began to infect Indian critiques of the genre as early as the *Guldastah-i Ḥairat*. But, as we will see, the critique mounted by the histories of Bakāwalī was not as thoroughgoing as those presented by elite Urdu literary critics such as Muḥammad Ḥusain Āzād (1830–1910) and Alṭāf Ḥusain Ḥālī (1837–1914) in the era when the Urdu novel began to come into its own. Just as Ḥālī and Āzād attacked the Urdu *ġhazal* for not being sufficiently "natural," so they dismissed *qiṣṣahs*, especially versified ones. Connected to the idea of the *qiṣṣah*'s unnaturalness, there arose a moral critique: insofar as an important purpose of literature was to edify and inculcate proper morals in the reader, the *qiṣṣah* was inadequate. Because the *qiṣṣah* did not reflect nature, it could not be morally exemplary either. Tied to these critiques was the subjection of the *qiṣṣah* to the Orientalist historical judgment that we have already glimpsed, shaped by ideas of British epistemological superiority. When the *qiṣṣah* genre at last became the subject of literary histories in the twentieth century, its depreciation continued along similarly epistemologically grounded lines. Despite the apparent sympathy of indefatigable *qiṣṣah* scholars like Gyān Chand Jain for the genre, their assessments perpetuated many aspects of the negative colonial evaluation of its worth.

In her study of the Urdu *ġhazal*, *Nets of Awareness*, Frances Pritchett (1994, chap. 7) has shown that during the latter half of the nineteenth century, Āzād and Ḥālī developed readings of Urdu poetry that painted its history in largely negative terms. In bygone days, so they claimed, the *maẓmūns* (themes or propositions) of the Urdu *ġhazal* were fresh and close to "nature," but later imitators merely remasticated and regurgitated the material that they should have discarded to make way for their own, original creations. Reuse and subtle reworking of preestablished themes were part of the game of the Urdu *ġhazal*, particularly via the method that Shamsur Rahman Faruqi (2006b) calls "*maẓmūn-āfirīnī*," or proposition creation, whereby, for example, the proposition that the beloved figuratively kills the lover is extended by degrees into a new proposition: the beloved is a hunter who slays the lover with the arrow of his gaze. To multiply this process was, for Āzād, to stretch originally quite natural poetic images to their breaking point by rendering them unnatural. This criticism was the most striking of many critiques directed by Āzād against Urdu poetry as it had been prior to the reformation that he and Ḥālī would prescribe for it (Pritchett 1994, chap. 11). The problem with Urdu literature generally, according to these critics, was that it was too "unnatural" in the decadent period immediately preceding British imperial rule and extending into the critics' lifetimes.

Given that the idea of nature as a closed system of laws that exclude the intervention of God was given to India by the British, the Urdu language did not have a directly equivalent term, and therefore we find Ḥālī importing the English noun "nechar" and the adjective "necharal" into his works of criticism. The concept of a "natural" poetry appears to have had both Romantic and rationalist-empiricist overtones. Natural poetry was faithful to nature and not padded with unnatural exaggerations, which might be caused, in the *ġhazal*, by prolonged *maẓmūn-āfirīnī* or, in the qiṣṣah, simply by the flights of imagination, the representations of jinns and heads growing on trees, and so forth that were the storytellers' staples. Good literary representations ought to aspire to the fidelity of photographs; they ought to be rooted in what really and empirically existed and in what could rationally exist.

It is not that Ḥālī was at all dismissive of the role of the imagination (*taḳhayyul*, which Ḥālī explicitly glosses as *imaijineshan*) in the *Muqaddamah*. On the contrary, imagination was for Ḥālī the most important prerequisite to being a poet, and it was something that a poet was born with, a thoroughly Romantic notion. Nevertheless, the supreme importance of the imaginative faculty was tempered by Ḥālī in several ways. In his enumeration of the qualities that a good poet ought to possess, the second quality that Ḥālī mentioned after imagination was the habit of observing the world. Critics like Ḥālī often performed the double gesture of adopting identifiably Western ideas but also giving them an indigenous veneer by relating them to germane Islamicate ideas. In this case, it was simple for Ḥālī to connect a British-derived naturalism to the Quranic injunction to observe the signs of God in the horizons and within oneself. Without quoting the Quran directly, he very clearly alluded to this verse, but his example was that of Walter Scott, who, according to Ḥālī, was discovered by a friend to be engrossed in the painstaking work of taking notes on minute wild plants and berries, the better to lend realism to his poem "Rokeby" (Ḥālī 1964, 165–66).[20] Empirical observation, which is not mentioned at all in previous poetological manuals, was thus given pride of place in Ḥālī's treatise. The freshness of personal observation was opposed to the spiritlessness of conventional poetry that simply regurgitated the endlessly masticated, used-up propositions of which Āzād had spoken.

Having expanded upon the importance of observation, Ḥālī implicitly set up reality as a limit upon the imagination's range by introducing a new faculty onto the scene: the discriminatory power *(quwwat-i mumayyizah)*. The imaginative faculty, he wrote, must be governed by discrimination to remain within its bounds and produce good poetry, free from an excess of fancy. Discrimination was made possible by the familiarity with the real world that Ḥālī had already advised. If the mind of the poet is deprived of "its proper food; that is, of the provisions of truths and real events," it will perforce feed upon the unhealthy wild vegetation of far-fetched fancies (Ḥālī 1964, 165–66). For a poet's mind to be able to discriminate between wild fancy and proper ideas based on reality, the poet must habitually regale himself or herself with intellectual food gathered from "nature."

The *Muqaddamah*'s subject is poetry rather than prose, and prose romances are therefore not touched upon. But romances in versified form—specifically, in maśnawī form—certainly are. Ḥālī singled out several for criticism. The poem "Ṭilism-i ulfat" (Love's ṭilism) by the Lucknow-based poet Ḵhwājah Asad 'Alī Ḵhān Qalaq was disparaged as self-contradictory, as well as bawdy, as was Dayā Shankar Nasīm's masterpiece *Gulzār-i Nasīm*, the versified *qiṣṣah* of Bakāwalī (Ḥālī 1964, 366–67). In casting such a sprinkling of aspersions, Ḥālī (1964, 368) was only warming to his real subject, namely, the unnaturalness of such romances:

> With regard to the *qiṣṣah*, it is necessary to take care that nothing is expressed that is contrary to experience and observation. Just as nowadays it is not becoming to ground the *qiṣṣah* in impossible and super-customary [*fauq al-'adah*] things, it is absolutely unacceptable to narrate episodes in the *qiṣṣah* that are belied by experience and observation. It is not simply the bad taste of the *qiṣṣah* writer that is thus proved, but his lack of knowledge, his unacquaintedness with the facts of the world, and his indifferent attitude toward the gathering of necessary information.

Without being oversimplistic about the roots of this new emphasis on nature, which no doubt looked to an already existing Islamicate rationalism for a buttress, it is safe to say that it was part and parcel of the overturning of traditional ways of thinking that was tied to the increased control asserted by the British over elite Indian education and culture after they had quelled the Rebellion of 1857, exiled Bahādur Shāh Ẓafar, and put India under the rule of the Crown. Infamously, in 1835 the British politician and litterateur Thomas Babington Macaulay championed both the withdrawal of British funding for traditional Indian educational institutions and support for English-medium education with a Western cultural slant. These insistences were enshrined in the 1835 English Education Act. Ḥālī's *Muqaddamah* in fact draws heavily upon Macaulay and upon the ideas of other Britons such as Walter Scott and John Milton.

In Muḥammad Ḥusain Āzād's project of literary reform, the effects of colonialist thought were even clearer. He directly advocated the imitation of British models of fiction, which represented what was natural and real. He argued that to continue to allow fantastical representation to run amok was to oppose the historical progress that India's British benefactors were sharing with the backward country. In the foreword to his literary-critical work *Nairang-i k̲h̲ayāl* (The enchantment of imagination), of which the first half was published in 1888, Āzād (1998, 46) adopted a fawning attitude toward the technology, culture, and literature of the British rulers of India: "Just as the English arts and sciences are improving our clothing, our dwellings, our living conditions, and our former knowledge, English literature, too, goes on correcting our literature." He painted an image of a befuddled and backward Urdu literature that was fortunate to be subject to the influence of the much more advanced literature of the English language. Like Ḥālī, Āzād attacked the faulty representation in which Urdu literature indulged. He singled out romances as principal perpetrators of this crime:

> That era has passed during which we would tell our boys stories from the mouths of parrots and mynah-birds. And if we made some progress we would have four faqirs tie on their loincloths and settle down,

or fly fairies, or produce demons, and waste the whole night speaking of them. The times are different, and so we too must act differently. (Āzād 1998, 49)

The changing times, the onward march of history, the eclipse of the old worldview: these necessitated the discarding of the fantastic forms of representation provided by the kinds of texts to which Āzād alluded. His readers would have understood that he was referring to well-known *qiṣṣah*s in the passage quoted above. The reference to the storytelling parrot or mynah-bird would have been understood as an allusion to the various versions of the *Ṭūṭī-nāmah* (Parrot's tale), and the four faqirs were the dervishes in the *Qiṣṣah-i Chahār darwesh* (Tale of the four dervishes), while the *parī*s might have been Princess Bakāwalī or any one of a number of such *qiṣṣah* characters. Such absurd stories must be done away with, according to Āzād, in favor of English-style representations, which have a solid basis in reality.

Representations that are incongruous with the rational-empirical world are not thrown out completely by Āzād, but their existence must be justified in one of two ways: either they should form useful allegories, or they should subvert themselves absurdly enough to be read as explosions of the romance genre. The latter is the way Ratan Nāth Sarshār's prose books might have been read, for example, while the allegorical romance—a subgenre of which there was a long tradition in South Asia—was represented by many of the essays in *Nairang-i ḳhayāl* itself. Later, Munshī Premchand's (1910) story "*Dunyā kā sab se anmol ratan*" ("The World's Most Precious Object") was another example of the allegorical romance. But in the absence of one of these two motives, romances were simply without utility, according to Āzād's logic. English literature, in contrast to literature in Urdu, always aims at a beneficial purpose, edifying and informing. English writings, according to Āzād (1998, 48), are only lightly garnished by the imagination. Their foundation is in reality.

While Āzād praised English literature for its faithfulness to reality, a similar form of literature in the Urdu language had already begun to gain sway, with British encouragement. First published in 1874, Naẕīr Aḥmad's *Taubaṯ al-Naṣūḥ* (The repentance of Naṣūḥ) was one of the earliest Urdu novels, along with other previous works by Naẕīr Ahmad: *Mir'at al-'arūs* (The bride's mirror, 1869) and *Banāt al-na'sh* (Daughters of the bier, 1872) (Naim 2004a, 132).[21] *Taubaṯ al-Naṣūḥ* narrates the moral and religious reawakening of its title character, Naṣūḥ, following a feverish dream. Abashed by his admonitory vision, Naṣūḥ sets out to reform not only himself but also his entire family. His dandyish elder son Kalīm, who is addicted to all manner of luxury in the style of Indian aristocrats, is, however, refractory. Naṣūh and his younger son 'Alīm resort to ransacking Kalīm's apartments and discarding the possessions that he keeps to cultivate his fashionable image. In a scene highly reminiscent of the burning of Don Quixote's library, Naṣūḥ and 'Alīm come upon Kalīm's book cabinet and resolve to consign his collection to the flames.[22] Another brother, Salīm, describes how the voluptuary Kalīm advised him to buy such distasteful romances as the *Fasānah-i 'ajā'ib* (Story of wonders), the *Tale of Bakāwalī*, the *Tale of Ḥātim Ṯā'ī*, and the *Bahār-i dānish* (Naẕīr Aḥmad 1964, 254). Similarly, 'Alīm speaks regretfully of the time that he has wasted at the traditional school (*maktab*), where he has only mouthed the Quran without understanding its words but has read worthless *qiṣṣah*s (Naẕīr Aḥmad 1964, 130). In both the critique that it made of the *qiṣṣah* genre and the circumstances of its production, Naẕīr Ahmad's novel was clearly subject to British ideas. Based in part on Daniel Defoe's conduct book *The Family Instructor*, *Taubaṯ al-Naṣūḥ* was written by Naẕīr Aḥmad in the hopes of winning a literary prize awarded each year by the British in the North-Western Provinces. He did win it, to the tune of five hundred rupees. The book, along with his other works, not only entered the twentieth-century canon of Urdu literature but also gained a long-lasting place on school syllabi (Naim 2004b, 129).

As in the case of the reform of the Urdu *ġhazal*, an ancillary objection to the *qiṣṣah* genre was that it was incapable of inculcating proper morals in its readers. Kalim's precious books, destroyed by his reform-crazed family, were described by Naẕīr Aḥmad (1964, 253) as "short *qiṣṣah*s, [containing] uncouth ideas, obscene meanings, and debased subjects; far from morals, distant from shame." Apart from Naẕīr Aḥmad's characterization of Kalīm's library, the novelist 'Abd al-Ḥalīm Sharar's indictment of the *qiṣṣah* of Ḥātim Ṭā'ī is an example of this critique. In presenting the "historical" circumstances of Ḥātim, the exemplar of generosity, Sharar decried the absurd and unhistorical *qiṣṣah* as a stumbling block to the effectiveness of Ḥātim's ethical exemplarity (Sharar, n.d., *Ṣad pārah-i dil* 110).[23] The logic at work in Sharar's critique was that the exemplarity of literature can only be effective if readers are able to believe in the would-be exemplars that it put forth as its protagonists or antagonists. This reasoning, like, and indeed tied to, the epistemological critique of the *qiṣṣah*, can be traced to eighteenth-century British literary criticism. Taking his cue from Aristotle's discussion of character in the *Poetics*, Samuel Johnson had made precisely this point about English romances. For Johnson, the doughty knight who battles dragons and mates with fairies was too far-fetched a figure for the reader to exchange places with (Williams 1970, 142–44). Epistemological change meant, for Johnson, that fantastic romances must fail to be exemplary any longer, for no right-thinking person could connect their characters to themselves. As in the case of the Western romance genre with which the *qiṣṣah* was identified, the *qiṣṣah*'s failure of moral exemplarity was tied to its epistemological failure.

Both the epistemological and the moral failures of the *qiṣṣah* were tied by the reforming elites to a declinist narrative of Indian history, which had a clear connection to the Orientalist notion that Indian nonrationalism and love of the "romance" proved the lingering premodernity of the Indian intellect. Proponents of this idea of Indian history, still popular in our own time despite the efforts of revisionist historians, averred that after the 1707 death of Aurangzeb, last of the "great Mughals," Indo-Muslim culture fell prey to decline. This decline was caused not only by warfare and a failing economy but also by the effeminacy and debauchery of the elites, their neglect of military duty, and their slothful reliance on the lowest and most depraved members of society as well as superstition, "man-worship," opium addiction, and other such horrors. The idea of Indian decline provided, of course, a convenient justification for colonialist intervention from the eighteenth century onward (Sarkar 1973, 335–61).[24]

It is not the father but the *qiṣṣah*-loving son Kalim who is cast as the representative of this debauched, decadent, and somnolent culture in *The Repentance of Nasuh*. The still-fashionable culture into which Kalīm figured was criticized even by Walī Ashraf Ṣabūḥī, the admirer and biographer of Delhi's "last" storyteller, Mīr Bāqir 'Alī. Despite his sympathetic portrayal of Bāqir 'Alī, Ṣabūḥī diagnoses the fortunes of the *qiṣṣah* genre in a way that accords exactly with the declinist historical narrative:

> [Properly military] feelings of bloodthirstiness were changed into thoughts of cock and quail fighting, hunting, music and dance, and other entertainments. A state of impassivity was cast over what had been an active life. Their limbs began to go numb in consequence of sitting on couch cushions all day, and at night the quality of their sleep was affected. They needed lullabies, and so, romances were begun. This was how storytelling began. Whether Iran invented it or India, it was the product of the people's slumber and the government's numbness. (Ṣabūḥī 1963, 43)

While Ṣabūḥī's idea of history is inherited from the British and from Indian reformers such as Sharar, to whose account of Awadhi decadence Ṣabūḥī's views can be compared, his narrative of Indian decline points toward the possibility of a more active future (Sharar 2000). It should not be surprising that nationalists swallowed colonialist historiography to provide a foil for their own struggles. Thus the view of the *qiṣṣah* that portrayed it as an outgrowth and enabler of a horridly backward *nawābī* India was well entrenched in the twentieth century, among nationalists as well as among admirers of the British.

By the middle of the twentieth century, Urdu literary critics were making systematic attempts to define the genre by listing the works supposed to belong to it. Some of the most impressive among these works of literary scholarship were Gyān Chand Jain's and Farmān Fatḥpūrī's volumes, which surveyed *dāstāns* in prose and verse respectively, aiming at comprehensiveness. While Jain and Fatḥpūrī bequeathed definitions of the genre to us by researching and describing every *qiṣṣah* they deemed even marginally important, they and other *qiṣṣah* scholars such as Waqār 'Azīm and Kalīm al-Dīn Aḥmad also attempted to encode the genre by explaining its traits directly. The views expressed by the twentieth-century critics regarding Urdu romances were extensions of the views held earlier by writers such as Ḥālī and Āzād, albeit in a more sophisticated and sympathetic form.

Shamsur Rahman Faruqi has shown that the most important among the Urdu critics of the twentieth century clung to Ḥālī's and Āzād's prejudices regarding the Urdu *qiṣṣah* and especially to the declinist historical narrative that had come to support these prejudices. They held such adverse views even while they defended the *qiṣṣah* from the partisans of the novel. The novel was by the mid-twentieth century in the ascendant in the hierarchy of prose genres, and the production of *qiṣṣah*s was not as visible, though it had not yet ceased. Prose criticism took the novel as its touchstone; the Urdu "romance" was increasingly being perceived as a thing of the past, just as its Western namesake had already been a hundred years before. Thus, for example, when the Indian writer Rāz Yazdānī mounted a defense against literary critic Rām Bābū Saksenah's (1966, 101) accusations that *qiṣṣah*s were deficient in the consistency of their characters, that they were far-fetched, and so forth, he seems to have been unable to take a step back from Saksenah's assumptions in refuting his argument (Faruqi 1999, 496). Faruqi shows that Yazdānī simply refuted Saksenah on Saksenah's own terms—that is, on the terms of the novel's genre code. If Saksenah argued that the novel was superior in its expression of characters' emotions, Yazdānī asserted that the *qiṣṣah* also represented its characters' interiority. If Saksenah belittled the plot of the *qiṣṣah* as disconnected, Yazdānī stood up for the *qiṣṣah*'s plot without telling the reader how it was different from the plots of novels (Faruqi 1999, 497–502). The novel had established itself as the dominant genre in the system. Its standards reigned paramount.

Apart from Rāz Yazdānī, Faruqi reviews the work of Suhail Bukhārī, Waqār 'Aẓīm, Rāhī Ma'ṣūm Raẓā, Suhail Aḥmad Ḳhān, Shamīm Aḥmad, and Muhammad Salim-ur-Rahman, but he devotes the most energy to a critique of Kalīm al-Dīn Aḥmad's *Urdū zabān aur fann-i dāstān-go'ī* (The Urdu language and the art of storytelling). In this work Kalīm al-Dīn Aḥmad, while affirming the usefulness of studying the romance, referred repeatedly to the genre as the work of "savages" or of "immature children" (Aḥmad 1965, quoted in Faruqi 1999, 504). Though writing in the 1960s, he followed a line of reasoning similar to that of the nineteenth-century Orientalists and Urdu literary reformers and insisted that irrational events such as those depicted in romances could be appreciated by readers only insofar as they were still possessed to some degree of a childlike mindset or, what was practically the same, a savage mindset:

> The similarity between a child and a savage lies in the fact that both enjoy stories, and do not weigh them upon the scales of ratiocination and criticism. When a child's mind has developed, and when the savage pushes forward through the stages of civilization, he feels that there is something lacking in these stories. (Aḥmad 1965, quoted in Faruqi 1999, 513)

Kalīm al-Dīn Aḥmad's criticism follows a familiar logic. According to this reasoning, the novel is the properly modern and rational form of fictional narrative. The *qiṣṣah* is useful mainly because it belongs to a previous era, going all the way back to a period of "savagery," and it can be studied as a relic of the past. Children, like savages, are credulous and imperfect in their appreciation of the strictures that reason and sense impose upon reality, and therefore they enjoy romances. Fully civilized adults, on the other hand, should only be able to enjoy romances insofar as there is some residuum of the child or savage left in them. We have already seen that British critics were asserting the childishness of *qiṣṣah*s and their audiences in the nineteenth century, parallel to the Orientalist strategy of legitimizing the reading of these "romances" for the production of knowledge about Indian society. This idea was bound up with a notion of Indian historical backwardness or medievalism, which was then taken up by Indian reformers themselves.

Gyān Chand Jain's masterpiece of literary history, *Urdū kī naṡrī dāstāneṅ* (Urdu prose romances), is perhaps the most sensitive and clear-minded work on the *qiṣṣah/dāstān* genre produced in the twentieth century. It is the only major work that Faruqi exempts from his criticism. In his introductory essays, Jain makes certain observations about the worldview of the *qiṣṣah* that pose a direct challenge to the dominant epistemology that privileges the novel. Most radically, Jain champions the validity of "supernatural" beings and events, pointing to the observations of institutions in the West such as the Society for Psychic Research and the Institute of Parapsychology (Gyān Chand Jain 1969, 62–69). In much of his argumentation Jain adheres to the strategy of appealing to Western authority, a practice that one sees earlier in the histories of Bakāwalī, for example. However, he also avails himself of the characterizations of jinns, demons, and *paris* that had been made by Sharar (Gyān Chand Jain 1969, 66).[25] As Zadeh (2011, 6) has written, "While we may readily admit that there are no islands populated with dog-headed men, or tribes of women who grow from trees, . . . we need not do so at the expense of understanding the conceptual frameworks that made such stories meaningful." Whether or not one agrees with Jain's positive assessment of British Air Chief Marshal Lord Dowding's claim that fairies still reside in English gardens, his willingness to take the epistemology behind the *qiṣṣah* seriously made him a more sensitive critic than his contemporaries (Gyān Chand Jain 1969, 64). Even if the very vocabulary of the "supernatural" (*fauq-i fiṭrat*) poses limitations, it is arguably a step forward from Waqār 'Aẓīm's acceptance that the *qiṣṣah* is "unnatural" (*ghair fiṭrī*) (Faruqi 1999, 527–28).

If it were the case that Jain's study presented a perfectly historicized picture of the genre, then we could rest assured of its benign influence. But this most important work on the *dāstān* genre is curiously divided within itself. The excellence and independence of Jain's readings of an awe-inspiring number of stories are far greater than the quality of his reading of Indian history. Like Kalīm al-Dīn Aḥmad, Jain does find it necessary to draw the reader's attention to the origins of the human species to fully trace the history of the *qiṣṣah* and present it as a document revealing the nature of the earliest humans, although in doing so he manages to be less egregious than Kalīm al-Dīn Aḥmad. Where Jain's study reverts most strongly to colonialist ideas is in his acceptance of the then-prevalent notion of the decline of Indo-Muslim society and culture after the death of Aurangzeb.

Jain's idea of Indian history was entirely consonant with the one that Sabūḥī assumed when he inveighed against the inactivity and love of luxury that were supposedly the primary characteristics of Indian nobles after the Mughal Empire began to decay. Jain claimed that the popularity of the *qiṣṣah* genre was in fact in direct proportion to the laziness of Indian society (Gyān Chand Jain 1969, 106). As one reads *Urdū kī nas̱rī dāstāneṅ*, it at first appears that, although he is in thrall to declinist historiography, he will allow his judgment of the *qiṣṣah* to escape determination by that history. He wrote, "*Dāstān*s are the product of an inactive society in search of repose. Nevertheless, they themselves are full of the heat of activity and life. There is no rest in them at all. Everywhere, there is speed, change, and revolution." However misguided this view of the societies in which *dāstān*s arose is, Jain is to be credited for not reducing them to mere reflections of elite Indian culture in this passage. But in his next chapter Jain argued that the activeness of the *qiṣṣah* and the inactiveness of the society supposedly reinforced one another. Exciting its listeners with fictional battles, the *qiṣṣah* stood as a substitute for real military activity. As the storyteller poured the *qiṣṣah* into his ear, "the nawab would feel as if one of his chiefs or deputies had accomplished some feat. In this state he would take himself away into dreamland, where he might perhaps subjugate some demons and fairies" (Gyān Chand Jain 1969, 107). The elite Indians who were the storytellers' primary audiences were so contented with the active scenes of the *qiṣṣah* as to forget that it behooved them to act themselves.

In the end, Jain, like most of the other *dāstān* scholars, told his readers that the onset of the blood-stirring age of the Indian independence movement spelled the *qiṣṣah*'s death knell. At last, Indians themselves were active and no longer had any need to engross themselves in book-bound battles and quests. With a hint of regret, Jain explained that the *qiṣṣah* is history—its time has passed, and its importance lies in its representation of the bygone time in which it was important. Many twentieth-century critics treated *qiṣṣah*s as mines of historical information; Rahi Masoom Raza (1979) does so in his study of *Ṭilism-i Hoshrubā*; Ibn-i Kanwal (2005) in his book on the *Bostān-i Ḳhayāl*; and Sayyid 'Abd Allāh (1965) in the preface to his edition of *'Ajā'ib al-qiṣaṣ*. In this antiquarian spirit, Jain pronounced his final verdict: "The importance [of *qiṣṣah*s] is like that of ancient ruins. Just as we preserve old things in museums, we shall keep *dāstān*s safe as literary souvenirs" (Gyān Chand Jain 1969, 110).

In the diminution of the *qiṣṣah* to a residue of a bygone era there is perhaps a kernel of wisdom. Jain's obituary recognizes, at least, that if the genre was unsuited to the present age, there was some reason for its flourishing during a previous historical age. The historicism of genre insisted on by Ralph Cohen (1986)—its inseparability from its ideological, cultural, and material contexts—is acknowledged. Jain had sympathy for the nonrationalist worldview that once supported the worth of the *qiṣṣah* genre and a willingness to read individual *qiṣṣah*s on their own terms rather than under the destructive light provided by the dominant poetics of the novel. But even he was blinded by a historiography that devalued the history of India prior to independence and that had once been twinned with the rationalist and moral critiques of the "Eastern romance." The revisionist narrative of this period of Indian history threatens, thankfully, to do away with many of the assumptions about colonial saviorhood that lurk behind the old historical narrative. But apart from demolishing problematic assumptions about cultures that existed at a relative remove from Western colonialism, it is also necessary to attempt to reconstruct what has been lost, though such an attempt is in itself fraught with risks.

The twentieth-century literary critics' antiquarianism should also alert us to the dangers of overemphasizing the *qiṣṣah* genre's decline. While the *qiṣṣah* came under pressure from a newly victorious epistemology and a rival genre, and while the storytelling tradition was eroded by socioeconomic changes, a story of absolute decline runs the risk of determining the *qiṣṣah* according to a simplistic historical origin. It also risks ignoring the rivulets running through the twentieth century and beyond, wherein the *qiṣṣah*, or new genres that draw upon it, may have survived. It is not enough to depend upon a historicism that anchors verbal art to its "original" context. Otherwise, we should be content to say, with Jain, that *qiṣṣah*s are "legacies of our past, of no use for the present, or for the future" (Gyāṇ Chand Jain 1969, 110).

Conclusion

WHAT WAS THE *QIṢṢAH,* if not a rudimentary precursor to the novel? How was its genre code constituted before the new devaluation inflicted by colonial epistemologies at the turn of the twentieth century? A genre code is always forged and modified by the force of worldviews arising in particular spatial and historical contexts. The *qiṣṣah* was always a genre with a contested code, as we have seen in chapters 4 and 5. Differing epistemologies led to different valuations of the *qiṣṣah* against the genre of history, for example, even before the challenge of the novel arose, alongside with India's permeation by colonial thought. But given the ubiquity of a nonrationalist worldview privileging the sincerity of narratives, Divine Power, and the judgment of the heart, the *qiṣṣah* held its own against many other genres to which it was related and with which it was in conflict. We could not have apprehended the *qiṣṣah*'s code or value except within the hierarchical matrix of a genre system that bore the imprint of the worldviews we have mentioned and in which each genre (*qiṣṣah*, history, *marśiyah*, *ġhazal*, etc.) had its relative worth.

Especially in the case of an orally performed genre such as the *qiṣṣah*, it has been necessary to consider how its best-known producers, the *qiṣṣah-ḳhwān*s, or storytellers, put their imprint upon the genre. It is facile to imagine that they were uplifted or cast down like autumn leaves in the wind, passively subject to the whims of the changing worldviews of audiences and others as they raised or lowered the worth of *qiṣṣah*s. Storytellers were very active participants in the valuation of the *qiṣṣah*, since their own worth and power were tied to it. We have seen how, from Darbār Ḳhān at Akbar's court to Mīr Bāqir 'Alī in his humble house in Delhi, storytellers employed a variety of strategies and made use of their social capital and multiple professional abilities to increase their worth and that of the genre with which they were identified, right down to the supposed sunset hour of storytelling in the first half of the twentieth century.

Their method of constructing *qiṣṣah*s in performance, through the weaving together of textual fragments in parataxis and through *munāsib-ḳhwānī*, points to a basic principle of the *qiṣṣah* genre, or any genre for that matter. A text is never traversed by one genre alone; every text is multigeneric. In the case of any *qiṣṣah*, we can clearly see the stitching that binds together the patchwork of textual fragments bearing diverse genres. The multigenericity of any *qiṣṣah* produces two complexities that must define the future study of *qiṣṣah*s far beyond the limits of the current book. First, within any given text dominated by the genre code of the *qiṣṣah*, we need to take into account the interrelations, symbioses, and conflicts of a multiplicity of participating genres and how they might have worked to produce a use value for the audience. Second, we must look for the *qiṣṣah* outside of texts that we would normally perceive as *qiṣṣah*s. We have sought out the *qiṣṣah* in histories in chapter 4. We have seen instances in which *tārīḳh*s were crisscrossed by fragments marked by the genre traits of the *qiṣṣah*. We have encountered histories that were legible in their entirety as *qiṣṣah*s—despite the fact that the *qiṣṣah* and history genres were often opposed to one another by proponents of pre-colonial rationalism.

At least at the elite level, *qiṣṣah*s and histories would gradually become sealed off from one another. By the end of the nineteenth century, both histories and novels would become more highly esteemed than *qiṣṣah*s. In chapter 5, I outlined the role of colonialism in the lowering of the *qiṣṣah*'s worth closer to our own time and the complicity of Urdu-knowing thinkers, from Ḥālī and Āzād to Kalīm al-Dīn Aḥmad and Gyān Chand Jain, in this devaluation. It goes without saying that this study itself cannot be neutral. It is another example of an ideological effort to change the value and the genre code of the *qiṣṣah* through an appeal to a particular narrative of the genre's history, namely, an anti-colonial one. It seeks to reshape the *qiṣṣah*'s genre code in a manner that would free it from Orientalist assumptions, in the name of the recovery of a precolonial genre code.

Historical recoveries always take place in an ideological manner, and the genre code is always formed through the force of worldviews, including ideologies. But at the same time, I would like to point out some of the limits and blindnesses of this study, especially with regard to its focus on storytellers. I have deemed it important to recover the lives of Indo-Persian and Urdu storytellers, who have for the most part been forgotten by scholars but without whose agency it is impossible to understand the genre dynamics of the *qiṣṣah*. What the sources give us, however, is only a certain cross-section of the storytellers who must have populated India in previous centuries.

The Forgotten Storytellers

The storytellers whose lives and productions of worth I analyzed in chapters 2 and 3 were almost uniformly male professionals performing in Persian or Urdu for elites. The sources that we have for the history of storytelling in India seem to yield the names of only these storytellers, whose gender, language, elite audience, and, especially, specialized profession work in concert to make them visible to us. Even these relatively privileged storytellers have been minimally visible and in some cases unknown to scholars. It is important to bring their names to light, but in doing so, we should consider who may have been left in the shadows. In the first place, we know next to nothing about female storytellers, although they certainly existed. For instance, the nawab of Cambay (Khambat) once sent to an ill and sleepless British friend

> two female story-tellers, of respectable Mogul families, but neither young nor handsome. Placing themselves on each side of his pillow, one of them in a monotonous tone commenced a tale, which in due time had a soporiferous effect; when he awoke the story was renewed exactly where it had left off. (J. Forbes 1834, 235–36, quoted in Pritchett 1991, 6–7)

In Lucknow there were female servants, *muġhlānī*s and *ustānī*s, who performed tales for noble women (Ja'far Ḥusain 1998, 168, 434, 453; Pritchett

1991, 15). The names of these storytellers go unrecorded. Like the male storytellers of Mughal lineage who wound up at the Rampuri court, many of these women were, or claimed to be, of noble birth, but they were possessed of little economic means, a condition born of the tumult of the eighteenth-century crisis of Mughal power. It is also clear that they are mentioned because of their connection with elite audiences.

Elite audiences and patrons could not, however, have been the only arbiters of the *qiṣṣah*'s worth, nor can we by any means assume that *qiṣṣah-ḳhwāns* themselves were always or even usually of elite status. To borrow Katherine Butler Schofield's distinction between "status" and "prestige," the status of most of the *qiṣṣah-ḳhwāns* we have looked at seems to have been at least intermediate and non-elite, even if their middling or even lower status was covered over by their prestige or worth in the eyes of elite patrons.[1] The languages that the remembered storytellers used are tied to their worth and to the fact of their being remembered at all. These languages were Persian, up to the eighteenth century, and Urdu, from the eighteenth century onward—both languages that were well patronized by courtly elites. Were we able to find instances of storytellers who told stories in other languages, we might be on our way to discovering other audiences for the *qiṣṣah* as well.

Colonial studies such as Richard Carnac Temple's *Legends of the Punjab* do exist to provide us with narrative *qiṣṣahs* in the Punjabi language, but they give only the barest idea of the performers of these tales. Even in the twentieth century, the excellent work of Saeed Bhutta on the life and tales of the low-status Punjabi *mīrāsī* storyteller Kamāl Dīn stands out as a unique example of scholarly attention paid to Punjabi-language storytelling. For Rajasthan, studies such as Susan Wadley's on the story of Ḍholā or John Smith's on the Pābūjī narrative are once more the fruits of ethnographical work, as is Wilma Heston's scholarship on Pashto storytelling, among others (Wadley 2004; Smith 1991; Heston and Nasir 2015; Lutgendorf 1991; Pandey 1982; Nath and Gold 1992; Sabnani 2012). Scholarly studies of non-elite Indian storytelling using scrolls, images, masks, and so on are similarly focused on the present, and I have been reluctant to project back into the colonial and precolonial past on their basis.[2] Nevertheless, the silence of the biographical dictionaries and histories regarding storytelling in languages other than Persian and Urdu is no doubt unrepresentative of the historical presence of such storytelling.

The evidence suggests, however, that Persian-language storytellers in Mughal India preferred to place their storytelling and its language within the elite sphere, especially if they had come from elite or socially mobile lineages, as Darbār Ḵhān and Mullā Asad had done and as Faḵhr al-Zamānī claimed to have done (Faḵhr al-Zamānī Qazwīnī 1983, 758). The practically exclusive emphasis in the sources upon courtly storytelling also tells us that Persian-writing elites had no knowledge, or covered over their knowledge, of both elite and non-elite appreciation of storytelling by non-elites, much of which would have taken place in languages other than Persian. As Pritchett has mentioned in *The Romance Tradition in Urdu* (1991), even storytelling in Urdu is only unambiguously known from the nineteenth century.

While most of the above lacunae can be blamed on the sources themselves, there is one final, more egregious assumption at work that has a bearing on the research methods for the study of storytellers. This assumption is that storytelling always occurred in professional contexts. Most if not all of the storytellers whose names have appeared in chapters 2 and 3 are recognized, sometimes in their very names, as professional storytellers: for example, Mulla Asad Qiṣṣah-ḵhwān and Mīr Bāqir ʿAlī Dāstāngo. We have seen that they very often performed other functions for which they were remunerated. But we have not dealt with the fact that there were storytellers for whom *qiṣṣah-ḵhwānī* was not an occupation but rather a casual activity, performed for the delight and benefit of family or friends. Two examples during the eighteenth century are ʿInāyat Allāh Bangālī, who told the *Tale of the Bakāwalī Flower* orally to his beloved Naẕar Muḥammad but who nowhere indicated that he was a professional, and the uncle of Sayyid Iḥsān ʿAlī, who told the Persian *Tale of Ḥātim Ṭā'ī* during a family gathering in Hyderabad, the audience for which included his young nephew (Sayyid Iḥsān ʿAlī 1755, fol. 14v). While it is likely that the techniques, flair, and craftiness of professional storytelling made it a touchstone for nonprofessionals, casual storytelling must have been much more common, and in this study, I could have read the sources with an eye to discovering instances of this mode of storytelling. Indeed, it will be worthwhile in the future to pay more heed to Orsini's argument (2009) that the content, form, and usage of nineteenth-century Hindi and Urdu lithographs link them to oral performance.[3] Similarly, it is likely that close readings and considerations of the material aspects of *qiṣṣah* manuscripts will better help us to understand casual and non-elite storytelling (see Orsini and Schofield 2015, esp. Novetzke 2015).

Survival and Revival

In remembering the possibilities of non-elite audiences for the *qiṣṣah* and their continuation into the twentieth century, we should also temper the idea of the *qiṣṣah*'s decline. While there certainly was a decline of the *qiṣṣah*—I have dealt with several aspects of it in chapters 2 and 5—certain questions remain. What was it that declined? What would be the measure of such a decline? Clearly the steady disappearance of Indian princes and potentates left elite storytellers bereft of much of their traditional patronage; as the twentieth century progressed, we hear less and less of storytellers who could find courtly support. Yet it appears that Mīr Bāqir 'Alī, for example, was able to adjust his strategy and find alternative patrons among the wealthier citizens of Delhi, including the well-to-do merchant Chhunnāmal and the politically influential physician Ḥakīm Ajmal Ḳhān. Bāqir 'Alī is remembered because of his vaunted connections to the nineteenth-century nobility of India, whereas storytellers like Ṭallan Miyāṅ and Kamāl Dīn, who had no such connections as far as we know, were sidelined by most scholars. But the cases of these two storytellers demonstrate that professional storytelling for non-elite audiences lived on into the postcolonial period, as do the practices of picture storytellers in various regions of India, the subject of a 2010 exhibition at the Indira Gandhi National Centre for the Arts in Delhi.

Similarly, when we look at written *qiṣṣah*s, the story is not one of simple decline. There are clear indications that Naval Kishore Press's *Dāstān-i*

Amīr Ḥamzah was popular into the twentieth century. Several *daftars* of the cycle went into multiple editions, with reprintings of *Ṭilism-i Hoshrubā* being particularly frequent. Pritchett's summary of the incomplete British records shows that printed chapbook editions of smaller romances were also quite common; for example, there are records of 108,500 copies of the *Tale of Ḥātim Ṭā'ī* printed in India from 1896 to 1945—69,000 copies of twenty-eight Hindi editions and 39,500 copies of twenty Urdu editions. From 1904 to 1945, at least 265,600 copies of the *Qiṣṣah-i Ṭoṭā mainā* (Tale of the parrot and the mynah-bird) were printed, and other short romances boast similar numbers (Pritchett 1985, app. A). As demonstrated by *Marvelous Encounters* (Pritchett 1985) and the chapbook *qiṣṣah*s in Pritchett's own collection, these tales were common into the 1960s and 1970s, and juvenilized versions are still published by the Pakistani bookstore Ferozsons.

Thus the decline of the *qiṣṣah*—the devaluation of the genre, the cessation of its performance, the loss of interest in printed versions—is only verifiable at the elite level. The privileging of colonially derived epistemologies, and the valuing of the novel and later the even more realist short story (*afsānah*) over the fantastical *qiṣṣah*, was the work of elites influenced by British ideas. We cannot rule out the possibility of a subterraneous survival of the *qiṣṣah*'s value, which we have not yet learned to see clearly. In the past decade or so, storytelling in India and Pakistan has returned to prominence under the name of *dāstāngo'ī*, and this development has been marketed, not unreasonably, as a revival. It will take work to understand to what extent the thread was really broken.

Throughout the twentieth century, highbrow Bollywood films depicting upper-middle-class romance were accompanied by popular cinema that often used *qiṣṣah* plots. Some of them, such as *Gul-e Bakawali*, *Hatim Tai*, or the *Arabian Nights*–inspired *Ali Baba*, were very successful indeed, as demonstrated by the number of versions that existed. One has only to watch the white-winged Ḥusn Parī wave her wand to save Ḥātim Ṭā'ī (Jeetendra) from a gang of murderous ensorcelled trees in the 1992 film to believe that the *qiṣṣah*, or at least the worldview that it represented, was still valued at the end of the twentieth century, if only as a lower-middle-class entertainment. While these films also owed a great deal to Orientalist costume films in Hollywood, they represented the legacy that the *qiṣṣah* genre had staked out in the Parsi theater. Very often they were being produced by Parsi businessmen like Homi Wadia. Parsi and Urdu theater traditions were making use of *qiṣṣah* narratives from the very beginning. They drew especially upon the episodes of the *Shāhnāmah*, due to its representation of a Zoroastrian past, but other *qiṣṣah*s, like *Ḥātim Ṭā'ī* and *Gul-i Bakāwalī*, were also staged in the nineteenth century (Hansen 2003, 396–97; 2016, 223; Nicholson 2016, 617). Particularly popular was the *Bakāwālī*-like play *Indrasabha*, by Sayyid Āġhā Ḥasan Amānat Lakhnawī, first performed as early as 1854 (Amānat 2007, 18).

Enthusiasts of Urdu pulp fiction, published in serial digests, can also be regarded as unwitting upholders of the *qiṣṣah*'s value in face of its apparent decline. Though digest stories generally do not reference *qiṣṣah*s directly, it is not difficult to see them as reflections of a worldview that is heir to the one that gave the *qiṣṣah* genre a respectable position in the genre hierarchy. The popular story *Devtā* (Demigod), by Muhyiuddin Nawab (serialized from 1977 to 2010), is an example of a pulp fiction narrative filled with elements of the strange and marvelous.[4] The protagonist, Farhād 'Alī Taimūr, is a young middle-class Lahori embroiled in a difficult family situation complicated by contested landholdings. Early on, he is instructed in three occult sciences: mind reading, telepathy, and hypnotic suggestion. He uses them to extricate himself from his family difficulties but creates new enemies in the process. His cousin Ġhazzālah resents this telepathic Yūsuf for rejecting her Zulaikhā-like advances. Her machinations land Farhād in a dire situation when one day he awakens bound and trapped within a magic circle. A beautiful young woman in a sari appears to check up on him but turns out to be entirely unsympathetic to his plight. But to Farhād's astonishment, he realizes that he is able to read the mind of a nearby cat. Establishing a telepathic connection with the cat, he communicates with her, and she narrates her life story.

Farhād's feline interlocutor informs him that she was not originally a cat but rather a young Anglo-Indian woman named Sāmī Pokar, the daughter of Colonel Pokar of Calcutta. Sāmī was playing badminton one day with a friend, when she was espied by the wizened sorceress Chhammiyā and her male assistant Kedār. The sight of Sāmī's body filled Kedār with lust and Chhammiyā with envy. The two made a pact: Chhammiyā would snatch Sāmī's body, and Kedār would deflower Chhammiyā in the body of Sāmī Pokar. The two kidnapped Sāmī and achieved their first goal, Chhammiyā using her knowledge of the occult to enter Sāmī's body. But Sāmī's spirit, instead of dispersing into nothingness, was able to enter the body of a nearby cat. Sāmī the cat, anxious to preserve the virginity of her true body, pursued Chhammiyā and Kedār across India. The three finally turned up in Delhi, where Chhammiyā's guru resided, for Chhammiyā hoped that he would teach her a mantra to annihilate Sāmī's soul altogether. However, during their joint residence in the metropolis, the cat's intelligence did not go unnoticed. It was discovered in *qiṣṣah*-like manner. As Chhammiyā and Sāmī walked through the bazaar one day, Sāmī spotted a fraudulent transaction taking place. She leaped onto the coin being tendered, and to the shopkeeper's astonishment, the coin was found to be counterfeit. The cat's fame spread; a story was written up in the papers, and the Hindus began to worship her. The denouement comes when Chhammiyā, Kedār, and Sāmī (who are living together) receive an imposing visitor who turns out to be an intelligence agent from the Indian secret service (Research and Analysis Wing, or RAW). Before taking them to RAW's base, he explains that the cat will be used in an espionage mission against Pakistan.

It is easy to see the textual fragments of many genres that we think of as Western running through a pulp fiction novel like *Devtā*. It incorporates elements of science fiction. It echoes the B-grade horror films of the 1970s and 1980s, which were being produced in Lollywood as well as Hollywood.[5] The powers possessed by its characters signal its debt to superhero comics. And, most importantly, it shares many if not most of its genre traits with the *jāsūsī*, or detective novels that were popular in India and Pakistan, especially those of Ibn-e Safi, which had an obvious relation to novels by the likes of Ian Fleming.[6] But we could just as easily focus on their local hypotexts and see *Devtā* and other pulp fiction and *jāsūsī* novels as pervaded by fragments bearing the *qiṣṣah* genre, for readers who are still able to recognize it. The epistemology that *Devtā* reflects—one in which hypnotism, telepathy, body transfer, and mantric spells are taken seriously—is similar in many regards to the epistemology that buttressed the romance. The new worldview, which credited both the existence of jinns and that of scientifically studiable (but not yet explicable) paranormal activity, was precisely the worldview to which Gyān Chand Jain drew his readers' attention in his partial defense of the *qiṣṣah*.

If we see the *qiṣṣah* not as the dominant genre enveloping and controlling the receptions of other minor genres in a text but as a minor genre itself, in the sense of a genre of textual fragments running through other texts, then the survival of the *qiṣṣah* in later texts, both written and visual, from pulp fiction to Bollywood films, begins to come into focus. But the survival of the genre from the twentieth century onward will only become visible when the older *qiṣṣah*s that are the hypotexts of such works of verbal and visual art are remembered. In postcolonial South Asia, this remembrance is becoming more and more possible, as the courtly storytelling traditions of Faḳhr al-Zamānī and Bāqir 'Alī are revived and reshaped by an increasing number of *dāstāngo*s and as the idea of the novel's superiority becomes irrelevant. South Asians at the beginning of the twenty-first century are more open than their parents to a recognition of the value of the *qiṣṣah* and of the older ways of thinking upon which it rested.

Appendix

The Preface and Introduction to the *Ṭirāz al-akhbār*

This translation is based on the Majlis manuscript in Tehran. I came to know belatedly of the existence of a recent edition of the *Ṭirāz al-akhbār* by Sayyid Kamāl Ḥājj Sayyid Jawādī (Tehran: Pazhuhishkadah-yi Hunar, 1322 [2013–14]). I regret not being able to avail myself of this much-needed work and thank an anonymous peer reviewer for telling me of it. I thank Timur Koraev of Moscow State University for his aid with certain passages. Headings in capital letters represent text in red ink in the manuscript. All errors of translation are my own.

God, bestow upon Nabī a tongue!
Without Your praise his tale cannot be told.
Let his heart share stories with his tongue—
then make it scatter pearls in Your praise.

THE EMBROIDERER OF THE reports [*ṭirāz-i akhbār*] of renowned sultans and the Ornament of the stories of the Lords of the Auspicious Conjunction is the Great Name of God, exalted be His Greatness! One of

His Auspicious Names is the Crown upon the imperial signature [*ṭuġhrā*] of the firmans of earthly rulers. By the eternally obeyed Order of His Emperorship—which is the Seat of the trustworthiness of the national and economic affairs of the kings of the impermanent world until the extinction of the universe by the stamp of the seal-ring of the Creator—the knowers of the Valley of Awareness and those intimate with innumerable secrets praise Him to no end, and grow acquainted with helplessness and humbleness.

Those who sit upon their thrones in the gathering of meaning-decoration, and those enthroned upon the sandalwood seats in the company of word-ornamentation, are confirmed in their agitation when attempting to describe His countless favors and benefits. And so what place is there for one like me, a tale-bearing speechifier, who thinks little and has a long tongue, an ignorant tale-teller, a loquacious know-nothing, even to breathe a word declaring His Unity and Praising Him whose Oneness and Besoughtness are undeniable?

POEM [FOL. 2A]
Who am I that in my poverty
I should establish neighborhood
    with him by my praise?
I praise God boldly,
and in the wine-tavern essay my wit.
The eloquent Arab,[1] when his speech began,
bored no pearl, except
    What do we know of You?
For those aware of God
    the path gives no pain,
but what place is there for one
    unaware of himself?
Better that I pull back my tongue from its desire
A wooden sword is better in its sheath.

1. That is, Muḥammad.

Since the best behavior in the way of servitude is thanks and illimitable praise of the Real God, he brings upon his tongue whatever his heart can get a hold of. With that which has burned his nature he inks the pen and writes upon the folio of fame.

BY THE AUTHOR
In the Name of the Emperor of emperors
Who is the Refuge of the refugeless;
The Lord Who created the universe,
and created Adam from swarthy clay.

Hurrah for that Powerful One, Displayer of Power, Who in the blink of an eye brought the two worlds [*kaunain*] into existence by compounding the letters *kāf* and *nūn*,[2] and Who brought the races of the sons of Adam from the unity-place of nonexistence into the multiplicity-city of existence and subsistence by His Power!

FROM THE ROSEGARDEN OF MYSTERY[3]
When the "P" of His Power blew upon the Pen,
it made thousands of images upon the Tablet of Nonexistence.

Hurrah for the adorning Power that has ornamented some men with the jewels of bravery so that at the age at which they have the ability to distinguish between good and evil on the Day of Strife—on the road to knowledge of Him—they, like the silvery-limbed cupbearers of the joyful gatherings, can quaff the pomegranate-red wine of the blood of the religionless in the midst of the battle, from the goblet of the sharp sword and the cup of the blade, atop this man-rearing, man-eating rubbish-heap!

He sets a group of these courage-essaying men upon the business of following the doings of the wheat-complexioned, guileful idols, the bow-stringing of whose eyebrows and the dagger-play of whose eyelashes

2. These letters make up the existentiating Divine Command "*kun*" ("Be!").
3. *Gulshan-i rāz* by Maḥmūd Shabistarī.

pierce the soul and the heart [fol. 2b] the way that water wears away earth, so that with the arrow and the javelin they might snatch the heart and soul from the chests of the enemies of the faith. He is the Powerful One Who, before the enemy's attack, orders those defenders to manipulate their maces, which are like the Alburz Mountains in size, so that at the time of combat they batter the head of the invidious Sky, and disturb the brains of the cow of the Earth.

The flight of the carrier-pigeon of the arrow from the coop of the bow is in accordance with His Command. The throwing of the lasso-serpent from the nest of the catapult is in accordance with the Command of the One Who must be obeyed. He is a Protector Whose Protection is a complete shield against evil. Every head that is protected by it is impervious to the hatchet. He is the Victor whose Victory's "V" causes Death to fall on its face before everyone to whom He gives aid.

BY THE AUTHOR
Swift-horsed Death goes flying
from the one over whom He watches.

Every battle in which the fire of combat blazes up is the effect of a spark from the fire of the Wrath of the Wrathful. Every revelrous gathering in which the ones who are busy with revelry and joy heighten their knowledge of pleasure thanks to the melody of the harp and the flute, and the ecstasy of the song, is by the grace of His blemishless sitar.

BY THE AUTHOR
When the candle-fire's spear spits flame,
it is the Divine Wrath, to be sure.
Those drunk on song and wine in every gathering
are so by His pleasure, unbounded as it is.

He is the lover-loving Beloved, by the quality of whose needlessness the flower-faced, jasmine-scented, musky-haired ones perform their blandishments. He is the seeker-supporting Besought by the blessing of Whose care for lovers the poetry-speaking idols throw signs to the heart-bereft, by means of their wrinkled brows and the twistings of their hairs. The idols of every idol-house are amazed at His perfect Beauty, and the stones of the Ka'ba are confounded at His Greatness and Beauty:

DISTICH

O You, desire for Whom brought
    I am here! to the Haram,
it is your memory that feeds
    the idol.

The sun stabbing with its dagger, and the wandering moon that it spears, are busy day and night [fol. 3a] upon the field of the sky, speeding about. By His command, the lights of this blue enclosure govern the past and future of every individual among humankind by their ascent and descent.

BY THE AUTHOR

By His Command, the stars in the high heavens
are seeking this and that both day and night.
One man they make to reach a throne and crown,
and cast another one into black muck.

He is the Sage for Whose House of Healing the ingenious sages of the hospital of Time write prescriptions. He is the Scholar before the book of Whose scholarship the perfect scholars of the school of the world are know-nothings. He is the Artificer by Whose various artifices the rarest of the artifice-makers of the world are amazed. He is the Inventor in Whose novel inventions the best of the inventors of the earth are absorbed. He is the First of every last, and the Last of every first. He is the Hidden Aspect of every apparent thing, and the Apparent Aspect of every hidden thing. In every form that you see, His meaning is revealed. Every apparent thing at which you look has emerged out of His Hidden Side.

BY THE AUTHOR

Everywhere you turn there is the Face
of His self-manifestation,
whether you pry into the marrow
or into the skin.
The rose breaks into laughter
in the Spring because of Him,
and thanks to Him the vernal cloud
bursts into tears.
Because of Him in every form
there is profit,
and because of Him, substance
gains its properties.
All trees have two seasons in the year.
They are enrobed by the hand of Power.
Springtime is green,
like the color of the charmers.
Autumn is red,
like the blood of the martyrs.
To one He gives beauty,
and trains him in blandishments.
To one He gives love,
and enflames his form.
From within the heart
he brings meanings to the tongue.
He orders that words
be recorded by fingers.
The Earth and the skies exist
on account of His artifice.
The two worlds are merely
a whiff of His power. [fol. 3b]
Because of Him, every thing
makes its appearance.

And because of Him, too,
in the end, it is said,
It is not in the Abode.

His Majesty is great, and His Bounty is universal. After penning the praise of God, Who is without any "why"—and after thanking and lauding the Creator of *Be and it is . . .* prayers beyond reckoning [for the Prophet], and blessings whose number is not encompassed by understanding—not even that of the cores of the hearts of the knowers of God, not even from the tongue-tips of the self-knowers, those who would sacrifice themselves for the perfumed tomb and illuminated shrine of the Master [Muḥammad], who is the breeze that the Maker [has sent] to the inhabitants of this turquoise-like enclosure. Day and night, gifts of blessings are sent upon his pure soul, the best of all created things. *God and the angels bless the Prophet.*

To the court of this powerful and majestic Messenger, He sent Gabriel the Trustworthy to tell stories. So by the Celestial Command Gabriel recited to him the mournful story of Joseph, and by having him listen to that wondrous tale Gabriel released his blessed mind from the prison-house of the anguish caused by his enemies. The verse *We tell you the best of tales* is verification of this—indeed, it is a proof of the singularity of this matter.[4]

BY THE AUTHOR
In what language could the tongue praise
the one for whom Gabriel turned storyteller?
Better for me to send benedictions upon him,
as the Lord, Alive and Loving, commands.
May the blessings of God be upon him and his pure family.

Let it not be veiled from the chief among the wordsmiths of the gathering of speech-crafting and the incomparable storytellers of the assembly of story-making that this confused one wandering in the desert

4. Qur'an 12.3.

of amazement—ʿAbd al-Nabī b. Ḵhalaf Faḵhr al-Zamānī—came from Iran, the Trace of Paradise, at the outset of his youth, the beginning of the spring of his life, to India, the Abode of Peace. In this image-filled land he fell into the valley of storytelling out of necessity—

BY THE AUTHOR

Whatever the work may be
    that comes before the needy man,
he will find himself prosperous
    when to the task he sets his hand.

To make a long story short, by the blessing [fol. 4a] of verbal artistry, he was freed from the whisperings of distress. Afterward, he thought to himself and considered in his own heart that this heavenly art was becoming his favorite pastime—that, indeed, it had become a veil upon other excellent pursuits and purposes, and that he must leave this work, and release himself from the infamy of this shame.

COUPLET

Not all that my heart wished for came to be—
what came true was just what God desired.

So, by the Order of the Lord and the Celestial Decree, he busied himself for ten years in traveling and trading. During these days and months and years he spent most of his time studying the verses of the divans of the ancient and modern poets, and he read from beginning to end whatever books of history and romance he could get hold of. He collected all the choice poetry and prose that would be of use for any activity. Sometimes, when he could not get a book to peruse, he settled down to write poetry, and his pen's crooked writing recorded good verses and interesting couplets. He also gained expertise in the science of divination, and committed just *jafr* to memory. In the art of composition he became the envy of his contemporaries.

But, strange to say, during his days of wandering the world, in every country that he reached, it was his storytelling that was loudly celebrated. He saw that the rank of the other arts was low, and the rulers of every land troubled this weakling to tell the story of the Prophet's and the Walī's [i.e., 'Alī b. Abī Ṭālib's] paternal uncle [Ḥamzah b. 'Abd al-Muṭṭalib]. Their interest was stretched to an exaggerated extent, beyond all limits. Indeed, the art of one's own genius is imbued with a certain musk that will make itself known however much you hide its fragrance. It is not possible that the hearer should hear it, and not become like a flower, laughing and in bloom.

BY THE AUTHOR

The smell of talent reveals it—like musk, [fol. 4b]
if it can be concealed, it is a wonder.
Speech fills hearts with joy. Everyone
who hears a lovely word laughs like a flower.

To sum it up, when he saw that this burden still lay upon his neck, and that this work had fallen upon his head, he was once again forced to make a regular custom of this beguiling practice. Indeed, he made it the means by which he earned his daily bread. For twelve years he has made himself comfortable in the province of Bihar, which is the mole upon the beautiful cheek of India, and the beard embellishing the face of this land of sugar. Every governor who has come to take up the guardianship of this country has remembered this weakling according to his desire, because of his knowledge of the [storytelling] art and his verbal performance. [Each one] has called him to his assembly and shown him perfect kindness.

BY THE AUTHOR

To the lord who is a master of discernment,
The wordsmith is as dear as his own soul.

When the years since the migration of the Seal of the Prophets by the revolutions of the curved blue heavens had reached 1037—

COUPLET

The World-seizing Khedive, Refuge of the World,
The cosmos of humanity, Jahangīr the Emperor

—according to *Every soul tastes death* took the cup of annihilation from the hand of the cupbearer of the death-hour, and Death, the beauty, became his bedfellow. The Creator of the beings of the world, the Crown-bestower upon those sitting upon the dirt, the One Who created the souls and the horizons, the Absolute Emperor, handed over to the most rightful and greatest successor, the most felicitous and noble son of Jahāngīr the Heaven-dwelling—who in the days of his princehood was named Shāh Ḵhurram and is now entitled Shāh Jahān, chosen from among all of his peers and all of the princes—the lofty degree of sultanhood and world-rule, the honorable degree of world-possessing and earth-capturing, as befitted his true nature and his natural ability, his inherited right, his acquired talent, his complete gentility and inexpressible fitness for the ordering of the affairs of the world and the organization of the whole of the human race. After the [fol. 5a] royal reins of control and the bridle of power had been given into the hands of his whim and will, he was given the title Shihāb al-Dīn Muḥammad, Honored Lord of the Auspicious Conjunction the Second.

At the beginning of the rule of this fortunate one, and the commencement of his vigilant guardianship of the realm, the days' events lazed upon the bed of ease. In the refuge of the shadow of favor, and in the shadow of endless mercy, all of Islamdom—indeed, the whole of mankind, whether elite or common, relaxed upon the couch of peace. The basis of his success became more solid by degrees, so that until its termination, no trouble could intrude upon the days. The foundation of the Law and justice became solid, so much so that until the termination of this endless period, the revolutions of day and night would not see despoliation. In the very first hour that he settled upon the throne, he made the state verdant and irrigated by the blessing of his good intention. In the first days of his enthronement, he created an abode of gladness by the grace of his instruction. The bonfire of his exalted power is the envy of the highest sky, and the impregnable gate of his dignity surpasses the zenith of the stars Arcturus or Spica. The high-soaring hawk of his lofty aspiration rivals in its altitude the eagle of the heavens. It flies as high as the great feather of the celestial phoenix and the golden bird of the sun. In his concurrence with the principle of Lordship of the Auspicious Conjunction, he renewed the rules of Akbar, the Lord of the Auspicious Conjunction, and with the power of Alexandrian pomp he made the renown of the Alexandrian law resound.

BY THE AUTHOR ʿABD AL-NABĪ FAKHR AL-ZAMĀNĪ

When the Conjunction-Lord turned twenty-two,
he set afoot Nausherwan's justice anew.
And Alexander was made glad by him,
for he had found his laws once again. [fol. 5b]
Through him, the world turned into a glad, green garden
that, like Eternal Heaven, never saw Autumn.
After this, sorrow vanished from the world,
and there appeared the key to felicity's door.
By his justice, oppression has waned so much
that no man has to bring its name to his tongue.

The state-adorning ministers, in thanks for this great gift—namely, that this eternally felicitous one became seated upon the throne of the court of greatness—gave the earnings of their lives to the poor and the beggars, the weak and worthy. The courageous nobles, in thankfulness for this great gift—that is, that such a connoisseur of value should have become the lord of the throne of the realm of fortune, gave over with sincere hands the jewels and cash of their spirits to be sacrificed in his service. To spread the felicitations of his noble reign, the poets of the time brought in their hands pearls of meaning and hidden jewels from the seas of their nature and the mines of their minds, by means of the courage of the diver of thought, and the aid of the face-veil of thought, and with the tips of the fingers of wisdom they strung them into verse. With the noise of the river and the melody of the sarod, the nightingale-voiced singers and the sunlike songsters made the sound of congratulations reach from the earth to the sky. When they heard this good news, the buds of the minds of the holy angels blossomed like the flower of the fortune of the Lord of the Auspicious Conjunction.

VERSE

When the King of noble blood sat with his seal-ring
like a jewel in the bezel of the throne of state,
his devotees scattered about their jewels,
just as the king's hand scattered gold, cloud-like.
They sprinkled so their silver to the skies
at last the very moon became a scaly fish.
Lips stretched out such vast felicitation-chains,
the sound of congratulations reached the heavens.
The scatterers of speech went round spreading acclaim,
from the caskets of their praise they scattered jewels.
So many jewels of acclaim were strewn about [fol. 6a]
that earrings became heavy hanging on men's ears.

When the happy news of the reign of the one intimate with good fortune—the joy-increaser of the gardens of success, the field-adorner of the flower-garden of Lordship of the Auspicious Conjunction, the spreader of the faces of the beauty of worldlings, the expresser of the mysteries of the sky, the mirror of the manifestations of God, the obliterator of the injustices and innovations of the past, Abū al-Muẓaffar Shihāb al-Dīn Muḥammad the Second Lord of the Auspicious Conjunction, Shāh Jahān the Emperor—came to the province of Bihar and to Patna, minds emerged from division, and hearts were freed from worry. This weakling thought it incumbent upon himself to send a panegyric [*qaṣīdah*], stringed in verse, in absentia, in order to felicitate the success of those standing upon the threshold of dignity and grandeur of His Majesty. Because, four years before he had become the crafter of robes of submission and the jewel upon the seal-ring of country-conquering, he had come from Bengal to Bihar in the days when he was a prince, and made this dominion verdant and irrigated with the auspiciousness of his gladness [*k̲hurramī*]. This lowly one produced a chronogram of his enthronement for good divination [*fāl*], and made a verse strophe [*qiṭ'ah*], and passed it on to the servants of his Divine Throne-like court. He received his gift from the incomparable sea of presents. Praise be to God, the effects of that good divination attached themselves to the days of fortune of this peerless emperor!

THIS IS THE CHRONOGRAMMATICAL STROPHE

My heart, Shāh K̲hurram has become the world's Khedive,
the uplifter of the parasol of Taimūr!
By Divine justice and kingly fortune
He has become the lighter of Conjunction-Lordship's candle.
With the laws of Alexander the Conjunction-Lord,
he has turned round the world and has conquered the earth. [fol. 6b]
Every way Shāh K̲hurram turns his face
Victory runs before him, like a fleet-footed horse.
Like the sun he has risen from the East
and with fortune he travels toward the West.
After conquering Bengal, by the pleasure of God
he came to Bihar, successful here too.
By the good fortune of his joy-bringing arrival,
Bihar became Paradise, after witnessing Autumn.
Its ground grew upon itself in its pride,
so much, it seemed as high as the sky.
With good fortune he set his sights on Delhi's throne—
and he took it, and became ruler of India.
When he sat on the throne, all the star-jewels
in the green-blue bowl scattered down upon him.
By the natural justice of this just king,
the old man of the world became young like Zulaik̲hā.

By dint of his justice in the world, everyone
let Nausherwān's justice fly out of their heads.
My heart, sit in comfort and in delight,
for again India is the Abode of Peace.
When the intellect grasped the year he was enthroned,
it said, "India's king is now the King of the World."[5]

THIS IS THE PANEGYRIC IN FELICITATION OF THE ENTHRONEMENT OF THE INTIMATE OF FORTUNE, EMPEROR ABŪ AL-MUẒAFFAR SHIHĀB AL-DĪN MUḤAMMAD SHĀH JAHĀN SECOND LORD OF THE AUSPICIOUS CONJUNCTION, PRODUCED BY THE AUTHOR OF THIS COMPOSITION ʿABD AL-NABĪ B. ḴHALAF FAḴHR AL-ZAMĀNĪ FROM THE SCREEN OF HIS IMAGINATION

A thousand thanks! Abū al-Muẓaffar Shāh Jahān
Shihāb al-Dīn is now emperor of the world!
When Ḵhurram became Conjunction-Lord the winter month
became spring-like thanks to his justice's auspiciousness.
Due to his lofty head his crown ascended to the heavens.
Due to his bravery his throne was filled with dignity.
The Sky, going to his enthronement, scattered
the stars from its heart, instead of unique pearls. [fol. 7a]
The phoenix of his parasol had cast its shade all round—
proud against the sun though it was standing on the ground.
His intentions are so straight that it would not be strange
if they should stop the water's crooked flow upon the earth.
Without his pleasure far be it from Destiny to cast
any person in these times down low from any cause.
The spread of his august command is like the monarch's gaze itself.
All the tongues of all the hearts recite his praises endlessly.
The Sky revolves about his head continuously because
his mind bestows tranquility due to his truthfulness.

5. "*Shāh-i Hind shāh-i jahān shud.*" The value of this chronogram is 1033 H, which is the year in which the future Shāh Jahān entered the city of Patna.

With wet luster, his domination's sword slays unbelievers' fire
and with his justice he makes populous true Faith's abode.
The World is decked out and adorned, and has become a bride
in the era of the rule of this monarch and his just laws.
On the threshold of his residence the Sun and Moon bow down
their foreheads in the nights and in the days with such sincere faith
that the fates upon their brows transfer their traces to the ground
so that you might say they were the stamps of seal-rings.
Against his majesty he saw the world, a dim star in vast skies,
which the mind espies after gazing for long ages.
Look! In the morning his dominion's forehead, fortune's flower
shines in the heavens like the Sun that warms the world.
Not accounting for his kitchen, the Sky has turned accountant
and takes lentils from Virgo's stars, and sometimes from the Pleiades.
If, mindful of his [Shah Jahan's] high aspiration, a traveler should take
out of the ground a stone according to the measure of his strength,
in the hand of his hope it would become a jewel in that same breath,
in such a manner that his doubt would turn into certainty.
Where is Hātim Tā'ī? Now, with the sleeve of generosity
he is reduced to killing flies, right and left, upon his dinner-spread.
How could I produce any description of his majesty?
The Sky is but his ring, and the jewel within it is the Sun.
Hurrah for that generous-natured one, by whose bounty
the world and everything that it contains are like the golden sun.
As it scatters gold, his hand puts the Sun to shame—
so much so that every night it sets, and travels out of sight.
The praise-expressing mouth turns the sky to gold
as if it were a golden coin, with stars as ashrafis. [fol. 7b]
He is like the Sun in Aries when he is at his greatest height,
whenever he is seated in the midst of a golden hall.
When the charger of my pen writes a description of his steed,
the speech becomes a beauty, it fills the poem with color.
God bless that fairy-faced steed of his—

it has no likeness in the art-gallery of China.
The coquetry of its strutting gait would make a beggar
out of any fairy-faced beauty, the envy of heaven's houris.
Out of rivalry with its ringlet-like hair,
the circle of its hoof has become like a musky lock.
It outstrips the speed of a flash of lightning
consider it to be as fast as a thousand arrows.
What a miracle! He flies without feather or wing,
with such speed that the eagle envies him.
Ah, the celestial paces of your horse's hoof!
It befits the Pleiades to be from that hoof's nail and shoe!
The earth, on which the Phoenix of his fortune casts its shade,
has reason always to be proud, against the lower sky.
Who are you, Nabī Storyteller, to sing his praise?
How can a beggar praise a King bearing Jamshed's laws?
No comparison I make to your dignity is true
Your majesty's extent has exceeded that of Heaven's gardens.
It is best that I should end my praising with a prayer,
for I have nothing in my hand but this, or better than this.
Forever, as long as power remains with this prayer,
always, as long as "Amen!" follows prayer,
May Gabriel's prayers be upon the friends of his door,
and Nabī's curses be on his court's enemies.

When the foundations of the sultanate and success of this bountiful being, the uplifter of the royal parasol, had become firm, and the basis of the power of the justice and world-possession of the divine-natured essence of the Second Lord of the Auspicious Conjunction had grown strong, according to the best mode—and may God give you the best!—by the celestially based high aspiration, borrowed from the Sun, he deemed it necessary [fol. 8a] to repel the greatest evil and repulse the wrongdoing of darkness from the heads of the servants of the Benign King, according to [the precept] *God commands justice and righteousness*, so that on the Day when humankind will be rewarded, the results [of this deed] would influence the happy days of the servants of the threshold of his majesty:[6]

Your justice is your candle,
illuminating the night,
and your Today is intimate
with your Tomorrow.

Consequently, he discharged the governors of provinces everywhere who, while governing during the days when Jannat-makānī [Jahāngīr] had ruled the world, had held that injustice and religious innovation were allowable attitudes toward subjects and soldiers. In place of the unjust ones of each region, he set up provincial governors who were just and righteous-minded from the core of their hearts. In short, in the second year of the august reign of the Emperor of Jamshedian grandeur and Alexandrian law—aided by the country's good fortune—there came to govern this realm [of Bihar] the encompassing sea [produced by] the cloud of high aspiration, the center of manhood, the luster of the sword of bravery, the hand in the sleeve of severity, the mole upon the forehead of generosity, the light of fortune's brow, the Saturn of the heaven of loftiness, the Jupiter of the sky of felicity, the Mars of majesty, the Sun of the heavens of honor, the Venus of the station of pleasure, the arrow-like pen of power, the foreword to the canon of wisdom, the opening *ġhazal* in the divan of capability, the origin of the volume of justice, the sincere friend [*safī*] of the gardens of creation, the Joseph of beautiful countenance, the Abraham of the table of bounty, the flower-bouquet of the garden of glory, the seller of the pearl of security, the ornament upon the face of piety, the comprehensive wisdom and insight into this portion of the world, the table of contents of the book of glorified God's Creation, the warrior of the faith, Ṣafī Ḳhān Saif Ḳhān—

BY THE AUTHOR
The sincere friend of creatures; because of his name
the sword [*saif*] has gained its renown,

6. A red heading is faded here, but it probably reads "BY THE AUTHOR."

the Emir who with his divine-natured justice [fol. 8b]
makes the world like the Garden of Paradise,
the generous one who by the cloud of his liberal hand
has flooded away the foundations of sorrow

—the felicitous one who due to his high aspiration declared his avid desire to strengthen the Clear Faith and his willingness to tread the path of the Leader of Messengers [Muḥammad], the fortunate one whose sun-like justice left the traces of the white hand [of Moses] in every place that he had governed, the wet luster of whose saber reddens the cheek of the flower-garden of justice, the bud of whose armor-piercing spear pulls out the thorn of injustice from the wounded breast of every weary heart, the judge who makes the tent-ropes of justice reach the tent-ropes of the limits of the East and the West, the just one whose hand of justice frees the collar of the helpless victims from the claws of tyrannous oppressors, the supporter of the poor—from the day that the sapling of his hopes grew tall in the meadow of his fortune, the shade of its giving has been cast continually upon the heads of those burned by affliction; and from the hour that the tree of his desire and the fruit of his wish have come to fruition, the days have been perfumed by the soul-sustaining breeze of his generosity—he of illumined sight, whose light reaches the body of the moon, and who gifts a wealth of light to the greater luminary until the morning of the Day of Resurrection—the administrator who, were he to claim world-rule like the world-warming sun, he would subjugate the world without evil or trouble, and without any clamor or violence.

BY THE AUTHOR
The sky's luminaries
  beg from his glances—
the sun's light within,
  and the stars in the dark nights.
The sun and celestial lights revolve
  round his hand and his pen,

for his hand is jewel-studded,
and his pen rains rubies.
Not to overdo it, but this enlightened man
possesses four qualities,
and each of those qualities
are worthy of complete regard:
The justice of Caesar, the generosity
of Ḥātim, the wisdom of Buzurjmihr,
the power of Rustam, in this world,
in these unhappy times.

[fol. 9a] Ever since his auspicious arrival made the province of Bihar verdant and moist like the springtime, he followed the Divine Command and obeyed the Shadow of God, and strove mightily to combat crimes. With the hand of power he barricaded the door of vice and iniquity in this land against the disobedient. Like the water of life, wine was hidden in the dark room of *Ẓulumāt*,[7] and the red vintage disappeared from among the drunkards.

COUPLET
His interdiction restricted the custom
of wine-drinking, so much that the stars
in the heavens at midnight
overturned their glasses.

He got rid of the repugnant innovations, whose infamy had made God's creatures weary of their own lives over the course of years and months. He wiped out the foul practices and clear injustices that the previous governors had made it their custom to carry out, in the violence of their greed. After he had commenced the work of provincial governorship and the establishment of firmness, he began to perform good works. For, from the

7. The country veiled in unceasing darkness, in which Alexander and Khiẓr discovered the water of life. Identified with Bactria, as mentioned in the first chapter of the Introduction.

beginning of his creation, to the present time, when he has reached the age of forty-five, he has expended many treasures upon God's Path, due to the grief in his mind. He has completed work on buildings, and he has been the architect of hearts as well.

Having picked the rose of delight from the victory-garden of this man of great fortune, and having heard of the defeat of 'Abd Allāh Ḳhān by him, some travelers arrived from Ahmedabad in Gujarat. Seeing the fort, and the river-like pool, they watched them with watering eyes, and knew them to be clear demonstrations and conclusive proofs of his high aspiration and bravery.

Every worshipper who prayed the Friday prayer at the Jama' Mosque of the knower of the Real [i.e., Saif Ḳhān] in the aforementioned city took from it the quality of abstinence and the reality of good character, having sensed that this was the hiding-place of favor. Every student [fol. 9b] who read his lesson in the school of this excellent sustainer of the scholar [*fāẓil*] was informed of his wisdom, sight, understanding, and good wishes. Every man who was far from being clean with even the external cleanliness that begged from the water and air of his hamam knew, from the construction of that house of cleanliness, of his inner purity, whose home is the Holy. Every poor patient who found strength from being healed in his healing-house said "Bravo!" with all his heart and soul to his sound nature, his direct understanding, his blessing-diffusing self. Hurrah for the felicitous, wealthy one who by his glorious grace does these kinds of good deeds, and hooray for the master of great fortune who, by the Divine Favor, leaves good traces as remembrances in this fleeting world!

BY THE AUTHOR

In this ancient world, no one dies
who leaves behind good traces on the earth.

To make a long story short, every structure that he had concluded in Ahmedabad, he also laid the foundation for in the city of Patna by the Ganges River. He added to them two magnificent serais with an enclosed market, whose revenue will always go toward the upkeep of the mosque and school, the expenses of the dwellers of those buildings, medications for the sick, and toward the meritorious ones of this good city. By the aid of the Divine Grace and by the courage of his innate aspiration, in a short time all of his buildings were brought from commencement to completion—and very well. He made all of these buildings strong, so that if, for example, the water of Noah's storm were to rise and engulf the two worlds, not even a wet dew would sit upon the hem of their minarets [*gul-dastah*]. And if the wind of the Day of Judgment were to appear, not a single carpet would move from the front room of his school. Speech coils up like a snake in jealousy at its firmness and enduringness. Trying to describe these buildings, the elect among the wordsmiths of this country are like fishes [fol. 10a] in a violent whirlpool.

From upon the screen of his imagination, this weakling produced these few couplets, by way of a chronogram of the date of the foundation of this good assemblage [of buildings]:

CHRONOGRAMMATICAL STROPHE ON THE ASSEMBLAGE OF GOOD, BY THE AUTHOR

Grace became the companion
of God's pure one [*safī*], Saif Ḳhān,
    and made him the adornment of the earth,
the generous man who implemented
    the excellence of the World-Creator
in this amazed land.
In the country of Bihar he has made
    magnificent buildings, for God's sake,
a troop of them in one place.
Among them there is a mosque,
    spreading grace, like the Ka'ba,
and there is none like it, or to rival it—
a place of worship in which
    the angels pray

the *tahajjud* prayer at night.
Because of the height of its grand arch
    the heavens fall
from the arches of men's hearts.
The eyebrow of its prayer-niche makes a lover
    of the sun, with a hundred eyes of its heart,
as if it were a beloved.
Its courtyard's floor is so clean
    that one could gaze
upon one's own reflection, as in a mirror.
Compared to each of its domes, the sky
    appears as large as a drop of water
due to their height and expansiveness.
There is a school for learning as well,
built, and accessible
    on one side of the mosque.
Every room in it is like the pure chamber
of the heart, and the treasury
of the Grace of God the Exalted.
Let us say that Ignorance itself
stood personified there;
he too would gain knowledge.
Due to the grace attached
    to that building, even a perfect *ʿālim*
can polish his knowledge.
On another side, he has built
a healing-house that the mind has named
    the Abode of Health—
a house of healing in which
    the very floor has become a cure
repelling illness, as if it were a physician.
Inside it, healing is granted
    to the ill, merely by gestures;

health, as if it were by the Messiah's breath.
On another side, he built
a coffeehouse, which rests in the heart
better than souls rest in bodies, [f. 10b]
a house of pleasure, in which instrument
and music become one,
like the gaze and the one gazing.
It is the specialty of its coffee that it
dispels the negligent dream
by farsangs from the eye of the wise.
When Nabī asked the Intellect,
that farseeing old man, about the year
of Saif Ḳhān's good assemblage,
It read from the Tablet
of God's Approbation, and it said:
"The Assemblage of the World's Good."[8]

When the appreciation and kindness of this generous-natured man became evident to the shaikhs and the scholars of near and far, from every direction they turned their faces toward this fortune-favored court of this exemplar of fortune. Every one of them was benefited by his full kindness and generous nature, each according to his situation. By the perfect bounty, the eloquence, and the blossoming mien of this humane man, they were made certain of his friendship for the poor. And [seeing] the orderliness of his good deeds, they put the finger of amazement upon the teeth of thought.

BY THE AUTHOR
Together they say by way of certainty,
"No doubt he is a man of the world and of religion!
"I have never seen his like in these times
"for knowledge, gentleness, generosity and dignity."

8. The chronogram is *majmūʿah-i ḳhair-i dunyā* (1039 H).

A group of worshippers of the Real, who were busy adoring the Provider in the near and distant corners of this land, sent needed money, according to their ability. And the doors of honest subjects—a group who had been sitting in the corner of seclusion and who had withdrawn the feet of rejection beneath their robes—were mysteriously opened.

BY THE AUTHOR
I have heard that in old times, Hātim
would sit in his grand tent, and do good deeds.
He was the host at his own dinner-spread,
and he showed his guest his favor.
But this bountiful-natured generous one
sent gifts right up to the doors of houses! [fol. 11a]
If I call him the envy of Hātim, it is just.
How much difference there is between the two![9]

Since, by the assistance of fortune and the stars, this one who is bewildered by the Factory of the Decree and the Power found a fixed place among the assembly of the attendants of this man of lofty essence, he saw among his peers many men of understanding and subtlety. He became a fellow-servant of all of the wordsmiths and songsters whose like had not been seen until that time. [But] whenever a storyteller recited a suitable verse or a phrase of prose in his service, he [Fakhr al-Zamānī] already held it in his memory. And that which he did not know he had [at least] heard, and what he listened to [for the first time] became part of his consciousness.

Into the heart of this lowly person there entered the intention to make available in writing some of the poetry and prose from the books he had studied. Books that he had not seen, he perused in the library of this summary list of the Book of Creation [i.e., Saif Ḳhān]. Everything that pertains to the art of storytelling and its like, he wrote down. He

9. This panegyric was first used by Faḳhr al-Zamānī in the *Maiḳhānah* to praise his then-patron Sardār Ḳhān (Faḳhr al-Zamānī Qazwīnī 1983, 781).

compiled a selection of the ancients' and the moderns' descriptions of all things, so that the current idiom and the mode of composition and versification of every era would be apparent to the knowers living in this morsel of time, and so that it would be a source of strength to the artists of speech.

As for the desiderata that were not seen in any writing, he composed them himself and strung them into verse. Indeed, in the case of some of the descriptions, he inserted his own name [i.e., with his own writings] in order to display his discernment. He transferred them all onto the blank page in a befitting manner. He composed a book for the storytellers of the company of this connoisseur of complexity [Saif Ḳhān], so that they may look at this anthology, and so that they may focus upon everything they need, whether poetry or prose, for the sake of *munāsib-ḳhwānī*, [f. 11b] so that perhaps at the time of their performance, they might make this knowledge-seeker [Saif Ḳhān] an audience to a choice and unheard-of couplet or a fresh prose phrase, and give him [Faḳhr al-Zamānī] credit in the presence of that subtle Ḳhān. However, this is an impossibility—this proposition is a vain thought!

HEMISTICH
What an impracticable idea, and what a vain thought!

In any case, by the aid of the fortune of this Man of Lofty Fortune, this broken-down fellow was set upon this work, and he made a book composed of an Introduction, four *ḳhabar*s, and a final section, named the *Ṭirāẓ al-aḳhbār*. The Introduction comprises five chapters, and as for the *ḳhabar*s, he provided one on courtly assemblies, one on war, one on love, and one on trickery, since the entire romance is made up of nothing more than these four elements. Each *ḳhabar* of the four is made up of twelve *ṭirāẓ*es, and every *ṭirāẓ* contains a description of all that relates to it. Whether it be poetry or choice prose, from whatever source, it is included. In some of them, two or three descriptions have been added to the writing as needed, so that it will not lack the blessing of the number twelve, which is the number of the names of the Infallible Imams.[10] The final section has to do with all sorts of different things that are not related to the four *khabars*, but that are useful for all tasks, whether they are prose or poetry. He has inscribed them separately.

Here he has inscribed a table of contents to the Introduction, along with all of the chapters and *ṭirāzes* making up the *khabars*. In the Introduction, and in the *khabars* and the final section, he has repeated [the abstracts] with his expressive pen, so that by the writing of a comprehensive and detailed list of contents those who seek a particular *ṭirāz* will have their search made easy for them. With his agitated pen, he has written at the head of [each] piece of prose or poetry the name of the historian or poet. In the case of [f. 12a] each couplet with an author whose name he does not know, a notice has sufficed to say that it is well established among men.

After this he has written in the Preface the list of *khabars* and so on from the books of which this anthology has made use, thanks to his study and perusal of them.

INTRODUCTION TO THE BOOK *ṬIRĀZ AL-AKHBĀR*, COMPRISING FIVE CHAPTERS

CHAPTER ONE: On the invention of the romance and the differences between the accounts of its invention.

CHAPTER TWO: On the characteristics of the romance and the storyteller and that which pertains to them.

CHAPTER THREE: On the superiority of the storyteller to the poet, shown by two proofs.

CHAPTER FOUR: On the creed and tolerance of the storyteller, and his understanding his own worth, and of his behaving toward everyone with humanity.

10. Of Twelver Shi'ism. Cf. Fakhr al-Zamānī's *Nawādir al-ḥikāyāt*, each volume of which was also to contain twelve chapters: "He made it so that each volume is made up of twelve chapters, and every chapter is made up of twelve choice tales, according to the [number of the] Lofty-Ranking Infallible Imams, may God bless all of them—and the celestial signs of the Zodiac, and the number of months" (Fakhr al-Zamānī Qazwīnī 1632, fol. 11a).

CHAPTER FIVE: On the *dar-āmad* and *bar-āmad* of the storyteller while telling his story, and on the customs of *munāsib-k͟hwānī*, which in the terminology of the artists of speech is known as *muraṣṣaʿ-k͟hwānī*, and the manners of sitting and rising and moving and all sorts of ways of speaking.

CONTENTS OF THE FIRST ḲHABAR, relating to battle, comprising twelve *t͟irāzes*.

FIRST T͟IRĀZ: On the Unity of the Lord of the Worlds, and the praise of the Leader of Messengers.

SECOND T͟IRĀZ: On the renowned sultans and the just *k͟hāqāns*, both male and female; and on crowns, thrones, rings, and parasols.

THIRD T͟IRĀZ: On well-advising ministers, secretaries decorating documents, fortunate pens, ink, paper and ink-holders.

FOURTH T͟IRĀZ: On battlefields of brave deeds, horsemen of the field of enmity, wrestling, javelin thrusting, sword striking, and overcoming the enemy and so on. [f. 12b]

FIFTH T͟IRĀZ: On weapons such as swords, bows, arrows, javelins, maces, and hatchets.

SIXTH T͟IRĀZ: On elephants, wolves, elephant herds, and armies of elephants.

SEVENTH T͟IRĀZ: On valuable steeds.

EIGHTH T͟IRĀZ: On the rising of the world-warming sun, by way of *barāʿat-i istihlāl*.

NINTH T͟IRĀZ: On the setting of the greatest luminary and gift-giver to the world.

TENTH T͟IRĀZ: On strong forts, well-fortified fortresses, ruined forts, the preparation and rebuilding of ruined forts, cannons, and guns.

ELEVENTH T͟IRĀZ: On defeating armies, the conversations of leaders with their soldiers, describing the state of the army to the emperor, the travel of soldiers to the place of battle, the formation of their lines, the battle itself, hacking, hiding weapons, and the racing of chariots by leaders and their sons.

TWELFTH ṬIRĀZ: On victorious battles at the rising or setting of the sun, the victory of the believers over infidels, forbidding the retreat of Indians, victory, that which must not follow after a great victory, spoils and ransom, the killing of a leader who has come into one's hands, and the teaching of Islam to an infidel who has formed the intention of becoming a Muslim.

CONTENTS OF THE SECOND ḲHABAR, relating to courtly assemblies, comprising twelve *ṭirāẓ*es.

FIRST ṬIRĀZ: On wine and wine-taverns, and jars of wine.

SECOND ṬIRĀZ: On cupbearers, wine-cups, decanters, glasses, and revelers.

THIRD ṬIRĀZ: [f. 13a] On male and female musicians, songsters and songstresses, instruments and their sounds, and songs.

FOURTH ṬIRĀZ: On world-adorning Spring, heart-expanding Nauroz, thunder and lightning, rain, clouds, and wind.

FIFTH ṬIRĀZ: On the month of Tammūz[11] and everything relating to it.

SIXTH ṬIRĀZ: On the Autumn and everything relating to it.

SEVENTH ṬIRĀZ: On the month of Dai[12] and everything relating to it.

EIGHTH ṬIRĀZ: On the rising of the sun by way of *barā'at-i istihlāl.*

NINTH ṬIRĀZ: On the setting of the sun by way of *barā'at-i istihlāl.*

TENTH ṬIRĀZ: On gardens full of fruit, mangoes, palaces, serais, mountains, meadows, and forests.

ELEVENTH ṬIRĀZ: On hunts, hunted animals, including birds, wild beasts; and on polo-playing and hitting the ball.

TWELFTH ṬIRĀZ: On assemblies of rogues, celebrations filled with decorations, table spreads, candles, and lanterns.

CONTENTS OF THE THIRD ḲHABAR, relating to love, comprising twelve *ṭirāẓ*es.

FIRST ṬIRĀZ: On love, lovers, beauty, the heart, and the gaze.

SECOND ṬIRĀZ: On beauty and types of beautiful people.

11. The summer.

12. The winter.

THIRD ṬIRĀZ: On nannies, female servants, and male servants.

FOURTH ṬIRĀZ: On horses, by way of *barā'at-i istihlāl.*

FIFTH ṬIRĀZ: [f. 13b] On falling in love and the conversation between the seeker and the sought.

SIXTH ṬIRĀZ: On the addresses of the lover and the beloved to one another, with never-before-repeated speeches on blandishments and the pride of beloveds, and the needfulness and lowliness of lovers.

SEVENTH ṬIRĀZ: On the rising and setting of the world-warming sun by way of *barā'at-i istihlāl.*

EIGHTH ṬIRĀZ: On the night of separation.

NINTH ṬIRĀZ: On the weeping and distress of the lover, and his speech to himself at the height of his agony, and other things, such as his throwing glances and speaking to his tears, his fortune, and the candle; and on the writing of letters by the lover to the beloved, and by the beloved to the lover.

TENTH ṬIRĀZ: On the night of union.

ELEVENTH ṬIRĀZ: On marriage and the morning of union.

TWELFTH ṬIRĀZ: On the marriage-night and the birth of children.

CONTENTS OF THE FOURTH ḴHABAR, relating to trickery, comprising twelve *ṭirāz*es.

FIRST ṬIRĀZ: On jewels and so on.

SECOND ṬIRĀZ: On thieves, tricksters, and messengers.

THIRD ṬIRĀZ: On the weapons of tricksters, including daggers, bows, slings, and bells.

FOURTH ṬIRĀZ: On deceitful women.

FIFTH ṬIRĀZ: On sorcerers.

SIXTH ṬIRĀZ: On ghouls, *nasnās*es, and the like.

SEVENTH ṬIRĀZ: [f. 14a] On wildernesses and hard roads.

EIGHTH ṬIRĀZ: On thin horses.

NINTH ṬIRĀZ: On masters of states [holy men] and of artifice [artists], and the like.

TENTH ṬIRĀZ: On the rising of the sun by way of *barā'at-i istihlāl.*

ELEVENTH ṬIRĀZ: On the setting of the sun by way of *barā'at-i istihlāl.*

TWELFTH ṬIRĀZ: On demons, those of hideous aspect, flayers, and Africans.

CONTENTS OF THE FINAL CHAPTER, relating to the descriptions of various things, comprising nineteen *ṭirāz*es.

FIRST ṬIRĀZ: On the human, the intellect, the spirit, and knowledge.

SECOND ṬIRĀZ: On speech and speech-crafters, the manners of speaking, and on writing, calligraphy, and the like.

THIRD ṬIRĀZ: On faith in the court of the Maker of the part and the whole, on gaining dominion, and the thanks given by sultans for the gifts of God, in particular the gift of having children; and the distribution of authority with justice and rectitude among one's children.

FOURTH ṬIRĀZ: On sincerity and truthfulness, patience, provision, and contentment.

FIFTH ṬIRĀZ: On advice to the commons and the elite, avoiding the company of sultans, assisting the nation, and accomplishing service.

SIXTH ṬIRĀZ: On aspiration, generosity, and the like, and on justice, ethics, and humility.

SEVENTH ṬIRĀZ: On administration [f. 14b], keeping secrets, and recognizing one's own limits.

EIGHTH ṬIRĀZ: On obedience, discipline, frankness, and old age.

NINTH ṬIRĀZ: On quieting sorrow with the hope of ease, on falling ill and convalescence, and on the illness and convalescence of the emperor.

TENTH ṬIRĀZ: On being at peace in the world, civility, ease before war, forbidding wine, building mosques, on mosques and schools, against impostors, and on hot baths.

ELEVENTH ṬIRĀZ: On the letters of kings, the answers from ministers, and on doorkeepers.

TWELFTH ṬIRĀZ: On the letters of sayyids, judges, censors, physicians, calligraphers, painters, poets, melodious musicians, songful singers, and rare storytellers to one another.

THIRTEENTH ṬIRĀZ: On the sending of letters between the seeker and the sought, between the father and the child; congratulations upon the marriage-night, upon Eid and Eid celebrations, and upon the convalescence of an ill person, exhorting someone who has gone into jail to be patient, asking after someone who has gone to jail, serving faqīrs, on advising and not advising, on avoiding a bad companion, and on bad behavior.

FOURTEENTH ṬIRĀZ: On high-ranking sayyids, sweet-tongued preachers, ascetics and worshippers, townsmen and citizens, deserted cities, markets, Indians of the market, shrines, the places of worship of Brahmans, and on Brahmans.

FIFTEENTH ṬIRĀZ: On the moon of Ramadan [f. 15a], on childhood, the days of youth, the days of old age, and the coming of death.

SIXTEENTH ṬIRĀZ: On the sea, shipwrecks, rivers, pools, fish, wells, springs, cups, glasses, winecups, and watering-places.

SEVENTEENTH ṬIRĀZ: On travel, famine, miserliness, and ungratefulness.

EIGHTEENTH ṬIRĀZ: On the Simorgh, dragons, snakes, camels, and cows.

NINETEENTH ṬIRĀZ: On fillers in speech, consoling, mourning, condoling, and prayers at the court of the Judge of the Needs of humankind.

THIS IS THE LIST OF BOOKS, SELECTIONS FROM WHICH MAKE UP THIS COLLECTION. INCLUDING POEMS AND PROSE, 200 IN NUMBER. FIRST, THE NAMES OF THE BOOKS OF PROSE.

Jāmiʿ al-ḥikāyāt, Muḥammad ʿAufī, 3 vols.—*Tārīkh-i Sindbād*, 1 vol.—*Nuzhat al-arwāḥ*, Amīr Ḥusainī Sādāt, 1 vol.—*Tārīkh-i muʿjam*, 1 vol.—*Maqāmāt-i Ḥamīdī*, 1 vol.—*Tāj al-maʾāsir*, Ḥasan Niẓāmī Dihlawī, 1 vol.—*Ẓafar-nāmah*, Maulānā Sharaf al-Dīn 'Alī Yazdī—*Rauẓat al-ṣafā*, Muḥammad b. Ḳhāwandshāh—*Al-Mushtahir*, Ḳhwāndmīr, 7 vols.—*Ḥabīb al-siyar*, by his son Mīr Ḳhwānd, 3 vols.—*Maṯla' al-sa'dain*, Kamāl al-Dīn 'Abdal-Razzāq Samarqandī, 2 vols.—*Bahāristān*, Maulānā Jāmī, 1 vol.—*Nigāristān*, Maulānā Mu'īn Juwainī, 1 vol.—*Anwār-i suhailī*, Maulānā Ḥusain Wā'iẕ Kāshifī, 1 vol.—*Ḥāṣil al-ḥayāt*, 1 vol.—*Majma' al-laṯā'if*, Maulānā Muẓaffar Qiṣṣah-ḳhwān, 1 vol.—*Mansha'āt-i Shaiḳh* Abū al-Faẓl, 3 vols.—*Maiḳhānah* and *Nawādir al-ḥikāyāt* by the author of this book, 2 vols.

LIST OF MASNAVIS [fol. 15b]

Shāhnāmah, Firdausī, 3 vols.—*Yūsuf Ẓulaiḳhā*, ditto, 1 vol.—*Garshāsp-nāmah*, Asadī Ṯūsī, 1 vol.—*Ḥadīqah*, Ḥakīm Ṡanā'ī, 1 vol.—*Gul o hurmuz*, Shaiḳh 'Aṯṯar, 1 vol.—*Manṯiq al-ṯair*, ditto, 1 vol.—*Maśnawī*, Maulavī-i Rūm, 3 vols.—*Wisah o Rāmīn*, Faḳhr-i Kirmānī, 1 vol.—*Mihr o Mushtarī*, Muḥammad 'Aṣṣār, 1 vol.—*Ḳhamsah*, Shaiḳh Niẓāmī—*Ḳhamsah*, Amīr Ḳhusrau Dihlawī—*'Ishqiyyah*, ditto, 1 vol.—*Qirān al-sa'dain*, ditto, 1 vol.—*Bostān*, Shaiḳh Sa'dī, 1 vol.—*Gulistān*, ditto, 1 vol.—*Jām-i Jam*, Shaiḳh Auḥadī, 1 vol.—*Ḳhwurshed-i Jamshed*, Salmān, 1 vol.—*Haft aurang*, Maulānā Jāmī—*Taimūr-nāmah*, Hātifī, 1 vol.—*Futūḥāt-i Shāhī*, ditto, 1 vol.—*Shahanshāh-nāmah*, Mīrzā Qāsim Junābādī, 1 vol.—*Ḳhāwarnāmah*, Ibn Ḥusām, 1 vol.—*Lailà o Majnūn*, Maktabī Shīrāzī, 1 vol.—*Shāh o gadā*, Hilālī, 1 vol.—*Gau chaugān*, ditto, 1 vol.—*Maẓhar-i āśār*, Hāshimī, 1 vol.—*Farhād o Shīrīn*, Waḥshī, 1 vol.—*Nāẓir o manẓūr*, ditto, 1 vol.—*Ḳhuld-i barrīn*, ditto, 1 vol.—*Nān o ḥalwā*, Shaiḳh Bahā' al-Dīn Muḥammad—*Maśnawī*, Taẕrū'ī Qazwīni, 1 vol.—*Majmū'ah-i ḳhayāl*, Ḥakīm Ruknā, 1 vol.—*Nal-Daman*, Shaiḳh Faiẓī, 1 vol.—*Maśnavī*, Zulālī Ḳhwānsārī—*Maśnavī*, Ẓuhūrī, 1 vol.—*Andarz-nāmah*, Ḥakīm 'Ārif, 1 vol. [fol. 16a]—*Ḳhusrau-Shīrīn*, Mirzā Ja'far Āṣaf Ḳhān, 1 vol.—*Maśnawī*, 'Urfī, 1 vol.—*Sikandar-nāmah*, Ḳhwājah Ḥusain Ṡanā'ī, 1 vol.—*Jahāngīr-nāmah*, Ṯālib Āmulī, 1 vol.—*Ẕikr al-'aish*, Yūsufī, 1 vol.—*Haft paikar*, 'Atābī Takalū, 1 vol.—*Ḳhusrau-Shīrīn*, ditto, 1 vol.—*Bāġh-i bahār*, author of this book, 1 vol.

LIST OF DIVANS OF THE ANCIENTS AND MODERNS

Rūdakī—'Unṣurī—Azraqī—Kisā'ī—Qaṣāwī Ummī—Ṣāni'ī Rāzī—Qawāmī—Adīb Ṣābir—Ṣafī al-Dīn Sirāj al-Dīn Qamarī—Jalāl 'Aẓud—Abū al-Ma'ālī Naḥḥās—Ḳhāqānī—Anwarī—Jamāl al-Dīn 'Abdal-Razzāq—Kamāl al-Dīn Ismā'īl—Manūchihr Shaṣt Kulah—Imāmī Harawī—Imām Faḳhr-i Rāzī—Sirāj Balḳhī—Amīrā Ḳhīkatī—'Imād Shahriyārī—'Uṡmān Muḳhtārī—Raẓī al-Dīn Nīshāpūrī—Rashīd Waṭwāṭ—Mas'ūd Sa'd Salmān—Saif Isfarang—Mujīr Bailaġhānī—Ṭayyān Bammī—Sharaf al-Dīn Muqbil—Ẓahīr Fāryābī—Aṣīr Aumānī—'Abd al-Wasī' Jabalī—Abū al-Faraj Rūnī—Kirmānī—Kāfī Ẓafar—Samān Sa'ujī—Lāmi'ī—Farīdā Ḥaul—Maulānā Niẓāmī Astarābādī—'Ubaid Zākānī—Ummīdī Rāzī—Mīrzā Sharaf Jahān Qazwīnī—Qāẓī Nūrī—Abū al-Ma'ālī Nīshāpūrī—Sā'ilī Mīrzā Qulī Mailī—Mīr Ḥājj—Shāh Ṭāhir Dakhanī—Walī Dasht-i Bayāẓ—Ḥusain Ṡanā'ī—Hilālī—Chalabī 'Allāmī—'Urfī—Ṭālib Āmulī—Shikebī—Naẓīrī—Mīrzā Ġhāzī—Aqdasī—Mīr Sanjar b. Ḥaidar Mu'ammā'ī—Mīrzā Faṣīḥī—Ḥakīm Shifā'ī—Maulānā Muḥammad Ṣūfī—Malik Qumī—Mīrzā Malik Mashriqī—Qudsī Mashhadī—Fāẓil Shīrāzī—Āqā Shāpūr—Muḥibb 'Alī Sindī—Nau'ī Ḳhabūshānī—Abū Turāb Beg [fol. 16b]—Mirzā Niẓām Dast-i Ġhaib—Ḥakīm Ruknā—Ġhiyāṡ Ḥalwā'ī—Ḥakīm 'Ārif—Ṭālib Kalīm—Muḥammad Qulī Salīm—Mīrzā Dānish—Mīr Dostī Samarqandī—Bāqir Ḳhwurdah—Sharārī Hamadānī—Ẓakī Hamadānī—Raunaqī Hamadānī—'Atābī Taklū—Mīr Wālihī Qumī—Murshid Burojirdī—Ġhurūrī Kāshī—Nādim Gīlānī—Ṣā'ib—Fuzūnī Astarābādī—Mīr Malikī Qazwīnī—Fā'iz Baghdādī—Ġhiyāṡā-i Munṣif—Mīr Ni'mat Allāh Waṣlī—Wajhī Harawī—'Askarī Kāshī—Ḥaidar Ḳhaṣātī—'Abd al-Nabī Faḳhr al-Zamāni, the author of this book.

CHAPTER ONE: ON THE INVENTION OF THE ROMANCE AND THE DIFFERENCES BETWEEN THE ACCOUNTS OF ITS INVENTION.[13]

LET IT NOT REMAIN hidden from the stringers of speech that there is much difference of opinion among the knowers of accounts with regard to the romance of the Arabian Amīr [Ḥamzah]. In their writings, some of them have alleged that one of the ʿAbbasid caliphs was once ill with a fever. The renowned physicians of that era tried to cure the Caliph, but they had no success. A wise physician from among the Arabs arranged this romance in order to rid him of the ailment. In the shape in which we now know it [fol. 17a], day after day, he recited it to the Caliph. He would halt his recitation in a perfectly sweet place, and the next day he would begin again at that very place, until slowly this sweet tale took away the ailment altogether. After the health of his body had been restored, the Caliph would often listen to this story in times of sorrow, in order to increase his happiness, until it became famous among men.

Once it became famous among the people of Persia, one of the sages of Bactria and Ẕulumāt added to it, and bound *t̤ilisms* to it, and all of the lords of wealth and pleasure would listen to it. Even if they had heard it before, most of them would be inclined to hear it again. The author of the *Maḵẖzan al-aḵẖbār*, Mīr Muḵẖtār Rāzī,[14] has suggested in his work that he [the Bactrian sage] brought this speech upon the correct path, and therefore in those times everyone, whether elite or common, heard it once more from beginning to end. All of them desired to hear it once more.

Some of the storytellers are of the opinion that the narrator of the romance was the Maulānā, esteemed and honored client of the kings of Arabia and Persia, ʿAmar b. Umayyah Ẓamrī.[15] Others say that the romance was composed in the days of the Emperor Ḵhusrau, and the

13. This chapter is largely reproduced by Shāh Naẕar Qiṣṣah-ḵẖwān in the introduction to the *Ẕubdat al-Rumūz*.

14. I have not been able to trace this work.

15. The original has Ẓamīrī. ʿAmr b. Umayyah b. Ḵhuwailid b. ʿAbd Allāh Ẓamrī was a Companion of the Prophet and a transmitter of hadith who participated in many battles during the early days of Islam.

rest trace the origin of the romance to the river-hearted, blue-blooded Ḳhwajah Buzurjmihr the sage.

Before this weakling came to India and resolved to produce the present composition, he had long striven in that Trace of Heaven, Iran, to discover the truth about the invention of this captivating work [the *Ḥamzah-nāmah*]. In the early days of his youth, he was quite intimate with storytellers, and had observed the mysteries [of the romance], both those that had been written down and those that he heard. But his mind was not satisfied with any of these accounts. In the year 1018, when he had arrived at the [Mughal] capital Agra,[16] he struck up an intimate acquaintance with the greatest of the historians of this morsel of time: the one who sought the truth of the accounts of prophets and of sultans of the age: Najīb al-Dīn [fol. 17b] Ġhiyāṡ al-Dīn 'Alī Naqīb Ḳhān, son of Mīr 'Abd al-Laṭ̤īf b. Mīr Yaḥyà, the author of the *Lubb al-tawārīḳh.*

At a certain ceremony in the same year, the Chosroes of Alexandrian Dignity and Jamshedian Power, the Emperor Nūr al-Dīn Muḥammad Jahāngīr, inquired of him [Naqīb Ḳhān] how many ministers who had served bygone kings had been blind. That preserved tablet of the accounts of the renowned sultans replied to His Majesty, "Your Highness, are you asking about the ministers who were blind in the left eye, or those administrators whose right eye was devoid of the honored robe of sight?" The Emperor, Refuge of the World, was struck with amazement at this question. He said, "I have heard a strange speech from you, and you have made a curious query! I am asking about both." Then and there, Naqīb Ḳhān set before the sight of the nobles the number and names of the ministers who were blind in their right eyes and left eyes, how many years old they were at the time when they took up their ministries, and the lifespans of the sultans whose kingdoms this administrative group ornamented with the jewelry of their administration—along with the names of the books

16. The text has 1028, but Naqīb Ḳhān passed away in 1023 H, so he could not have conversed with Faḳhr al-Zamānī in the year that appears in the manuscript. Faḳhr al-Zamānī's initial sojourn in Agra shortly after his arrival in India took place from 1018 to 1022 H, and so it is possible that a "2" has been mistakenly substituted for a "1."

in which their particulars were included. Jahāngīr the World-Possessor ordered that the books that the aforementioned Ḳhān had named should be presented. Having looked at all of them they found his speech to be according to the writing.

When this weakling witnessed his ability in the art of historiography, he asked him about the invention of the romance of the Leader of Martyrs Amīr Ḥamzah, the Lord of the Auspicious Conjunction. He answered that when the Sultan Mas'ūd b. Sultan Maḥmūd Ġhaznawī was leaning on the four cushions of sultanate, the most knowledgeable of knowers of that time was Ḥakīm Abū Bakr Bāqillānī. The aforementioned sultan developed epilepsy during his rule. The sages of that time tried to cure the sickness of the Sultan, but were unable to do so. [fol. 18a] The aforementioned Ḥakīm laid the foundation of this romance and wrote it down from heart in an hour when he was given full leisure to compose it. At a perfectly felicitous time he began to read it before Ma'sūd, the successor of Maḥmūd. Day by day he performed it for him, and he did not let go of the skein of his speech until the tale had come to an end. In the space of four months, the Sultan found release from the prison of epilepsy by the blessing of this sorrow-dispelling composition. The author of the romance, Ḥakīm Abū Bakr Bāqillānī, finished the romance for the Sultan in six months the first time. After him, Ḥakīm Rūdakī also made some contribution to this irreplaceable work, and dreamed up the manners of stately [*bah ṭumṭarāq*] reading. Naqīb Ḳhān also said that this romance is a peerless composition and that for the removal of sadness there is no better activity than the hearing of it.

As for the narrators who contributed to this lovely romance and colorful tale in later times, one of them is the Sīmurġh of the mountain of imagination, Mullā Jalāl Balḳhī. Others are Naṣr Bāzargān, Abū al-Ma'ālī Nīshāpūrī, and Maulānā Ḥusain Mushtāqī. *Badī' o Qāsim* was produced by Mullā Jalāl during the time of the Chosroes of Alexandrian Dignity, the Khedive with the banner of Darius, the world-seizing, country-conquering candle of the race of the Prophet, Shāh 'Ismā'īl Ḥusainī Ṣafawī.

The ornamenter of new and old accounts, the decorator of the cheek of the bride of speech, the beloved of the hearts of the sultans of his time, Zain al-ʿĀbidīn Takaltū Ḳhān, wrote the *Nūr al-Dahr-nāmah* and *Īraj-nāmah* in Tabriz the Warlike City, and presented them in the service of that World-Refuge in a new pavilion. The World-Refuge King was holding a great celebration that day, on account of the completion of the pavilion. When Takaltū Ḳhān had [fol. 18b] recited a story from the *Īraj-nāmah*, he [the emperor], laughing and sporting, made a present to the maulawī of thousand two tomans for the tale, and he named the pavilion the Pavilion of Takaltū Ḳhān and bestowed it upon him with its furnishings. To this day the pavilion's traces are visible in Tabriz. Modesty aside, that rara avis of the world of romances put the speech and ability and capability of his contemporaries upon the shelf of oblivion. No one has surpassed him in this art. He introduced fine additions and interesting complexities into the romance, and therefore the beauty of the narration that emerged from within him was one in a hundred.

This pinnacle of fame was so famous that the Emperor, with the Rank of Jamshed, with as many soldiers as there are stars in the sky, was completely inclined toward the romance. Therefore whenever God the Exalted granted him a son, he would give the son the name of one of the heroes of the romance. They say that when Takaltū Ḳhān had brought the romance's course to the battle of Ṭ̤ahmāsp, that day a new creature was brought to the side of the World-Possessor, and he named him Ṭ̤ahmāsp. It happened the same way with the battle of Alqāṣ, and so he named one of his sons Alqāṣ.

One time, when Takaltū Ḳhān presented the story of the battle between Qahrish and Landhūr b. Saʿdān in the service of the king, in the fashion of this old storytellers he slew the aforementioned stalwart and also had Qahrish slain at the hands of Ḳhusrau. The king had a great deal of love for the nonexistent Qahrish, and he declared, "I ask the Maulawī to spare the blood of Qahrish!" Zain al-ʿĀbidīn said, "Give me the blood money so that I do not kill him." The king paid blood money amounting to ten tomans. He also paid blood money for Ṭ̤ahmāsp b. ʿAnqawīl Dew, out of his own desire and according to the time, with twenty tomans. From that day [fol. 19a] to this, storytellers do not kill these two brave men in the romance. When the aforementioned Ḳhān told me the reality of the birth of the romance in the detail that is recorded, I kept it safe in my mind so that one day afterward I would use it in this composition.

STROPHE

To men of sense, a sage's company
  is life increased twofold. Pay heed to this!
For what you gather during your long life
  intervenes for you upon the Day of Need.

CHAPTER TWO: ON THE CHARACTERISTICS OF THE ROMANCE AND THE STORYTELLER AND THAT WHICH PERTAINS TO THEM.

It is not hidden from the wise and perspicacious that the romance of the Lord of the Auspicious Conjunction is a tale of surpassing sweetness, in spite of its being a lie, devoid of the form of sincerity. From reading it and listening to it, certain benefits accrue to the hearers and readers of the romance. First, it makes the speaker, along with the listener, eloquent and fluent and knowledgeable regarding the current speech [*rozmarrah*]. Second, it makes them appear knowledgeable regarding the administration of worldly things and activities related to the kingdom, and it makes storytellers dear in the sight of the nation's rulers. In spite of its own vanity, it shakes the people of fortune off of the skein of vain thoughts. There is no better medium for the gaining of intimacy with sultans, ministers, nobles, and nobles' sons than the romance.

As an example, this lowly one and Ni'mat Allāh Safāhānī (who was a world-wanderer) attained to the perfection of a connection with a son of one of the nobles of Kashmir. Both of us were seeking to become the companion of the desired one, so that for a moment the effect of his [?] would remove the sorrow from our hearts.[17] The aforementioned traveler knew the occult sciences. He showed some whiffs of the occult works to the beloved, according to the time. But not a single knot from among his strange matters opened the knots of his [the young nobleman's] love, He

17. There are several words in this phrase that I was not able to decipher.

could not bring the friend in his direction [fol. 19b], and he could not wound the hearts of his rivals. And yet, by reading a single chapter of the romance [of Amir Hamzah], this weakling [Faḳhr al-Zamani] became to this friend as if they were two brains housed together under one skin. Like the candle that adorns the gathering he became united [?] with him.

To make a long story short, storytellers are quick to gain proximity to the emperors of the world, as did Maulānā Zain al-'Ābidīn Takaltū Ḳhān, who was in the service of that Potentate—as mighty as heaven, the Sun of fame whose court is the sky, with as many soldiers as there are stars—Shāh Ismā'īl, like Jamshed in his power. And as did the rara avis of his time, 'Ināyat Allāh Darbār Ḳhān in the employ of that Potentate—he whose fortune is young and lofty, the august Emperor of happy omen—Jalāl al-dīn Muhammad Akbar Pādshāh Ġhāzī.

[Note in the right margin of the manuscript:] *Zain al-'Ābidīn Takaltū Ḳhān was storyteller to Shāh Ismā'īl Bahādur Ḳhān. It is recorded in the* Zubdat al-aḳhbār[18] *that Zain al-'Ābidīn Takaltū Ḳhān would recite poetry extemporaneously while reading the romance, and sometimes he would recite a* barā'at-i istihlāl *relating to the speech on his tongue. Such storytellers are superior to the poets of the world, according to two proofs.*

The things that the storyteller must possess are strength of memory, sensory focus, and natural absorptiveness. He must not overdo food that causes forgetfulness. He must not give way to distraction while he is speaking, lest he should say something absurd out of negligence. He must not go careening from wars to courtly gatherings or from the tale that he is telling to another tale. The master of this art must have such natural absorptiveness that he can grab hold of whatever he hears and remember it right away, in such a way that he never forgets it. To top it off, he must see in his mind the suitable gestures [that he learned] from his teacher, to such an extent that he is able to copy his teacher in his absence.

For improving the memory, this prayer is tried and true, and he ought to read it 340 times a day: *O Knower of the Hidden, Who needs no aid for His Memory.*

18. The *Zubdat al-aḳhbār* was a historical work by Faḳhr al-Zamānī's friend Ġhiyāṡ al-Dīn 'Alī Naqīb Ḳhān (see above). It was mentioned by Rieu (1879, 122) in his catalog of British Museum manuscripts. Otherwise I cannot find this work.

CHAPTER THREE: ON THE SUPERIORITY OF THE STORYTELLER TO THE POET SHOWN BY TWO PROOFS.

WHEN THE STORYTELLER TELLS his story in the assembly of one of the successful sultans, [fol. 20a] it is certain that in the gathering there will be more or less ten men of capability and excellence. If the speaker performs amid this sort of assembly—of men who enjoy difficulty—and if he utters fluent and eloquent and easy words; and if, over the course of the verbal performance he makes elegant movements and sweet gestures and [recites] good verses and interesting couplets; and he performs *munāsib-khwānī* when his speech thirsts for it; (and if, when he cannot think of a non-repetitious verse, he recites a *barāʿat-i istihlāl* ex tempore in the midst of his telling of the story; and if he uses the prose that comes to his tongue);[19] and if, when his speech comes to an close, he has not spoken a single word of nonsense from beginning to end, then he is by many degrees greater than a poet!

The second proof is that if a poet does read out a verse, he has [previously] returned to it ten times and revised it. It is only after he is satisfied with it in his heart that he reads it before an audience. But as for the poor storyteller, everything that he says extemporaneously must possess continuity, and must not be incorrect in terms of the speech that is current. On top of this, he must make suitable gestures, quite aside from his speech. Everything that he brings upon his tongue is just as it is. He may not indulge in revision. In the light of these two proofs it is a certainty that the labor of the men of prose outstrips the tribulations of the men of verse.

It is the opinion of the ornamenters of meaning, the illumined minds, and the just ones that this has been demonstrated. If this kind of storyteller utilizes all of the trickery mentioned by the author of the *Ṭirāz al-akhbār*, ʿAbd al-Nabī Fakhr al-Zamānī, and if someone hears from him a chapter of the aforementioned kind of story, that person [i.e., the listener]—even if he be unjust himself—must do him justice: he is better than a poet. But I do not know whether in the whole wide world there are even two such

19. The passage in parentheses is given in the left margin. It appears to have been meant as an addition to the main body of the text.

storytellers who can give the lie to the ignominy [of storytellers as against poets] with such color and fragrance that it would cause the wise ones of the times to be enraptured with their stories and their enchantments.

CHAPTER FOUR: ON THE CREED AND TOLERANCE OF THE STORYTELLER AND HIS UNDERSTANDING HIS OWN WORTH, AND OF HIS BEHAVING TOWARD EVERYONE WITH HUMANITY.

[FOL. 20B] THE POSSESSOR of this heart-stealing art and the master of this assembly-adorning craft must be confined by his creed, not by the bonds of religious prejudice, because every one of the sultans of the day and the high-ranking nobles has a different religion and a separate law. Some are Sunni, a few are Shiʿa. There is a group that affirms the unity of God, and a lot that disbelieve the resurrection of the dead. The storyteller must deal with each differing faction in each region according to need. First of all, he must not proclaim his own creed inconsistently in order to mix with the great men of each kingdom. For if he makes himself out to be Sunni in one place and makes himself known as a Shiʿa in another, he will not be able to maintain this to the end. Because it is possible that, before he shifts locations, the reality of his religion will have been disseminated to every corner of the kingdom where he has long resided. The best conduct for the speaker is toleration.

With all people he should behave with humanity, so that in this way perhaps he will win the heart of some afflicted person, and ease a frustrated mind—so that it might be the cause of expiation in this world for his telling of lies, and of being red-faced with pride in the next.

And whenever he has influence over the mood of a ruler, he should try to assist those of his contemporaries who are in distress. And in the case of a man with no connections, there too, he should not excuse himself! For it has been said—

COUPLET

God grants forgiveness to the man
whose existence brings comfort to humankind.

A storyteller who is not a story knower is incomplete in his craft. He must be so ready with his romances that he is able to recite whatever story the audience wants extemporaneously, even if he has only just looked at it. To know the value of his own art is for the storyteller [fol. 21a] more necessary than anything else, and safeguarding the honor of his acquisition is more vital than anything, so that in the eyes of the people of the heart he does not become lowly and untrustworthy. The more he engages in this beguiling art in an independent manner, the more amiable and well liked he becomes.

CHAPTER FIVE: ON THE *DAR-ĀMAD* AND *BAR-ĀMAD* OF THE STORYTELLER WHILE TELLING HIS STORY AND ON THE CUSTOMS OF *MUNĀSIB-ḴHWĀNĪ,* WHICH IN THE TERMINOLOGY OF THE ARTISTS OF SPEECH IS KNOWN AS *MURAṢṢAʿ-ḴHWĀNĪ,* AND THE MANNERS OF SITTING AND RISING AND MOVING AND ALL SORTS OF WAYS OF SPEAKING.

LET IT BE CLEAR to the rare appraisers of the jewels of speech and the unique knowers of new and old reports that in storytelling the *dar-āmad* is of three kinds: first, in the style of Iran; second, in the way of the people of Turan; and third, according to the rules of India. The customs of the people of Rūm have not been recalled in this chapter. The reason is that this lowly one has not reached that country, and he does not trust that which he has heard, for they have said—

HEMISTICH

When has the heard ever been like the seen?

One thing that has been heard with regard to the storytelling of the Rūmīs, to which his heart bears witness that it is correct, is that they recite the romance in Rūmī Turkish or a mixture of Arabic and Qizilbāsh Turkish. This work does not need to expound upon each particular instance.

The mode of the *dar-āmad* of the people of Iran is that whenever they begin to tell the romance, they first recite a versified tale that bears some relation to the romance that they will recite, with something of battle and something of courtly gatherings, something of lovemaking and something of trickery. After that they begin to describe the narrators of the romance, until little by little they reach the praise of the Leader of the Martyrs Amīr Ḥamzah. Once they bring to their tongues around to the praise of his renowned name, they recite two verses of the following kind—

STROPHE [FOL. 21B]
It is he—if it lacked
his brand of servitude, Destiny
would not descend from
the sky to the earth's surface.
It is he—if it lacked the seal
of his treasurer, the sun
would not deposit its hidden
treasure in the ground.

Then they pick up the thread of their performance with *munāsib-ḳhwānī* of the greatest possible delicacy, not stepping outside the bounds of *barā'at-i istihlāl*. Thus it is in an amorous[20] way that they describe the description of the horse upon which a certain woman rides on some occasion within the romance. And so it is when it comes to battle, courtly assemblies, trickery, love, the rising and setting of the sun, and so forth. During the speech performance they do not stint in their delicate expression of whatever [material] they must deal with. During *muraṣṣa'-ḳhwānī*, when their performance is thirsty for suitable speech, they lend luster and color to their performance with a prose passage or with two or three verses (in the manner that has been mentioned). They choose to recite poetry infrequently because it keeps the listener away from the main issue. Indeed, it distances him by far from the real issue, which is the hearing of the romance.

As long as his romance takes the form of a regular narrative, the possessor of this captivating art must sit upon one knee and use words that

20. The text has *'āshiqān*, but here I follow Maḥjūb's (1991, 194) amendment to *'āshiqānah*.

are well considered and weighed. When he comes to military affairs, and the performance waxes hot—at the time of the clashing of swords and the brandishing of maces—he must sit upon two knees and attain to such fervor that while he is reciting his story the hearer of the romance sees the deeds of war. When the tapestry of the speaker's speech reaches the point at which one of the warriors performs the rite of the shattering of fetters, he must sit up on two legs, and he must perform and express the act as if he were doing the shattering, so that one would think that he himself was snapping chains, and the hearers would think that he was in this state. When pulling a bowstring, sitting on a sandalwood throne, [fol. 22a] or wrestling, he must not fail to make use of the things that pertain to these [actions]. [He must recite the tale of] a courtly assembly in a blossoming, easy manner. [He must recite a tale of] love with the coquetry of those who are sought in love and the desire of those who seek—as well as their haughtiness and their wretchedness [respectively]. [In reciting a tale of] trickery he must become like a piece of sugar-candy,[21] presenting himself as a comic figure to the audience. And during a conversation between 'Amar and Bakhtak he must use his captivating arts in order to excite them.

Some of the speech-crafters of Iraq begin with a panegyric during the *dar-āmad* of the romance. When the reciter of the panegyric speeds toward the praise of the one who would be praised, they insert instead of his name, the name of the Amīr [Ḥamzah], the Lord of the Auspicious Conjunction. Having recited a few verses in his praise from that panegyric, they move on to the [main] performance. They [i.e., the Iraqi storytellers] accept the practice of *barā'at-i istihlāl*, but they do not view as allowable the description of the narrators of the romance in the preface of the story. What is well known in India—and it is indeed the foremost thing in the *dar-āmad* of the [Indian-style] romance—is that the storyteller ought to recite a few verses in praise of the grandee in whose service they are presenting the speech. After that they busy themselves in the telling of the romance. For in these lands flattery is very well received at the commencement of all works.

21. The text has "*pārah kard wa qand shawad*," whereas Maḥjūb (1991, 194) amends it to "*pārah-i qand gardad.*"

The potentates of India have made this a favored way of proceeding, and they endure flattery.

In Turan during *muraṣṣa'-khwānī* they are not bound to use *barā'at-i istihlāl*. The rule of their *dar-āmad* during the performance is that at the beginning of it they first recite a few verses on the Unity of God, and after that they recite a few other verses in praise of the Prophet. Then they praise the Four Friends and begin to recount the names of the narrators of the romance, and when they have brought forth the names of them all, they begin to recite the romance. While speaking they are not bound to use the current speech. [fol. 22b] Therefore, in the assemblies of the potentates of India, the Land of Sugar, this weakling has repeatedly heard from good storytellers of Turan, during their speech performances, [odd or antiquated phrases such as the following]: "Ten thousand four score and eight riders."[22] They use so many fillers in their speech that if one were to remove "it so happened" and "to make a long story short" from the romance as they recite it, there would be nothing else left! It is as if their natural energy were dependent upon these two phrases. But, in their own manner[23] they recite their tales with great sweetness and saltiness in places. And in their own way they recite stories of trickery better than other stories.

The manner of bringing to an end the thread of this colorful tale, and the rule of finishing a section of the story—which [manner and rule] is called the *bar-āmad*—is this. One must break the necklace strung with the jewels of speech in such a place that the hearer of the romance will imagine that there will never be a better tale in the entire romance, and he will be restless and eager to hear the end of it. If, in the meantime, he pleads with the performer a hundred times a day to recite up to the end of the chapter, the performer must not recite it, as far as this is possible. He must increase the eagerness of the listeners. When the people assembled become insistent and the storyteller grows helpless, even if he has recited

22. "*Hashtād o nuh-dād o hazār sawār.*"

23. Here the manuscript contains a non-Persian string of words that appears to be "*khūk hī wa hī qaltāq.*" Ja'far Maḥjūb (1991, 210n21) was unable to decipher it, but it may be in a Turkic language of Transoxiana.

[the story] a hundred times, each time he must recite it better by far than on the previous occasion. The narrators term this *pāband-ḳhwānī.* In this matter all three traditions of the preeminent artists are as one. In all countries the rare subtilizers bring [the section of the romance] to its finale in this way.

Let it not be hidden from the nightingale-voiced ones of the flower-garden of narration and the musicians of the assembly of tales that all of the descriptions of the four *ḳhabar*s and *barā'at-i istihlāl* that this weakling has brought upon the pages of this book, in verse and in prose, connected and separate, he has recorded with his sputtering pen, as well as he has been able. First he has recorded and expressed with his pen the choice tales and poems and opening panegyrics [to be used] in *pesh-ḳhwānī* in the aforementioned way, from every of the twelve from among the four *majlis*es and so on. After that he has written down the four *majlis*es. But first, the *dar-āmad*. . . .

Notes

Introduction

1. Haase (2010) makes the argument for the decolonization of folktale/ fairy-tale studies in a compelling manner.
2. See Pritchett 1994 for a study of the depreciation of the ghazal in the late nineteenth century.
3. Muhammad Salim-ur-Rahman, e-mail message to author.
4. One effect of our different approaches is that, whereas Faruqi excludes from the genre and from the scope of his study certain texts like Mīr Amman's *Baġh o bahār* (Garden and springtime) and Rajab 'Alī Beg Surūr's *Fasānah-i 'ajā'ib* (The tale of wonders), I find myself unable to do so. Thus this study includes within its sweep anything that might have been called a *dāstān, qiṣṣah*, or *ḥikāyat.*
5. For Blanchot's critique, see Todorov 1990, 194. For Croce's, see Jameson 1981, 160.
6. Todorov (1990) uses the precise but unwieldy term "discursive property" for what I call a "trait" or "mark." Derrida uses either "mark," "remark," or "trait." It is also Derrida (1980) from whom I borrow the term "code."
7. On "para," see Miller 1979, 219–20.
8. Derrida's point in "The Law of Genre" is that the genre traits within the text, the "marks" of genre, in effect "remark" upon the text's genre and are themselves paratextual. This leads to a certain autodeconstruction of the text's body via genre—"degenerescence" as Derrida (1980) calls it.
9. See Todorov (1990, 198–200) on reading and writing "in function of genre." According to Fredric Jameson (1981, 106), "Genres are essential-

ly literary *institutions*, or social contracts between a writer and a specific public, whose function is to specify the proper use of a particular cultural artifact." Ralph Cohen (1986, 211) suggests that the regulation by which genre produces meaning can be thought of in terms of Hans Robert Jauss's (1982) reception theory.

10. Cf. Honko 1980, 23, on genre as a system of rules of reproduction.
11. "*Qiṣṣah-jāt-i nas̤r*" and "*qiṣṣah-jāt-i naẓm*" (Qamar 1915, 2).
12. ʿAbd al-Nabī Fak̤hr al-Zamānī also made this connection in the *Ṭirāz al-ak̤hbār* (Fak̤hr al-Zamānī Qazwīnī 1633, fol. 3b).
13. For more on the *shahr-āshob* genre, see Khan 2009.

Chapter 1

1. Faridany-Akhavan (1989) effectively critiqued an older opinion that the text relevant to each illustration was provided on the verso of each illustrated folio. Having the text and illustration on separate folios would have made it easier for two men to work with the image on the one hand and the text on the other in the performance situation.
2. It bears repeating that we are dealing with texts that are *embodied* artworks; as Shamsur Rahman Faruqi (1999) has insisted, even written *dastans* bear the traces of oral performance.
3. Contrary to both the *Tūzuk* and the *ʿArafāt al-ʿāshiqīn*, the 1978 Aligarh edition of the *Maʾās̤ir-i Jahāngīrī* has Mullā Asad coming from Patna instead of Thattha. Taqī al-Dīn Auḥadī states in the *ʿArafāt* that after the death of his patron Mīrzā Ġhāzī, Asad returned to Thattha for a time before entering the royal camp of Jahāngīr (Auḥadī 2009, 581).
4. Seemingly the importance—indeed, the possibility—of conversion to economic capital diminishes very much after the death of the storyteller, when he is commemorated by later generations but cannot reap his reward. However, this line of thinking assumes that cultural capital should be convertible only by the artist in whose name it accrues. It is easy to see how the cultural capital accruing to dead storytellers could financially benefit their students or those involved in the production of a romance that invokes their names.

5. This manuscript, extremely interesting insofar as it is the only known counterpart to the *Ṭirāz al-akhbār*, was once in Maulwi Muhammad Shafi'’s collection (Muḥammad Bashīr Ḥusain 1972, 192). I have been unable to locate it thus far, but I am very grateful to Hamid Ali, senior librarian at Punjab University Library, for his efforts to find it.
6. Sayyid Kamāl Hājj Sayyid Jawādī has edited the *Ṭirāz al-akhbār* recently (1292 Hijrī Shamsī / 2013–14). It is unfortunate that the publication of this edition came to my knowledge too late for me to obtain and cite it.
7. See chapter 4 for a discussion of transmission-based historiography and its distastefulness to certain rationalists.
8. The known manuscripts of Fakhr al-Zamānī's writings are enumerated in Khan 2017a. See Khan 2015 for a preliminary analysis of the *Ṭirāz*.
9. For an explanation of the figure of the *mirzā* and his elite masculinity, see Ahmad 1975 and O'Hanlon 1999.
10. In the seventeenth century it seems that some remnant of this building existed, but if so it has long since passed into oblivion.
11. The photograph of the painting is in the British Library ("Photograph of Portrait of Darbār Khān" 1911).
12. Only the *Tarkhān-nāmah* disagrees, making the claim that Mullā Rashīd and Mullā Asad both came from Iran "dressed as beggars" before being patronized by Mirzā Ghāzī (Muḥammad b. Jalāl Tattawī 1965, 85).
13. For his Shirazi origins, see Auḥadī 2009, 581. His relationship to Shah 'Abbas's storytellers is noted in the same *tarjamah* in Ḥusain Qulī Khān 'Aẓīmābādī 1981, 110, and Wālih 2005, 208.
14. Note Rashidi's problematization of the dates of this encounter (Rāshidī 1970, 450–53).
15. Fakhr al-Zamānī, who was in the service of Mahābat Khān's son, met him there (Fakhr al-Zamānī Qazwīnī 1983, 601–2).
16. Asad migrated to Thatta and entered Mirzā Ġhāzī's service while the latter was still a boy ("*dar martabah-i ṭufūliyyat*"), according to Taqī al-Dīn Auḥadī (2009, 581).
17. See Amān Allāh's biographical notice in Shāh Nawāz Khān Aurangābādī 1888, 1:740–48.

18. Sayyid Sulaimān Ḥusain (1988, 13–14) has disputed the date of composition that Jain deduced for Mihr's *qiṣṣah*, that is, 1203 H (1888–89). On the basis of the Karachi manuscript, Ḥusain understands its date to be 1218 H (1803), which would put it some years after the establishment of Fort William College.

Chapter 2

1. The father of Muḥammad Feroz Dihlawī asserted that Bāqir 'Alī said this to Ṣabūḥī when they were both at Bāqir 'Alī's home one day after the 'Aṣr prayer (Muḥammad Feroz Dihlawī 2014, 65).
2. Both Bukhārī and Shāhid Aḥmad pin the blame on the rise of the cinema (Sayyid Yūsuf Bukhārī Dihlawī 1987, 21; Shāhid Aḥmad Dihlawī 1979, 190).
3. For accounts of Gilchrist's role at Fort William College, see Kidwai 1972 and Siddiqi 1960.
4. In the College Council's June 7, 1802, memo of the revised composition of the Hindustani department, Jawān's name appears. He is listed as a translator, with a salary of eighty rupees per month (Siddiqi 1963, 123).
5. Prior to 2004, Harington had been on the council of Gilchrist's seminary but does not seem to have been on the initial College Council (Siddiqi 1963, 98, 104).
6. It is not clear whether Gilchrist had already met Ashk by the time he sent this letter or, if he did, whether he had other storytellers in mind when he asked the council to give him the fallback option of employing two "inferior" storytellers.
7. Ashk wrote in his *Intikhāb-i Sulṭāniyyah* that Gilchrist made him a munshi of the "first class" (*darjah-i awwal*).
8. That a storyteller should produce such a treatise might seem odd given the modern understanding of the romance as a frivolous genre, unconnected to knowledge. However, Bāqir 'Alī's publications, as well as the statements of Fakhr al-Zamani, Ashk, and Ghalib Lakhnawi, to be examined in the next chapter, should remind us that knowledge sharing

was understood as an important aspect of the romance genre and a factor in the raising of its worth.

9. Our information regarding the production of Ashk's *Ḥamzah-nāmah* is muddled, due to the lack of a first edition (Pritchett 1991, 11). In general, it is agreed, on the basis of the preface that appears in most editions, that the book was published in 1801; see Ashk 1863, 2; Faruqi 2006b, 180–82. However, as we have seen, Gilchrist did not make his request for a storyteller to the College Council until the beginning of 1802, and Ashk indicates that he was unable to complete his writing while he was unemployed. Furthermore, the manuscript of the first volume of Ashk's work at the British Library contains a postscript in which Ashk indicates that he submitted this volume to Gilchrist in 1802 (Barelvī 1965, 17). Besides this, as we shall see below, Gilchrist indicated in 1802 that Ashk's project was ongoing. Thus it appears quite possible that the actual date of publication of the book was later than 1801, although before August 1803, as the book is mentioned by Gilchrist in his August 9, 1803, list of Fort William College publications that he nominated for awards (Siddiqi 1960, 194).
10. *Nigārḳhānah-i Chīn* was originally written for the East India Company servant Jonathan Henry Lovett, who, however, passed away in 1805. It was therefore rededicated to Mordaunt Ricketts (Gyān Cand Jain 1969, 253). The *Intiḳhāb-i sulṭāniyyah* was written for Mordaunt Ricketts, then in a relatively minor position in the Bengal Civil Service, later Lucknow Resident (Barelvī 1965, 7, 18).
11. Ashk mentions the names of the *daftar*s of the proposed twenty-two-volume *Hamzah-nāmah*, some of which correspond with the *daftar* names mentioned by Faḳhr al-Zamānī or with the names of the later Urdu versions: *Qiṣṣah-i Ḳhurd sāl*, *Hurmuz-nāmah*, *Bālā Bāḳhtar*, *Kochak Bāḳhtar*, *Pā'īn Bāḳhtar*, *Iraj-nāmah*, *Ṣandalī-nāmah*, *Tūraj-nāmah*, and *La'l-nāmah* (Barelvī 1965, 17). Shamsur Rahman Faruqi (1999, chap. 1) understands the Naval Kishore version's *daftar*s to be eight in number, but several of the names are the same as in Ashk's projected version.
12. For studies of the Urdu *marṡiyah*, see Masud 1990 and Hyder 2006.

13. I thank Razak Khan for sharing information and materials gained during his extensive research on the Rampur state.
14. Jain (1969, 706) disputes Rāz Yazdānī's claim, also found in Aṡar's account, that Mīr Aḥmad 'Alī came to Rampur during the rule of Yūsuf 'Alī Ḳhān. He does so on the basis of the dates of the four *Ḥamzah-nāmah daftars* in the Rampur Raza Library.
15. Compare Rasā's and Mīr Nawwāb's salaries below.
16. Jain (1969, 706) considers Mīr Aḥmad 'Alī's *Hoshrubā* to be preliminary. See also the statements regarding Mīr Aḥmad 'Alī in the Naval Kishore *Hoshrubā*, laid out in the next chapter.
17. Some storytellers of the later generation may have interacted with Mīr Aḥmad 'Alī themselves. For instance, Anbā Parshād's son Ġhulām Raẓā and Aṣġhar 'Alī's son Jalāl may have had this opportunity (Gyān Cand Jain 1969, 706; Yazdānī 1952, 6). Much information about Mīr Aḥmad 'Alī and other Urdu storytellers is provided in Musharraf Ali Farooqi's introduction to his translation of Jāh 2009.
18. In poetry he used the pen name "Rasā" and was the disciple of Mirzā Muḥammad Taqī Ḳhān "Hawas" (Aṡar Rāmpūrī 1950, 110; Nāṣir 1970, 461).
19. Rāz Yazdānī, however, claims that he came earlier, during the reign of Nawab Muḥammad Sa'īd Ḳhān (Yazdānī 1952, 11; Aṡar Rāmpūrī 1950).
20. 'Ishrat, who mistakes Anbā Parshād's name, tells a version of this anecdote in which Anbā Parshād himself arrested his tale.
21. I must thank Katherine Schofield and David Lunn for pointing out this invaluable source to me.
22. Sayyid Ḥusain was the son of the storyteller Sayyid 'Alī b. Mirzā Makkhū Beg Lakhnawī (d. 1886–87), who worked in Rampur in Kalb-i 'Alī Ḳhān's time (Aṡar Rāmpūrī 1950, 110).
23. Faruqi discusses the first edition dates of the Naval Kishore volumes, as well their narrative order, in 2006b, chaps. 2 and 4. For an extensive study of Naval Kishore and his press, see Stark 2007.
24. Faruqi is, however, skeptical with regard to 'Ishrat's statement, followed by

Rāz and Jain, that Fidā was a storyteller as well as a *naṡr-ḳhwān* (Ḳhwājah 'Ishrat Lakhnawī 1935, 59).

25. Jāh himself had a student, apparently in *naṡr-ḳhwānī*, named Sayyid Kāẓim Ḥusain Murādābādī (Faruqi 2006b, 150–51).
26. Part of the difficulty in assessing whether this account of Qamar is facetious lies in the fact that, of the two copies that Faruqi has seen, one from the Bodleian Library and one from the University of Toronto, the Bodleian copy is missing four important pages, while the Toronto copy, a later edition, lacks the obsequious passage entirely (Faruqi 2006b, 159).
27. See Pernau 2013 for an excellent study of the *sharīf* upper/middle class in India.
28. Furthermore, in storytelling, Qamar had a pupil, Mirzā Raẓā 'Alī, who was the author of a *dāstān* entitled *Ṣaulat al-ẓaiġham* (The lion's fury).
29. Qamar's death is announced by his son Ishtiyāq Aḥmad Suhail in his *taqrīẓ* to Qamar (1901, 814).
30. On Bāqir 'Alī, see Pritchett's previous English-language account (1991, 16–21). I am grateful to Zahra Sabri for providing me with Aqeel Abbas Jafri's edition of many of the biographical sketches of Bāqir 'Alī and his short works (*Mīr Bāqir "Alī Dāstāngo: Dāstāneṅ aur dāstān-go"ī* 2014).
31. Feroz and Shāhid Aḥmad record the price of Bāqir 'Alī's home performances as one anna. Mullā Wāḥidī says that he charged eight annas or one rupee. Shāhid Aḥmad mentions that he had previously charged two rupees for performances in Delhi (not necessarily at home) (Muḥammad Feroz Dihlawī 2014, 68; Shāhid Aḥmad Dihlawī 1979, 192; Mullā Wāḥidī Dihlawī 2013, 97).
32. For the anecdote regarding Bāqir 'Alī's turban, see Sayyid Yūsuf Buḳhārī Dihlawī 1987, 23.
33. For an excellent study of tea under British rule in India, see Lutgendorf 2012.
34. Though Ṣabūḥī does not say so, the *dāstān* that he recounted from memory was previously published in *Ṭilism-i Hosh-afẓā*. Cf. Ṣabūḥī 1963, 49ff., to Mīr Bāqir 'Alī Dāstān-go 1892, 2.
35. *Sharāfat* has the senses of "nobility, respectability, genteelness," and so

forth. By Bāqir 'Alī's time it referred, more or less, to a rising (or risen) middle class, but a variety of individuals claimed respectability by using the term. For an important discussion of this category and its shifting meaning in the nineteenth century, see Pernau 2013.

36. Compare the discussion of the *qiṣṣah/dāstān/ḥikāyat* distinction in chapter 5.

37. However, in his radio broadcast on storytelling, Shāhid Aḥmad increased this amount to 10–15 rupees (Shāhid Aḥmad Dihlawī 1944, 38–41)!

38. The title "*muqarrir-i kā'ināt*" appears in Bāqir 'Alī's own publications; see 1922, title page, and 1920a, front matter.

39. The recordings are Mīr Bāqir 'Alī Dāstān-go 1920c and Mīr Bāqir 'Alī Dāstān-go 1920b. See Chattophadhyay 2011 with regard to Shahid Amin's research. For Bāqir 'Alī's lists of weapons and jewelry, see Shāhid Aḥmad Dihlawī 1944, 40. For a list of wrestling moves, see Mīr Bāqir 'Alī Dāstān-go 1892, 40.

40. For a discussion of the use of the *ṡaqal-dān*, see Faruqi 2012, 141–42. More generally, Bāqir 'Alī dedicated a section of his 1920a to the etiquette of dining (4–8).

41. Bāqir 'Alī replied, "I give thanks to God, but these days life has no *mazah* [taste, pleasure]." The Westernized gentleman responded, using an English word, "Yes, Mīr Ṣāḥib, these days the ṭaisṭ of life has changed." At this, Bāqir 'Alī spat forth a long string of Urdu words that the ignoramus could have used instead.

42. For an example of a chapbook with Bāqir 'Alī's notes on vocabulary, see Mīr Bāqir 'Alī Dāstān-go 1922.

43. I am very grateful to Muhammad Salim-ur-Rahman for providing me with his edition of *Kānā-bātī*.

44. Bāqir 'Alī's other stories of Gāṛhe Ḳhān also sold for eight annas each: *Gāṛhe Ḳhān kī Ḍhākah-wālī se mulāqāt* (Gāṛhe Ḳhān's meeting with his wife from Dhaka) and *Gāṛhe Ḳhān aur Malmal Jān kī jang* (The war of Gāṛhe Ḳhān and Malmal Jān); *Gāṛhe Ḳhān kā dukhṛā* (The misery of Gāṛhe Ḳhān) sold for six annas. There was also the didactic *Ādāb o aḳhlāq* (Manners and ethics, six annas), three volumes of *Ustānī* (The teacher, volumes 1 and 2 for six annas each, volume 3 for three annas), and *Ārārārādhūn* (three an-

nas), and the tale of the last Mughal's elephant, *Maulā Bakhsh hāthī* (Maulā Bakhsh the elephant, three annas) (Mīr Bāqir 'Alī Dāstān-go 1922, 16).

45. See Muḥammad Feroz Dihlawī 2014, 69, for Bāqir 'Alī's final resting place.
46. Bāqirī Begam, who passed away in 1952, had moved to Pakistan after Partition with her husband, Sayyid Ẓamīr Ḥasan Naqwī, who wrote the preface to the new edition of Bāqir 'Alī's 1966. Their sons were named Sayyid Raẕī Ḥusain and Sayyid Shahanshāh Ḥusain (Sayyid Yūsuf Bukhārī Dihlawī 1987, 20).

Chapter 3

1. For a fascinating study of Ṭibbiyah College and its epistemological significance, see Pernau 2013, 312ff.
2. For a more detailed discussion, see Khan 2017a.
3. See Prasad 1962, 91, for the list of governors.
4. When it came to sources of information on Fakhr al-Zamānī's life, aside from Fakhr al-Zamānī's own writings, Muḥammad Shafī' was aware only of the *Tārīkh-i Muḥammad Shāhī*, which provides a short notice of Fakhr al-Zamānī showing that he was known as a storyteller in the mid-eighteenth century (1740 CE) when the Tārīkh was written. Quoted in Muḥammad Shafī', "Muqaddamah," ix n3. Muḥammad Bakhtāwar Khān's *Mir'āt al-'ālam*, which was written in 1078 H (1667–68), not long after Fakhr al-Zamānī's death, provides no new information beyond what the *Maikhānah* already tells us (Muḥammad Bakhtāwar Khān 1667, fol. 487b).
5. Fakhr al-Zamānī set out for Mashhad at nineteen years of age, and he appears to have reached Agra not many years later, by 1018 H.
6. 'Abd Allāh Anṣārī Harawī was a Ḥanbalī scholar and Sufi who lived from 396 to 481 H.
7. While in Lahore, Fakhr al-Zamānī made the acquaintance of a number of poets, including "Mauzūn al-mulk" Luṭfī Shīrāzī, recently honored with a title by Jahāngīr; Muḥammad Mīrak 'Ārifī Mūsawī; and the aged Sufi Darwesh Jāwed Qazwīnī (Fakhr al-Zamānī Qazwīnī 1983, 818, 907, and 919).

8. *Mauzūn* can also refer to metrical correctness, but this would hardly apply to a prose *dāstān*.

9. Mīrzā Niẓām al-Dīn Aḥmad's career, according to the *Maikhānah*, was as follows. He was attached to Akbar's court in some capacity in 999 H, in which year Akbar asked him to look in upon the mortally ill poet 'Urfī Shīrāzī and bring news of his health back to his court (Fakhr al-Zamānī Qazwīnī 1983, 222). In 1018 H, when Fakhr al-Zamānī first encountered him, he was a *wāqi'ah-nawes* at Jahāngīr's court in Agra. He set off with Jahāngīr for Ajmer in 1022 H (762), but by 1023 H he was no longer at the imperial court, having taken up *wāqi'ah-nawesī* in Kashmir (Khwājah Kāmgār Ḥusainī 1978, 497). By 1025 H, when Fakhr al-Zamāni took up with him again, he was *dīwān* and *bakhshī* of Kashmir, and finally at the end of 1026 H he was summoned to Jahāngīr in Mandu and appointed *dīwān* of Bihar (770). In 1028 H, when Fakhr al-Zamānī was writing his own *tarjamah*, Mīrzā Niẓāmī was still in this post (763, 771).

In his brief biography in the *Encyclopedia Islamica*, Muḥammad Bāqir asserts that the *wāqi'ah-nawes* whom Fakhr al-Zamānī met early on was not the same as the *dīwān* and *bakhshī* of Kashmir with whom he took refuge later. Yet, oddly, the article refers to both men as Mīrzā Niẓāmī, whereas the *Maikhānah* edition (surely the article's source) refers to the first as Mīrzā Niẓāmī and to the second as Mīrzā Niẓām al-Dīn Aḥmad. It is not clear on what basis Muḥammad Bāqir believed Mīrzā Niẓāmī and Mīrzā Niẓām al-Dīn Aḥmad to be two separate men. Writing in 1028 H, Fakhr al-Zamānī says that Mīrzā Niẓāmī "is now the diwan of the province of Bihar" (763), and later on he describes Mīrzā Niẓām al-Dīn Aḥmad's appointment to this very post (770). Muḥammad Shafī' certainly makes them one and the same, calling them both Mīrzā Niẓāmī in his preface (xi–xii) and only making one clarification: that Mīrzā Niẓāmī was not the same as Niẓām al-Dīn Aḥmad, the historiographer who authored the *Ṭabaqāt-i Akbarī* (762n1). This is despite that Khushḥāl Cand in the eighteenth-century *Tārīkh-i Muḥammad Shāhī* conflated Mīrzā Niẓāmī and the author of the *Ṭabaqāt* (Khushḥāl Cand is quoted in Muḥammad Shafī' 1983, ix n3).

10. Naqīb Khān is noticed in Shāh Nawāz Khān Aurangābādī 1888, 3:812–

17. See Chandra 1976, 178, for information regarding his family and their flight from Iran.

11. Naqīb Ḳhān's work, regarding which I have not yet discovered any further information, is excerpted in the *Afṣaḥ al-akhbār* of Muḥammad Bāqir Afṣaḥ (Rieu 1879, 122).
12. For a translation of Mīr 'Alā' al-Daulah's passage on the illustrated *Ḥamzah-nāmah*, see Chandra 1976, 180–81.
13. Faḳhr al-Zamānī cites Mīr 'Alā' al-Daulah in the *Maiḳhānah*, Faḳhr al-Zamānī Qazwīnī 1983, 860.
14. Seventeen days after setting out from Agra, Jahāngīr stopped at the town of Rup Bas (in modern Rajasthan), where he remained hunting for fifteen days altogether before going on to Ajmer. The *Tūzak* tells us that Jahāngīr subsequently renamed Rup Bas "Amanābād" in honor of Mīrzā Amān Allāh, though it is not entirely clear whether this occurred on that very trip or afterward. The timeline, as given in the *Tūzak* according to the solar months, is as follows. Jahāngīr left the Agra fort on the night of 24 Shahrīwār and came to the Dahrah Garden (Ārām Bāgh) southwest of Agra proper. He remained there for eight days and left on 1 Mihr. He reached Rup Bas on 10 Mihr, spending eleven days there, according to the *Tūzak*'s account, but he left on 25 Mihr. Therefore, he evidently remained in Rup Bas for fourteen or fifteen days. He did not enter Ajmer until a month later, on 26 Ābān / 5 Shawwāl, the holy month of Ramaẓān having gone by in the interval (Nūr al-Dīn Muḥammad Salīm Jahāngīr, Mu'tamad Ḳhān, and Hādī 1914, 123–25).
15. See the *Maiḳhānah*, Faḳhr al-Zamānī Qazwīnī 1983, 878–79, for Faḳhr al-Zamānī's account of Anwar.
16. See Faḳhr al-Zamānī Qazwīnī 1983, 764–68, for the entire account of his early relation with Amān Allāh.
17. For a complete conspectus of Faḳhr al-Zamānī's work, see Khan 2017a.
18. See Faḳhr al-Zamānī Qazwīnī 1983, 769, for Faḳhr al-Zamānī's description and one version of the chronogram. The Majlis Library's manuscript of the *Maiḳhānah* presents a variant chronogram (Faḳhr al-Zamānī Qazwīnī n.d., fol. 170b). Both chronograms are incorrect (see Khan 2017a).

19. Glosses on the allusions in this passage may be found in Khan 2017a.
20. Waṣlī was a disciple of the poet Murshid Burojirdī, mentioned earlier. When Murshid was summoned to India by Mīrzā Ghāzī, Waṣlī came with him and entered Mīrzā Ghāzī's service. When Jahāngīr made Mīrzā Ghāzī governor of Qandahar, Waṣlī went to the royal court in Ajmer (where Fakhr al-Zamānī dwelled in Mīrzā Amān Allāh's service). Not finding it to his liking, he set out for Lahore, meeting Fakhr al-Zamānī and Maḥmūd Beg Turkmān on the way (Fakhr al-Zamānī Qazwīnī 1983, 269–70).
21. By 1028 H, Fakhr al-Zamānī had not heard any news of the pair.
22. Ṣafdar Khān was appointed governor of Kashmir in 1023 H (Nūr al-Dīn Muḥammad Salīm Jahāngīr, Mu'tamad Khān, and Hādī 1914, 126).
23. See Fakhr al-Zamānī Qazwīnī 1983, 770, for Fakhr al-Zamānī's account of his time in Kashmir.
24. Fakhr al-Zamānī also met Aḥwālī Sīstānī in Kashmir, a dependent of Ṣafdar Khān b. Mīrzā Yūsuf Khān, who wrote poems in praise of the Shi'ite imams rather than the rightly guided caliphs (Fakhr al-Zamānī Qazwīnī 1983, 909).
25. In this edition, Fakhr al-Zamānī tells us that he met Nadīm in Kashmīr in 1020 H, which seems unlikely.
26. For the meeting with Waṣlī, see Fakhr al-Zamānī Qazwīnī 1983, 971.
27. The spectacle of the elephant is detailed in Khan 2017a.
28. The *Qiṣṣah-i Hatim Ta'i* and *Qiṣṣah-i Gul-i Bakawali* are examples of short romances situated in the eighteenth century that show traces of it.
29. See the conspectus of Fakhr al-Zamānī's works in Khan 2017a.
30. For a description of *barā'at-i istihlāl*, see Maḥjūb 1991, 210n16. Manuals of poetic language also tended to describe this device. For example, see Muḥammad al-Dīn 1876, 4.
31. The painting is reproduced in Seyller and Thackston 2002, 171. The translation is based on Thackston's in the same volume (301).
32. For the picture storytellers of India, see Jyotindra Jain 1998 and chap. 1, this volume.
33. Aside from the account in the *Bostān* (cited above), there are earlier accounts in Ibn Kathīr 1998, 77–78.

34. *Para*, as J. Hillis Miller (1979, 219) explains, is "an antithetical prefix which indicates at once proximity and distance, similarity and difference, interiority and exteriority."
35. Apart from being produced in the city where he was possibly resident at this time, the manuscript contains marginal notes that appear to be additions by the author.
36. Peter Mundy (1907, 159–62), who was in Patna during 'Abd Allāh Khān's governorship, is very critical of the current governor and recounts the Biharis's positive view of Saif Khān by contrast.

Chapter 4

1. Editor Ġhulām Rasūl Mihr tells us that Wilāyat 'Alī is *muhtamim* of the press, a detail that Ḳhalīq Anjum appears to have left out.
2. See also the newer edition edited by Ṭāhirah Parwīn Akram, Tawakkul Beg 2005.
3. I am grateful to Charles Melville for sharing with me a draft of his very informative Lahore conference paper on the Indian reception of the Shamsher-Ḳhānī.
4. Given that Berūnī was himself an Iranian, this cannot be a sweeping criticism.
5. The *Encyclopedia of Islam* notes that there is much confusion regarding T͟ha'ālibī's identity, but in any case his patronage context can be established (Bosworth 2011).
6. Chief among these was probably the same New Persian translation of the Pahlawi *Ḳhwadāy-nāmag* from which Firdausī's predecessor Daqīqī evidently derived his material. See Nöldeke 1979, 63.
7. Distance in terms of time and space is a common emollient offered to naysayers of such far-fetched accounts. The British traveler in Iran John Malcolm (1827, 78) received the following explanation from his companion Ḥājī Ḥusain of the endangered status of *ġhūl*s in the nineteenth century: "The number of these ghools . . . has greatly decreased since the birth of the prophet, and they have no power to hurt those who pronounce his name in sincerity of heart."

8. The translation is Zadeh's.
9. I have modified Zadeh's translation very slightly. In this case Yāqūt al-Rūmī is claiming that he is sincere *even if the account is false.*
10. See also Culler 1982, especially his commentary on illocutionary utterances: "to mean something by an utterance is not to perform an inner act of meaning that accompanies the utterance" (111).
11. This is, not strictly speaking, a proper translation of *isnād*; the figure of the "chain" is not implied within it, and in certain contexts "warrant" is better.
12. Peacock (2007, 80) goes on, however, to point out that Ṯabarī himself fell a bit short of being the model "hadith historian."
13. Ibn Kalbī's genealogy is as follows: Ḥātim b. 'Abd Allāh b. Sa'd b. al-Ḥashraj b. Imrū al-Qais b. 'Adī b. Akhzam b. Hazūmah b. Rabī'ah b. Jarwal b. Tha'al b. 'Amr b. Al-Ġhauth b. Ṭayyi' b. Udad b. Zaid b. Yaḥshub b. 'Arīb b. Zaid b. Kahlān b. Saba' b. Yaḥshub b. Ya'rib b. Qaḥṭān.
14. Qaḥṭān is the putative ancestor of all Southern Arabs, while his descendant Kahlān is the forebear of most of the nomadic branch of this family (accounts of Ḥātim generally bear witness to his nomadism and that of his tribe).

Chapter 5

1. The *Guldastah* commits a puzzling error with regard to the year, giving it as 1866 Faṣlī, equivalent to 2456 CE! (Muḥammad Ya'qūb Lakhnawī 1876, 6). Later accounts such as *Tārīkh-i ṭilism-i Bakāwalī* and the 1905 *Tārīkh-i Riyāsat-hā-i Baghelkhanḍ* understand this as 1866 CE (Muḥammad Ismā'īl Ḍāsnawī 1895, 52; Farmān Fatḥpūrī 2006, 63). Both of these accounts refer to the chief commissioner as "John Temple," whereas the *Guldastah* simply omits his first name.
2. My hasty look through Temple's correspondence did not yield any mention of a Bakāwalī Fortress expedition. As Simon Digby has noted, Temple does not refer to any such investigative effort in his biography either (Digby and Harrow 2000, 284).
3. My summary of the *Qiṣṣah-i Gul-i Bakāwalī* is based largely on Nihāl Chand 2008, according to which Tāj al-Mulūk is cast into the ocean and

washes up on the shore of some enchanted land. It is, however, Nasim (2007, 191) who understands this country as a *ṭilism*.

4. The story in fact continues after the marriage of Bakāwalī and Tāj al-Mulūk, when King Indra interferes by summoning Bakāwalī to dance for him at his court in the clouds, causing the hapless Tāj al-Mulūk to follow her and initiate a new series of disasters. Simon Digby has translated Nihāl Chand's version of the *qiṣṣah* into English (Digby and Harrow 2000). W. A. Clouston also wrote an English translation in 1889 as part of his collection. His translation was based on Garcin de Tassy's French version, *La Rose de Bakawali*, initially published in two parts in the *Journal Asiatique* from September to October 1835.
5. For an excellent survey of the sources on the "true story" of Bakāwalī, see Farmān Fatḥpūrī 2006.
6. "Pindas" appear to be the Pindaris.
7. What I have before me is a photocopy of the same copy of the *Tārīkh-i Ṭilism-i Bakāwalī* that Fatḥpūrī saw and summarized in his study. Fatḥpūrī points out that the initial publication of the *Tārīkh* took place from December 1894 to January 1895. The 1895 edition is held by the Liaquat Memorial Library in Karachi. I am grateful to Zahra Sabri for obtaining a copy of the text for me.
8. Digby identifies the plant, also known as the Baka tree, which has long been known for its usefulness as a remedy for ocular ailments (Digby and Harrow 2000, 285–86).
9. I thank Matthew Melvin-Koushki for sharing a draft of his article with me.
10. Muḥammad Ismā'īl refers to the tablet as the *ṭilism-kushā*, or *ṭilism* opener, whereas in the *Ḥamzah-nāmah* and other *qiṣṣah*s the term "*ṭilism-kushā*" usually meant the conqueror of the *ṭilism* (Muḥammad Ismā'īl Ḍāsnawī 1895, 8).
11. The earliest importation of the English word into Urdu, as *injinīr*, occurred around 1847, according to Abū al-Lais̤ Ṣiddīqī's and Nasīm Amrohwī 1977, 911.
12. It is not clear whether the idea of the *uṛan khaṭolā* had anything to do with an incipient interest in the *vimānas*—the supposed Vedic-period flying

proto-airplanes whose mechanisms are detailed in G. R. Josyer's probably fabricated *Vaimānika shāstra* (see Deb 2015). Muḥammad Ismāʿīl instead glosses the aircraft with the Sanskrit word *mrchchhakatika*.

13. Ibn ʿArabi distinguished between reason (*nuṯq*) and intellect (*ʿaql*), which, however, does not seem to have caught on in the post-Akbarian Islamicate world (Khan 2008).
14. A recently published study argues that an "enchanted" worldview persisted into the twentieth century in Euro-America, even if "Occidentals" desired to be seen as distinguished by their rationalism (Josephson-Storm 2017).
15. See also the hadith in which the Prophet exhorts Muslims to contemplate creation but not the Creator (Zadeh 2010, 29).
16. Studies of *maʿnī-āfirīni* can be found in Faruqi 1996; 2004; 2006d; and Pritchett 1994. A well-known example of meaning creation leading to bewilderment is the opening verse (*maṯlaʿ*) to Mirzā Ġhālib's ghazal, "*Nah thā kuchh to ḳhudā thā*" (Ġhālib and ʿArshī 1958, ghazal 44).
17. Quran 36.82: "When He wills a thing, He has only to command it: 'Be!' And it comes to be." Cf. Rūmī 1925, vv. 4056–76.
18. Ibn ʿArabī (2004, 91) explained that *ʿādat* was valid only in the sensory world and not beyond it.
19. Fielding (1998, 773) alluded to these romances in *Tom Jones*, as a foil for the new and better form of fiction: "The Arabians and Persians had an equal advantage [to the ancients] in writing their tales from the genii and fairies, which they believe in as an article of their faith, upon the authority of the Koran itself. But we have none of these helps. To natural means alone we are confined."
20. The Quranic verse is 41.53.
21. Ratan Nāth Sarshār's *Fasānah-i Āzād* started being published serially prior to 1869 but was not collected into book form until 1880.
22. *Don Quixote* was well known to Urdu writers. The 1880 *Fasānah-i Āzād* took much of its inspiration from Cervantes, and his 1894 *Ḳhudā'ī faujdār* was a translation of *Quixote*.
23. I thank Prashant Keshavmurthy for alerting me to this reference.

24. For critiques of the colonialist/nationalist historiography of the eighteenth century, see Bayly 2012; Perlin 2003; Stein 2003.
25. It is not clear from Sharar's words that he was in fact defending the existence of such beings, however.

Conclusion

1. Schofield (2006, 75) uses the term "status" in order "to differentiate between communities across the whole of Mughal society" and "prestige" to "differentiate between communities of musicians."
2. One example is Jyotindra Jain 1998, which is otherwise highly important.
3. Orsini makes this point regarding manuscripts in Orsini and Schofield 2015.
4. The following account is from the novel's opening narrative published in the 1970s (Nawab 1993).
5. See Ali Khan and Ahmad 2010 for a study of Lollywood horror films.
6. For an excellent account of the early development of *jāsūsī* novels, see Orsini 2009, chap. 7.

Works Cited

'Abd al-Bāqī Nihāwandī. 1910. *Ma'āsir-i Raḥīmī*. Ed. Muḥammad Hidayat Hosain. Vol. 3. Calcutta: Asiatic Society of Bengal.

'Abd al-Ḥāmid Lāhaurī. 1867. *Bādshāhnāmah*. Asiatic Society: Calcutta.

Abū al-Faraj al-Iṣfahānī, 'Alī b. Al-Ḥusain. 1970. *Kitāb al-Āġhānī*. Vol. 19. Cairo: Dār al-sha'b.

Abū al-Fazl b. Mubārak. 1877. *Akbar-nāmah*. Ed. Maulawī 'Abd al-Raḥīm. Vol. 2. Calcutta: Baptist Mission Press.

———. n.d. *'Iyār-i dānish*. Manuscript. Montreal: McGill University Blacker-Wood Rare Books. MS BW Ivanow 0020.

Āftābchī, Jauhar. 2009. "Tazkirat al-wāqi'āt." In *Three Memoirs of Humayun*, ed. W. M Thackston, 75–215. Costa Mesa, CA: Mazda.

Ahmad, Aziz. 1967. *Islamic Modernism in India and Pakistan, 1857–1964*. London: Oxford University Press.

Ahmad, Qeyamuddin. 1973. *Corpus of Arabic & Persian inscriptions of Bihar (A.H. 640–1200)*. Patna: K. P. Jayaswal Research Institute.

Ahmed, Manan. 2008. "The Many Histories of Muhammad b. Qasim: Narrating the Muslim Conquest of Sindh." PhD diss., University of Chicago.

Alam, Muzaffar. 2003. "The Culture and Politics of Persian in Precolonial Hindustan." In *Literary Cultures in History: Reconstructions from South Asia*, ed. Sheldon Pollock, 131–98. Berkeley: University of California Press.

Alam, Muzaffar, and Sanjay Subrahmanyam. 2009. "Frank Disputations: Catholics and Muslims in the Court of Jahangir (1608–11)." *Indian Economic and Social History Review* 46 (4): 457–511.

Althusser, Louis. 2008. *On Ideology*. London: Verso.

Amānat, Sayyid Āġhā Ḥasan. 2007. *The Court of Indar and the Rebirth of North Indian Drama*. Ed. Afroz Taj. New Delhi: Anjuman Taraqqī-i Urdū (Hind).

Amīr Mīnā'ī, Amīr Aḥmad. 1982. *Intikḥāb-i yādgār*. Lucknow: Uttar Pradesh Urdu Academy.

Asar Rāmpūrī, Muḥammad 'Alī Ḳhān. 1950. "Dībāchah." In *Musaddas-i tahnīyat-i jashn-i Benazīr*, by Mīr Yār 'Alī Jān Ṣāḥib, 5–130. Rampur: Rampur State Press.

Asher, Catherine B. 1992. *Architecture of Mughal India*. Cambridge: Cambridge University Press.

Ashk, Ḳhalīl 'Alī Ḳhān. 1863. *Dāstān-i Amīr Ḥamzah*. Vol. 1. Bombay: Maṭba'-i Ḥaidarī.

Atkinson, James. 1892. *The Sháh námeh of the Persian Poet Firdausí*. London: F. Warne.

Auḥadī, Taqī al-Dīn. 2009. *'Arafāt al-'āshiqīn wa 'araṣāt al-'ārifīn*. Ed. Muḥsin Nājī Naṣrābādī. Vol. 1. Tehran: Intishārāt-i Asāṯīr.

Austin, John L. 1975. *How to Do Things with Words*. Cambridge, MA: Harvard University Press.

Āzād, Muḥammad Ḥusain. 1998. *Nairang-i ḳhayāl*. Ed. Muḥammad Ṣādiq. 3rd ed. Lahore: Majlis-i Taraqqī-i adab.

Babur, Ẓahīr al-Dīn, and 'Abd al-Raḥīm Ḳhān-i Ḳhānān. 1993. *Bâburnâma*. Ed. W. M. Thackston. Vol. 2. Cambridge, MA: Dept. of Near Eastern Languages and Civilizations, Harvard University.

Badā'ūnī, 'Abd al-Qādir b. Mulūk Shāh. 1864. *Muntaḳhab al-tawārīḳh*. Ed. Maulwī Aḥmad 'Alī and William Nassau Lees. Vol. 2. Calcutta: College Press.

Baihaqī, Abū al-Faẓl Muḥammad b. Ḥusain. 2009. *Tārīḳh-i Baihaqī*. Tehran: Intishārāt-i Suḳhan.

Bakhtin, Mikhail. *The Dialogic Imagination: Four Essays*. Trans. Caryl Emerson and Michael Holquist. Austin: University of Texas Press, 2004.

Baqir, M. 1982. "'Abd-Al-Nabī Qazvīnī." *Encyclopedia Iranica, Online Edition*. http://www.iranicaonline.org/articles/abd-al-nabi-qazvini-india.

Barelvī, 'Ibādat. 1965. "Muqaddamah." In *Risālah-i kā'ināt*, by Khalīl 'Alī Khān Ashk, 5–23. Karachi: Urdū dunyā.

Bascom, William R. 1955. "Verbal Art." *Journal of American Folklore* 68 (269): 245–52.

Bauman, Richard. 1975. "Verbal Art as Performance." *American Anthropologist* 77 (2): 290–311.

Bayly, C. A. 2012. *Rulers, Townsmen and Bazaars: North Indian Society in the Age of British Expansion, 1770–1870*. New Delhi: Oxford University Press.

Beglar, J. D. 1878. *Report of a Tour Through the Bengal Provinces of Patna, Gaya, Mongir, and Bhagalpur: The Santal Parganas, Manbhum, Singhbhum, and Birbhum ; Bankura, Raniganj, Bardwan, and Hughli : in 1872–73*. Vol. 8. Calcutta: Office of the Superintendent of Government Printing.

Ben-Amos, Dan. 1976. "Analytical Categories and Ethnic Genres." In *Folklore Genres*, ed. Dan Ben-Amos, 215–42. Austin: University of Texas Press.

Bhutta, Saeed. 2006. *Kamāl kahānī*. Lahore: Sānjh.

Bilgrāmī, 'Abdullāh Ḥusain, and Mirzā Amān Allāh Ġhālib Lakhnawī. 2007. *The Adventures of Amir Hamza: Lord of the Auspicious Planetary Conjunction*. Trans. Musharraf Ali Farooqi. 1st ed. New York: Modern Library.

Boase, Roger. 1977. *The Origin and Meaning of Courtly Love: A Critical Study of European Scholarship*. Manchester: Manchester University Press.
Bosworth, C. E. 2011. "al-T̲H̲aālibī, Abū Manṣūr." Ed. P. Bearman, Th. Bianquis, C. E. Bosworth, E. van Donzel, and W. P. Heinrichs. *Encyclopaedia of Islam, Second Edition*. BrillOnline. http://referenceworks.brillonline.com/browse/encyclopaedia-of-islam-2.
Bourdieu, Pierre. 2007. "The Forms of Capital." In *Sociology of Education: A Critical Reader*, ed. Alan R Sadovnik, 83–95. New York: Routledge.
Busch, Allison. 2010. *Poetry of Kings: The Classical Hindi Literature of Mughal India*. New York: Oxford University Press.
Chandra, Pramod. 1976. *The Tuti-nama of the Cleveland Museum of Art and the Origins of Mughal Painting*. Chicago: P. Chandra.
Chattophadhyay, Sohini. 2011. "Voices from Colonial India." *Open*, February 26. http://www.openthemagazine.com/article/arts-letters/voices-from-colonial-india.
Clouston, W. A. 1889. *A Group of Eastern Romances and Stories from the Persian, Tamil, and Urdu*. Privately printed.
Cohen, Ralph. 1986. "History and Genre." *New Literary History* 17 (2): 203–18.
Culler, Jonathan. 1982. *On Deconstruction*. Ithaca, NY: Cornell University Press.
Dargāh Qulī Ḳhān. 1993. *Muraqqaʿ-i Dihlī*. Ed. Ḳhalīq Anjum. New Delhi: Anjuman Taraqqī-i Urdū (Hind).
Deb, Siddharta. 2015. "Those Mythological Men and Their Sacred, Supersonic Flying Temples." *New Republic*, May 14. https://newrepublic.com/article/121792/those-mythological-men-and-their-sacred-supersonic-flying-temples.
Derrida, Jacques. 1980. "The Law of Genre." Trans. Avital Ronell. *Critical Inquiry* 7 (1): 55–81.
Digby, Simon, and Leonard Harrow. 2000. *Wonder-Tales of South Asia*. Oxford: Oxford University Press.
Faḳhr al-Zamānī Qazwīnī, ʿAbd al-Nabī. 1632. *Nawādir al-ḥikāyāt wa ġharāʾib al-riwāyāt*. Manuscript copied in Ahmedabad. London: British Library. MS Or. 1874.
———. 1633. *Ṯirāz al-aḳhbār*. Manuscript copied in Patna. Tehran: Mūzah-i Markaz-i asnād-i Majlis-i shūrā-i Islāmī. MS 358.
———. 1983. *Maiḳhānah*. Ed. Aḥmad Gulcīn-i Maʿānī and Muḥammad Shafīʿ. 3rd ed. Tehran: Iqbāl.
———. 2014. *Ṯirāz al-aḳhbār*. Ed. Sayyid Kamāl Ḥājj Sayyid Jawādī. Tehran: Pazhuhishkadah-yi Hunar.
———. n.d. *Maiḳhānah*. Manuscript. Tehran: Mūzah-i Markaz-i asnād-i Majlis-i shūrā-i Islāmī. MS 797 sīn sīn.

Falsafī, Naṣr Allāh. 1954. "Tarikh-i qahwah wa qahwah-ḳhānah dar Īrān." *Suḳhan* 5 (4): 258–68.
Farīd Bhakkarī. 1961. *Ẕaḳhīrat al-ḳhawānīn*. Ed. Sayyid Mu'īn al-Ḥaqq. Vol. 1. Karachi: Pakistan Historical Society.
Faridany-Akhavan, Zahra. 1989. "The Problems of the Mughal Manuscript of the Hamza-nama: 1562–1577: A Reconstruction." PhD diss., Harvard University.
Farmān Fatḥpūrī, Dildār 'Alī. 2006. "Qiṣṣah Gul-i Bakāwalī: Afsānah yā ḥaqīqat?" In *Urdū fikshan kī muḳhtaṣir tārīḳh*, 41–67. Lahore: Beacon Books.
Faruqi, Shamsur Rahman. 1996. *Urdū ġhazal ke ahamm moṛ: Īhām, ri'āyat, munāsibat*. New Delhi: Ġhālib Academy.
———. 1999. *Sāḥirī, shāhī, sāḥib-qirānī: Dāstān-i Amīr Ḥamzah kā mutāla'ah*. Vol. 1. New Delhi: Qaumī Council barā'e furoġh-i Urdū zabān.
———. 2004. "A Stranger in the City: The Poetics of Sabk-i Hindi." *Annual of Urdu Studies* 19:1–93.
———. 2006a. "Maẓmūn-āfirīnī." In *Shi'r-i shor-angez: Ġhazaliyāt-i Mīr kā muḥaqqiqānah intiḳhāb, mufaṣṣal muṭāla'e ke sāth*, 4:77–113. New Delhi: Qaumī Council barā'e furoġh-i Urdū zabān.
———. 2006b. *Sāḥirī, shāhī, sāḥib-qirānī: Dāstān-i Amīr Ḥamzah kā mutāla'ah*. Vol. 2. New Delhi: Qaumī Council barā'e furoġh-i Urdū zabān.
———. 2006c. *Sāḥirī, shāhī, sāḥib-qirānī: Dāstān-i Amīr Ḥamzah kā mutāla'ah*. Vol. 3. New Delhi: Qaumī Council barā'e furoġh-i Urdū zabān.
———. 2006d. *Shi'r-i shor-angez: Ġhazaliyāt-i Mīr kā muḥaqqiqānah intiḳhāb, mufaṣṣal muṭāla'e ke sāth*. 4 vols. New Delhi: Qaumī Council barā'e furoġh-i Urdū zabān.
———. 2012. *Luġhāt-i rozmarrah*. 4th ed. Karachi: Āj.
Fielding, Henry. 1986. *Joseph Andrews*. Ed. R. F Brissenden. Harmondsworth: Penguin.
———. 1998. *Tom Jones*. Ed. John B. Bender and Simon Stern. Oxford: Oxford University Press.
Forbes, Duncan. 1830. *The Adventures of Hatim Taï: A Romance*. London: Oriental Translation Fund.
Forbes, James. 1834. *Oriental Memoirs*. 2nd ed. Vol. 2. London: R. Bentley.
Frye, Northrop. 1973. *Anatomy of Criticism*. Princeton, NJ: Princeton University Press.
Genette, Gérard. 1997a. *Palimpsests: Literature in the Second Degree*. Lincoln: University of Nebraska Press.
———. 1997b. *Paratexts: Thresholds of Interpretation*. Cambridge: Cambridge University Press.

Ġhālib Lakhnawī, Mirzā Amān 'Alī Ḳhān. 1855. *Tarjamah-i Dāstān-i Ṣāḥib-qirān*. Calcutta: Maṭba'-i Imdādiyyah.
Ġhālib, Mirzā Asad Allāh Ḳhān. 1967a. "Dībācah-i Gulzār-i Surūr." In *'Ūd-i Hindī*, ed. Murtaẓà Ḥusain Fāẓil Lakhnawī, 445–48. Lahore: Majlis-i taraqqī-yi adab.
———. 1967b. *'Ūd-i Hindī*. Ed. Murtaẓà Ḥusain Fāẓil Lakhnawī. Lahore: Majlis-i Taraqqī-i adab.
———. 1969a. *Ḳhuṭūṭ-i Ġhālib*. Ed. Ġhulām Rasūl Mihr. Vol. 2. Lahore: Panjab University.
———. 1969b. *Urdū-i mu'allà*. Vol. 1. Lahore: Majlis-i Taraqqī-i adab.
———. 1984. *Ġhālib ke ḳhuṭūṭ*. Ed. Ḳhalīq Anjum. Vol. 1. New Delhi: Ġhālib Institute.
———. 1993. *Ġhālib ke ḳhuṭūṭ*. Ed. Ḳhalīq Anjum. Vol. 4. New Delhi: Ġhālib Institute.
Ġhālib, Mirzā Asad Allāh Ḳhān, and Imtiyāz 'Alī Ḳhān 'Arshī. 1958. *Dīwān-i Ġhālib, nusḳhah-i 'Arshī*. Aligarh: Anjuman Taraqqī-i Urdū Hind.
Ġhulām Ḥusain b. Hidāyat Allāh Ṭabāṭabā'ī. 1897. *Siyar al-muta'āḳhirīn*. Vol. 2. Lucknow: Naval Kishore.
Ġhulām Rasūl 'Ālampūrī. 2000. *Aḥsan al-qiṣas*. Lahore: Sang-i Mīl Publications.
Haase, Donald. 2010. "Decolonizing Fairy-Tale Studies." *Marvels & Tales* 24 (1): 17–38.
"Haft inṣāf-i Ḥātim." 2007. In *Ḥātim-nāmah*, vol. 2. Tehran: Intishārāt-i Mu'īn.
"Haft sair-i Ḥātim." 2007. In *Ḥātim-nāmah*, vol. 1. Tehran: Intishārāt-i Mu'īn.
Ḥaidarī, Sayyid Ḥaidar Baḳhsh. 1972. *Qiṣṣah-i Ḥātim Ṭā'ī*. Ed. Aṭhar Parwez. New Delhi: Maktabah-i Jāmi'ah.
Hakala, Walter N. 2014. "A Sultan in the Realm of Passion: Coffee in Eighteenth-Century Delhi." *Eighteenth-Century Studies* 47 (4): 371–88.
Ḥālī, Alṭāf Ḥusain. 1964. *Muqaddamah-i shi'r o shā'irī*. Ed. Rafīq Ḥusain. Allahabad: Rā'e Ṣāḥib Lālah Rām Dayāl Agarwālā.
Hanaway, William L. 1970. "Persian Popular Romances Before the Safavid Period." PhD diss., Columbia University.
Hansen, Kathryn. 2003. "Languages on Stage: Linguistic Pluralism and Community Formation in the Nineteenth-Century Parsi Theatre." *Modern Asian Studies* 37 (2): 381–405.
———. 2016. "Passionate Refrains: The Theatricality of Urdu on the Parsi Stage." *South Asian History and Culture South Asian History and Culture* 7 (3): 221–38.
Ḥasan, Muḥammad. 1956. *Jalāl Lakhnawī: Sawāniḥ-i ḥayāt*. Karachi: Anjuman-i taraqqī-i Urdū Pākistān.

Heston, Wilma Louise, and Mumtaz Nasir. 2015. *The Bazaar of the Storytellers*. 2nd ed. Islamabad: Lok Virsa.

Honko, Lauri. 1980. "The Lament: Problems of Genre, Structure and Reproduction." In *Genre, Structure and Reproduction in Oral Literature*, ed. Lauri Honko and Vilmos Voigt, 21–40. Budapest: Akademiai Kiado.

Hujwerī, 'Alī 'Us̤mān. 1978. *Kashf al-maḥjūb*. Ed. 'Alī Qawīmī. Islamabad: Markaz-i Taḥqīqāt-i Fārsī-i Īrān o Pākistān.

Ḥusain, Muḥammad Bashīr. 1972. *Fihrist-i makḥṭūtāt-i Shafī' bah Fārsī o Urdū o Panjābī dar kutub-ḳhānah-i Maulwī Muḥammad Shafī'*. Lahore: Punjab University.

Ḥusain Qulī Ḳhān 'Az̤īmābādī. 1981. *Taẕkirah-i Nashtar-i 'ishq*. Ed. Aṣġhar Jānfidā. Vol. 1. Dushanbe: Nashariyāt-i Dānish.

Ḥusain, Sayyid Sulaimān. 1988. "Muqaddamah." In *Nau ā'īn-i Hindī*, by Mihr Chand Khatrī Mihr, 7–50. Lucknow: Uttar Pradesh Urdū Academy.

Hyder, Syed Akbar. 2006. *Reliving Karbala: Martyrdom in South Asian Memory*. New York: Oxford University Press.

Ibn al-'Arabī, Muḥyī al-Dīn. 1966. *Fuṣūṣ al-ḥikam*. Beirut: Dār al-kitāb al-'Arabī.

Ibn 'Arabī, Muḥyī al-Dīn. 2004. *The Ringstones of Wisdom*. Trans. Caner K. Dagli. Chicago: Kazi Publications.

Ibn Isḥāq, Muḥammad b. Isḥāq b. Yasār. 1963. *Sīrat al-nabī*. Ed. Muḥammad Muḥyī al-Dīn 'Abd al-Ḥamīd. Vol. 4. Cairo: Maṭba'aṭ al-Madanī.

Ibn Kat̲h̲īr, 'Imād al-Dīn Ismā'īl b. 'Umar. 1964. *Al-Sīraṭ al-nabawiyyah*. Ed. Muṣṭafā 'Abd al-Wāḥid. Vol. 1. Cairo: Maṭba'āt 'Īsà al-Bābī al-Ḥalabī.

———. 1998. *The Life of the Prophet Muhammad*. Trans. Trevor Le Gassick. London: Garnet.

Ibn-i Kaṅwal, Nāṣir Maḥmūd Kamāl. 2005. *Bostān-i Ḳhayāl: Ek muṭāla'ah*. Delhi: Kitābī Dunyā.

Iskandar Beg Turkmān. 1956. *Tārīḳh-i 'ālam-ārā-i 'Abbāsī*. Vol. 1. Tehran: Amīr Kabīr.

'Izzat Allāh Bangālī. 2007. "Gul-i Bakāwalī." In *Gulzār-i Nasīm*, ed. Rashīd Ḥasan Ḳhān, 603–724. Lahore: Majlis-i Taraqqī-i adab.

Jāh, Muḥammad Ḥusain. 1874. *Ṭilism-i faṣāḥat*. Lucknow: Naval Kishore.

———. 1988. *Ṭilism-i Hoshrubā*. Vol. 3. Patna: Ḳhudā Baḳhsh Oriental Public Library.

Jah, Muhammad Husain. 2009. *Hoshruba: The Land and the Tilism*. Trans. Musharraf Ali Farooqi. Vol. 1. New York: Urdu Project.

Jahāngīr, Nur al-Din Muhammad Salīm. n.d. *Tuzuk-i Jahāngīrī*. Manuscript. London: British Library. MS Add. 6554.

Jahāngīr, Nūr al-Dīn Muḥammad Salīm, Muḥammad Sharīf Mu'tamad Ḳhān, and Mirzā Muḥammad Hādī. 1914. *Tūzuk-i Jahāngīrī*. Lucknow: Naval Kishore.

Ja'far Ḥusain, Mirzā. 1998. *Qadīm Lakhna'ū kī āḳhirī bahār*. New Delhi: Qaumī Council barā'e furoġh-i Urdū zabān.
Jain, Gyān Chand. 1969. *Urdū kī nas̤rī dāstāneṅ*. Karachi: Anjuman-i Taraqqī-i Urdū.
Jain, Jyotindra. 1998. *Picture Showmen: Insights into the Narrative Tradition in Indian Art*. Mumbai: Marg Publications.
Jameson, Fredric. 1981. *The Political Unconscious: Narrative as a Socially Symbolic Act*. Ithaca, NY: Cornell University Press.
Jān Ṣāḥib, Mīr Yār 'Alī. 1950. *Musaddas-i tahnīyat-i jashn-i Benaẓīr*. Ed. Muḥammad 'Alī Ḳhān As̤ar Rāmpūrī. Rampur: Rampur State Press.
Jauss, Hans Robert. 1982. *Toward an Aesthetic of Reception*. Trans. Timothy Bahti. Minneapolis: University of Minnesota Press.
Josephson-Storm, Jason A. 2017. *The Myth of Disenchantment: Magic, Modernity, and the Birth of the Human Sciences*. Chicago: University of Chicago Press.
Kāshifī, Kamāl al-Dīn Ḥusain Wā'iẓ b. 'Alī. 1941. *Risālah-i Ḥātimiyyah*. Ed. Sayyid Muḥammad Riẓā Jalālī Nā'īnī. Tehran: Nahẓat.
Khalidi, Tarif. 1994. *Arabic Historical Thought in the Classical Period*. New York: Cambridge University Press.
Khan, Ali, and Ali Nobil Ahmad. 2010. "From Zinda Laash to Zibahkhana: Violence and Horror in Pakistani Cinema." *Third Text* 24 (1): 149–61.
Khan, Pasha M. 2008. "Nothing but Animals: The Hierarchy of Creatures in the Ringstones of Wisdom." *Journal of the Muhyiddin Ibn 'Arabi Society* 43:21–50.
———. 2009. "From The Lament for Delhi." In *Nationalism in the Vernacular: Hindi, Urdu, and the Literature of Indian Freedom*, ed. Shobna Nijhawan, 88–92. Delhi: Permanent Black.
———. 2015. "A Handbook for Storytellers: The Ṭirāz al-akhbār and the Qissa Genre." In *Tellings and Texts: Music, Literature and Performance in North India*, ed. Francesca Orsini and Katherine Butler Schofield, 185–207. Cambridge: Open Book Publishers.
———. 2017a. " 'Abd al-Nabī Faḳhr al-Zamānī and the Courtly Storytellers of Mughal India." In *Non Momento Vasta: Essays in Honor of Shamsur Rahman Faruqi*, ed. Alireza Korangy, 23–72. Leiden: Brill.
———. 2017b. "Preface to a Romance (1866)." In *Ghalib: Selected Poems and Letters*, ed. Frances W. Pritchett and Owen T. A Cornwall, 91–94. New York: Columbia University Press.
Ḳhān, Rashīd Ḥasan. 2007. "Muqaddamah." In *Gulzār-i Nasīm*, by Dayā Shankar Nasīm, 11–67. Lahore: Majlis-i Taraqqī-i adab.
Ḳhayāl, Mīr Taqī Al-Ja'farī Al-Ḥusainī. 1742. *Bostān-i Ḳhayāl*. Manuscript. London: British Library. MS I.O. Islamic 1773.

———. n.d. *Bostān-i Ḳhayāl*. Manuscript. London: British Library. MS I.O. Islamic 2442.
Ḳhwājah 'Ishrat Lakhnawī. 1935. "Lakhna'ū kī dāstān-go'ī." *Nigār*, May.
Ḳhwājah Kāmgār Ḥusainī. 1978. *Ma'āsir-i Jahāngīrī*. Ed. 'Azrā 'Alwī. Aligarh: Aligarh Muslim University.
Kidwai, Sadiq-ur-Rahman. 1972. *Gilchrist and the 'Language of Hindoostan.'* New Delhi: Rachna Prakashan.
Lafont, Jean. 2002. *Maharaja Ranjit Singh: Lord of the Five Rivers*. New Delhi: Oxford University Press.
Lory, Pierre. 2003. "Kashifi's Asrār-i Qāsimı and Timurid magic." *Iranian Studies* 36, no. 4 (December): 531–41.
Lutgendorf, Philip. 1991. *The Life of a Text: Performing the Rāmcaritmānas of Tulsidas*. Berkeley: University of California Press.
———. 2012. "Making Tea in India: Chai, Capitalism, Culture." *Thesis Eleven* 113 (1): 11–31.
Maḥjūb, Muḥammad Ja'far. 1991. "Taḥawwul-i naqqālī wa qiṣṣah-ḳhwānī." *Īrānnāmah* 9:186–211.
Malcolm, Sir John. 1827. *Sketches of Persia*. Vol. 2. London: Cassell.
Manjhan Rājgīrī, Mīr Sayyid. 2000. *Madhumālatī: An Indian Sufi Romance*. Trans. Aditya Behl. Oxford: Oxford University Press.
Masud, Naiyer. 1990. *Marsiyah-ḳhwānī kā fann*. Lucknow: Uttar Pradesh Urdū Academy.
Meisami, Julie Scott. 1993. "The Past in Service of the Present: Two Views of History in Medieval Persia." *Poetics Today* 14 (2): 247–75.
———. 1999. *Persian Historiography to the End of the Twelfth Century*. Edinburgh: Edinburgh University Press.
Melville, Charles. 2009. "The Tarikh-i Dilgusha-yi Shamshir Khani and the Reception of the Shahnama in India." Paper presented at the Biennial Conference of the Association for the Study of Persianate Societies, Lahore, February 28.
Melvin-Koushki, Matthew. 2017. "Powers of One: The Mathematicalization of the Occult Sciences in the High Persianate Tradition." *Intellectual History of the Islamicate World* 5 (1–2): 127–99.
Mihr, Mihr Chand Khatrī. 1988. *Nau ā'īn-i Hindī*. Ed. Sayyid Sulaimān Ḥusain. Lucknow: Uttar Pradesh Urdū Academy.
Miller, J. Hillis. 1979. "The Critic as Host." In *Deconstruction and Criticism*, ed. Harold Bloom, 177–215. New York: Seabury Press.
Mīr 'Alā' al-Daulah b. Mīr Yaḥyà Qazwīnī. 1674. *Nafā'is al-ma'āsir*. Manuscript copied. Munich: Bayerische Staatsbibliothek. MS Pers. Codex 3.
Mīr Bāqir 'Alī Dāstān-go. 1892. *Ṭilism-i Hosh-afzā*. Delhi: Maṭba'-i Rizwī.
———. 1920a. *Ādāb o akhlāq*. Dehli: Dehli Printing Works.

———. 1920b. "Parable of the Prodigal Son in Urdū." Gramophone Recordings from the Linguistic Survey of India (LSI). Dehli. London: British Library. 6825AK. http://dsal.uchicago.edu/lsi/6826AK. Accessed August 11, 2011.

———. 1920c. "A Story in Urdū." Gramophone Recordings from the Linguistic Survey of India (LSI). Dehli. London: British Library. 6826AK. http://dsal.uchicago.edu/lsi/6826AK. Accessed August 11, 2011.

———. 1922. *Risālah-i Kapaṛ gand, al-ma'rūf, Gāṛhe Ḳhān ne Malmal Jān ko t̤alāq de dī*. Delhi: Almās Press.

———. 1966. *Ḳhalīl Ḳhān Fāḳhtah*. Delhi: Sang-i Mīl Publications.

———. 2011. *Kānā-bātī*. Ed. Muhammad Salim-ur-Rahman. Lahore: Majlis-i Taraqqī-i adab.

———. 2014a. "Bātoṅ kī bāteṅ." In *Mīr Bāqir "Alī Dāstāngo: Dāstāneṅ aur dāstān-go"ī*, ed. 'Aqīl 'Abbās Ja'frī, 190–237. Karachi: Anjuman-i taraqqī-i Urdū Pākistān.

———. 2014b. "Maulā Baḳhsh hāthī." In *Mīr Bāqir "Alī Dāstāngo: Dāstāneṅ aur dāstān-go"ī*, ed. 'Aqīl 'Abbās Ja'frī, 179–89. Karachi: Anjuman-i taraqqī-i Urdū Pākistān.

Mīr Bāqir 'Alī Dāstāngo: Dāstāneṅ aur dāstān-go'ī. 2014. Ed. 'Aqīl 'Abbās Ja'frī. Karachi: Anjuman-i taraqqī-i Urdū Pākistān.

Mir, Farina. 2010. *The Social Space of Language: Vernacular Culture in British Colonial Punjab*. Berkeley: University of California Press.

Mīr Ḳhwānd, Muḥammad b. Ḳhāwandshāh. 1959. *Tārīḳh-i Rauẓat al-ṣafā*. Vol. 2. Tehran: Markazī-i Ḳhayyām Pīrūz.

Mīr, Mīr Muḥammad Taqī. 1979. *Nikāt al-shu'arā'*. Karachi: Anjuman-i taraqqī-i Urdū.

Miyāṅ Muḥammad Baḳhsh. 2002. *Safar al-'ishq: Saif al-Mulūk*. Ed. Muḥammad Sharīf Ṣābir. Lahore: Sayyid Ajmal Ḥusain Memorial Society.

Monier-Williams, Monier. 1863. *Indian Epic Poetry: Being the Substance of Lectures Recently Given at Oxford: With a Full Analysis of the Rámáyana and of the Leading Story of the Mahá-Bhárata*. London: Williams and Norgate.

Mottahedeh, Roy. 1997. "'Aja'ib in the Thousand and One Nights." In *"The Thousand and One Nights" in Arabic Literature and Society*, ed. Richard G. Hovannisian and Georges Sabagh, 29–39. Cambridge: Cambridge University Press.

Muḥammad al-Dīn. 1876. *T̤ibyān al ṣanā'i'*. Lahore: Mat̤ba'-i Aftāb-i Panjāb.

Muḥammad b. Jalāl Tattawī. 1965. *Tarḳhān-nāmah*. Ed. Ḥusām al-Dīn Rāshidī. Hyderabad, Sindh: Sindhī Adabī Board.

Muḥammad Baḳhtāwar Ḳhān. 1667. *Mir'āt al-'ālam*. Manuscript. London: British Library. MS Add. 7657.

Muḥammad Feroz Dihlawī. 2014. "Mīr Bāqir ʿAlī Dāstāngo." In *Mīr Bāqir ʿAlī Dāstāngo: Dāstāneṅ aur dāstān-go'ī*, ed. ʿAqīl ʿAbbās Jaʿfrī, 63–70. Karachi: Anjuman-i Taraqqī-i Urdū Pākistān.

Muḥammad Ismāʿīl Ḍāsnawī. 1895. *Tārīkh-i Ṭilism-i Bakāwalī*. Meeruth: Gulzār-i Muḥammadī.

Muḥammad Najm al-Ġhanī. 1918. *Akhbār al-ṣanādīd*. Vol. 2. Lucknow: Naval Kishore.

Muḥammad Shafīʿ. 1926. "Dībācah." In *Maikhānah*, by ʿAbd al-Nabī Fakhr al-Zamānī Qazwīnī, i–xl. Lahore: ʿItr-chand Kapūr and Sons.

———. 1938. *Dillī kā sanbhālā*. Delhi: Maktabah-i Jāmiʿah.

———. 1983. "Muqaddamah." In *Tazkirah-i Maikhānah*, by ʿAbd al-Nabī Fakhr al-Zamānī Qazwīnī, ix–xxxv. 3rd ed. Tehran: Iqbāl.

Muḥammad Yaʿqūb Lakhnawī. 1876. *Guldastah-i ḥairat*. Lucknow: Gulzar-i Muḥammad.

Mullā ʿAbd Allāh. 1799. *Haft sair-i Ḥātim*. Manuscript. Lahore: University of the Punjab, Sherani. MS 4279/1226.

Mullā Wāḥidī Dihlawī. 2013. *Mere zamāne kī Dillī*. Karachi: Anjuman-i Taraqqī-i Urdū.

Mumtāz, Barkhwurdār b. Maḥmūd Turkmān Farāhī. 1957. *Maḥbūb al-qulūb*. Tehran: Mu'assasah-i Maṭbūʿāt-i Amīr Kabīr.

Mundy, Peter. 1907. *The Travels of Peter Mundy in Europe and Asia, 1608–1667*. Ed. Richard Carnac Temple and Lavinia Mary Anstey. Vol. 2. Cambridge: Hakluyt Society.

Munshī, Mūl Chand. 1844. *Qiṣṣah-i Khusrawān-i ʿAjam*. Delhi: Urdū akhbār Press.

———. 1846. *Qiṣṣah-i Khusrawān-i ʿAjam*. Calcutta: Ġhulām Ḥaidar.

Munzawī, Aḥmad. 1988. *Fihrist-i mushtarak-i nuskhah-hā-i khaṭṭī-i Fārsī-i Pākistān*. Vol. 10. Islamabad: Markaz-i Taḥqīqāt-i Fārsī-i Irān o Pākistān.

Naʿīm Aḥmad. 1968. *Shahr-āshob*. New Delhi: Maktabah-i Jāmiʿah.

Naim, C. M. 2004a. "Afterword." In *The Repentance of Nussooh*, ed. C. M. Naim, 117–40. Delhi: Permanent Black.

———. 2004b. "Prize-Winning Adab: Five Urdu Books Written in Response to the Gazette Notification No. 791A (1868)." In *Urdu Texts and Contexts: The Selected Essays of C. M. Naim*, 120–50. Delhi: Permanent Black.

Narayana Rao, Velcheru, David Shulman, and Sanjay Subrahmanyam. 2003. *Textures of Time: Writing History in South India*. New York: Other Press.

Nasīm, Dayā Shankar. 2007. *Gulzār-i Nasīm*. Ed. Rashīd Ḥasan Khān. Lahore: Majlis-i Taraqqī-i adab.

Nāṣir, Saʿādat ʿAlī Khān. 1970. *Tazkirah-i khwush maʿrakah-i zebā*. Vol. 1. Lahore: Majlis-i Taraqqī-i adab.

Nath, Madhu Natisar, and Ann Grodzins Gold. 1992. *A Carnival of Parting: The Tales of King Bharthari and King Gopi Chand as Sung and Told by Madhu Natisar Nath of Ghatiyali, Rajasthan*. Berkeley: University of California Press.

Nawab, Mohiyudin. 1993. *Devtā*. Karachi: Kitābiyāt.

Naẕīr Aḥmad. 1964. *Taubat an-Naṣūḥ*. Ed. S. M. Shafīq. Lahore: Majlis-i Taraqqī-i adab.

Nicholson, Rashna Darius. 2016. "Corporeality, Aryanism, Race: The Theatre and Social Reform of the Parsis of Western India." *South Asia: Journal of South Asian Studies* 38 (4): 613–38.

Nihāl Chand Lāhorī. 2008. *Maẕhab-i ʿishq*. Ed. Ḳhalīl al-Raḥmān Dā'ūdī. 2nd ed. Lahore: Majlis-i Taraqqī-i adab.

Nisyānī Tattawī, Ṭāhir Muḥammad. 1964. *Tārīḳh-i Ṭāhirī*. Ed. Nabī Baḳhsh Ḳhān Baloc. Haidarabad, Sindh: Sindhī Adabī Board.

Niẓām al-Dīn Aḥmad b. Muḥammad Muqīm. 1913. *Ṭabaqāt-i Akbarī*. Vol. 2. Calcutta: Asiatic Society of Bengal.

Nöldeke, Theodor. 1979. *The Iranian National Epic, or, The Shahnamah*. Philadelphia, PA: Porcupine Press.

Novetzke, Christian Lee. 2015. "Note to Self: What Marathi Kirtankars' Notebooks Suggest about Literacy, Performance, and the Travelling Performer in Pre-Colonial Maharashtra." In *Tellings and Texts: Music, Literature and Performance in North India*, ed. Francesca Orsini and Katherine Butler Schofield, 169–84. Cambridge: Open Book Publishers.

O'Hanlon, Rosalind. 1999. "Manliness and Imperial Service in Mughal North India." *Journal of the Economic and Social History of the Orient* 42 (1): 47–93.

Orsini, Francesca. 2009. *Print and Pleasure: Popular Literature and Entertaining Fictions in Colonial North India*. Ranikhet: Permanent Black.

Orsini, Francesca, and Katherine Butler Schofield, eds. 2015. *Tellings and Texts: Music, Literature and Performance in North India*. Cambridge: Open Book Publishers.

Pandey, Shyam Manohar. 1982. *The Hindi Oral Epic Canainī: The Tale of Lorik and Candā*. Allahabad: Sahitya Bhawan.

Patil, D. R. 1963. *The Antiquarian Remains in Bihar*. Patna: Kashi Prasad Jayaswal Research Institute.

Payeur, Brittany. 2010. "The Lilly Shamshir-Khani in a Franco-Sikh Context: A Non-Islamic 'Islamic' Manuscript." In *The Islamic Manuscript Tradition: Ten Centuries of Book Arts in Indiana University Collections*, ed. Christiane Gruber, 221–50. Bloomington: Indiana University Press.

Peacock, A. C. S. 2007. *Mediaeval Islamic Historiography and Political Legitimacy: Balʿamī's Tārīkhnāma*. New York: Routledge.

Perlin, Frank. 2003. "The Problem of the Eighteenth Century." In *The Eighteenth Century in Indian History: Evolution or Revolution?* ed. P. J. Marshall, 53–61. New Delhi: Oxford University Press.

Pernau, Margrit. 2013. *Ashraf into Middle Classes: Muslims in Nineteenth-Century Delhi*. New Delhi: Oxford University Press.

"Photograph of Portrait of Darbār Ḳhān." 1911. Photograph. London: British Library. Photo 1010/10(148) Delhi Museum (Darbar Loan Exhibition).

Prasad, Beni. 1962. *History of Jahangir*. Allahabad: Indian Press.

Premchand. 2010. "The World's Most Precious Object." In *Nationalism in the Vernacular: Hindi, Urdu, and the Literature of Indian Freedom*, ed. Shobna Nijhawan, trans. Allison Busch, 128–38. Ranikhet: Permanent Black.

Prior, Katherine. 2004. "Harington, John Herbert (1764/5–1828)." *Oxford Dictionary of National Biography*. Oxford University Press. Accessed May 24, 2017.

Pritchett, Frances W. 1985. *Marvelous Encounters: Folk Romance in Urdu and Hindi*. New Delhi: Manohar Publications.

———. 1991. *The Romance Tradition in Urdu: Adventures from the Dastan of Amir Hamzah*. New York: Columbia University Press.

———. 1994. *Nets of Awareness: Urdu Poetry and Its Critics*. Berkeley: University of California Press.

Qamar, Aḥmad Ḥusain. 1901. *Homān-nāmah*. Lucknow: Naval Kishore.

———. 1915. *Ṭilism-i Haft paikar*. Vol. 2. Lucknow: Naval Kishore.

———. 1988. *Ṭilism-i Hoshrubā*. Vol. 6. Patna: Ḳhudā Baḳhsh Oriental Public Library.

Qāniʻ Tattawī, ʻAlī Sher. 1959. *Tuḥfat al-kirām*. Trans. Ḥusām al-Dīn Rāshidī. Hyderabad, Sindh: Sindhi Adabi Board.

Qāṭiʻī Harawī, Mullā. 1979. *Tazkirah-i Majmaʻ al-shuʻarā-i Jahāngīr Shāhī*. Ed. Muḥammad Salīm Aḳhtar. Karachi: Karachi University.

Rāshidī, Ḥusām al-Dīn. 1970. *Mirzā Ġhāzī Beg Tarḳhān aur us kī bazm-i adab*. Karachi: Anjuman-i taraqqī-i Urdū.

Raza, Rahi Masoom. 1979. *Ṭilism-i Hoshrubā: Ek muṭālaʻah*. Bombay: Ḳhiyābān Publications.

Reeve, Clara. 1930. *The Progress of Romance*. New York: Facsimile Text Society.

"Review of The Adventures of Hatim Tai." 1830. *Asiatic Journal and Monthly Miscellany* (August): 66–69.

"Review of The Adventures of Hatim Tai." 1883. *Quarterly Review* 39, no. 98 (July): 506–12.

Rieu, Charles. 1879. *Catalogue of the Persian Manuscripts in the British Museum*. Vol. 1. London: British Museum.

Rūmī, Jalāl al-Dīn. 1925. *The Mathnawí of Jalálu'ddín Rúmí*. Ed. Reynold Alleyne Nicholson. Vol. 1. London: Brill.

Perkins, Ryan. 2013. "From the Mehfil to the Printed Word: Public Debate and Discourse in Late Colonial India." *Indian Economic and Social History Review* 50 (1): 47–76.

Sabnani, Nina. 2012. "Prompting Narratives: The Kaavad Tradition." *India International Centre Quarterly* 39 (2): 11–19.

Ṣabūḥī, Walī Ashraf. 1963. *Dillī kī chand 'ajīb hastīyāṅ*. Lahore: Maktabah-i Ṣabūḥī Water Works.

Sa'dī Shīrāzī, Abū 'Abd Allāh Musharrif al-Dīn b. Muṣliḥ. 1977. *Bostān*. Ed. Nūr Allāh Irānparast. Tehran: Dānish.

Ṣafawī, Muḥammad Ṣādiq. 1989. *Dabīr aur Shamsābād*. Shamsabad: Dānish Maḥall.

Ṣafī, Aḥmad. 1984. *Wājid 'Alī Shāh aur shāh-i jinn*. 'Alīgaṛh: Markaz-i Adab-i Urdū.

Said, Edward W. 1979. *Orientalism*. New York: Vintage Books.

Saksenah, Rām Bābū. 1966. *Tārīkh-i-Adab-i-Urdū*. Trans. Mirzā Muḥammad 'Askarī. Dehli: Caman Book Depot.

Sām Mīrzā. 2005. *Taẕkirah-i Tuḥfah-i Sāmī*. Ed. Rukn al-Dīn Humāyūn Farrukh. Tehran: Intishārāt-i Asāṯīr.

Sarkar, Jadunath. 1973. *History of Aurangzib: Based on Persian Sources*. Vol. 5. Bombay: Orient Longman.

Saussure, Ferdinand de. 1986. *Course in General Linguistics*. LaSalle, IL: Open Court.

Sayyid 'Abd Allāh. 1965. "Muqaddamah." In *'Ajā'ib al-qiṣaṣ*, ed. Rāḥat Afzā Bukhārī, 11–27. Lahore: Majlis-i taraqqī-i adab.

Sayyid Iḥsān 'Alī. 1755. *Gulshan-i Iḥsān*. Karachi: Anjuman-i Taraqqī-i Urdu. 3/288.

Sayyid Yūsuf Bukhārī Dihlawī. 1987. *Yārān-i raftah: Shakhṣī khākoṅ kā majmū'ah*. Karachi: Maktabah-i Uslūb.

Schofield, Katherine Butler. 2006. "If Music Be the Food of Love: Masculinity and Eroticism in the Mughal Mehfil." In *Love in South Asia: A Cultural History*, ed. Francesca Orsini, 61–83. Cambridge: Cambridge University Press.

Seyller, John William, and W. M Thackston. 2002. *The Adventures of Hamza: Painting and Storytelling in Mughal India*. Washington, DC: Freer Gallery of Art.

Shabistarī, Mahmud ibn 'Abd al-Karim. 1978. *Gulshan-i rāz*. Ed. E. H Whinfield. Islamabad: Markaz-i Taḥqīqāt-i Fārsī-i Īrān o Pākistān.

Shāfi'ī-Kadkanī, Muḥammad Riẓā. 2002. "Nigāhī bah Ṯarāz al-akhbār." *Nāmah-yi Bahāristān* 1 (5): 109–22.

Shāh Nawāz Ḳhān Aurangābādī. 1888. *Ma'āsir al-umarā'*. Ed. Maulawī Majd al-Raḥīm. 3 vols. Calcutta: Asiatic Society of Bengal.

Shāh Nazar Qiṣṣah-ḳhwān. n.d. *Zubdat al-rumūz*. Manuscript. Tehran: Mūzah-i Markaz-i asnād-i Majlis-i shūrā-i Islāmī. MS 2141.

Shāhid Aḥmad Dihlawī. 1944. "Dāstāngo'ī." *Sāqī*, November.

———. 1979. *Chand adabī shaḳhṣiyyateṅ*. New Delhi: Modern Publishing House.

Sharar, 'Abd al-Ḥalīm. 2000. *Guzashtah Lakhna'u*. Ed. Rashīd Ḥasan Ḳhān. Delhi: Maktabah-i Jāmi'ah.

———. n.d. *Florā Florindā*. N.p.: Maktabah-i Urdū.

———. n.d. *Ṣad pārah-i dil: Tazkirah-i mashāhīr-i 'ālam*. Delhi: Rangīn Press.

Sharma, Sunil. 2002. "Amir Khusraw and the Genre of Historical Narratives in Verse." *Comparative Studies of South Asia, Africa and the Middle East* 22 (1): 112–18.

———. 2013. "The Production of Mughal Shāhnāmas." In *Ferdowsi's Shāhnāma: Millennial Perspectives*, ed. Olga M. Davidson and Marianna Shreve Simpson, 86–103. Boston, MA: Ilex Foundation.

Shiblī Nu'mānī. 1962. *Shi'r al-'Ajam*. Ed. Mas'ūd 'Alī Nadawī. 6th ed. Azamgarh: Maṭba'-i Ma'ārif.

Ṣiddīqī, Abūllais, and Nasīm Amrohwī. 1977. *Urdū lughat*. Vol. 1. Karachi: Taraqqī-i Urdū Board.

Siddiqi, M. Atique. 1960. *Gilchrist aur us kā 'ahd*. Aligarh: Anjuman Taraqqī-i Urdū Hind.

———. 1963. *Origins of Modern Hindustani Literature*. Aligarh: Naya Kitab Ghar.

Smith, John D. 1991. *The Epic of Pābūjī*. Cambridge: Cambridge University Press.

Stark, Ulrike. 2007. *An Empire of Books: The Naval Kishore Press and the Diffusion of the Printed Word in Colonial India*. Ranikhet: Permanent Black.

Stein, Burton. 2003. "Eighteenth-Century India: Another View." In *The Eighteenth Century in Indian History: Evolution or Revolution?* ed. P. J. Marshall, 62–89. New Delhi: Oxford University Press.

Surūr, Rajab 'Alī Beg. 1975. *Surūr-i sulṭānī*. Ed. Āghā Suhail. Lahore: Majlis-i taraqqī-i adab.

———. 2008. *Fasānah-i 'ajā'ib*. Ed. Rashīd Ḥasan Ḳhān. Lahore: Majlis-i taraqqī-i adab.

Ṭabarī, Abū Ja'far Muḥammad b. Jarīr. 1960. *Tārīḳh al-Ṭabarī: Tārīḳh al-rusul wa al-mulūk*. Vol. 1. Cairo: Dār al-ma'ārif.

Taftāzānī, Mas'ūd b. 'Umar. 2001. *Al-Muṭawwal*. Ed. 'Abd al-Ḥamīd Hindāwī. Beirut: Dār al-kutub al-'ilmiyyah.

Tawakkul Beg. 1999. *Tārīḳh-i dil-gushā*. Ed. Iḥyā Muḥammad Āqāzādah. Tehran: Ḥauzah-i Hunarī.

———. 2005. *Tārīkh-i Dilgushā-i Shamsher-Khānī*. Ed. Ṭāhirah Parwīn Akram. Islamabad: Markaz-i Taḥqīqāt-i Fārsī-i Irān o Pākistān.

Tha'ālibī, Abū Manṣūr. 1900. *Ghurar akhbār mulūk al-Furs wa siyari-him*. Ed. Hermann Zotenberg. Paris: Imprimerie Nationale.

Todorov, Tzvetan. 1984. *Mikhail Bakhtin: The Dialogical Principle*. Minneapolis: University of Minnesota Press.

———. 1990. *Genres in Discourse*. Cambridge: Cambridge University Press.

Truschke, Audrey. 2011. "The Mughal Book of War: A Persian Translation of the Sanskrit Mahabharata." *Comparative Studies of South Asia, Africa and the Middle East* 31 (2): 506–20.

———. 2016. *Culture of Encounters: Sanskrit at the Mughal Court*. New York: Columbia University Press.

Wadley, Susan Snow. 2004. *Raja Nal and the Goddess: The North Indian Epic Dhola in Performance*. Bloomington: Indiana University Press.

Wālih, 'Alī Qulī Khān. 2005. *Riyāz al-shu'arā*. Ed. Muḥsin Nājī Naṣrābādī. Vol. 1. Tehran: Asāṭīr.

Williams, Ioan. 1970. *Novel and Romance, 1700–1800: A Documentary Record*. New York: Barnes & Noble.

Yazdānī, Rāz. 1952. "Maṭbū'ah Ṭilism-i Hoshrubā." *Nigār*, November.

Zadeh, Travis. 2010. "The Wiles of Creation: Philosophy, Fiction, and the 'Ajā'ib Tradition." *Middle Eastern Literatures* 13 (1): 21.

———. 2011. *Mapping Frontiers across Medieval Islam: Geography, Translation, and the 'Abbāsid Empire*. New York: I.B. Tauris.

Zotenberg, Hermann. 1900. "Préface." In *Ghurar akhbār mulūk al-Furs wa siyari-him*, by Abū Manṣūr al-Tha'ālibī, i–xlv. Paris: Imprimerie Nationale.

Index

'Abd al-Bāqī Qiṣṣah-khwān, Mīr, 38
'Abd Allāh, Mullā, Ḥātim-nāmah, 8, 50, 133, 152–61
'Abd Allāh Anṣārī, Khwājah, 98
'Abd Allāh Bilgrāmī: Ashk as predecessor of, 58; "Love is ever fertile in ploy and stratagem," 114
'Abd Allāh Khān Uzbeg, 36, 131
Abū al-Faraj al-Iṣfahānī, 'Alī, *Book of Songs*, 155, 159–60
Abū al-Faẓl b. Mubārak: death of, 30; *Kalīlah wa Dimnah*, 48
Abū Lahab, 34
Abū al-Muẓaffar Naṣr, 150
'ādat, 185–86, 280n18
Adīnah Beg, 113
The Adventures of Hatim Tai (Forbes), 192–93
Āftābchī, Jauhar, 48–49
Āghā Ḥaidar Afsūn, Nawāb, 71–72
Aḥmad, Kalīm al-Dīn, *Urdū zabān aur fann-i dāstān-go'ī*, 5, 204
Aḥmad, Na'īm, *Fughān-i Dihlī*, 20
Aḥmad, Naẓīr, *Taubat al-Naṣūḥ*, 200–202
Aḥmad 'Alī, Mīr: disciples of, 62–65; Faruqi on, 117–18; interaction with other storytellers by, 270nn16–17; and Qamar, 71; Rampur arrival of, 270n14; *Ṭilism-i Hoshrubā*, 62, 64; *Ṭilism-i Tahmūras De'oband*, 64
Ahmed, Manan, *Chachnāmah*, 154
Aḥwālī Sīstānī, 276n24
Ajā'ib al-makhlūqāt, 182–83

Ajā'ib al-qiṣaṣ (Shāh 'Ālam II), 56, 112
Akbar, Emperor: Abū al-Faẓl as courier to, 48; as Darbār Khān's patron, 46; illustrated *Hamzah-nāmah*, 23–24, 27, 118, 119 fig 2; *Mahābhārata*, 30; and Naqīb Khān, 101–2; as patron of storytellers, 29; successor of, 38
akhlāq genre, 126, 133
Akmal al-maṭābi' Press, 137–38
'Alā' al-Daulah, Mīr, 102
"Alas, alas! For Maḥẓūẓ Khān has left!" (Murshid), 42
"Alas for anyone whose garment's hem" (Faghfūr), 40
'Alīm al-Dīn Wafā, Mīrzā, 72
'Alī Wardī Khān, Nawab, 36, 51
Alqāṣ Mīrzā, 35
Amān, Khwājah Badr Al-Dīn, *Hadā'iq-i anẓār*, 138
Amān Allāh, Mīrzā, 44, 46–47, 102–4, 106
Amān Allāh Khān "Amānī," Mīrzā, 102
Amānat Lakhnawī, Sayyid Āghā Ḥasan, 216
'Amar 'Ayyār painting (Keshav Dās, Māh Muhammad), 118, 119 fig 2
Amarkantak jungle (map), 171 fig 4. See also *Tale of the Bakāwalī Flower* ('Izzat Allāh Bangālī)
Amin, Shahid, 81
Amīr al-Dīn "Mīrzā Kallan," Mīrzā, 72

Amīr ʻAlī, Mīr, 76–77, 80–81
Amīr Ḥamzah, characterization of, 2. *See also Dāstān-i Amīr Ḥamzah*; *Ḥamzah-nāmah*; Naval Kishore Press; *Qiṣṣah-i Amīr Ḥamzah*
Amīr Ḳhān, Muḥammad, 66
Anbā Parshād Rasā, Munshī, 62–66, 68, 76, 80, 270nn17–20
Anīs, Mīr, 65
ʻaqlī, 135, 147, 172–73, 181
Arabic Historical Thought in the Classical Period (Khalidi), 147–52
Aristotle: *Poetics*, 201; *On the Soul*, 148
Asad Qiṣṣah-ḳhwān, Mullā: lineage of, 213, 266n3, 267n16; patron of, 45–46, 135, 267n12; and worth of storytellers, 25, 32, 37–43
Aṣġhar ʻAlī, Ḥakīm Sayyid, 62, 63, 65–66, 76, 270n17
Ashʻarī Abū Bakr al-Bāqillānī, 185
Ashk, Ḳhalīl ʻAlī Ḳhān: on *dāstān* for practical purposes, 92; at Fort William College, 54, 56–61; *Ḥamzah-nāmah daftars*, 269n11; *Ḥamzah-nāmah* production by, 58–61, 269n9; Intiḳhāb-i sulṭāniyyah, 60, 269n10; legacy of storytelling by, 86, 88–89; and linguistic exemplarity, 49–50; *Nigārḳhānah-i Chīn*, 60, 269n10; political knowledge of, 48; *Risalah-i Kāʼināt-i jau*, 58
Asiatic Journal, 193
Atkinson, James, 142, 143
ʻAṭṭar, Farīd al-Dīn, *Conference of the Birds*, 119, 122–23, 183
Auḥadī, Taqī al-Dīn, 42
Aurangzeb, Emperor, 31
Austin, John, 153
ʻayyārī (trickery), 111–14
Āzād, Muḥammad Ḥusain, 4, 9, 164, 194–95, 197–99, 203, 210; *Nairang-i ḳhayāl*, 198–99
Aẕīm al-maṭābiʻ Press, 137
Bābur, Emperor, 27
Badāʼunī, *Muntaḳhab al-tawārīḳh*, 36
Bahādur Shāh Ẓafar, Emperor, 4, 56, 76–77, 80, 84, 198
Bahrām, Prince, 98
Baihaqī, Abū al-Faẓl Muḥammad, *History (Tārīḳh-i Baihaqī)*, 148–49, 156
Bakāwalī, Princess. *See Tale of the Bakāwalī Flower* (ʻIzzat Allāh Bangālī)
Bakhtin, Mikhail, 7
Bāqir, Muḥammad, 274n9
Bāqir ʻAlī, Mīr, 72–90; biographical information, 75–78; *Dillī kā sanbhālā*, 77; disciples of, 87–88; education of, 84, 91; *Gāṛhe Ḳhān* chapbooks, 85–87, 272n44; *Kānā-bātī*, 83–84; *Ḳhalīl Ḳhān Fāḳhtah*, 87; as last *dāstāngo* of Delhi, 53–54, 72–73, 87; and linguistic exemplarity, 49–50, 82–83; patrons and compensation of, 74, 78–81, 83, 88, 91, 213, 271n31, 272n37; print technology used by, 86–87; and professional vs. casual storytellers, 213; *qiṣṣah* devaluation in time of, 187; storytelling skill of, 73–75, 81–85, 114, 115; *Ṭilism-i Hosh-afzā*, 75, 77, 82, 86, 88, 112, 271, 271n34; title and worth of, 78–81; and worth of romance genre, 88–90
Bāqirī Begam, 87, 273n46
barāʼat-i istihlāl, 114
bar-āmad, 116
Barbieri, Giammaria, 191
Bascom, William, 1
Bauman, Richard, 1
Bāyqārah, Sulṭān Ḥusain, 156
bazm, 111–14
Bedil, ʻAbd al-Qādir, 121
Ben-Amos, Dan, 18
al-Berūnī, Abū Raiḥān, 147–48, 277n4

Bhutta, Saeed, 90, 212
Biography of the Prophet (Ibn Isḥāq), 149, 156, 158
Blanchot, Maurice, 10
Bollywood films, 215–16
Book of Songs (Abū al-Faraj al-Iṣfahānī), 155–56, 159–60
Bostān-i Ḳhayāl (Ḳhayāl): composition of, 15; as *dāstān*, 9; Ġhālib on, 137–38
Bostān (Sa'dī), 120, 126
Buḳhārī, Yūsuf, 73–81, 84–87
Bukhari, Zulfiqar Ali, 87, 89
Busch, Allison, 3

Chachnāmah (Ahmed), 154
Chhunnāmal, 79–81, 214
chronogrammatical verse set, 42
Cohen, Ralph, 17, 19–20, 207, 266n9
colonialism: and Bāqir 'Alī's storytelling worth, 83; *qiṣṣah/* romance genre devalued during, 163–65; *rākshasa*, 174–75; romance genre decline during, 2–6. *See also* rationalist epistemology
Conference of the Birds ('Aṯṯar), 119, 122–23, 183
Croce, Benedetto, 10

daftars, 35, 47, 59–62, 65–66, 71, 269n11
Dakkani language (Urdu-Hindi), 5
Darbār Ḳhān, 'Ināyat Allāh: Faḳhr al-Zamānī on, 44; lineage of, 213; and Naqīb Ḳhān, 101–2; patron of, 46; political knowledge of, 47–48; portrait of, 39 fig 1; sources of worth as storyteller, 34–37, 43
Dargāh Qulī Ḳhān, 109
Darwesh Muḥammad Samarqandī, 28–29
dāstān: arresting of, 64, 80–81, 116; *dāstāngos*, 1, 9–10; defined, 9–10, 144; devaluation of, 5; practical uses of, 91–94; *Shāhnāmah* (Firdausī) as source of, 136–40; traits of, 13; as verbal art, 1. *See also* storytellers and storytelling; verbal art
Dāstān-i Amīr Ḥamzah: *Bostān-i Ḳhayāl* (Ḳhayāl) composition and, 15; Ġhālib Lakhnawī's version of, 112; performed by Darbār Ḳhān, 36; *Qiṣṣah-i Amīr Ḥamzah* vs., 9; *Ṭilism-i Hoshrubā*, 61–62, 67, 70, 117–18, 207, 214–15
Dastūr al-fuṣaḥā (Faḳhr al-Zamānī), 105–6, 108
Defoe, Daniel, 200
Derrida, Jacques, "The Law of Genre," 11, 265n6
Devtā (Nawab), 216–17
Dillī kā sanbhālā (Bāqir 'Alī), 77
Ḍomoṅ kī galī, 75–76
"Dunyā kā sab se anmol ratan" (Premchand), 199
Durrat al-tāj (Quṯb al-Dīn Shīrāzī), 179

East India Company, 56–57, 269n10
Encyclopedia Islamica, 274n9
English Education Act (1835), 198

Faġhfūr Lāhījī, Hakim, 40
Faiẓ Aḥmad Ḳhān, Nawab, 79
Fā'iz Dihlawī, Ṣadr al-Dīn, 173
Fajjū, Miyāṅ, 74
Faḳhr al-Zamānī, 'Abd al-Nabī: Amān Allāh as patron of, 44, 46–47, 102–4, 106; biographers' knowledge about, 7, 97–98, 130–31; *Dastūr al-fuṣaḥā*, 105–6, 108; early storytelling craft of, 98–104; on Faġhfūr Lāhījī, 40; health of, 106–7, 130–31; lineage of, 213; *Maiḳhānah*, 31–33, 31–34, 40, 97, 99, 105–7, 274n9, 275–76n18, 275n13; multiple roles of, 44–45; *Nawādir al-ḥikāyāt*, 31–32, 98, 105–6, 131; patron of, 46–47, 267n15; pen names of, 98; *Ṭirāz al-aḳhbār*, 28–29, 31, 92, 94–97,

Fakhr al-Zamānī, ʻAbd al-Nabī (*cont'd.*) 109–17; travels by, 100–109; and worth of romance genre, 45–50. *See also Ṭirāz al-akhbār*
The Family Instructor (Defoe), 200
Faridany-Akhavan, Zahra, 118, 266n1
Farmān Fatḥpūrī, Dildār ʻAlī, 5, 165; on *qiṣṣah* genre, 202–3; on *Tārīkh-i ṭilism-i Bakāwalī* (Muḥammad Ismāʻīl), 172, 278n1, 279n7; *Urdū kī manẓūm dāstāneṅ*, 13
Faruqi, Shamsur Rahman: on *Dāstān-i Amīr Ḥamzah*, 111; on Naval Kishore storytellers, 67, 69–70; on romances as patchwork texts, 129; *Sāḥirī, shāhī, ṣāḥib-qirānī*, 5–6, 265n4; on *silsilah-jātī* romances, 117; on verbal/oral performance, 266n2
Fatḥī Beg Shahnāmah-khwān, 38
female storytellers, 211–12
Fidā ʻAlī "Fidā" Naśr-khwān, Mīr, *Ṭarīq-i naśr-khwānī*, 67–68, 271n24
Fielding, Henry: *History of the Adventures of Joseph Andrews*, 187–90; *The History of Tom Jones, A Foundling*, 188–89, 280n19
film industry: Bollywood films as continuance of *qiṣṣahs*, 215–16; early cinema and decline of *qiṣṣahs*, 54, 268n2
Firdausī, *Shāhnāmah*, 9, 20, 135–47, 150–51, 216
Forbes, Duncan, 159; *The Adventures of Hatim Tai*, 192–93
Fortress of Bakāwalī, 166–69, 175–80. *See also Tale of the Bakāwalī Flower* (ʻIzzat Allāh Bangālī)
Fort William College: Ashk's employment with, 50, 54, 56–61; *Maẕhab-i ʻishq* (Nihāl Chand Lāhorī), 125, 167, 169
Fuġhān-i Dihlī (Aḥmad), 20
Gāṛhe Khān chapbooks (Bāqir ʻAlī), 85–87, 272n44
genealogy, sincerity effect and, 159–60, 278nn13–14
Genette, Gérard, 10, 14, 93, 128
genre: *akhlaq*, 126, 133; akhlāq genre example, 126; code of, 13–17, 20, 93, 125, 147–52, 265n6; *dāstān*, *qiṣṣah*, and *ḥikāyat*, defined, 9–10, 144; determining, 11; genre system as hierarchy, 19–21, 26–32; as ideology (worldview), 16, 20, 164–65, 181; "instituted-ness" of, 14, 20–21; literary modernism on, 10–11; paratexts, 124, 128, 277n34; as system, 17–19, 21; traits (marks) of, 11–13, 265n6; uses of multigenre romance, 122–30; Western vs. Eastern "genre equation," 190–92. *See also* historiography; rationalist epistemology
George V, King, 37
Ghafūr ʻAṣrī, 108
Ġhālib, Mirzā Asad Allāh Khān: on *Bostān-i Khayāl* (Khayāl), 137–38; and judgment of heart, 148; and *Shāhnāmah* as history in India, 141–47; on Sīmurġh narrative, 136–42, 150–51
Ġhālib Lakhnawī: Ashk as predecessor of, 58; on *dāstān* for practical purposes, 91; *Dāstān-i Amīr Ḥamzah*, 112; political knowledge of, 48
ġhazal: and Amān Allāh, 104; and genre hierarchy, 19; genre traits of, 12; *Nets of Awareness* (Pritchett), 195; and rationalist epistemology, 184; uses of, 121, 129, 158
Ġhāzī Beg Tarkhān, Mirzā, 25, 38, 40–43, 46, 135, 267n16
Ġhulām ʻAlī, 143
Ġhulām Ḥaidar, 144–45
Ġhulām Ḥusain, 51
Ġhulām Ḥusain, Sayyid, 68

Ġhulām Mahdī, 65
Ġhulām Raẓā, 64
Ġhurar akhbār mulūk al-Furs (T͟haʿālibī), 141, 148, 150–52, 277n5
Gilchrist, John, 50, 56, 58, 59–60
God, power of intellect and, 183, 185–86
Gulāb Singh and Sons, 70
Gulchīn-i Maʿānī, 97
Guldastah-i Ḥairat, maʿrūf bah Tawārīkh-i Bakāwalī (Muḥammad Yaʿqūb Lakhnawi), 169–75, 170 fig 3, 171 fig 4, 177, 194, 278n1
Gul-i Bakāwalī. See Tale of the Bakāwalī Flower (ʿIzzat Allāh Bangālī)
Gulistān (Saʿdī), 120
Gulshan-i rāz (Shabistarī), 183
Gulzār-i Muḥammadī Press, 173
Gulzār-i Nasīm (Nasīm), 12, 17, 167–68, 197

Ḥadāʾiq-i anẓār (Amān), 138
hadith: chain of transmission used for, 154–56; and *naqlī*, 149
Ḥaidar Qiṣṣah-k͟hwān, 38
Hājj Sayyid Jawādī, Sayyid Kamāl, 267n6
Ḥakīm ʿAbd al-Majīd K͟hān, 80
Ḥakīm Ajmal K͟hān, 80, 83, 91, 214
Ḥakīm Aṣġhar ʿAlī, 62, 63, 65, 76
Ḥālī, Alṭāf Husain, 4, 9, 164, 194–98, 203, 210
Hamdard (Maulānā Muḥammad ʿAlī), 86
Ḥamzah-nāmah: and Akbar, 102; Akbar's illustrations of, 23–24, 118; Ashk's production of, 58–61, 269n9; *daftars* of, 35, 47, 59–62, 65–66, 71, 269n11; *Ḥamzah-nāmah* (Takaltū K͟hān), 35–36; *Hoshruba*, 117–18; illustrations of, 23–24, 27, 118, 119 fig 2; "Love is ever fertile in ploy and stratagem" (Abd Allah Bilgrāmī), 114; and political knowledge, 48; popularity of, in late nineteenth/early twentieth centuries, 3–5; published by Naval Kishore Press, 4, 55, 68–69, 214–15; *Sāḥirī, shāhī, ṣāḥib-qirānī* (Faruqi), 5–6, 265n4; Shi'i performance in Lucknow and Rampur, 61–67; story of Badīʿ al-Zamān in, 75; Ṭanbūrah as storyteller of, 33. *See also* Ashk, K͟halīl ʿAlī K͟hān; Urdu-language storytellers
Harington, John Herbert, 57, 268n5
Ḥasan, Mīr, *Siḥr al-bayān*, 11–12, 17
Ḥasan, Sayyid Ẓamīr, 76
Hāshim "Muḥtaram" Samarqandī, Mīr Muḥammad, 29–30
Ḥātim-nāmah (ʿAbd Allāh): historiography of, 8, 133, 152–61; as *Qiṣṣah-i Ḥātim Ṭāʾī*, 8, 50, 126, 133, 153, 160; *Seven Deeds of Justice of Ḥātim Ṭai*, 158; story of Saffānah in, 155, 158, 160–61
heart, judgment of, 148, 181–86, 209
ḥikāyat, 9–10, 144
The Histories of Bakāwalī (Muḥammad Yaʿqūb Lakhnawi), 169, 172
historiography, 133–61; genre as historical, 17; genre code of, 147–52; on genre identification, 136–47; and *Ḥātim-nāmah* (ʿAbd Allāh)/*Qiṣṣah-i Ḥātim Ṭāʾī*, 8, 133, 153–61; Oriental historiogarphy decline, 134–35; overview, 8; *qiṣṣah* and relationship to histories, 133–36; *qiṣṣah/tārīkh* divide, 174; romance, novel, and history, defined, 188–89; romance genre vs. history, 126–27; and sincerity effect, 151–61; storytellers mentioned in histories, 31; *tarīkh*, defined, 133. *See also Qiṣṣah-i Ḥātim Ṭāʾī*; *Shāhnāmah* (Firdausī)
The History of Charoba Queen of Aegypt (Reeve), 190–91

History of Prophets and Kings (Ṭabarī), 156
"The History of Romances" (Lewis), 188
History of the Adventures of Joseph Andrews (Fielding), 187–90, 280n19
The History of Tom Jones, A Foundling (Fielding), 188–89, 280n19
History (Tārīkh-i Baihaqī), (Baihaqī), 148–49
hookahs, 66, 80, 84
Huet, Pierre Daniel: "De l'origine des romans," 191; "Sur l'origine des Romans," 188
Humāyūn, Emperor, 27, 46, 48–49
Hunar Faiẓābādī, Ja'far Ḥusain, 117–18
Ḥūrī Ustād, 33
Ḥusain, Ḥājī, 277n7
Ḥusain 'Alī, Mīr, 76–77
Ḥusainī Press, 70
ḥusn o 'ishq, 111–14
Hussein, Abdullah, *Udās nasleṅ*, 14
hypotexts: Genette on, 93; textual fragments as, 119–22

Ibn 'Arabī, Muḥyī al-Dīn: on rationalism, 148; *Ringstones of Wisdom*, 183–86
Ibn Isḥāq, Muḥammad, *Biography of the Prophet*, 149, 156, 158
Ibn Kalbī, Hishām, 159–60, 278n13
"I have heard that in Muṣṭaf's days" (Ṭanbūrah), 34
India: declinist narrative of Indian history, 201–8; East India Company, 56–57, 269n10; Mughal family members as storytellers, 71, 72; Orientalists on *rākshasa*, 174–75; Rebellion of 1857, 3, 53–56, 166, 198. *See also* Persian-language storytellers; rationalist epistemology; Urdu-language storytellers; *individual names of emperors*
Indrasabha (Amānat Lakhnawī), 216
intellect, epistemology of, 181–86
intertextuality: four elements of storytelling, 111–14; *taẓmīn*, 157–58; textual fragments and memory in romance genre, 117–22
Intikḥāb-i sulṭāniyyah (Ashk), 60, 269n10
iqtibās, 157–59
Isḥāq Ḳhān, Nawab, 83
'Ishrat Lakhnawī, Ḳhwājah, 89–90
Iskandar Munshī, 38
Iskandar Qiṣṣah-ḳhwān, 30–31, 43
Ismā'īl (Shāh), 26, 35
isnād, 149, 154–59, 161
I'timād Ḳhān, 36
'Izzat Allāh Bangālī, *Tale of the Bakāwalī Flower*, 124, 127–28, 164–81, 213

Ja'far Āṣaf Ḳhān, Mīrzā, *Ḳhusrau-Shīrīn*, 116
Jāh, Muḥammad Ḥusain: on Aḥmad 'Alī, 270n17; Ḥusainī Press, 70; *Mātam-i Ḥusainī*, 68; publishing of *Ḥamzah-nāmah*, 4; student of, 271n25; *Ṭilism-i Faṣāḥat*, 68; *Ṭilism-i Hoshrubā*, 67–71, 117
Jahān, Ḳhwājah, 36
Jahāngīr, Emperor: and Asad, 25, 42; and Faḳhr al-Zamānī, 100–103, 107–9, 124–25, 273n7, 274n9, 275n14, 276n20; and hierarchy of poetry and storytelling, 28; and Iskandar Qiṣṣah-ḳhwān, 30–31; and *Jahāngīrnāmah*, 125, 134; and Niẓāmī, 44; and sons' rivalry, 124–25; Ṭanbūrah as storyteller to, 33; and worth of storytellers, 25, 37
Jain, Gyān Chand: and rise of novel, 202–8; studies of the Urdu *qiṣṣah* by, 165; *Surūr-i Sulṭāni* excluded from list of romances by, 145; *Urdū kī naṡrī dāstāneṅ*, 5, 13, 205–8
Jālib Dihlawī, Mīr, 86

Jameson, Fredric, 15–16, 181, 265–66n9
Jauss, Hans Robert, 123
Jawān, Kāẓim 'Alī, 56
Jawān Bakht, Mirzā, 56, 57, 268n4
Johnson, Samuel, 189, 201

Kalb-i 'Alī Ḳhān, Nawab, 63–64, 66
Kalīlah wa Dimnah (Abū al-Faẓl), 48
Kamāl Dīn, 90, 212, 214
Kānā-bātī (Bāqir 'Alī), 83–84
Kāẓim 'Alī, Mīr, 77
Keshav Dās, 118, 119 fig 2
ḳhabars, 111
Ḳhalaf Beg, 98
Khalidi, Tarif: *Arabic Historical Thought in the Classical Period*, 147–52; on *isnād*, 154–55
Ḳhalīl, Muḥammad, 173
Ḳhalīl Ḳhān Fāḳhtah (Bāqir 'Alī), 87
Ḳhān, Rashīd Ḥasan, 167
Ḳhān-i Ḳhānān, 'Abd al-Raḥīm, 27, 29–31, 43
Ḳhān-i Zamān, 36
Ḳhān Turkmān, Amīr, 28
ḳharq al-'ādat, 185–86
Ḳhayāl, Mīr Taqī, 91–92; *Bostān-i Ḳhayāl*, 15
Ḳhiẓr, Prophet, 2
Ḳhurram, Prince. *See* Shāh Jahān, Emperor
Ḳhusrau-Shīrīn (Ja'far Āṣaf Ḳhān), 116
Ḳhwushgo, Brindāban Dās, 30
Kitab al-Āġhānī. *See Book of Songs* (Abū al-Faraj al-Iṣfahānī)
Kitab al-Āġhānī (Abū al-Faraj al-Iṣfahānī), 155–56, 159–60

Lālah Āsā Rām Sāth, 63, 135
Lālah Chāndī Parshād, 63
"The Law of Genre" (Derrida), 11, 265n6
Legends of the Panjab (Temple), 166, 212
Lewis, Stephen, "The History of Romances," 188
Lilly Library (University of Indiana), 143
linguistic exemplarity: by Bāqir 'Alī, 49–50, 82–83; Dakkani, 5; at Fort William College, 56–61; Linguistic Survey of India archives, 78, 81–82; and romance genre, 49–50
Linguistic Survey of India, 78, 81–82
"Love is ever fertile in ploy and stratagem" (Abd Allah Bilgrāmī), 114
Lovett, Jonathan Henry, 269n10
Lucknow, performance of *Ḥamzah-nāmah* in, 61–67

Ma'āṡir-i Raḥīmī (Hāshim), 29–30
Macauley, Thomas Babington, 198
Mahābat Ḳhān, 42–44, 46–47, 102–4, 124, 267
Mahābhārata: and Hāshim, 30; and Naqīb Ḳhān, 102
Maḥjūb, Muḥammad Ja'far, 110
Maḥmūd Beg Turkmān, 107
Māh Muhammad, 118, 119 fig 2
Maiḳhānah (Faḳhr al-Zamānī), 31–34, 40, 97, 99, 105–7, 274n9, 275–76n18, 275n13
Majma' al-laṭā'if (Muẓaffar), 28, 113, 267n5
Malcolm, John, 113, 277n7
al-Ma'mūn, Caliph, 148
marṡiyah-ḳhwānī: importance of, 55; story of, 61
Mashdī Galīn Ḳhānum, 159
Masīḥ Beg, 103
maṡnawī, genre traits of, 11–12, 17
Masud, Naiyer, 62–63, 67
Mātam-i Ḥusainī (Jāh), 68
Matba'-i Riẓwī, 86
mathematics, occult and, 178–81
Maulānā Muḥammad 'Alī, *Hamdard*, 86

Mazhab-i 'ishq (Nihāl Chand Lāhorī), 125, 167, 169
Meisami, Julie: on Ġhālib, 140, 146–48; *Persian Historiography*, 147–52; on rhetorical aspects of Persian histories, 135–36
Melville, Charles, 142
Melvin-Koushki, Matthew, 179
memory, in romance genre, 117–22
Mihr Chand Khatrī, *Nau ā'īn-i Hindī*, 50
Mihr Ġhulām Rasūl, 277n1
Miller, J. Hillis, 277n34
Mīr, Mīr Taqī, 135
Mīran, Mīr, 51
Mīrḳhwānd, *Rauẓat al-ṣafā*, 121, 141, 149, 156, 158
Mīr Sarbarahnah, 27
Mottahedeh, Roy, 182
Mughal Empire. *See* India; *individual names of emperors*
muġhlānīs, 211–12
Muḥammad, Prophet: Amīr Ḥamzah and relationship to, 2; poem by Ṭanbūrah about, 34
Muḥammad Baḳhsh, Miyāṅ, *Tale of Saif al-Mulūk*, 183–84
Muḥammad Baḳhtāwar Ḳhān, 31, 273n4
Muḥammad Hāshim, Mīr, 43
Muḥammad Ḥusain Ḳhān, Risāldār Nawāb, 71–72
Muḥammad Ismā'īl Ḍāsnawī, Sayyid, *Tārīḳh-i ṭilism-i Bakāwalī*, 13, 172–74, 177, 180–83, 185, 202, 278n1, 279n7
Muḥammad Ḳhwurshed Isfahānī, "Maulānā, 38
Muḥammad Murtaẓà Ḥusain "Wiṣāl," 65
Muḥammad Sa'īd Ḳhān, Nawab, 62, 270n19
Muḥammad Shafī', Ḳhwājah, 77, 97, 106
Muḥammad Ya'qūb Lakhnawi: *Guldastah-i Ḥairat, ma'rūf bah Tawārīḳh-i Bakāwalī*, 169–75, 170 fig 3, 171 fig 4, 177, 194, 278n1; *The Histories of Bakāwalī*, 169, 172
mumtana' al-wuqū', 146–47
munāsib-ḳhwānī, 113
Mundy, Peter, 109–11, 277n36
Munshī, Mūl Chand, *Qiṣṣah-i Ḳhusrawān-i 'Ajam*, 143–45
Muntaḳhab al-tawārīḳh (Badā'unī), 36
Munzawī, Aḥmad, 142
Muqaddamah, 197–98
Murshid Burojirdī: "Alas, alas! For Maḥẓūẓ Ḳhān has left!," 42; "Alas for anyone whose garment's hem," 38; and Faġhfūr, 40–41; and Ġhāzī, 41–43, 46; "Your servant of heavenly stature, Asad," 41
Muṣṭafā'ī Press, 168–69
Mu'taman al-Daulah, 15
Mu'tazilism, 148
Muẓaffar Ḥusain, Mīr, 63
Muẓaffar Ḥusain, *Majma' al-laṭā'if*, 28, 113, 267n5

Nadīm Gīlānī, 108
Nādir Mirzā, 72
Nairang-i ḳhayāl (Āzād), 198–99
Nannhe Ḳhān, Nawab, 79
Naqīb Ḳhān, Najīb al-Dīn Ġhiyās̱ al-Dīn 'Alī, 30, 101–3
naqlī: defined, 135, 181; and *isnād*, 149, 154–59, 161; *Shāhnāmah* (Firdausī) as basis of derivative histories, 150–51. *See also* historiography
Narayana Rao, Velcheru, *Textures of Time*, 134–35, 148
Nasīm, Dayā Shankar, *Gulzār-i Nasīm*, 12, 17, 167–68
Naṣīr, Muḥammad 'Abd Allāh Ḳhān, 181, 183
nas̱r-ḳhwānī, 55, 61, 67–68

National Museum (New Delhi), 142–43
nature, rationalist epistemology and, 184–86
Nau ā'īn-i Hindī (Chand Khatrī), 50
Naushād 'Alī, Rājah, 84
Naval Kishore Press, 4, 55, 68–69, 214–15; and Bāqir 'Alī, 74–75; collection at Columbia University, 5; *Ḥamzah-nāmah daftars*, 269n11; *Ḥamzah-nāmah* storytellers, 67–72; and Munshi Naval Kishore, 67, 68, 70–71; *Ṭilism-i Hoshrubā*, 61–62, 67, 70, 117–18, 207, 215. *See also* *Ḥamzah-nāmah*
Nawab, Muhyiuddin, *Devtā*, 216–17
Nawādir al-ḥikāyāt (Fakhr al-Zamānī), 31–32, 98, 105–6, 131
Nawwāb, Mir, 72
Naẓar Muḥammad, 167, 213
Nets of Awareness (Pritchett), 195
Nigārḵhānah-i Chīn (Ashk), 60, 269n10
Nihāl Chand Lāhorī, *Maẕhab-i 'ishq*, 125, 167
Ni'mat Allāh Ṣafāhānī, 44
"Nishapuri" family, 71–72
Niẓām al-Dīn Aḥmad (Mīrzā Niẓāmī), 44, 100–101, 103, 108, 274n9
Niẓāmī, Ḵhwājah Ḥasan, 79–80
Niẓām Shīrāzī, 25
novel genre: code of genre for, 14; eighteenth-century emergence of, 4–5; *qiṣṣah* as precursor to, 209–11; *qiṣṣah* devaluation and emergence of, 187; rise of, 194–206; romance, novel, and history, defined, 188–89
Nu'mānī, Shiblī, 141

occult, mathematics and, 178–81
On the Soul (Aristotle), 148
opium, 30, 74–75, 80, 89–90
Orsini, Francesca, 2, 55, 58–59, 62, 86, 214

pāband-ḵhwānī, 116
panegyrics, 29–31, 41, 122, 124, 126, 129, 133
paratexts, 14, 124, 128, 277n34
pardah-ḵhwānī, 23
parīs, 22, 166, 199. *See also* *Tale of the Bakāwalī Flower* ('Izzat Allāh Bangālī)
Paristān-i ḵhayāl (Ṣafīr Bilgrāmī), 136–40
Parnak, Muḥammad Qulī Ḵhān, 41
Parwez, Prince, 94, 124–25
patahs, 117–18, 122
Peacock, A. C. S., *Translation of Ṭabarī's History*, 156
Pernau, Margrit, 62
Persian Historiography (Meisami), 147–52
Persian-language storytellers, 23–51; elite vs. non-elite audiences of, 213–14; and *Ḥamzah-nāmah*, 23–24; overview, 6–7; Persian language exemplarity in storytelling, 49; poetry and storytelling in hierarchy of genres, 27–32; romance genre and increased worth by storytellers, 43–51; sources of storytellers' worth, 32–43; study of storytellers from sixteenth to seventeenth centuries, 27; worth of romances and their producers, 24–27
Poetics (Aristotle), 201
poetry: chronogrammatical verse set, 42; *ġhazal*, 12, 19, 104, 121, 129, 158, 184, 195; *mas̱nawī*, 11–12; panegyrics, 29–31, 41, 122, 124, 126, 129, 133; quatrain, 40, 103–4; romance genre vs. worth of, 43–45; *sāqī-nāmahs*, 33; satire vs. praise genres, 18; *shahr-āshob*, 20; *shi'r* vs. *tārīḵh*, 144; by Ṭanbūrah, 34. *See also* genre; *individual poems*
Premchand, Munshī, "Dunyā kā sab se anmol ratan," 199

print technology: effect on verbal/oral storytelling, 55, 60–61; and Naval Kishore storytellers, 67–72
Pritchett, Frances: on Ashk, 59; and Naval Kishore collection at Columbia University, 5, 164; *Nets of Awareness*, 195; and rationalist epistemology, 184; *The Romance Tradition*, 213; and Western vs. Eastern "genre equation," 191
processuality, 19–20
The Progress of Romance (Reeve), 190–92
pulp fiction (Urdu), 216–17
Punjabi-language storytellers, 212–13
Punjab State Archives, 142–43

Qalaq, Ḳhwājah Asad ʻAlī Ḳhān, "Ṭilism-i ulfat," 197
Qamar, Aḥmad Ḥusain, 4, 67–72, 271n26, 271n28–29
Qamar, Bandah Ḥasan, 70
Qamar, Bandah Ḥusain, 70
Qāsim ʻAlī, Mīr, 62
Qāẓi Sarfarāz Ḥusain, *Saẕā-i ʻaish*, 86
qiṣṣah: defined, 9–10, 144; equating *qiṣṣah* and romance, 186–94; and factuality, 138–39, 151–54, 161; genre traits pf, 12–13; hierarchy of, 19; knowledge sharing in, 55, 268–69n8; modern-day survival in new forms, 214–18; as precursor to novel, 209–11; *qiṣṣah-ḳhwāns*, 1, 9–10; relationship to histories, 133–36; romance genre devalued during colonialist era, 163–65; study of Urdu storytellers from nineteenth century to early twentieth century, 27; as verbal art, 1. *See also* genre; historiography; rationalist epistemology; storytellers; storytellers and storytelling; *Tale of the Bakāwalī Flower* (ʻIzzat Allāh Bangālī); verbal art
Qiṣṣah-i Amīr Ḥamzah: *Dāstān-i Amīr Ḥamzah vs.*, 9; Faḳhr al-Zamānī as storyteller of, 44–46
Qiṣṣah-i Gul-i Bakāwalī. *See Tale of the Bakāwalī Flower* (ʻIzzat Allāh Bangālī)
Qiṣṣah-i Ḥātim Ṭāʼī, 8, 50, 126, 133, 153, 160, 215. *See also Ḥātim-nāmah* (ʻAbd Allāh)
Qiṣṣah-i Ḳhusrawān-i ʻAjam (Munshī), 143–45
Qiṣṣah-i Raushan Jamāl (Aṣġhar ʻAlī), 65
Qiṣṣah-i Ṭoṭā mainā, 215
qiṣṣah-ḳhwāns, 1. *See also* Persian-language storytellers
Quran: and genre hierarchy, 19; memorization of, 157
Quṭb al-Dīn Shīrāzī, *Durrat al-tāj*, 179

Al-Rāġhib al-Iṣfahānī, 182
Raḥīm al-Dīn Ḥayā, Mirzā, 72
rākshasa, 174–75
Rambler (Johnson), 189
Rampur, performance of *Ḥamzah-nāmah* in, 61–67
Ranjīt Siṅgh, 142–43
Rashīd, Mullā (Mullā ʻAbd al-Rashīd), 38, 42, 266n3, 267n12
rationalist epistemology, 163–208; and epistemologies of intellect, 181–86; equating *qiṣṣah* and romance, 186–94; and judgment of heart, 148, 181–86, 209; overview, 8–9; and precolonial rationalism, 173; *qiṣṣah*/romance genre devalued during colonialist era, 163–65; and rise of novel, 194–206; *Tale of the Bakāwalī Flower* (ʻIzzat Allāh Bangālī) criticism, 164–81. *See also* novel genre; *Tale of the Bakāwalī Flower* (ʻIzzat Allāh Bangālī)
Rauẓat al-ṣafā (Mīrḳhwānd), 121, 141, 149, 156, 158
razm, 82, 111–14

Razmnāmah, Naqīb Ḳhān and, 102
Rebellion of 1857: critiques of *qiṣṣah*, 166; exile of Bahādur Shāh Ẓafar, 198; storytelling decline and, 3, 53–56. *See also* rationalist epistemology
Reeve, Clara: *The History of Charoba Queen of Aegypt*, 190–91; *The Progress of Romance*, 190–92
Ricketts, Mordaunt, 269n10
Rieu, Charles, 134
Ringstones of Wisdom (Ibn 'Arabī), 183–86
Risalah-i Kā'ināt-i jau (Ashk), 58
romance genre: Bāqir 'Alī and worth of, 88–90; colonial-era decline of, 2–6; equating qiṣṣah and romance, 186–94; intertextuality in, 111–14, 117–22; knowledge sharing in, 268–69n8; and linguistic exemplarity, 49–50; Persian storytellers of India and hierarchy of, 28–29; poetry value vs., 43–45; political knowledge contained in, 47–49; *qiṣṣah* distinction from, 1; quantifying worth of, 50–51; romance, novel, and history, defined, 188–89; as worldview, 16; worth of storytellers of, 24–27; young patrons of storytellers, 46–47. *See also* genre; rationalist epistemology
The Romance Tradition (Pritchett), 213
rozmarrah, 49

Ṣabūḥī, Walī Ashraf, 53–54, 73–75, 89, 91, 114, 202
Sa'dī: *Bostān*, 120, 126; *Gulistān*, 120
Ṣafā'ī Tabrezī, 98
Ṣafdar Ḳhān, 108, 276n22
Ṣafīr Bilgrāmī, Sayyid Farzand Aḥmad, *Paristān-i ḳhayāl*, 136–40
Sāḥirī, shāhī, ṣāḥib-qirānī (Faruqi), 5–6, 265n4
Said, Edward W., 16
Sa'īd al-Dīn, Maulwī, 57
Saif Ḳhān, 44, 105, 109–11, 130–31
Saksenah, Rām Bābū, 203
Salim-ur-Rahman, Muhammad, 5
Sām Mīrzā, 35, 36
sāqī-nāmahs, 33
Sardar Ḳhān Ḳhwājah Yādgār, 108
Sarshār, Ratan Nāth, 199
Sayyid Aḥmad Ḳhān, Sir, 184
Sayyid 'Alī (father), 270n22
Sayyid Ḥusain 'Alī (son), 66, 270n22
Sayyid Iḥsān 'Alī, 213
Saẓā-i 'aish, Q̱āẓi Sarfarāz Ḥusain, 86
Schofield, Katherine Butler, 212
Scott, Walter, 196
Scott, William, 57
Shabistarī, Maḥmūd, *Gulshan-i rāz*, 183
Shafī'ī-Kadkanī, Muḥammad, 111
Shāh 'Abbās I, Emperor, 38–39, 135
Shāh 'Alam II, Emperor, *'Ajā'ib al-qiṣaṣ*, 56, 112
Shahid, Rifaqat Ali, 69–70
Shāhid Aḥmad, 81
Shāh Jahān, Emperor, 33–34, 44, 94, 124–25
Shāhnāmah (Firdausī): as basis for derivative histories, 150–51; Bollywood films based on, 216; as *dāstān*, 9; as historiography vs. romance genre, 20; as history in India, 140–47; manuscripts of, 135; as romance vs. historical text, 135; as source of *dāstāns*, 136–40; Ṭanbūrah as storyteller of, 33. *See also naqlī*
Shāh Naẓar Q̱iṣṣah-ḳhwān, 91, 112
shahr-āshob, 20
Shāh Ṭahmāsp, 35, 98
Shaiḳh Muḥammad Ḥusain "Mitthan," 112
Shakespear, John, 50
Shamsah-i Zarrīn Q̱alam, 42

Shamsher-Khānī (Tawakkul Beg), 141–46, 150
sharāfat, 76, 78, 88–89, 271–72n35
Sharar, Abd al-Ḥalīm, 61, 112, 164, 185, 201–2, 205
sharīf, 70, 73
Sharma, Sunil, 135, 141
Sher Shāh Sūrī, 48–49
Shi'i performance of *Ḥamzah-nāmah*, 55, 61–67
shi'r, 144
Shulman, David, *Textures of Time*, 134–35, 148
Siḥr al-bayān (Ḥasan), 11–12, 17
silsilah-jātī romances, 117
Sīmurġh narrative, Ġhālib on, 136–42, 150–51
sincerity effect: genealogy example of, 159–60, 278nn13–14; intention of author vs. factuality, 151–54, 161; and source indication, 157–59; transmission claim for, 149, 154–59, 161, 181
source indication, 157–59
speech act theory, 153
Story of Amīr Ḥamzah. See Dāstān-i Amīr Ḥamzah; *Ḥamzah-nāmah*; *Qiṣṣah-i Amīr Ḥamzah*
storytellers and storytelling: Awadhi nawabs family members as storytellers, 71–72; compensation for, 59–65, 74, 78, 268n4, 271n31, 272n37; eighteenth century scarcity of, 51; female storytellers, 211–12; hookahs used by, 66, 80, 84; *mauzūniyyat* by, 100, 104; opium used by, 30, 74–75, 80, 89–90; patrons, 46–47, 55, 133, 213–14 (*See also individual names of storytellers*); performance skills of, 7, 61–67, 73–75, 80–85, 114–17; Punjabi-language storytellers, 212–13; and romance genre's worth, 43–51; *sharāfat*, 76, 78, 88–89, 271–72n35; storytelling as professional vs. casual activity, 213–14; storytelling as verbal art, defined, 1; vocalization by Aṣġhar 'Alī, 65–66; worth and cultural capital of, 24–26, 266n4. *See also* Persian-language storytellers; *individual names of storytellers*
Subrahmanyam, Sanjay, *Textures of Time*, 134–35, 148
Sufistic commentary: critique on intellect, 148; and historiography, 133; intellect and bewilderment, 183–84
Sulṭān Ibrāhīm Mīrzā, 98
"Sur l'origine des Romans" (Huet), 188
Surūr, Mirzā Rajab 'Alī Beg, 145–47, 150, 152

al-Ṭabarī, Jarīr: Peacock on, 156; *Tārīkh al-Rusul wa al-mulūk*, 141, 149–52; *Tārīkh-i Bal'amī*, 141
Taftazānī, Sa'd al-Dīn, 157
Ṭahmāsp Mīrzā, 35
Takaltū Khān, Zain al-'Ābidīn, 26, 44, 102; *Ḥamzah-nāmah*, 35–36
Tale of Saif al-Mulūk, (Bakhsh), 183–84
Tale of the Bakāwalī Flower ('Izzat Allāh Bangālī), 164–81; *Guldastah-i Ḥairat, ma'rūf bah Tawārīkh-i Bakāwalī* (Muḥammad Ya'qūb Lakhnawi), 169–75, 170 fig 3, 171 fig 4, 177, 194, 278n1; and *qiṣṣah*/romance genre devalued in colonialist era, 164–66; story and characters of, 124–25, 127–28, 177–78; Temple's expedition to find Fortress of Bakāwalī, 8, 166–69, 175–80; variations of and printings of, 167–69
Ṭallan, Mirzā, 89–90, 214
Ṭanbūrah, Muḥammad: "I have heard that in Musṭaf's days," 34; sources of worth as storyteller, 32–34, 43

tārīkh: defined, 7, 133; *qiṣṣah/tārīkh* divide, 174; *shi'r* vs., 144. *See also* historiography
Tārīkh al-Rusul wa al-mulūk (Ṭabarī), 141, 149–52
Tārīkh-i Bal'amī (Ṭabarī), 141
Tārīkh-i Dil-gushā-i Shamsher-Khānī (Tawakkul Beg), 141–46, 150
Tārīkh-i ṭilism-i Bakāwalī (Muḥammad Ismā'īl), 13, 172–74, 177, 180–83, 185, 202, 278n1, 279n7
Ṭarīq-i naṡr-khwānī (Fidā 'Alī), 67–68
Taṣadduq Ḥusain, 4, 67–68
Taubaṭ al-Naṣūḥ (Aḥmad), 200–202
Tawakkul Beg, *Tārīkh-i Dil-gushā-i Shamsher-Khānī*, 141–44, 150
tazmīn, 157–58
Temple, Richard Carnac, *Legends of the Panjab*, 166, 212
Temple, Sir Richard: *Guldastah-i Ḥairat, ma'rūf bah Tawārīkh-i Bakāwalī* (Muḥammad Ya'qūb Lakhnawi) on, 169–75, 170 fig 3, 171 fig 4, 177, 194, 278n1; Temple's expedition to find Fortress of Bakāwalī, 8, 166–69, 175–80
Textures of Time (Narayana Rao, Shulman, Subrahmanyam), 134–35, 148
al-Ṯha'ālibī, Abū Manṣūr, *Ġhurar akhbār mulūk al-Furs*, 141, 148, 150–52, 277n5
"There is no place in existence like the Chashmah-i Nūr" (Masīḥ Beg, Fakhr al-Zamānī), 103
Thousand and One Nights, 16, 116, 182, 191, 215
Ṭilism-i Faṣāḥat (Jāh), 68
Ṭilism-i Hosh-afzā (Bāqir 'Alī), 75, 77, 82, 86, 88, 112, 271, 271n34
Ṭilism-i Hoshrubā (Naval Kishore Press), 61–62, 67, 70, 117–18, 207, 215
Ṭilism-i Ṭahmūraṡ De'oband (Aḥmad 'Alī), 64
"Ṭilism-i ulfat" (Qalaq), 197
ṭilisms, defined, 2, 112. *See also individual titles*
Ṭirāz al-akhbār (Fakhr al-Zamānī): on advantages of *qiṣṣah-khwānī*, 45; appeal to young patrons by, 47; biographical information found in, 44, 98, 99, 101, 102, 105–6; on *dāstān* for practical purposes, 91; Fakhr al-Zamānī on *Ḥamzah-nāmah* in, 47; Fakhr al-Zamānī on storytelling in, 44; on four elements of storytelling, 111–14; Hājj Sayyid Jawādī on, 267n6; on Iranian, Turanian, Indian, Rūmī styles of storytelling, 113–14; manuscripts of, 110–11; organization of, 111; on performance devices, 114–17; production of, 94–97, 109–10; on textual fragments and memory, 111, 117–22, 119 fig 2; and uses of multigenre romance, 122–30; verbal/oral performance demonstrated by, 7
ṭirāzes, 111
Todorov, Tzvetan, 10, 13, 17, 265n6
Translation of Ṭabarī's History (Peacock), 156
transmission claim, 149, 154–59, 161, 181
Ṭūr, Mirzā, 67

Udās nasleṅ (Hussein), 14
umarā-zadāgān, 46–47
University of Indiana, 143
Urdū kī naṡrī dāstāneṅ (Jain), 5, 13, 205–8
Urdu language: Bāqir 'Alī's expertise in, 82–83; exemplarity in storytelling, 49–50; pulp fiction of, 216–17; rise of novel in Urdu literature, 194–206; romance genre in late nineteenth/early twentieth centuries, 3–5. *See also* Urdu-language storytellers

Urdu-language storytellers, 53–90; after Rebellion of 1857, 53–56; by Ashk, 56–61; Bāqir 'Alī, 72–90 (*See also* Bāqir 'Alī, Mīr); Dastangoi revival (twenty-first century), 1; Dastangoi storytelling revival, 1; Naval Kishore storytellers, 67–72; overview, 6–7; political knowledge of, 47–49; Shi'i performance in Lucknow and Rampur, 61–67; study of storytellers from nineteenth century to early twentieth century, 27. *See also ġhazal*; *individual names of storytellers*
Urdū zabān aur fann-i dāstān-go'ī (Aḥmad), 5, 204
ustānīs, 211–12

Ventura, Jean Baptiste, 143
verbal art: defined, 1; effect of print technology on, 55, 60–61; performance skills of storytellers, 7, 61–67, 73–75, 80–85, 114–17; vocalization by Aṣġhar 'Alī, 65–66; written works as embodying verbal performance, 266n2. *See also individual names of storytellers*

Wāḥidī, Mullā, 76, 79, 86–87, 114, 271n31
Waisī Hamadānī, Ḳhwājah, 33–34
Wājid 'Alī Shāh, Nawab, 63, 65, 70, 145, 169–72
Walī al-Dīn "Mirzā Mallan," Mirzā, 72
Wālih Dāġhistānī, 42
warfare: *razm*, 82, 111–14; storytellers and worth as soldiers, 32–43
Wāriṡ Shāh, 121
Warton, Thomas, 191–92
Waṣlī, Mīr Ni'mat Allāh, 107, 276n20
Wazīrī Begam, 87
Wellesley, Lord (Baron Cowley), 50, 56, 60
Wilāyat 'Alī, Mīr, 137, 277n1
wonderment, 182–83

Yāqūt al-Rūmī, 151–53
Yazdānī, Rāz, 62, 203
"Your servant of heavenly stature, Asad" (Murshid), 41
Yūsuf 'Alī Ḳhān, 62
Yusuf (Prophet), 19

Zadeh, Travis, 151–52, 182, 205
Ẓāmin 'Alī Jalāl, 66

www.ingramcontent.com/pod-product-compliance
Lightning Source LLC
Chambersburg PA
CBHW051536230426
43669CB00015B/2614
9780814345993